R. Gupta's®

POPULAR MASTER GUIDE

Indian Coast Guard

YANTRIK

Recruitment Exam

2020
EDITION

Ramesh Publishing House, NEW DELHI

Published by
O.P. Gupta *for* Ramesh Publishing House

Admin. Office
12-H, New Daryaganj Road, Opp. Officers' Mess,
New Delhi-110002 ✆ 23261567, 23275224, 23275124

E-mail: info@rameshpublishinghouse.com
Website: www.rameshpublishinghouse.com

Showroom
- Balaji Market, Nai Sarak, Delhi-6 ✆ 23253720, 23282525
- 4457, Nai Sarak, Delhi-6, ✆ 23918938

Book Code: R-1037

ISBN: 978-93-86845-33-7

HSN Code: 49011010

CONTENTS

SELECTION PROCEDURE

The written tests will be objective type. The questions paper will contain questions from their respective branch (Mechanical/Electrical/Electronics & Telecommunication) and will also include some questions of general knowledge, reasoning aptitude & English. Those who qualify written tests will undergo Physical Fitness Test (PFT) and initial Medical Examination.

1

MECHANICAL ENGINEERING

Thermodynamics—Steam Engine—Internal Combustion Engine (I.C. Engine)—Refrigeration and Air Conditioning—Gas Turbines, Compressor and Jet Engines—Theory of Machines—Machine Design—Objective Type Questions—Answers

Heat : *It is a form of energy which produces in us the sensation of warmth.*

4.1. THERMODYNAMICS

Thermodynamics deals in the study of various concepts and laws describing the conversion of energy from one form to another. In engineering, the energy transformation is restricted to the study of heat and work and conversion from one form to another. The quantity of matter under consideration is called the *system*. In a closed system, there is no interchange of matter between system and surroundings. The mass does not cross the boundary whereas the energy transfer takes place along the boundary. In an open system, there is such interchange in which the mass as well as energy both transfer across its boundaries.

4.1.1 Zeroth law of Themodynamics

This law states that "when two systems A and B are in thermal equilibrium with a third system C, then A and B are in thermal equilibrium with each other.

The physical quantity that determines whether or not the given system A is in thermal equilibrium with another system B is called *temperature*.

4.1.2. First Law of Thermodynamics

According to this, in a cyclic process, the total amount of heat supplied to the system is proportional to the amount of work done by the system. If dU, dV and dW all are in the same units, then

$$d\theta = dU + dW$$
$$= dU + P.dV$$

This law has been stated in a number of ways, some of the typical statements are:

A. Energy can neither be created nor destroyed
B. The sum total of all energy remains constant
C. Whenever energy is transformed from one form to another, energy is always conserved.

4.1.3. The Second Law of Thermodynamics

Kelvin's statement : It is impossible to derive a continuous supply of work by cooling a body to a temperature lower than that of the coldest of its surroundings.

Clausius statement : It is impossible for a self-acting machine, unaided by any external agency, to transfer heat from a body to another at higher temperature.

Kelvin - Planck's statement : It is impossible to get a continuously supply of work from a body or engine which can transfer heat with a single heat reservoir.

4.1.4. Ideal Gas Laws

Boyle's Law : Keeping the temperature constant, the volume of a given mass of a gas varies inversely as its absolute pressure

$$V \propto \frac{1}{P}$$

or $$P.V. = \text{constant.}$$

Charle's Law : Keeping pressure constant, the volume of a given mass of a gas varies directly as its absolute temperature

$$V \propto T$$

or $$\frac{V}{T} = \text{constant.}$$

Gay Lussac's Law : Keeping the volume constant, the pressure of a given mass of a gas varies directly as its absolute temperature

$$P \propto T$$

or $$\frac{P}{T} = \text{constant.}$$

Gas Equation : At low pressure and high temperaturs, in the absence of chemical reaction, all gases approach a condition such their P-V-T properties may be expressed by the relation

$$PV = RT$$

Where V is the volume of 1 mole of the gas.

If M is the molecular weight of the gas and V is the volume of 1 gram of a gas at constant pressure P and temperature T, then perfect gas equation for 1 gram of the gas is

$$PV = \frac{RT}{M} = rT$$

where r (= R/M) is a gas constant for 1 gram of the gas.

Entropy : For reversible cyclic process in whch the temperature varies during heat absorption and rejection, *i.e.* For any reversible cycle $\int \frac{dQ}{T} = 0$. Consequently for any reversible process, $\int \frac{dQ}{T}$ is not a function of the particular reversible path followed. This intergral is called the *entropy change*, or

$$\int ds = \int_1^2 \frac{dQ}{T} = S_2 - S_1 = S_{1-2}$$

The entropy of a substance is dependent only on its state or condition. For any reversible process, the change in entropy of the system and surroundings is zero, whereas for any irreversible process, the net entropy change is possible.

4.1.5. The Third Law of Thermodynamics

It states that the total entropy of pure substances approaches zero as the absolute thermodynamic temperature approach zero. The third law approaches further that the partial derivatives with respect to temperature of generalised force and generalized displacement also vanish at absloute zero.

Relation between Internal Energy (i), Enthalpy (h), and Entropy (s) of an ideal gas

If an ideal gas with constant specific heats changes from an initial state P_1, V_1, T_1, to a final state P_2, V_2, T_2, the following equations hold.

$$u_2 - u_1 = mC_v(T_2 - T_1)$$

$$= A(P_2V_2 - P_1V_1)/(k-1)$$

$$h_2 - h_1 = m\,C_P(T_2 - T_1)$$

$$= Ak(P_2V_2 - P_1V_1)/(k-1)$$

$$S_2 - S_1 = m\left[C_v \log_e\left(\frac{T_2}{T_1}\right) + AR\log_e\left(\frac{V_2}{V_1}\right)\right]$$

$$= m\left[C_p \log_e\left(\frac{T_2}{T_1}\right) + AR\log_e\left(\frac{P_2}{P_1}\right)\right]$$

$$= m\left[C_p \log_e\left(\frac{V_2}{V_1}\right) + C_v \log_e\left(\frac{P_2}{P_1}\right)\right]$$

Special Changes of States for Ideal gases:

A. Constant Volume:

$$\frac{P_2}{P_1} = \frac{T_2}{T_1}$$

$$Q_{12} = u_2 - u_1 = mC_v\,(T_2 - T_1)$$

$$W_{12} = 0$$

$$S_2 - S_1 = mC_v \log_e\left(\frac{T_2}{T_1}\right)$$

B. Constant Pressure :

$$\frac{V_2}{V_1} = \frac{T_2}{T_1}$$

$$Q_{12} = m\,C_p\,(T_2 - T_1)$$

$$W_{12} = P\,(V_2 - V_1)$$

$$= mR\,(T_2 - T_1)$$

$$S_2 - S_1 = mC_p \log_e\left(\frac{T_2}{T_1}\right)$$

C. Isothermal (Constant Temperature):

$$\frac{P_2}{P_1} = \frac{V_1}{V_2}$$

$$U_2 - U_1 = 0$$

$$W_{12} = mRT \log_e\left(\frac{V_2}{V_1}\right)$$

$$= P_1\,V_1 \log_e\left(\frac{V_2}{V_1}\right)$$

$$Q_{12} = AW_{12}$$

$$S_2 - S_1 = Q_{12}/T$$

$$= mAR \log_e\left(\frac{V_2}{V_1}\right)$$

D. Reversible Adiabatic (Isentropic):

$$P_1V_1^{k} = P_2V_2^{k}$$

$$\left(\frac{T_2}{T_1}\right) = \left(\frac{V_2}{V_1}\right)^{k-1} = \left(\frac{P_2}{P_1}\right)^{k-\frac{1}{k}}$$

$$AW_{12} = U_1 - U_2 = m\,C_v\,(T_1 - T_2)$$

$$Q_{12} = 0$$

$$S_2 - S_1 = 0$$

$$W_{12} = \frac{P_1V_1 - P_2V_2}{k-1} = \frac{P_1V_1 - \left[1 - \left(\frac{P_2}{P_1}\right)\right]^{k-\frac{1}{k}}}{k-1}$$

4.1.6. Polytropic Change

For a polytropic change of an ideal gas (for which C_v is constant), the specific heat is given by the relation

$$C_n = \frac{C_v(n-k)}{n-1}$$

Hence $1 < n < k$, C_n is negative

In polytropic process

$$P_1V_1^{n} = P_2\,V_2^{n}$$

$$\frac{T_2}{T_1} = \left(\frac{V_1}{V_2}\right)^{n-1} = \left(\frac{P_2}{P_1}\right)^{n-1/n}$$

$$W_{12} = \frac{P_1V_1 - P_2V_2}{n-1}$$

$$= \frac{P_1V_1\left[1 + \left(\frac{p_2}{P_1}\right)\right]^{n-\frac{1}{n}}}{n-1}$$

$$Q_{12} = mC_n\,(t_2 - t_1)$$

4.1.7. Heat Engines

A heat engine is a device for converting heat energy into work. In the most general form it operates through the input as heat Q at temperature T, the output of work W, and the rejection of heat Q_s to a receiver or sink at temperature T_s. For a cycle,

$$dU = 0 \text{ and } Q - Q_s = W$$

Hence for any such process,

$$\text{Actual efficiency} = \frac{W}{Q} = \frac{Q - Q_s}{Q} = 1 - \frac{Q_s}{Q}$$

For a reversible cycle operating between the constant temperature T and T_s, Q = Td_s and $Q_s = T_s d_s$, hence for this ideal process,

$$\text{Ideal efficiency} = \frac{T - T_s}{T}$$

Any irreversibility in the cycle makes Q_s greater than $T_s d_s$ reduces the efficiency.

4.1.8. Power Cycles :

The Carnot Cycle : It consists of

A. A reversible isothermal expansion during which heat Q is received from a source at constant temperature T with output of work,
B. A reversible adiabatic expansion during which the temperature of the fluid decreases from T to the receiver temperature T_s with output of work,
C. A reversible isothermal compression during which heat Q_s is rejected to a receiver at temperature T_s , and
D. A reversible adiabatic compression to the original temperature T with output of work.

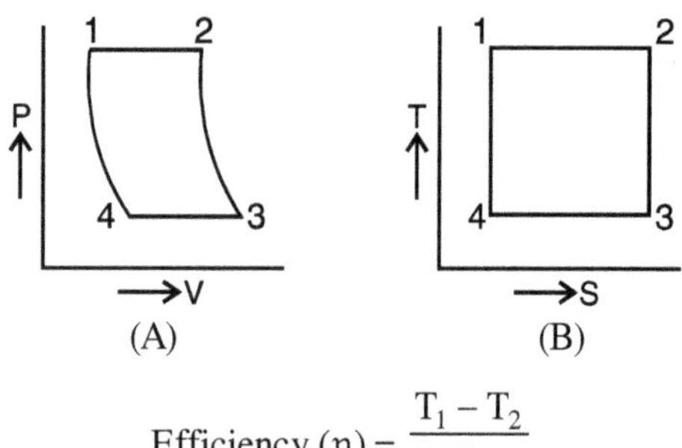

(A) (B)

$$\text{Efficiency } (\eta) = \frac{T_1 - T_2}{T_1}$$

Carnot theorem : No heat engine working between two given temperatures of source and sink can be more efficient than a perfectly reversible engine (Carnot engine, say) working between the same two temperatures.

The Joule Cycle : It is used in gas turbines consists of

A. Adiabatic compression of fuel air mixtures,

B. Combustion of mixture at constant pressure,
C. Adiabatic expansion, and
D. Heat rejection at constant pressure.

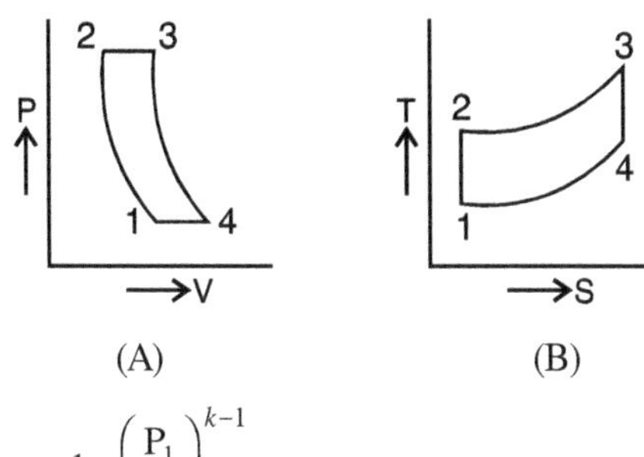

(A) (B)

Ideal Efficiency = $1-\left(\frac{P_1}{P_2}\right)^{k-1}$

The Otto cycle : In idealized from the Otto cycle assumes intake of air-fuel mixture without pressure loss. It consists of :

A. Adiabatic compression of mixture,
B. Combustion of mixture at constant volume,
C. Adiabatic expansion of combustion products with output of work, and
D. Discharge at constant volume.

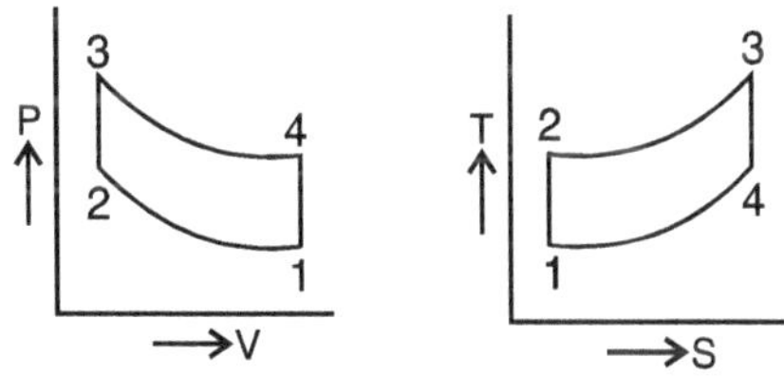

Ideal Efficiency = $1-\frac{1}{(r_c)^{k-1}}$

Where r_c is the compression ratio and $k=\frac{C_p}{C_v}$

The Diesel Cycle : In idealized form, the Diesel cycle consists of intake air without pressure loss

A. Adiabatic compression of air,
B. Liquid fuel injection at constant pressure maintained by vaporisation during expansions 2-3,
C. Adiabatic combustion and exapansion with output of work 3-4, and
D. Discharge of the products of combustion at constant volume 4-1.

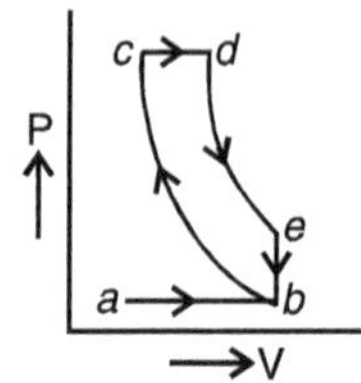

$$\text{Ieal Efficiency} = 1 - \frac{(r_c)^{1-k}}{k}\left(\frac{r_c^{\ k} - 1}{r_c - 1}\right)$$

Where r_c = Compression ratio = $\frac{V_1}{V_2}$

The Rankine Cycle : The Rankine cycle consists of

A. Heating, vaporising and super-heating from T_1 to T_2 at constant pressure P_1,

B. Adiabatic expansion from P_1 to P_3 with output of work,

C. Isothermal condensation at constant pressure P_3 with rejection of heat, and

D. Adiabatic compression of condensed fluid from P_4 to P_1 with input of work.

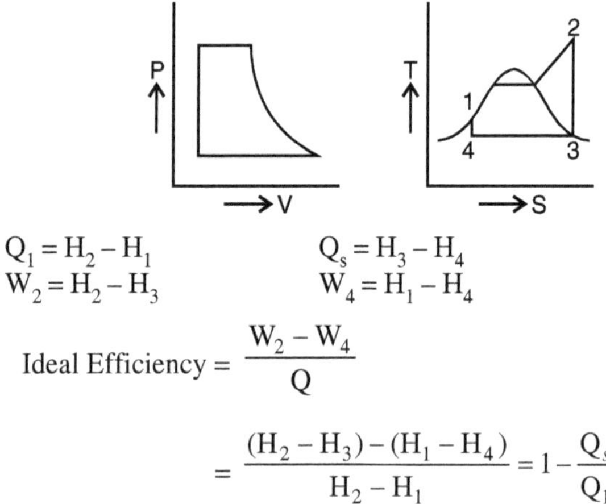

$Q_1 = H_2 - H_1$ $\qquad$ $Q_s = H_3 - H_4$

$W_2 = H_2 - H_3$ $\qquad$ $W_4 = H_1 - H_4$

$$\text{Ideal Efficiency} = \frac{W_2 - W_4}{Q}$$

$$= \frac{(H_2 - H_3) - (H_1 - H_4)}{H_2 - H_1} = 1 - \frac{Q_s}{Q_1}$$

4.1.9. Heat Transfer

Heat is transferred from one place to another by the following processes:

Conduction : Heat conduction is due to the property of matter which allows the passage of heat energy, even if physical body is impermeable to any kind of rays and its parts are not in motion relative to one antoher.

The fundamental relation for steady flow of heat by conduction originates from the French Physicists Biot and is expressed by

$$q = -kA\frac{dT}{dx}$$

Convection : When convective heat transfer is caused by density difference produced by temperature gradients, this is known as free or natural convection. On the other hand, the rate of heat transfer increases substantially if external agency, e.g., pump or blower is used, so that fluid moves faster. Such a convective heat transfer is known as forced convection.

Radiation : Heat radiation is due to the property of matter to emit and to absorb different kinds of rays, and to the fact that an empty space is perfectly permeable to rays and that matter allows them to pass more or less.

Heat transfer by radiation is important in boiler furnaces billet reheating furnaces etc. Solar radiation plays an important role in the design of heating and ventilating system.

Stefan's-Boltzmann's law : The amount of energy radiated per second per unit area of a perfectly black body is directly proportional to the fourth power of the absolute temperature of the surface of the body, i.e.,

$$E \propto T^4$$

or $$E = \sigma T^4$$

where σ is a constant of proportionality and is called constant. It's value is $5.67 \times 10^{-8}\ Wm^{-2}\ k^{-4}$.

4.2. STEAM ENGINE

In all steam engines, steam is used as the working fluid. These engines operate on the principle of first law of the thermodynamics, *i.e.,* heat and work are mutually convertible. In steam engine heat of steam is converted into work by means of a piston reciprocating in a cylinder. The mechanical work produced, is made available at the flywheel of the engine. Types of steam engines are :

I. Horizontal or vertical.
II. Single cylinder or multicyclinder.
III. Single acting or double acting.
IV. Slow speed, medium speed or high speed engines.
V. Condensing or non-condensing type.
VI. Throttle governed or automatic cut off governned.

Theoretical mean effective pressure, p_m is given by

$$P_m = \frac{p_1}{r}[1 + 2 - 3\log r] - p_b$$

where p_1 =admission pressure of steam,
p_b = back pressure of steam, and
r = expansion ration.

I. H. P. : It is the theoretical power developed in the engine cylinder. Indicated horse power of a steam engine is given as

$$\text{I.H.P} = \frac{p_m \text{LAN}}{4500} \text{ h.p. for double acting engine}$$

$$\text{I.H.P} = \frac{2p_m \text{LAN}}{4500} \text{ h.p. for double acting engine}$$

$$\text{I.H.P} = \frac{p_m \text{LAN}(2\text{A} - \text{Q})}{4500} \text{ h.p. taking into account piston rod.}$$

where P_m = Actual mean effective pressure in kg/cm^2
L = Lenght of stroke in m
A = Area of the piston rod in cm^2
N = Engine rpm

B.H.P. : It is the total power available on the shaft of the engine. Brake horse power is given as

$$\text{B.H.P.} = \frac{2\pi N\tau}{4500}, \text{ where } \tau \text{ be the forque.}$$

$$\text{Mechanical efficiency} = \frac{\text{B.H.P.}}{\text{I.H.P.}}$$

Fules : A fuel is substance which on burning with oxygen in the atmospheric, it produces a large amount of heat. The amount of heat liberated is known as *calorific value of fuel.* The fuel exist in all the three forms.

A. Solid fuels : Coal, wood.
B. Liquid fuels : petrol, diesels, alcohals, molases etc.
C. Gaseous fuels : Natural gas, coal gas, producer gas, water gas, blast furnace gas.

4.2.1. Calorific Value

The amount of heat obtained by the complete combustion of 1 kg of a fuel when the products of its combustion have been cooled down to the temperature of surrounding air.

Calorific value of solid and liquid fuels may be determined with the help of Bomb Calorimeter, a Boys Gas Calorimeter is used to determine calorific value of gaseous fuels.

4.2.3. Combustion of Fuels

Atmospheric air contains 21% by volume of oxygen and 79% by volume of nitrogen. By weight oxygen is 23% and nitrogen 77%. Knowing the composition of fuel, e.g., carbon, hydrogen and other constituents present in fuel, the amount of air required for combustion can be estimated.

When pure carbon is burnt with minimum quantity air, the maximum carbon dioxide content of fuel gases by volume is 20.9%. Thus CO_2 content of fuels can not exceed 21%. Presence of any other constituent of excess air supplied during combustion will reduce the percentage of carbon dioxide in the gases.

4.2.3. Steam Boilers

Steam Boilers are closed vessels in which steam is produced by the application of the heat produced by the combustion of fuel. The boilers may be smoke tube type in which hot gases from the furnace pass through a tube or a bank of tubes. These tubes are surrounded by water. Due to transfer of heat from hot gases to water, wet steam is produced. Simple vertical boiler, Cochran boiler, Scotch marine boiler, Lancashire boiler, and Locomotive boiler are examples of fire tube or smoke tube boilers.

In water tube boiler, the water circulates inside the tubes which are heated from outside by hot gases from the furnace, Babcock and Wilcox boiler, La Mont boiler, Loeffer boiler are the examples of water tube boilers.

Performance : The performance of a boiler is measured in terms of its evaporative capacity, *i.e.*, quantity of steam produced per hour or per day. The equivalent evaporation at 100°C is the amount of water evaporated from feed water at 100°C and formed into dry and saturated steam at 100°C at normal atmospheric pressure. Mathematically, equivalent evaporation at 100°C is expressed as

$$E = \frac{W_e(H - h)}{5390} kg.$$

where W_e = Weight of water actually evaporated or actual evaporation in kg/hr, and

H= Total enthalpy of evaporated steam

$$\text{Boiler efficiency} = \frac{W_s(H - h_1)}{W_f \times C}$$

4.2.4. Efficiency of the Engine

The ratio of work done to the energy supplied, expressed in identical units is a measure of the efficiency of the engine. Thus

$$\text{Indicated thermal efficiency} = \frac{\text{I.H.P} \times 4500}{\text{W(H} - h\text{)J}}$$

$$\text{Overall efficiency} = \frac{\text{B.H.P} \times 4500 \times 60}{\text{W}_f \times \text{C} \times \text{J}}$$

$$\text{Brake thermal efficiency} = \frac{\text{Heat in B.H.P}}{\text{Total heat}}$$

$$\text{Relative efficiency} = \frac{\text{Thermal efficiency}}{\text{Rankine efficiency}}$$

4.2.5. Steam Condenser

Steam condenser is a closed vessel into which the steam is exhausted, and condense after doing work in an engine cylinder or turbine. A steam condenser is used to maintain a low pressure so as to obtain the maximum possible energy from steam with the object of getting a high efficiency. Another purpose of steam condenser is to supply pure feed water of hot well, from where it is pumped back to the boiler.

Condensers are mainly of two types

I. Jet condenser or mixing type condenser

II. surface condensers or non-mixing type condenser.

The vacuum efficiency of a condenser is given by

$$\text{Vacuum Efficiency} = \frac{\text{Actual Vacuum}}{\text{Ideal Vacuum}}$$

$$= \frac{\text{Barometric pressure} - \text{Actual pressure}}{\text{Barometric pressure} - \text{Ideal pressure}}$$

$$\text{Condenser Efficiency} = \frac{\text{Temperature rise of cooling water}}{\text{Vacuum temperature} - \text{Inlet cooling temperature}}$$

4.2.6. Steam Nozzles

Steam nozzles is a passage of varying cross-section, which converts heat energy of steam into kinetic energy. During the first part of the nozzle, the steam increases its velocity, but in its later part steam gains more in volume than in velocity. As the mass flow of steam remains constant, the variation of steam pressure depends upon

I. Dryness fraction of steam.

II. Specific volume of steam.

III. Velocity of steam.

The smallest section of the nozzle is know as *throat.* Velocity of steam through nozzle is given by

$$v = 44.7\sqrt{U}$$

4.2.7. Steam Turbine

In a steam turbine rotatory motion is obtained by the gradual change of momentum of the steam. The steam turbine may be of two types.

I. Impulse turbine

II. Reaction type

Performance of steam turbines

I. Diagram of blading efficiency $= \dfrac{\text{Work done on the blades}}{\text{Energy supplied}}$

$$= \frac{2\left(V_w + V_{w_1}\right)V_b}{V^2} \; or \; \frac{V^2 - V_1^{\,2}}{V^2}$$

II. Gross efficiency $= \dfrac{\text{work done on blades / kg of steam}}{\text{Total energy supplied per stage per kg of steam}}$

$$= \frac{\left(V_{w_1} + V_{w_2}\right)V_b}{gJU}$$

III. Max. efficiency of an impulse turbine $= \cos^2\alpha$

IV. Max. efficiency of a reaction turbine $= \dfrac{2\cos^2\alpha}{1+\cos^2\alpha}$

4.3. INTERNAL COMBUSTION ENGINE (I.C. ENGINE)

The compressed fuel air mixture is ignited inside the cylinder of engine. During combustion, at very high temperature and pressure gases are produced which expand, inside the cylinder. The hot gases so produced pushes the piston outward and momentum of the flywheel pushes the piston inside the engine cylinder. Due to the movement of piston, the power is obtained and it is transmitted to the shaft of the engine.

I.C. engine is also called Spark Ignition Engine (S.I. Engine) Which is used in automobile, locomotive, civil aviation, agriculture equipment, marine, heavy earth moving machines and so many other machines.

Various stroke of internal combustion engines are

I. Intake stroke
II. Compression stroke
III. Ignition stroke
IV. Exhaust stroke.

Internal combustion engines are either four stroke engines or two stroke engines. In four sroke engines all the operation complete in four strokes mentioned above, whereas in two-stroke engine all the operations are completed in two strokes of the piston or in one revolution of the crankshaft.

4.3.1. The Dual Combustion Cycle

The Dual Combustion Cycle consists of

I. Heat added during constant volume process 2-3

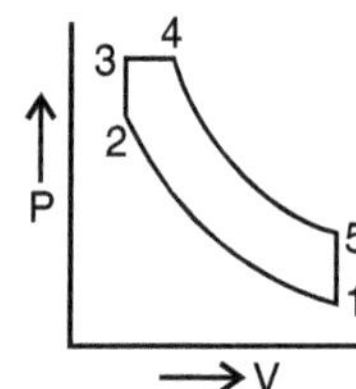

II. Heat added during constant pressure process 3-4.
III. Heat rejected during constant volume process 5-1.

$$\text{Efficiency} = 1 - \frac{2}{r^{k-1}}\left[\frac{\alpha\rho^{k} - 1}{(\alpha - 1) + \alpha\gamma(\rho - 1)}\right]$$

where $r =$ compression ratio
$\rho =$ cut of ratio
$\alpha =$ pressure ratio

4.3.2. Brake Thermal Efficiency

$$\text{B.T.E.} = \frac{\text{B.T.P.} \times 4500}{\text{W} \times \text{C.V.} \times \text{J}}$$

$$\text{Relative Efficiency} = \frac{\text{Themal efficiency}}{\text{Air standard efficiency}}$$

4.4 REFRIGERATION AND AIR-CONDITIONING

4.4.1. Refrigeration

It is defined as the production of temperature lower than those of the surroundings and maintaining the lower temperature within the boundary of a given space. Various methods for producing refrigerating effect are

(i) Ice refrigeration
(ii) Vapour absorption refrigeration
(iii) Liquid gas refrigeration
(iv) Vapour compression refrigeration
(v) Steam jet refrigeration
(vi) Air expansion refrigeration

Refrigerating Effect : The cooling effect produced by a machine is called as refrigerating effect.

Coefficient of Performance: The performance of a referigerating machine is measured in terms of coefficient of performance, which is given by the relation

$$\text{Coefficient of performance} = \frac{\text{Refrigeration effect}}{\text{Work input}}$$

$$\Rightarrow \qquad \beta = \frac{Q_2}{Q_1 - Q_2}$$

If a machine has the capacity to produce cooling effect of 50 kcal/min is said to have one tonne capacity of refrigeration.

Refrigerants : In a refrigerating system, the heat carrying medium is known as *refrigerant.* The refrigerant absorbs heat at one place which is at low temperature level and rejects it at some other place having higher temperature and pressure. In a refrigeration cycle, the refrigerant changes from liquid to vapour during the heat absorption process and condenses again to liquid while liberating heat. An ideal refrigerant should liberate all the heat it is capable of absorbing.

Properties of a Good Refrigerant

(i) Low boiling and freezing point
(ii) High latent heat value and low specific value
(iii) No corrosive effect on metals
(iv) Should be safe and non-toxic
(v) Ability to operate on a positive pressure
(vi) Capacity to mix with oil

Classification of Refrigerants : Refrigerants may be classified as

***(i)* Primary Refrigerants :** Those which cool the substances by absorption of latent heat. These are generally used in vapour compression systems. Some of the primary refrigerants are Ammonia, Carbon-dioxide, Sulphur-dioxide, Methyl chloride, Metholene chloride and Fluorinated hydrocarbons.

***(ii)* Secondary Refrigerants :** Those which cool substances by absorbing their sensible heat. Some of the secondary refrigerants are:

Air, water, calcium chloride brine, sodium chloride, brine, glycol etc.

4.4.2. Psychrometry

It is a branch of science which mainly deals with the study of the mixture of dry air and water vapour. The air is a mixture of gases like hydrogen, oxygen, argon, carbon dioxide, water vapour and traces of other gases. In air conditioning estimations air is taken as a mixture of dry air and water vapour.

4.4.3. Working of Refrigerating Machine

The coefficient of performance of a refrigeration machine working on reversed Carnot cycle is given by

$$COP = \frac{T_2}{T_1 - T_2}$$

Where T_1 is high temperature reservoir temperature where heat is rejected and T_2 is temperature of refrigerated space, *i.e.,* low temperature reservoir. The C.O.P. of a carnot heat pump is more than the C.O.P. of carnot refrigerator by unity.

Vapour Compression Cycle : Vapour compression cycle is used for all purpose refrigeration. It is generally used from small domestic machines to an airconditioning plant of large capacity.

The four fundamental operations of a simple vapour compression system are

(i) Compression,
(ii) Condensation,
(iii) Expansion, and
(iv) Vaporisation

The vapour compression cycle depends upon

(i) The conversion of a substance from liquid to vapour form (evaporation) involving the absorption of a considerable quantity of latent heat by the substance.

(ii) For a given substance the temperature at which evaporation or condensation takes place depends only on the pressure prevailing and can be varied by varying the pressure.

Vapour Absorption Cycle : Vapour absorption cylce differs from compression cycle in a way that it uses heat energy instead of mechanical energy to make a change in the conditions necessary to complete the refrigeration cycle. The heat energy for the cycle may be obtained from the gas burner, kerosene oil lamp or electric heater. This system has minimum number of moving parts. The working of this sytem depends upon the use of two substances which have great affinity for each other and which can be easily separated by the application of heat:

Dry Air : International Joint Committee on Psychrometric Data has fixed the following composition of air in mole fraction.

Oxygen	-	0.2095
Nitrogen	-	9.7809
Argon	-	0.0093
Carbon dioxide	-	0.003

Moist Air : It is a mixture of dry air and water vapour. The quantity of water vapour in air depends upon the temperature of air.

Saturated Air : Moist air is said to be saturated when it contains maximum amount of water vapour that it can hold. If water vapour added to air in more than that of saturated air, the drops of water will remain in suspension and will make the air foggy or moisty.

Degree of Saturation : It is the ratio of the prevailing humidity raio of moist air to the humidity ratio of saturated air at the same temperature and pressure.

4.4.4. Air -Conditioning

It involves the control of following factors :

(i) Temperature,
(ii) Humidity control,
(iii) Air movement and circulation, and
(iv) Filteration, cleaning and purification of air

Comfort air-conditioning is sub-divided into three groups :

(i) Summer air-conditioning
(ii) Winter air-conditioning, and
(iii) Year round air-conditioning

4.4.5. Cooling Loads

The total amount of heat which is required to be pumped out from the space to be kept at the desired level of temperature by the refrigerating equipment is known as cooling load. The total load determines the size of plant required.

Various load on an air-conditioning plant arise due to:

(i) Sensible heat gear, and
(ii) Latent heat gear

4.5. GAS TURBINES, COMPRESSOR AND JET ENGINES

4.5.1. Gas Turbines

Gas Turbines operate on Brayton cycle. A compressor usually coupled with turbine, compresses air which is then transferred to combustor. A *combustor* is a heat exchanger, where fuel is burnt, and temperature of air from compressor is raised. This high pressure high tempeature air expands in turbine doing mechanical work.

When the gas is ideal so that cp is constant, the thermal efficiency is given by

$$n = \frac{(T_c - T_b) - (T_d - T_a)}{(T_c - T_b)}$$

The efficiency of cycle can be improved by

(i) Multistage compression with intercooling

(ii) Reheating of expanding ash.

(iii) Use of regenerator.

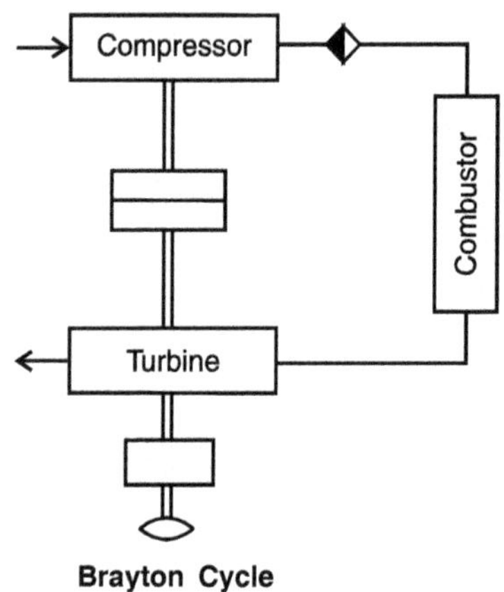

Brayton Cycle

Types of Gas Turbines

(1) Open Cycle Gas Turbine : During each cycle of operation fresh working fulid enters the system. The atmospheric air is drawn in the compressor and after compression it is used for the combustion of fuel in the combuster. The combustible gases after passing through the turbine are rejected to the atmosphere.

(2) Closed Cylce Gas Turbine : In this system same working fluid is circulated again and again afer completing the cycle. In this system, the heat is added from an external source and it is rejected from top, a cooling medium in a heat exchanger.

4.5.2. Steam Turbines

Steam Turbines convert energy in steam to shaft energy steam turbines may be classified as

(i) Impulse type

(ii) Reaction type

(iii) Combination of impulse and reaction

Steam Turbines may also be classified as

(i) Condensing type

(ii) Non-condensing type

Other classifications are

I. With respect to number of stages

(*i*) Single stage

(*ii*) Multi stage

II. With respect to the direction of steam flow

(*i*) Axial

(*ii*) Radial

(*iii*) Mixed

(*iv*) Helical

(*v*) Re-entry

(*vi*) Tangential

III. With respect to the pressure of steam as

(*i*) High pressure

(*ii*) Medium pressure

(*iii*) Low pressure

A steam turbine works on Rankine cycle and takes advantage of expansion upto the lowest pressure. The thermal efficiency of a steam turbine is higher than that of steam engine. In an impulse turbine, the expansion takes place in the nozzle only, where the pressure decreases and velocity increases. This pressure remains constant while steam passes over the blades of the turbine. In case of pure reaction turbine the steam expands as it flows over the blades which therefore act as nozzle.

The velocity of a simple impulse wheel is too high for practical purposes and as such the speed has to be reduced by some suitable means.

In case of single stage impulse, the blade efficiency is $= \dfrac{2V_b(V_{w_1} - V_{w_0})}{V_1^2}$

and stage efficiency $= \dfrac{V_b(V_{w_1} - V_{w_0})}{gJHD}$

In case of impulse turbine with several blade rings diagram efficiency

$$= \frac{2V_b \Sigma(V_{w_1} - V_{w_0})}{V_1^2}$$

4.5.3. Air Compressor

Air Compressor is used to increase the pressure of atmospheric air. For compressing the air, the work is done on it by a prime mover, which may be a electric motor, diesel engine etc.

Types of Air Compressors : Rotary Compressor : Machines which developes pressure on rotary principle are called *Rotary Compressors.* They generally run at very high speeds and are often coupled with prime movers like steam turbines or gas turbines. The compression of gas in a rotary compressor follows the law PV^n = constant, where index n depends on the properties of gas operating conditions.

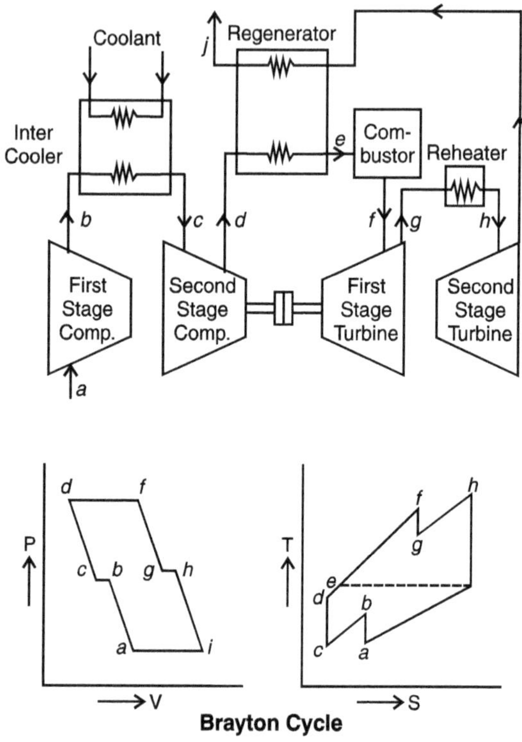

Brayton Cycle

Centrifugal Compressor : In centrifugal compressor, impeller consists of a large number of vanes and is mounted on a shaft, inside a stationary casing.

Pressure rise through impeller and diffuser as shown in the figure.

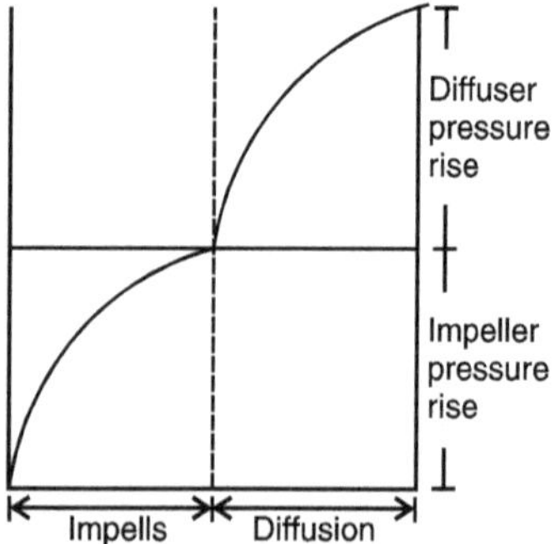

Work done is given by

$$W = \frac{V_{w_2} . V_{b_2}}{g}$$

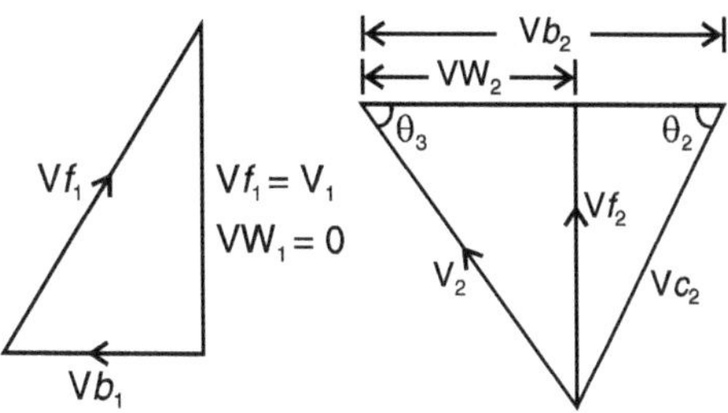

Isentropic efficiency of compressor

$$= \frac{\text{Isentropic temp. rise}}{\text{Actual temp. rise}}$$

Axial Flow Compressor : In axial flow compressor, air flows in an axial direction. There are alternate layers of rotating blades and stator blades.

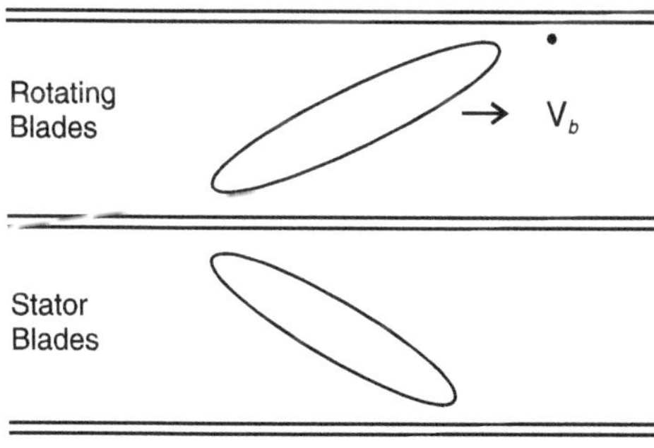

Degree of reaction,

$$R = \frac{1V_f}{2V_b} \tan(\beta_1 + \beta_2)$$

When degree of reaction is 0.5

$$\alpha_1 = \beta_1 \, and \, \alpha_2 = \beta_2$$

4.5.4. Jet Engines

In jet engines the propulsive force is produced by imparting momentum to the working fluid and then ejecting the gases at a very high velocity through the nozzle. The jet of gases from the nozzle produces a reaction in the opposite direction in the form of propulsive force.

Various types of jet engines are:

(A) Atmospheric engines

(B) Rocket engines

In atmospheric jet engines, the oxygen required for the combustion of fuel is taken from the atmosheric air. The performance of such engines depends upon the atmospheric pressure and temperature. But rocket engines carries both the fuel and the oxidising agent for combustion of fuel. The performance of such engine is independent of the atmospheric air.

Types of Atmospheric Jet Engines : Atmospheric jet engines are classified as

(a) Turbojet engines

(b) Turbojet with after burner

(c) Turbo prop

(d) Ram jet

(e) Pulse jet

Types of Rocket Engines : Rocket Engines are classified as

(a) Liquid propellant rocket engine

(b) Solid propellant rocket engine

4.6 THEORY OF MACHINES

A machine constains a number of inter-related parts, each having a different function, kinematics of machines deals with the relative motion between the parts, neglecting the consideration of force. Kinematic link is a resistant body or an assembly of resistant bodies which go to make a part or parts of a machine connecting other parts which have motion relating to it.

4.6.1. Kinematic Pair

A pair is a joint of two elements that permits relative motion. The relative motion between the elements or links that form a pair is required to be completely constrained or successfully contrained. Pairs may be classified as follows:

1. Depening upon the nature of contact between elements

   (a) Lower pairs

   (b) Higher pairs

2. Depending upon the nature of the mechanical constraints

   (a) Closed pairs

   (b) Open pairs

3. Depending upon the nature of relative motion between elements.

   (a) Sliding pair

(*b*) Turning pair
(*c*) Rolling pair
(*d*) Spherical pair
(*e*) Helical pair

4.6.2. Kinematic Chain

When a number of links are connected in space that the relative motion of any point on a link with respect to any other point on the other link follow a law, the chain is called a *kinematic chain.*

4.6.3. Mechanism

If one of the links of a constrained kinematic chain is fixed, the result is a *mechanism*

4.6.4. Inversion of Mechanism

Inversions are the different mechanism obtained by fixing different links in a kinematic chain. Thus as many inversions are possible as the number of links. The motion of a point or a link in a kinematic chain relative to some other point or a link is the property of the chain and not of the mechanism.

4.6.5. Gears

A gear drive is smooth and positive in action. Also, large power can be transmitted by gear drives. Gears are common in several mechanical engineering applications such as machine tools, automobiles, hoists, rolling mills etc. For parallel shafts, straight, stepped parallel helical gears are used, for intersecting shaft straight, bevel, spiral gears are used and for non-parallel, non-intersecting shafts cross, helical, worm, hypoid gears are used.

Terminology Used in Gears

(*a*) ***Pitch circle diameter :*** It is the diameter of a circle which by pure rolling action would produce the same motion as the toothed gear wheel.

(*b*) ***Pitch point :*** It is the point of the tangency or the point of contact of the two pitch circles of the mating gears.

(*c*) ***Circular pitch :*** The distance along the circumference of the pitch circle from a point on one tooth to a corresponding point on the adjacent tooth is called *circular pitch.* Thus, the circular pitch denoted by p_c for the spur gear of pitch circle diameter *d*, having 'T' as the number of teeth can be expressed by

$$p_c = \frac{\pi d}{T}$$

(*d*) ***Diametral pitch :*** The number of teeth per unit length on the pitch circle diameter is known as *diameteral pitch.*

$$p_d = \frac{T}{d}$$

(*e*) ***Module :*** The length of the pitch circle diameter per tooth is called *module.*

$$m = \frac{d}{T}$$

(*f*) ***Addendum :*** The radial height of the tooth above pitch circle is defined as *addendum.* Its standard value is one module.

(*g*) ***Addendum circle :*** A circle bounding the tops of the teeth is known as *addendum circle.* Diameter for this circle for standard tooth gear = pitch circle diameter + 2 m.

(*h*) ***Dedendum :*** The radial depth of a tooth below the pitch circle is defined as the *dedendum.* Its standard value is $\left(1+\frac{\pi}{20}\right)$ module = 1.157 m.

(*i*) ***Dedendum circle :*** A circle passing through the roots of all the teeth is defined as *dedendum circle.* Diameter of the dedendum circle for standard teeth is equal to pitch diameter – 2 × 1.57 m.

(*j*) ***Clearance:*** The radial height difference between the addendum the dedendum of a tooth is known as *clearance.* Thus standard teeth clearance value will be given by 2.157 m – 1 m = 0.157 m.

4.6.6. Cams

A cam is a mechanical member for transmitting a desired motion to a follower by direct contact. The driver is called the *cam* and driven member is called the follower.

The follower may be classified in three types.

(*a*) Construction of the surface in contact e.g., knife edge, roller, flat faced mushroom or spherical shape mushroom.

(*b*) The type of motion-translatory or oscillatory.

The location of the line of motion, with respect to cam centre, radial and off set.

4.6.7. Friction

Ridges and depression are there in all surfaces. When one surface has contact with another surface, these ridges and depression interlock and thus the relative motion of one surface over the other is resisted. This resistive force is known as the *force of friction.* Force of friction will always oppose motion. Mainly there could be three possible states of surfaces.

(i) Dry
(ii) Greasy or partially lubricated
(iii) Completely lubricated or flim lubricated

4.6.8. Pivots and Collars

The rotaing shafts are quite frequently subjected to axial thrust. This thrust is carried by bearing surfaces. The loss of horse power, in case of flat pivots, is given by the relation.

I. Uniform pressure

$$\text{H.P. lost in friction} = \frac{4}{3}\frac{\mu W_{r_1} \pi N}{4500}$$

II. Uniform wear

$$\text{H.P. lost in friction} = \frac{\mu W_{r_1} \pi N}{4500}$$

Where W is total lead in kgf, r_1 is the radius of the pivot, μ is the coefficient of friction and N is the shaft r.p.m. In case of collars, relation for horse power lost in friction is

$$\text{H.P. lost in friction} = \frac{2\pi N}{4500}\cdot\frac{2}{3}\mu W\left(\frac{r_1^{\,3} - r_2^{\,3}}{r_1^{\,2} - r_2^{\,2}}\right)$$

4.6.9. Belt, Rope and Chain Drive

They are known as flexible drives which are used to transmit power between shafts whose centre distance is too great, where gear trains are not possible.

Flat belts are mostly used to connect parallel shafts. The belts are made of leather, fabric, rubber impregnated fabric and synthetics. When d_1 is the diameter of driven pulley and ω_1 is the speed of driven pulley in rad/sec, and d_2 and ω_2 are the corresponding values of driver pulley, then

$$\frac{\omega_1}{\omega_2} = \frac{d_2}{d_1} \text{ and } \frac{\omega_1}{\omega_2} = \frac{d_2 + t}{d_1 + t}$$

Where t is the belt thickness.

Length of flat Belts

I. Open belt:

$$L = 2D + 1.57\,(d_2 + d_1) + \left(\frac{d_2 - d_1}{4D}\right)^2$$

Where D is the centre distance.

II. Cross belt.

$$L = 2\left[D\cos\alpha + \left(\frac{d_2 + d_1}{2D}\right)\left(\frac{\pi}{2} + \alpha\right)\right]$$

III. Angle of contact :

$$\theta = 2\left[\pi - \cos^{-1}\left(\frac{r_1 + r_2}{D}\right)\right]$$

Maximum power is transmitted by a belt where centrifugal tension

$$T_c = \frac{1}{2} \times \text{Maximum tension}$$

Maximum permissible velocity of belt is given by the relation

$$T = \frac{3wv^2}{I}$$

where w is the weight of belt per meter length.

4.6.10. Governor

The function of a governor is to maintain the speed of an engine within prescribed speed limits for varying load conditions. Thus a governor comes into action when the load on the engine varies. Various types of governors are:

I. Simple governor-watt type
II. Proel governor
III. Portor governor
IV. Hartnell governor
V. Spring control governor

4.6.11. Sensitiveness

Sensitiveness of governor is defined as the ratio of the difference between the maximum and minimum equilibrium speed to the mean equilibrium speed. Thus between speeds N_1 and N_2,

$$\text{Sensitiveness} = \frac{N_1 - N_2}{2(N_1 + N_2)}$$

4.6.12. Stability

A governor is said to be stable when for each speed within the working range the ball weights occupy a definite specified position. In other words, there is only one radius of the governor weights for each equilibrium speed.

4.6.13. Isochronism

A governor is said to be isochronous if the equilibrium speed is constant for all radii of rotation of the balls within the working range. Isochronism is desirable when approximately one constant speed is desired to be kept for all loads.

4.6.14. Hunting

A very sensitive governor may not be very stable. The speed controlled by it may fluctuate continuously. Thus in case of a very sensitive governor, the sleeve may shuttle between extreme position causing hunting.

4.6.15. Vibrations

Dynamically unbalanced masses in rotating machines cause oscillatory forces which result in mechanical vibrations. Some of the terms used in mechanical vibrations are:

(i) Frequency
(ii) Cycle
(iii) Period
(iv) Free vibrations
(v) Natural frequencies
(vi) Forced vibrations
(vii) Resonance
(viii) Damping

4.7. MACHINE DESIGN

Designing of machine is done to create a structure that can convert and control motions either with or without transmitting power. To comply with the commercial aspect, not only should the design be capable of performing required task, but its initial cost, running cost and maintenance charges should also be minimum. Thus, the best design should involve the least cost and also the consistent with weight appearance and other general requirements.

For the designers, analysis is the first step. The detailed analysis of the parts involved is carried out. Then individual components are designed keeping in view the stresses involved, various motion etc. Selectin of proper material is one of the most important aspects of design. Thus, a designer must have knowledge of metallurgy, strength of materials, theory of machines, manufacturing processes and also concepts of asthetic appearance design etc. As far as possible standard components like nuts, bolts of the sizes normally available arc selected.

4.7.1. Process for Designing a Machine Part

(i) Design of all components and preparation of all necessary drawings and detail specification.

(ii) A preliminary design of the machine structure, system or process to wire specifications for major components.

(iii) Forces acting on the elements are determined and the element is designed as link, beam, shaft or column.

(iv) Suitable material is selected for the component alongwith allowable stress and factor of safety.

(v) The consideration of different schemes for solving the problem and the selection of one to be investigated in more detail. Feasibility studies, backed up by special research if necessary, are feature of this stage in the process.

4.7.2. Stresses in Simple Machine Member

With other considerations, machine design involves the proper sizing of machine member to satisfy withstand the maximum stress which is induced within the member when it is subjected separately or to any combination of bending, torsional, axial or transverse loads. In general ductile materials, such as the soft steels are weaker in shear and are designed on the basis of maximum shear stress; while brittle materials, such as cast iron and certain hard steels are usually designed on the basis of the maximum normal stress in either tension or compression.

4.7.3 Pulley Design

Pulleys are wheels used to transmit power from one shaft to another by means of belts or ropes. The main parts of the pulley are the hub, rim and arms. While designing the pulley, following points must be considered:

Diameter (D) : Diameter of pulley is calcualted either by velocity ratio consideration or from the centrifugal stress consideration

$$D = \frac{60V}{\pi N}$$

Where P = Density of rim material

V = Velocity of rim in cm/sec

$$ft = \frac{PV^2}{g}$$

Thickness of the Pulley : Thickness of the pulley rim is calculated by using the relation $\left(\frac{D}{300} + 2\,\text{mm}\right)$ to $\left(\frac{D}{200} + 3\,\text{mm}\right)$ for single belt and $\left(\frac{D}{300} + 2\,\text{mm}\right)$ to $\left(\frac{D}{300} + 6\,\text{mm}\right)$ four double belt.

Width of the Pulley : If the width of the belt is known, then the width of the face of the pulley is taken 25% greater than the width of belt

$$B = 1.25\, b$$

where b = Width of Belt.

Arm Dimensions : Number of arms = 4 for 20 to 60 cm diameter and 6 for 60 to 150 cm diameter.

If the dia. is less than 20 cm, solid disc is used.

The arm is condidered as a cantilver fixed at hub and carries a concentrated load at the rim end

Length of arm = radius of pulley.

Hub : Diameter of hub $d_1 = 1.5\, d$

$$= 25 \text{ mm of } 2d$$

$$\text{Length of hub} = \frac{2}{3}\text{B or } \frac{\pi}{2}d$$

where d = Diameter of shaft.

4.7.4. Rolling Bearings

Rolling Bearings are known as anti-friction bearings. For satisfactory functioning proper selection mounting, lubrication and possibly shielding whenever required, are the major considerations. The coefficient of friction in rolling bearing varies with speed, load, amount of lubrication assembly,

Basic staitc load rating C_0 is given by

$$C_0 = f_0\, i\, Z\, D^2 \cos\alpha$$

where

i = Number of rows of balls in any one bearing

α = Nominal angle of contact

Z = Number of balls per row

D = Ball diameter

4.7.5. Gears Designing

While designing the gears, following considerations must be kept in mind :

(i) Suitable material

(ii) Velocity ratio

(iii) Horse power transmitted

(iv) Wear characterstics of teeth

(v) Lubrication arrangement

(vi) Strength of teeth to withstand the static loading due to starting torque or dynamic loading during normal running conditions.

4.7.6. Buckling of Machine Members

Rigidity may in some cases determine the design of a machine memeber. The member may be strong enough to prevent a stress failure, but may not sufficiently rigid for satisfactory operation.

Axial deflection δ due to axial load F is based on Hook's Law and is given by

$$\delta = \frac{FL}{AE}$$

where L = Axial length of member

E = Modulus of elasticity

A = Cross-sectional area.

Torsional deflection $\theta°$ due to a torsional load on a solid circular section is

$$\theta° = \frac{K\tau L}{\eta D^4}$$

For a hollow member of a circular cross-section, the angular deflection is

$$\theta° = \frac{K\tau L}{\eta\left(D_0{}^4 - D_i{}^4\right)}$$

where τ = Torque

L = Axial length of rigidity

η = Modulus of rigidity

D = Diameter of solid member

D_0 = Outside diameter of hollow member

D_1 = Inside diameter of hollow member

K = Numeric constant.

Lateral deflection due to bending only may be determined by solving the differential equation of the electric curve of the neutral axis

$$\frac{d^2y}{dx^2} = \frac{M}{EI}$$

where M = Bending moment

E = Modulus of elasticity

I = Rectanguler Moment of inertia

y = Deflection

x = Distance from the end of member to the section where the deflection is to determined. The deflection of beam may be determined by any one of the following methods:

(a) Area of moment method

(b) Step function method

(c) Conjugate beam method

(d) Graphical integration

(e) Theorem of Castigliano.

OBJECTIVE TYPE QUESTIONS

1. Calorific value of a fuel is based on
A. 1 kg of fuel B. 1 kg/m^3 of fuel
C. 1 m^3 of fuel D. its specific volume

2. The bomb calorimeter is an apparatus to measure the
A. calorific value of a gaseous fuel
B. calorific value of soild and gaseous fuels
C. calorimetric composition of any solid bomb material
D. calorific value of a solid or liquid fuel

3. The maximum heat content at 100°C in cal/m^3 is possessed by the following gas.
A. CH_4 B. SO_2
C. O_2 D. CO_2

4. The major constituents of a fuel are
A. Carbon, Hydrogen and Oxygen
B. Carbon, Hydrogen, Oxygen and Nitrogen
C. Carbon, Oxygen, Hydrogen, Nitrogen, Phosphours and sulphur
D. Carbon and Hydrogen

5. For combustion of gaseous fuels the following is of great use
A. Mendeleef's periodic table B. Dalton's Law
C. Brayton Cycle D. Avogadro Hypothesis

6. Lower Calorific value of a fuel is the
A. Vaule of heat produced by a fuel under constant pressure and volume
B. Value of heat produced which can be utilised for commercial purposes
C. Lowest amount of heat produced by a fuel by burning 1 m^3 of fuel
D. Lowest amount of heat produced by any fuel

7. Which one of the properties given below is an intensive property of the system?
A. Volume B. Temperature
C. Kinetic energy D. Potential energy

8. Which one of the properties given below is an extensive property of the system?
A. Pressure B. Temperature
C. Potential energy D. Viscosity

9. The mechanical equivalent of heat 'J' is equal to
A. 4.1868 kg/k.cal B. 4.186 J/cal.
C. 4.1868 k.cal/kg D. 4.1868 kJ

10. In metric system, the unit of heat is given as
A. C.H.U. B. B.TU.
C. k.cal D. Kelvin

11. The ratio of the specific heat at constant pressure to specific heat at constant volume for air is equal to

A. 1.4
B. 0.14
C. 14
D. 140

12 The general gas equation is given as

A. $PV = mT$
B. $\frac{P}{V} = mT$
C. $PV = RT$
D. $\frac{P}{V} = mRT$

13. In S.I. units, pressure is expressed in

A. kgf/cm^2
B. mm of mercury
C. N/m^2 or bar
D. None of the above

14. For any gas

A. $C_P = C_v$
B. $C_P < C_v$
C. $C_P > C_v$
D. None of the above

15. Gases have

A. Two specific heats
B. Three specific heats
C. One specific heat
D. None of the above

16. The value of C_P for air is equal to

A. 2.38 k.cal/kg °K
B. 0.024 k.cal/kg °K
C. 3.238 k.cal/kg °K
D. 0.424 k.cal/kg °K

17. In a closed system

A. Energy transfers from surrounding to system
B. Energy transfers from system to surrounding
C. Energy transfers from system to surrounding and vice versa
D. Energy as well as mass cross the boundaries

18. Centrifugal pump is an example of

A. Isolated system
B. Closed system
C. Steady flow system
D. None of the above

19. Heat engine is a device which

A. Convert mechanical energy into heat energy
B. Convert heat energy into mechanical energy
C. Delivers the heat flow from low temperature to a high temperature in a cyclic process
D. Delivers the heat from high temperature to a low temperature in a cyclic process

20. Molar volume is equal to

A. 22.41 m^3 at N.T.P.
B. 2.241 m^3 at N.T.P.
C. 29.27 m^3 at N.T.P.
D. 1.03 m^3 at N.T.P.

21. Equal volumes of different perfect gases at same temperature and pressure contain

A. Unequal number of molecules

B. Equal number of molecules

C. Any number of molecules depending upon other conditions also

D. None of the above

22 General energy equation for steam boiler is given by

A. $Q = H_2 - H_1$ B. $Q = H_1 + H_2$

C. $Q = H_2 - H_1 +$ work done D. $Q = H_2 - H_1 + K.E.$

Where Q is the heat supplied and $H_2 - H_1$ is change in enthaply

23. Change in entropy during constant pressure process is given by the relation

A. $mC_P \log_e \frac{T_1}{T_2}$ B. $mC_P \log_e \frac{T_2}{T_1}$

C. $m\,C_v \log_e \frac{T_2}{T_1}$ D. $m\frac{R}{J}\log_e \frac{T_2}{T_1}$

24. When a gas is heated at constant volume, the change in entropy is given by the relation

A. $mCp\log_e \frac{T_2}{T_1}$ B. $m\frac{R}{J}\log_e \frac{T_2}{T_1}$

C. $mR\log_e \frac{T_2}{T_1}$ D. $mC_v \log_e \frac{T_2}{T_1}$

25. In isobaric process, the

A. Temperature remains constant B. Volume remains constant

C. $p \times v =$ constant D. Pressure remains constant

26. A refrigeration system works on

A. Second Law of thermodynamics B. First Law of Thermodynamics

C. Zeroth Law of thermodynamics D. None of the above

27. Total heat supplied at constant volume is

A. $Q = m \times C_P \times (T_2 - T_1)$ B. $Q = m \times R \times (T_2 - T_1)$

C. $Q = m \times C_v \times (T_2 + T_1)$ D. $Q = m \times C_v \times (T_2 - T_1)$

28. Internal combusttion engine works on

A. First Law of Thermodynamics B. Second Law of Themodynamics

C. Zeroth Law of Thermodynamics D. None of the above

29. In Orsat's apparatus, the pyrogalic acid is used to absorb

A. CO_2 B. CO

C. O_2 D. N_2

30. In Orsat's apparatus $CuCl_2$ is used to absorb

A. CO_2 B. CO

C. O_2 D. N_2

31. The maximum steam pressure of a locomotive boiler is

A. Above 10 kg/cm^2 B. Seldom below 30 kg/cm^2

C. 14.7 kg/cm^2 at N.T.P. D. Limited to 18 kg/cm^2

32. The type of boilers which have greater reliability are the

A. Fire tube boilers B. Water tube boiler

C. Both have equal reliability D. Those which have single pass flow

33. The danger of an explosion is more serious in the case of

A. Water tube boilers

B. Fire tube boilers

C. Both are equally dangerous

D. It is more dangerous in water tube boilers because of its large water capacity

34. The boiler should conform to the safety regulations of the following

A. I.S. Specifications B. B.S. Code

C. DIN Specifications D. Boiler's Act

35. The use of an economiser with a boiler

A. Raises the plant efficiency

B. Helps bring down the feed water temperature

C. Is that it utilises the exhaust steam in raising the feed water temperature

D. Helps utilise the heat carried by the exhaust flue gases

36. In a boiler the fusible plug is fitted

A. Near the chimney before the exit steam opening

B. On the flange of the water level indicator

C. Inside the combustion chamber

D. At the fire box crown or over the combustion chamber

37. In a steam engine the fluid used for the expansion of work is

A. Coal B. Diesel

C. Steam D. Air fuel mixture

38. A steam engine can be a horizontal, vertical or inclined. This classification is according to the

A. Expansion of steam B. Speed of the engine

C. Position of cylinder D. Field of application

39. Steam engine works on

A. Joule's cycle B. Rankine cycle

C. Constant pressure cycle D. Constant volume cycle

40. The thermal efficiency of steam engine is

A. more than steam turbine B. less than steam turbine

C. equal to steam turbine
D. unpredictable

41. In uniflow steam engine the type of valve used for controlling the steam is
A. Corliss valve
B. Drop valve
C. Slide valve
D. None of the above

42. Eccentric is used to
A. Reduce the speed of steam
B. Control the flow of steam
C. Convert the rotatary motion into reciprocating
D. Convert the reciprocating motion into rotary motion

43. The function of crank is to
A. Control the speed
B. Control the flow of steam
C. Operate the valve of engine
D. Convert reciprocating motion into rotary

44. A steam engine having a speed of 275 R.P.M. is termed as a
A. High speed engine
B. Low speed engine
C. Medium speed engine
D. Very slow speed engine

45. Diagram factor is always
A. More than one
B. Less than one
C. Equal to one
D. None of the above

46. The approximate value of diagram factor is
A. 0.2
B. 0.5
C. 0.7
D. 1.2

47. Which of the following is an example of a fire tube boiler?
A. Locomotive boiler
B. Sterling boiler
C. Babcock and Wilcox boiler
D. All the above

48. High pressure boilers are those which produce steam at a pressure of
A. 80 kg/cm^2 or more
B. 20 kg/cm^2
C. Above 40kg/cm^2 but below 70kg/cm^2
D. Two atmospheres and above

49. The Cornish boiler differes from the Lancashire boiler in that
A. It contains one flue tube instead of two
B. Flow of gases is in the reverse direction
C. The cornish boiler is fire tube boiler whereas Lancashire is water tube boiler
D. All the above points of difference

50. Diagram factor is given by the relation

A. $\text{D.F.} = \dfrac{\text{Area of actual indicated diagram}}{\text{Area of hypothetical diagram}}$

B. $\text{D.F.} = \dfrac{\text{Area of actual indicated diagram}}{\text{Length of actual indicated diagram}}$

C. $\text{D.F.} = \dfrac{\text{Area of hypothetical diagram}}{\text{Length of hypothetical diagram}}$

D. $\text{D.F.} = \dfrac{\text{Area of hypothetical diagram}}{\text{Area of actual indicated diagram}}$

51. The relationship between stage efficiency, heat factor and overall efficiency of a multistage turbine is given by

A. $e_{\text{overall}} = \dfrac{e_{\text{stage}}}{\text{H.F.}}$

B. $e_{\text{overall}} = e_{stage} \times \text{H.F.}$

C. $e_{\text{overall}} = \dfrac{\text{H.F.}}{e_{stage}}$

D. $e_{\text{overall}} \times e_{stage} \times \text{H.F.} = 1$

52 The efficiency of the Rankine Cycle is given by

A. $\dfrac{H_1 - H_2}{H_1 - H_{w_2}}$

B. $\dfrac{H_1 + H_2}{H_1 - H_{w_2}}$

C. $\dfrac{H_1 + H_2}{H_1 + H_{w_2}}$

D. $\dfrac{H_1 - H_2}{H_1 + H_{w_2}}$

53. Indicated horse power developed inside the steam engine cylinder is given by the relation

A. $\text{I.H.P.} = \dfrac{P_m LAN}{75 \times 60}$

B. $\text{I.H.P.} = \dfrac{2P_m LAN}{75 \times 60}$

C. $\text{I.H.P.} = \dfrac{4P_m LAN}{75 \times 60}$

D. $\text{I.H.P.} = \dfrac{2P_m LAN}{60}$

54. The boiler that is most suitable for meeting fluctuating demands of steam is the

A. Lancashire boiler
B. Cornish boiler
C. Locomotive boiler
D. Cochran boiler

55. The draught in the Locomotive boiler is produced by

A. Means of the vacuum pump in it
B. The flow of steam from the fire box into the engine cylinder
C. The combined action of suction action of pump and pressure of steam
D. The motion of locomotive on rails

56. At the critical pressure of the steam the heat is equal to

A. 100
B. 250

C. Zero D. 80

57. The function of the fusible plug in a boiler is to

A. Lift the lever and start the pump for water supply in case of failure

B. Extinguish the fire if the water level in it falls below a certain level

C. Extinguish the fire if the water supply pump trips off

D. act as a safety valve

58. Boiler efficiency is the ratio of the

A. Energy absorbed by feed water to the energy supplied by the fuel

B. Energy released by feed water to the energy supplied by fuel

C. Energy utilised by feed water to energy absorbed by feed water

D. Boiler H. P to the pump H.P multiplied by the thermal efficiency of the system

59. Boiler H.P. is defined as

A. The evaporation of 15-65 kg of water per hour at 100°C into dry saturated steam

B. The work done for evaporation of 1 kg of steam per hour at 100°C into dry saturated steam

C. The amount of work done by the boiler in evaporating per unit kg of steam at 100°C into dry saturated steam at the same pressure

D. The net work done plus the frictional loss incurred to evaporate 1 kg of steam at saturation pressure into dry superheated steam

60. A balanced draught is one which

A. Contains the correct amount of draught

B. Is a combination of the forced and induced draughts

C. Produces the desired draught in the chimney

D. Gives a continuous state of balanced flow of air

61. A fuel which has a higher self ignition temperature

A. Detonates less

B. Helps detonation

C. Results in smooth burning of charge

D. Increases the rate of ignition

62. Pre-ignition

A. Is the spontaneous ignition of the last part of charge

B. Is resorted to at higher altitudes

C. Increases the efficiency and saves unburnt fuel

D. Causes reduced efficiency and loss of power

63. The efficiency of internal combustion engine ranges from

A. 15 to 35% B. 20 to 40%

C. 25 to 30% D. 30 to 35%

64. The firing order in a four-stroke I.C. engine is

A. 1-2-3-4
B. 1-4-3-2
C. 1-3-4-2
D. 1-2-4-3

65. The firing order in a six-stroke engine is

A. 1-5-3-4-2-6
B. 1-3-4-2-5-6
C. 1-5-3-4-6-2
D. 1-5-2-4-3-6

66. The quantity control method of governing is used in

A. Diesel engines
B. Rocket engines
C. Petrol engines
D. Steam engines

67. The delay period in S.I. engine is about

A. 0.10 secs
B. 0.0002 secs
C. 0.002 secs
D. The ignition time lag

68. The unstable compounds which cause detonation are

A. Oxides and intert substances formed during the course of reaction
B. Ketones and sulphur compounds
C. Petroxides, aldehydes and ketones
D. Aldehydes, oxides and sulphides

69. In the liquid cooling system in I.C. engines the thermostat allows the water to go to the radiator when the temperature of the water reaches about

A. 60°C to 65°C
B. 80°C to 85°C
C. 95°C to 97°C
D. Slightly below 100°C

70. Using a perfect combustion chamber in a gas turbine it is possible to get a combustion efficiency of about

A. 80-90%
B. 78%
C. 99%
D. Two-third, the theoretically calculated efficiency

71. Which among the following can be used for Turbojet engines?

A. Kerosene
B. Methyl Alcohol
C. High speed diesel
D. Demethylated spirit

72 Dopes is added to the engine fuel

A. to reduce its detonation tendency
B. to improve lubrication
C. to improve lubrication and reduce detonation
D. None of the above

73. The thermal efficiency of an I.C. engine is

A. More than external combstion engine
B. Less than external combustion engine
C. Equal to exteral combustion engine
D. Independent of method of fuel ignition

74. If a four-stroke engine is revolving of at 1200 R.P.M., then the number of explosions are equal to

A. 1200
B. 600
C. 2400
D. 300

75. If 'L' is the stroke length and r is the crank radius then

A. $L = r$
B. $L = 4r$
C. $L = \frac{r}{2}$
D. $L = 2r$

76. In I.C. engine the type of governing used is

A. Quality governing
B. Quantity governing
C. Hit and miss governing
D. None of the above

77. Which one is not related to I.C. engine?

A. Gas turbine
B. Four-stroke I.C. engine
C. Two-stroke S.I. engine
D. Steam turbine

78. Which is related to I.C. engine only?

A. Distributor
B. Spark plug
C. Atomiser
D. Carburettor

79. Spark ignition engine works on

A. Carnot cycle
B. Rankine cycle
C. Constant pressure cycle
D. Constant volume cycle

80. The term 'Bore' in I.C. engine is used for

A. Diameter of the piston
B. Inside diameter of cylinder
C. diameter of piston ring
D. None of the above

81. Displacement volume or swept volume is the volume displaced by the piston in

A. Two strokes
B. Four strokes
C. One stroke
D. Half stroke

82 The piston of an I.C. engine completes two strokes in

A. 180° of crank rotation
B. 360° of crank rotation
C. 540° of crank rotation
D. 720° of crank rotation

83. Ignition quality of pertol is expressed by

A. Octane Number
B. Cetane number
C. Calorific value
D. None of these

84. The pistons are usually given a coating such as tin plating in order to

A. Conduct heat efficiency
B. Reduce possibility
C. Reduce friction
D. None of these

85. Ignition quality of diesel fuel oil is expressed by an index called

A. Cetane number
B. Calorific value
C. Octane number
D. None of these

86. High speed diesel engines need an approximate cetane number of

A. 1 B. 10

C. 50 D. 100

87. Carbon residue in diesel oil should not be more than

A. 0.01% B. 0.1%

C. 0.5% D. 1%

88. Piston rings are usually made of

A. Steel B. Cast iron

C. Aluminium D. Metal

89. Which is false about V-type engines?

A. Less over head clearance B. Casting less liable clearance

C. Compact design D. All of the above

90. In loop scavenging, the top of piston is

A. Contoured B. Depressed

C. Slanted D. Flat

91. The refrigeration is used for

A. Food preservation B. Comfort

C. Cold storage and ice factories D. All the above three

92. The coldest part in the domestic refrigerator is

A. Condenser B. Evaporator

C. Receiver D. Compressor

93. The refigeration system works on

A. First law of thermodynamics B. Second law of thermodynamics

C. Zeroth law of themodynamics D. None of the above

94. The capacity of a refrigerating machine is expressed in

A. Tonnes of refrigeration

B. Terms of lowest temperature attained

C. Term of weight of a machine

D. Terms of voulume of a space to be cooled

95. Tonnes of refrigeration means

A. The weight of machine is one tonne

B. The weight of refrigerant used is one tonne

C. The rate of abstraction of heat from the space to be cooled

D. None of the above

96. The domestic refrigerator works on the principle of

A. Vapour absorption refrigeration system

B. Vapour compression refrigeration system

C. Thermo-electric refrigeration system

D. Liquid gas refrigeration system

97. The refrigerant used in the domestic refrigerator is
A. Ammonia
B. Freon (CCl_2F_2)
C. Fluorine
D. Methyl chloride

98. The liquid refrigerant which enters the evaporator is at
A. Low pressure
B. Low temperature
C. Low pressure and temperature both
D. High pressure and temperature both

99. Air refrigerator works on
A. Rankine cycle
B. Otto cycle
C. Carnot cycle
D. Bell coleman cycle

100. The working fluld in Bell Coleman cycle is
A. Freon-12
B. CO_2
C. Ammonia
D. Air

101. In refrigeration system using ammonia as refrigerant, the piping are made of
A. Copper
B. Aluminium
C. Brass
D. Steel

102. The unit of refrigerating effect is
A. kcal
B. kcal/J
C. kcal/min
D. Degree Kelvin

103. The refrigerant used for domestic refrigerator must be
A. Non-corrosive
B. Non-toxic and odourless
C. Of high working pressure
D. All the above three

104. The compressor of the refrigerator
A. Sucks the refrigeration from the evaporator
B. Deliver the compressed refrigerant to the condenser
C. Both A and B
D. Regulates the quantity of refrigerant

105. Cooling of water in an earthen pitcher is an example of
A. Steam jet refrigeration
B. Evaporation refrigeration
C. Vapour absorption refrigeration
D. Vapour compression refrigeration

106. Aqua ammonia is a solution of ammonia and
A. Freon-12
B. Freon-22
C. Water
D. CO_2

107. Aqua ammonia solution is used in
A. Vapour compression system
B. Vapour absorption system
C. Air refrigeration system
D. Evaporative cooling

108. The circulation of the refrigerant in an electrolux refrigerator takes place by
A. A pump
B. A compressor
C. gravity
D. None of the above

109. The condenser of domestic refrigerator is fitted

A. Below the evaporator
B. On the back of the refrigerator
C. Near the compressor
D. On the top of the refrigerator

110. The function of the expansion valves is

A. To control the pressure
B. To control the temperature
C. To regulate the flow of refrigerant
D. All the above three

111. The temperature of air measured by an ordinary thermometer is called the

A. Dry bulb temperature
B. Wet bulb temperature
C. Saturation temperature
D. None of the above

112 The temperature at which condensation of moisture begins when the air is cooled, is known as

A. Dry bulb temperature
B. Dew point temperature
C. Saturation temperature
D. Condensation temperature

113. The device used to regulate the flow of the refrigerant in a system is known as

A. Capillary tube
B. Solenoid valve
C. Thermostatic valve
D. All of the above

114. The use of compressor is not required in

A. Vapour compression system
B. Bell coleman refrigerator
C. Vapour absorption system
D. Air refrigeration system

115. In a vapour compression system, the compression of refrigerant vapour follow the law

A. $pvr = C$
B. $pv = C$
C. $pvn = C$
D. None of the above

116. In case of dry compression, the vapours

A. Enter the compressor in a wet state
B. Leave the compressor in dry saturated state
C. Enter the compressor in dry saturated state
D. None of the above

117. The Bell Coleman Cycle consists of

A. Two adiabatic processes and two constant pressure processes
B. Two adiabatic processes and two constant volume processes
C. Two isothermal processes and two adiabatic processes
D. Two constant volume processes and two constant pressure processes

118. C.O.P. is always

A. More than one
B. Less than one
C. Equal to one
D. Unpredictable

119. Too much freezing around the freezer is due to

A. Defective door seal
B. Frequent opening of door

C. Storing of hot food stuff
D. Low vlotage

120. The air which does not come in contact with the cooling coil while passing over it, is known as
A. Wet air
B. Saturated air
C. Dry air
D. By pass air

121. Which one of the following compressors is a displacement compressor?
A. Reciprocating air compressor
B. Vane blower
C. Centrifugal blower
D. Axial flow compressor

122. Under standard atmospheric condition, the velocity of air is
A. 236 m/s
B. 336 m/s
C. 436 m/s
D. 536 m/s

123. Critical pressure for steam is
A. 185.85 kg/cm^2
B. 212.55 kg/cm^2
C. 225.65 kg/cm^2
D. 245.55 kg/cm^2

124. Which of the following fluid can be used in binary vapour cycle?
A. Mercury
B. Diphenyl oxide
C. Aluminium bromide
D. Any of the above

125. Which of the following loss in steam turbines is negligible?
A. Residual velocity loss
B. Leakage loss
C. Mechanical friction loss
D. Radiation

126. Ljungstrom steam turbine is a
A. Radial flow turbine
B. Axial flow turbine
C. Mixed flow turbine
D. Any of the above

127. Which of the following is preferred for supercharging of internal combustion engines?
A. Roots blower
B. Axail flow compressor
C. Both fixed and moving blades
D. Reciprocating compressor

128. An axial flow compressor has
A. Larger blades at gas entry and smaller blades at exit
B. Smaller blades at gas entry and larger blades at exit
C. Identical blades at exist as well as entry
D. Size of blades remains same only angles changes

129. Gas turbine used in aircraft is of
A. Open cycle type
B. Closed cycle type with reheating
C. Closed cycle with reheating and regeneration
D. Open cycle type with reheating, regeneration and inter-cooling

130. In which of the following plant inferior quality fuel can be used?
A. Open cycle gas turbine with regeneration
B. Open cycle gas turbine with inter-cooling

C. Open cycle gas turbine with reheating and regeneration
D. Closed cycle gas turbine

131. The ratio of actual velocity to the local velocity of sound is called
A. Velocity ratio B. Velocity factor
C. Speed ratio D. Mach number

132. In a nozzle, once the critical conditions are achieved at the throat then which of the following remains constant?
A. Density of fluid B. Velocity of fluid
C. Flow rate D. All of the above

133. In a nozzle under choked flow conditions pressure waves travel, in the divergent portion, at
A. Subsonic speed B. Sonic speed
C. Supersonic Speed D. Subsonic to supersonic speed

134. Which of the following is a pressure compounded turbine?
A. Parson's turbine B. Curtis turbine
C. Rateau turbine D. All of the above

135. Which of the following steam turbine has indentical fixed and moving blades
A. Curtis turbine B. Rateau turbine
C. Parson's turbine D. None of the above

136. Thermal efficiency of a gas turbine is in the range
A. 50 to 60% B. 40 to 50%
C. 30 to 40% D. 20 to 30%

137. A diffuser
A. Converts kinetic energy into thermal energy
B. Converts potential energy into kinetic energy
C. Converts pressure energy into kinetic energy
D. Converts thermal energy into kinetic energy

138. The advantage of a gas turbine over a reciprocating engine is
A. Perfect balancing of rotor B. Continuous and uniform power
C. Usually small working pressures D. All of the above

139. Overall efficiency of a gas turbine is
A. Equal to Rankine cycle efficiency
B. Equal to Carnot cycle efficiency
C. Less than Diesel cycle efficiency
D. More than Otto or Diesel cycle efficiency

140. The flow on two sides of a normal shock wave is
A. Sub-sonic
B. Sonic
C. Supersonic
D. Supersoinc on one side and sub-soinc on the other side

141. The power transmitted by belt drive will be maximum if the maximum tension in the belt is

A. Twice the tension in the slack side
B. Equal to the tension in the slack side
C. Three times the tension due to centrifugal force
D. Equal to the tension due to centrifugal force

142. The efficiency of transmitting power will be maximum in case of

A. Rope drive B. Open belt drive
C. V-belt drive D. Chain drive

143. The power transmitted by a belt drive is maximum when the centrifugal tension as compared to the maximum tension is

A. One-third B. Equal
C. Double D. Three times

144. The radial distance between the top of the tooth and the bottom of the tooth space in the mating gear is known as

A. Addendum B. Dedendum
C. Pitch D. Clearance

145. A simple gear train is one in which each shaft carries

A. One wheel B. Two wheels
C. Three wheels D. Any number of wheels

146. Which amongst the following constitute a link?

A. Piston and piston rod
B. Piston rod and cross head
C. Piston crankpin and crank shaft
D. Piston, piston-rod and cross head of a steam engine

147. A flexible link is one which

A. Is deformed to the extent of its flexbility
B. While transmitting motion is not deformed at all
C. Can under go any amount of deformation above yield point
D. While transmitting motion is partly deformed but in a manner which does not have any affect on the transmission of motion

148. When motion is transmitted by means of a fluid it is known as

A. Flexible link B. Rigid link
C. Fluid link D. None of the above

149. Links which do not suffer any deformation while transmitting motion are called

A. Flexible links B. Rigid links
C. Fluid links D. None of the above

150. A simple mechanism has

A. One link B. Two links

C. Three links | D. Four links

151. The three types of links are

A. Cross, rigid, fluid
B. Rigid, elastic, fluid
C. Rigid, flexible, fluid
D. Strength, rigid, flexible

152 When two elements have surface contact and relative motion between them, it is called as

A. Higher pair
B. Turning pair
C. Lower pair
D. Sliding pair

153. The fluid under pressure in hydraulic crane act as a

A. Rigid link
B. Fluid link
C. Flexible link
D. All the above

154. Belts used for power transmission is an example of

A. Rigid link
B. Fluid link
C. Flexible link
D. None of the above

155. Any two links which have constrained relative motion between them, constitute a

A. Kinematic pair
B. Couple
C. Joint
D. Structure

156. The automobile steering gear is an example of

A. Higher pair
B. Lower pair
C. Closed pair
D. None of the above

157. In a higher pair, the relative motion is

A. Purely turning
B. Purely sliding
C. Due to surface contact
D. The combination of sliding and turning

158. When one element is constrained to roll over the other element the pair so formed is known as

A. Turning pair
B. Sliding pair
C. Rolling pair
D. Spherical pair

159. The temp. of the surface of the sun can be inferred from the study of the

A. Solar flares
B. solar shots
C. solar corona
D. solar spectrum

160. In a turning pair

A. One link is constrained to have only a turning motion relative to the other
B. One element is constrained to have sliding motion relative to another
C. One elements is constrained to have rolling motion over the other
D. One link turns about the other by means of threads

161. Flat belts running over a pulley forms

A. A closed pair
B. An open pair

C. A screw pair
D. A spherical pair

162. For a kinematic chain, if L represents the number of links and J respresents the number of joints, then

A. $J = \frac{2}{3}(L+2)$
B. $L = \frac{2}{3}(J+2)$
C. $J = \frac{3}{2}(L+1)$
D. $L = \frac{3}{2}(J+2)$

163. The relation between numbers of links *(l)* and number of pairs *(p)* is given as
A. $l = (2p - 1)$
B. $l = (2p - 4)$
C. $p = (2l - 2)$
D. $p = (2l - 1)$

164. In doulbe slider crank chain the number of possible inversion are
A. Two
B. Three
C. Four
D. Six

165. In slider crank the number of possible inversion are
A. Three
B. Four
C. Five
D. Six

166. Crankshaft rotating in a journal bearing of an engine forms a
A. Rolling pair
B. Sliding pair
C. Turning pair
D. Screw pair

167. A kinematic chain should have a minimum of
A. One link
B. Two links
C. Three links
D. Four links

168. The Oldham's coupling is used to connect
A. Two parallel shafts distance between whose axes is small and variable
B. Two parallel shafts distance between whose axes is fixed and small
C. To parallel shafts distance between whose axes is small
D. Shafts which are non-intersecting

169. The Scott-Russell mechanism consists of
A. Sliding pairs
B. Turning pairs
C. Sliding as well as turning pairs
D. Sliding pair with a crank mechanism of the Scott-Russell type

170. The Ackermann steering mechanism is prefered to the Davis type because
A. the former has sliding pair
B. the former has turning pair
C. it is mathmatically accurate
D. it is correct in all the positions

171. Spin lock screws are used under the conditions of
A. Severe temperature vibrations
B. Severe vibrations
C. Stess reversals
D. All of the above

172. Tap end studs are generally used on
A. Bearing brackets B. Cylinder heads
C. Fixtures D. All of the above

173. Flexible shafts are made of
A. Thin mild steel rod B. Hollow mild steel
C. Wavy steel wires D. Aluminium

174. Lubricant is not required in
A. Gas bearings B. Hydrostatic bearings
C. Electromagnetic bearings D. Foil bearings

175. The life of ball bearing is usually given in
A. Hours of service B. Total rpm
C. Either of A or B above D. None of the above

176. Bearings provided on passenger coaches in railway are
A. Bush bearing B. Cast iron bearings
C. Ball bearings D. Roller bearings

177. An eye bold is generally provided on
A. Furnaces B. Bench vices
C. Electric motors D. Overhead cranes

178. A ball bearing cannot be provided for
A. Low speed shafts B. Variable speed shafts
C. Variable load shafts D. Automobiles gear shafts

179. Which of the following types of gears are free from interference?
A. Cyclodial B. Hypocycloidal
C. Epicyclodial D. Stub

180. For which of the following gear material the noise level is relatively low
A. Alloy steel B. Graded cast iron
C. Porous materials D. Non-matallic materials

181. Low pressure angle on gears is likely to result in
A. Weaker teeth B. Stronger teeth
C. Pitting D. Abrasion

182 Which steel will have maximum percentage of carbon?
A. C 14 B. 15 Cr 65
C. 20 Cr 18 Ni 2 D. 40 Cr 40

183. In case of steels, as the percentage of carbon content increases
A. Tensile strength decreases B. Percentage elongation decreases
C. Hardness decreases D. Weldability increases

184. Which of the following bearing will have least coefficient of friction?
A. Self-aligning bearing B. Cylindrical roller bearing
C. Thrust ball bearing D. Tapered bearing

185. The coefficient of friction in a rolling bearing is of the order of
A. 0.1 B. 0.2
C. 0.01 D. 0.001

186. Which pair of gears usually has high friction losses?
A. Spur gears B. Bevel gears
C. Helical gears D. Worm and worm wheels

187. The natural frequency of a shaft in bending is
A. Nearly the same as the critical speed
B. Nearly half the critical speed
C. Nearly double the critical speed
D. Exactly the same at which it is running

188. Springs are used
A. to store energy
B. to reduce the magnitude of the transmitted force due to impact or shock
C. to alter vibratory characteristics of a member
D. Any of the above

189. Normally a spring operates within
A. Elastic limits B. Plastic limits
C. Visco-elastic limits D. Para-elastic limits

190. A taper bearing has
A. Tapered inner race B. Tapered outer race
C. Tapered case D. Tapered roller

191. Spring stiffness is
A. Load carrying capacity of spring
B. Load per unit area of base
C. Load/cross sectional area of spring
D. Load/unit deflection

192. In a ball bearing sleeve is fixed to
A. Carry more load
B. Reduce friction
C. Reduce wear
D. Prevent relative axial movement between the shaft and bearing

193. The balls in a ball bearing remain in position
A. Due to dead load on bearing B. Due to centrifugal force
C. By lubricant D. In a cage

194. Small steel balls are manufactured by
A. Casting B. Turning in lathe
C. Rolling D. Cold heading

195. In a ball bearing steel balls are made of
A. Cast iron B. Carbon steel

C. Stainless steel D. Carbon chrome steel

196. In oilless bearings

A. There is no external supply of lubricant
B. The lubricant is achieved by adding solid lubricants
C. Grease is used for lubrication
D. Graphite is used for lubrication

197. Rivets are used as

A. Temporary fastening
B. Permanent fastening
C. Permanent or removable fastening
D. Weak fastening

198. In a rivetted joint if the rivets are spaced opposite to each other in adjacent rows the joint is

A. Zig-zag rivetted B. Lap rivetted
C. Butt rivetted D. Chain rivetted

199. The efficiency of a rivetted joint is taken to be the

A. Shearing efficiency B. Crushing efficiency
C. Tearing efficiency D. Lowest of the three efficiencies

200. The unit of heat is

A. Ampere B. Calorie
C. Ohm D. Voltage

ANSWERS

1	**2**	**3**	**4**	**5**	**6**	**7**	**8**	**9**	**10**
C	D	B	D	C	B	B	C	B	C
11	**12**	**13**	**14**	**15**	**16**	**17**	**18**	**19**	**20**
A	C	C	C	A	C	C	C	B	A
21	**22**	**23**	**24**	**25**	**26**	**27**	**28**	**29**	**30**
B	A	B	D	D	A	D	A	C	B
31	**32**	**33**	**34**	**35**	**36**	**37**	**38**	**39**	**40**
D	A	B	D	A	D	C	C	B	B
41	**42**	**43**	**44**	**45**	**46**	**47**	**48**	**49**	**50**
D	C	D	A	B	C	A	A	A	A
51	**52**	**53**	**54**	**55**	**56**	**57**	**58**	**59**	**60**
B	A	B	C	D	C	B	A	A	B
61	**62**	**63**	**64**	**65**	**66**	**67**	**68**	**69**	**70**
A	D	A	C	C	C	C	C	B	C
71	**72**	**73**	**74**	**75**	**76**	**77**	**78**	**79**	**80**
A	A	A	B	D	A	D	C	D	B

81	82	83	84	85	86	87	88	89	90
C	B	A	B	A	C	B	B	A	A
91	**92**	**93**	**94**	**95**	**96**	**97**	**98**	**99**	**100**
D	B	B	A	C	B	B	C	D	D
101	**102**	**103**	**104**	**105**	**106**	**107**	**108**	**109**	**110**
D	C	D	C	B	C	B	C	B	D
111	**112**	**113**	**114**	**115**	**116**	**117**	**118**	**119**	**120**
A	B	D	C	A	C	A	A	C	D
121	**122**	**123**	**124**	**125**	**126**	**127**	**128**	**129**	**130**
B	B	C	D	D	D	A	A	A	D
131	**132**	**133**	**134**	**135**	**136**	**137**	**138**	**139**	**140**
D	D	B	C	C	C	A	D	C	D
141	**142**	**143**	**144**	**145**	**146**	**147**	**148**	**149**	**150**
C	D	A	D	A	D	D	C	B	D
151	**152**	**153**	**154**	**155**	**156**	**157**	**158**	**159**	**160**
C	C	B	C	A	B	D	C	D	A
161	**162**	**163**	**164**	**165**	**166**	**167**	**168**	**169**	**170**
B	B	B	B	B	C	D	A	C	B
171	**172**	**173**	**174**	**175**	**176**	**177**	**178**	**179**	**180**
B	D	C	C	C	D	C	D	A	D
181	**182**	**183**	**184**	**185**	**186**	**187**	**188**	**189**	**190**
A	D	B	D	D	D	A	D	A	D
191	**192**	**193**	**194**	**195**	**196**	**197**	**198**	**199**	**200**
D	D	D	D	D	A	B	D	D	B

2

ELECTRICAL ENGINEERING

Units—Machines—Heating—Power Systems—
Control Systems—Electric Traction—
Objective Type Questions—Answers

This chapter provides a brief amount of work containing units, ohm's law, D.C. circuits, electrostatics, electromagnetism, A.C. circuits and electrical measurements etc.

6.1. UNITS

***(i)* Force :** A force is that physical cause which when acting on a body changes the state of rest or of uniform motion of the body in a straight line. It is a vector quantity.

- S.I. unit of force is Newton (N) : *one Newton* (1 kgm s^{-2}) is that much force, which produces an acceleration of 1 ms^{-2}) in a mass of one kg.
- C.g.s. unit of force is dyne (dyn): *One dyne* (1 gcm sec^{-2}) is that much force, which produces an aceleration of 1 cm sec^{-2}) in a mass of one gram.
  1 N = 10^5 dyn.
- Dimensional formula of F = $[MLT^{-2}]$

***(ii)* Work :** The *work done by a force* is the product of the force and the distance through which the force acts.

$$W = \vec{F}.\vec{S}$$

If θ is the small angle between $\vec{F}$ and $\vec{S}$, then

$$W = Fs \cos \theta.$$

It is a scalar quantity.

- S.I. unit of work done is Joule (J): Work done is said to be 1 *Joule,* is a force of 1 (one) N displaces a body through 1 m in the direction of force
- c.g.s. unit of work done is erg. Work done is said to be 1*erg,* if a force of 1 dyne displaces a body through 1 cm is the direction of force.

$$1 \text{ (one) } J = 10^7 \text{ ergs.}$$

- Dimensional formula of W = $[ML^2T^{-2}]$

(iii) **Power :** The rate of doing work is called *power.* It is a scalar quantity.

- S.I. unit of power is watt (W): Power of an agent is said to be 1watt, if 1 joule of work is done in 1 second.
  Bigger units are kilowatt (= 10^3 watt), and Megawatt (= 10^6 watt)
- c.g.s. unit of power is erg/sec
  $$1 \text{ W} = 10^7 \text{ erg/sec.}$$
- Dimensional formula of P = $[ML^2T^{-3}]$

(iv) **Horse Power :** It is the practical unit of power in M.K.S. system and equal to 746 watt. In metric system of units,

1 H.P. (metric) = 75 × 9.81 Nm = 7355 Watts

(v) **Watt-hour :**

$$\begin{aligned} 1 \text{ kWh} &= 1000 \text{ watt-hour} \\ &= 1000 \times 3600 \text{ Watt-sec} \\ &= 36 \times 10^5 \text{ Joules} \\ &= 3.6 \times 10^6 \text{ Joules or Watt-sec} \end{aligned}$$

(vi) **Conversion of Electrical Units :** 1 kW = 1000 Watts = 1000 Joules/sec

$$\begin{aligned} &= 1000 \text{ Nm/sec} = 10^{10} \text{ ergs/sec.} \\ &= \frac{1000}{735.5} = 1.36 \text{ H.P. (metric)} \end{aligned}$$

Also,
$$\begin{aligned} 1 \text{ kWh} &= 3.6 \times 10^6 \text{ Watt sec} \\ &= \frac{3.6 \times 10^6}{4.180 \times 1000} \text{ k cals} \end{aligned}$$

6.1.1. Ohm's Law

If the temperature and other conditions remain constant, the current through a conductor is proportional to the aplied potential difference and it remains constant. Thus we can say:

$$\text{Current} = \frac{\text{Applied voltage}}{\text{Resistance of the conductor}}$$

$$\text{Resistance} = \frac{\text{Applied voltage}}{\text{Current in the circuit}}$$

Potential across resistance = Current × Resistance.

Conditions for Ohm's Law

1. Voltage-current graph is a *straight line* passing through the origin.

Example : An electrolyte like $CuSo_4$ solution with copper electrodes and a pure metal.

2. The Ohm's law can be applied to D.C. as well as A.C. circuits.

6.1.2. D.C. Circuits

A closed loop of conductors around which the movement of electricity can take place is known as electric circuit. Circuits may be of the following types:

1. Closed circuit
2. Open circuit
3. Short circuit
4. Dead circuit.

(i) **Series Circuit :** When the resistance are connected end to end so that they form any one path for the flow of current, then the resistance are said to be connected in series and such circuits are known as *series circuits.*

(ii) **Parallel Circuits :** When a number of resistanc are connected in such a way that one end of each one is jointed to a common and the other end being jointed to another common point then the resistances are said to be connected in parallel. Such circuits are known as *parallel circuits.*

(iii) **Series-Parallel Circuits :** The combination of series and parallel grouping is known as *series-parallel circuits.*

(iv) **Kirchoff's law :** There are two laws as follows.

Kirchoff's first law : The algebraic sum of all currents at a junction in any network is zero or the sum of incoming current towards any point is equal to the sum of the outgoing currents, away from that point. This law also known as *current law* or junction rule. It is based on *law of conservation of charge,* and is applicable for *parallel circuits.*

Kirchoff's second law : In any closed circuit (or mesh), the algebraic sum of the products of the current and resistance of each part of the circuit is equal to the resultant e.m.f. of the circuit. This law also known as *voltage law* or loop rule. *It is based on* law of conservation of energy, and is applicable for *series circuits.*

6.1.3. Electrostatics

(i) **Electric field :** Any charge *(q)* produces an electric field in the space surrounding it. The field exists whether there are other charges present in the space or not. Thus any point surrounding the charge where some other electric charge experiences an electric force is called an *electric field.* Thus an electric field is said to exist at a point if a force of electric origin is exerted on a charged body placed at that point.

The electric field E(r) at the point r in space is defined as

$$\mathrm{E}(r) = \lim_{q \to 0} \frac{\vec{\mathrm{F}}}{q}$$

(ii) **Coulomb's law :** The force of attraction or repulsion between two charges varies directly as the product of the charges and inversely as the square of the

distance between them. If q_1 and q_2 are the two charges at a distance r apart, then force F between these two points:

$$F = K\frac{q_1 q_2}{r^2}$$

where K is a positive constant.

In SI units, r is in metres, F in newton and charges are in a unit called coulomb (C). In SI units, the constant K is given by

$$K = \frac{1}{4\pi\varepsilon_0} = 9 \times 10^9 \text{ Nm}^2 \text{ C}^{-2}$$

where ε_0 is 8.85×10^{-12} $C^2 N^{-1} m^{-2}$ is called the permittivity of free space.

One coulomb is that charge which when placed at a distance of 1 m from an identical charge, in free space, repels it with a force of 9×10^9 N.

Unit of charge in c.g.s. system is stat-coulomb

1 coulomb = 3×10^9 stat-coulomb or e.s.u. of charge.

Thus, Coulomb's law for vacuum becomes

$$F = \frac{1}{4\pi\varepsilon_0}\frac{q_1 q_2}{r^2}$$

In a material medium, ε_0 is replaced by $\varepsilon = K\varepsilon_0$ where ε is called the permittivity of the medium and K is known as the dielectric constant of the medium.

***(iii)* Laws of electrostatic :**

1. *First law :* Like charges repel each other, whereas unlike charges attract each other.

2. *Second law :* The force exerted between two point charges:

(a) is directly proportional to the product of their strengths,

(b) is inversely proportional to the square of the distance between them and

This law is also known as Coulomb's law and may be expressed mathematically as

$$F \propto \frac{q_1 q_2}{r^2} \text{ or } F = K\frac{q_1 q_2}{r^2}$$

where K is the constant of proportionality.

***(iv)* Equipotential Surface :** *Equipotential surface* is any surface in an electric field which has same electric potential at every point.

***(v)* Potential Gradient :** The potential gradient is the rate of change of potential with distance measured in the direction of electric force. Electric intensity at a point is equal to the negative potential gradient at that point.

***(vi)* Electric intensity :** The electric intensity at any point in the field space around the charge is measured by the force which will act on a unit positive charge placed at that point. Thus,

Electric intensity, $$E = \frac{q}{4\pi\varepsilon_0 r^2}$$

where $\in_0$ is permettivity of the evacuated free space.

***(vii)* Electrostatic lines of force :**

(a) The electrostatic lines of force originate from a positive charge and terminate on a negative charge.

(b) are always normal to the surface of a charged body.

(c) represent the path which a positively charged conductor will follow.

(d) No two lines of force intersect each other.

***(viii)* Electric flux :** The *electric flux* through a given area is the total number of lines of force passing normally through that area.

Numerically, the electric flux (ϕ) through any surface S, open or closed, is equal to the surface integral of the electric field E(r), over that surface S, i.e.,

$$\phi = \int_S E(r).ds$$

Gauss' s theorem : Total electric flux that radiate outward from q coulomb of positive charge kept in vacuum is $1/\varepsilon_0$ times one total charge q contained inside the conductor.

Mathematically,

$$\phi = \oint_S E(r).ds = \frac{1}{\varepsilon_0}\sum_{i=1}^{N} q_i$$

***(ix)* Electric potential :** The electric potential at any point in an electric field surrounding a charged body is equal to the work done in moving a unit positive charge from a point where the potential is zero to that point where the potential is to be measured against the electrostatic force in the field.

The potential at distance r from q is given by $V = \frac{q}{4\pi\varepsilon_0 r}$ Volts

The potential difference between two points A and B is

$$V_B - V_A = \frac{q}{4\pi\varepsilon_0}\left[\frac{1}{r_B} - \frac{1}{r_A}\right]$$

***(x)* Capacitor or Condenser :** A capacitor or condenser consists of two conductors separated by an insulator or dielectric. The presence of second conductor which is usually connected to the earth, enhances the capacity of the system to store charge.

Some important characteristics of capacitors

(a) The current through a capacitor is zero if the voltage across it is not changing with time.

(b) A capacitor is sort of open circuit to DC.

(c) A finite amount of energy can be stored in a capacitor even if the current through the capacitor is zero, such as when the voltage across it is constant.

(d) It is impossible to change the voltage across a capacitor by a finite amount of current in zero time. For this it requires infinite current through the capacitor.

(e) A capacitor resists an abrupt change in the voltage across it in a manner analogous to the way a spring resists an abrupt change in its displacement.

(f) The capacitor never dissipates energy, but only stores it.

Example 1 : Determine the force between two free electrons spaced 1°A (0.01 nm) apart (a typical atomic dimension).

Solution : F is repulsive and $F = (kq_1q_2)/r^2$ with $q_1 = q_2 = 1.6 \times 10^{-19}$ C, and $r = 1.0 \times 10^{-2}$ m. Then

$$F = [(9.0 \times 10^9)(1.6 \times 10^{-19})^2]/(1.0 \times 10^{-2})^2 = 2.3 \times 10^{-8} \text{ N}$$

Example 2 : How many electrons are contained in –1C of charge? What is the total mass of these electrons?

Solution : The electron has charge $-e$, where $e = 1.6 \times 10^{-19}$C. Therefore, in –1.0 C of charge, there are $n = 1.0/1.6 \times 10^{-19} = 6.2 \times 10^{18}$ electrons. Mass of these electrons:

$$M = nm_e = (6.2 \times 10^{18})(9.11 \times 10^{-31} \text{ kg})$$
$$= 5.6 \times 10^{-12} \text{ kg.}$$

6.1.4. Electromagnctism

When a current is passed through a conductor, a magnetic field is set up in concentric circles around the conductor, thus the magnetic field set up due to current carrying conductor is called *electromagnetism.*

Determination of direction of magnetic field around a current carrying conductor : The direction of magnetic field can be determied by the following rules:

(i) Maxwell's cork screw rule : If a right handed screw be rotated along the wire so that it advances in the direction of current, then the direction in which the thumb rotates gives the direction of the magnetic field.

Flux density due to straight conductors is given by

$$B = \frac{\mu_0 IN}{2\pi r} \text{ (in air)}$$

where I is the current in amperes

N is the number of conductors

r is the perpendicular distance of the point from the conductor.

Flux density at the centre of circular loop of conductor is given by

$$B = \frac{\mu_0 I}{2r}$$

where r is the radius of the loop.

Right hand rule : If an observer holds a current carrying conductor in his hand with the extended thumb pointing in the direction of the current, the fingers encircling, the conductor will then point along the direction of the lines of force.

(i) **Electromagnet :** An electromagnet consists of a large number of turns wound on a soft iron piece as shown in Fig. 1.1 given below.

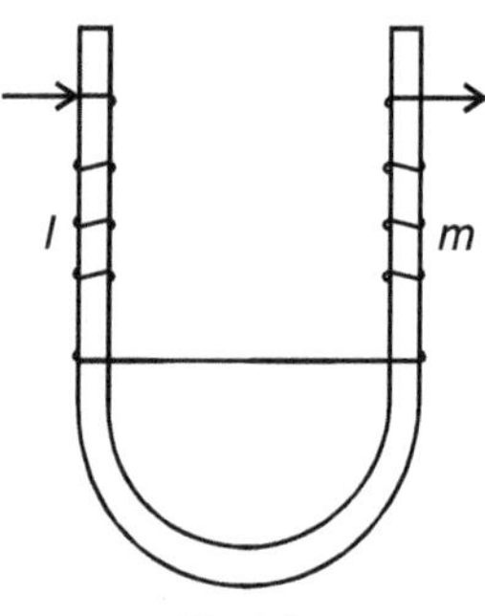

Fig 6.1

The coil is bound oppositely on the limbs l and m so that one end becomes north pole (N) and the other south pole (S).

(ii) **End rule for finding out the polarity :** When current flows in a solenoid (coil) it behaves like a bar magnet. When looked from one end, if the current flowing in the turns of solenoid is clockwise, the pole at the nearer end is south pole and at the further end is north pole.

If the current is flowing in anticlockwise direction, the nearer pole is north pole and further end is south pole.

(iii) **Flux :** The total magnetic lines of force set up by a magnet is called *flux*.

Magnetic flux (ϕ) is given by

$$\phi = \vec{B}.\vec{A}$$

where θ is the angle made by the field $\vec{B}$ with normal drawn to the closed area $\vec{A}$·

- S.I. unit of flux is webe (Tesla-meter^2). Magnetic flux is said to be 1 *weber,* if a uniform magnetic flux of 1 tesla acts normally over a plane area 1 m^2.
- c.g.s. unit of flux is Maxwell (Mx).

$$1 \text{ Wb} = 10^8 \text{ Mx}$$

- Dimensional formula of flux = $[ML^2T^{-2}A^{-1}]$

(iv) **Flux intensity :** The flux per unit area in air is called *flux intensity.* It is denoted by symbol H.

(v) **Flux density :** The flux per unit area in a magnetic matterial is called *flux density.* It is denoted by symbol β.

$$\beta = \text{Flux/Area} = \phi/A;$$

where ϕ = flux;

A = area of cross-section

(v) **Permeability :** It is defined as the ratio of the magnetic induction B to the magnetising field intensity H.

$$\mu = \frac{B}{H}$$

(vi) **Relative permeability :** The ratio of permeability of a medium to the permeability of air is called *relative permeability.*

$$\text{Relative permeability of any material} = \frac{\text{Permeability of medium}}{\text{Permeability of air}}$$

or $\mu_r = \mu/\mu_0 \Rightarrow \mu = \mu_0 \mu_r$

where μ_r = Relative permeability,

μ_0 = Permeability of air, and

μ = Permeability of medium

Also $\mu_0 = 4\pi \times 10^{-7}$ henery/m.

(vii) **Magneto-Motive Force (M.M.F.) :** It is defined as the force which drives or tends to drive magnetic flux through a magnetic circuit.

An m.m.f. is produced, when an electric current flows in a coil consisting of number of turns. This m.m.f. is measured by the product of current in ampere and the number of turns. The unit of m.m.f. is ampere turns.

∴ m.m.f. = N.I. amp. turns (AT)

where N = no. of turns. and

I = current in amp.

(viii) **Reluctance :** The reluctance is the resistance offered by the magnetic circuit to the flow of flux produced in that part of the circuit. Thus

$$R = \frac{m.m.f.}{\phi} \text{ ampere turns/weber}$$

The reluctance of a substance is

(i) directly proportional to the length of flux path (*l*), and

(ii) inversely proportional to the cross-section (A).

Thus $R \propto l/A$

or, $$R = \frac{ATwb}{\mu_0 \mu_r A}$$

The constant of proportionality $\frac{1}{\mu_0 \mu_r}$ or $\frac{1}{\mu_0}$ show that reluctance depends on the *relative permeability.*

$$\therefore \qquad R = \frac{m.m.f}{\text{flux}} \text{AT/W}b$$

It is also determined by the formula

$$R = \frac{l}{\mu_0 \mu_r a}$$

where l = length of the gap
μ_0 = permeability of air
μ_r = relative permeability
a = area of cross-section of magnetic material used.

(ix) **Fleming left hand rule :** This rule is applicable for finding out of one of the unknown quantities out of flux, current and direction of motion.

Keep thumb, first finger and middle finger of your left hand at right angles of each other is a stretch position as shown in Fig. 6.2.

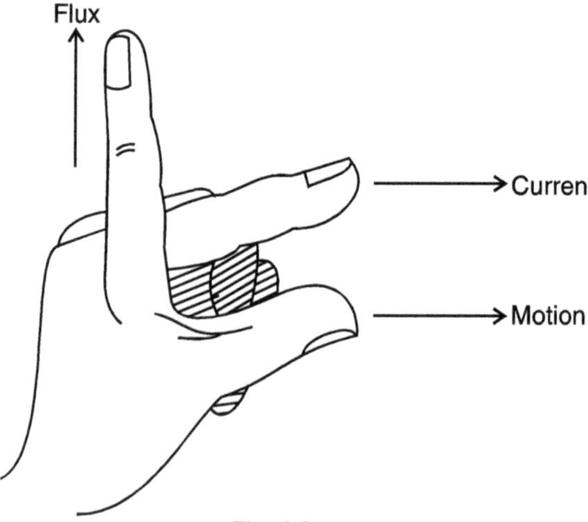

Fig. 6.2

When the first finger points towards the direction of field, midle finger points towards the direction of current, then the direction of force experienced by the conductor will be pointed by the thumb.

(x) **Laws of Electro-magnetic Induction :**

Faraday's first law : Whenever there is a change in the magnetic flux linked with a circuit, an induced e.m.f. is produced in it.

Faraday's second law : The magnitude of induced e.m.f. is equal to the rate of change of the magnetic flux linked with the closed circuit.

Therefore, Faraday's laws gives the magnitude of the induced e.m.f. i.e.,

$$\in \alpha \left|\frac{d\phi}{dt}\right|$$

Lenz's law : The direction of induced e.m.f. (or current) is such that it always opposes the cause that produces it.

Therefore, Lenz's law gives the direction of the induced e.m.f., i.e.,

$$\in = -\frac{d\phi}{dt}$$

Neumann's Law : This infact is the combined effect of the Faraday's law and Lenz's law.

(xii) **Difference between Electric and Magnetic circuits:**

Magnetic Circuits	*Electric Circuits*
1. Strictly speaking, flux does not actually flow in the sense in which current flows.	**1.** Current actually flows.
2. The value of permeability does not vary to a great extent and there is no material which can be called as "*insulator*" to magnetic flux.	**2.** Electical resistance varies very largely for different materials so much so that some substances act as insulators and some as conductors and even super conductors.
3. At a particular temperature, the permeabilities depend upon the total flux.	**3.** At a particular temperature, conductivity (resistance) is constant and is independent of strength of current.
4. There is an expenditure of energy to create a magnetic flux.	**4.** There is an expenditure of energy so long as the current flows.

6.1.5. A.C. Circuits

1. Fundamental of A.C.

An alternating electric or e.m.f. is one which passes through a definite cycle of changes.

Alternating currents and e.m.f. can be represented graphically or vectorially.

(i) **Cycle :** The distance between two consecutive indentical values is called

cycle as shown in Fig. 6.3.

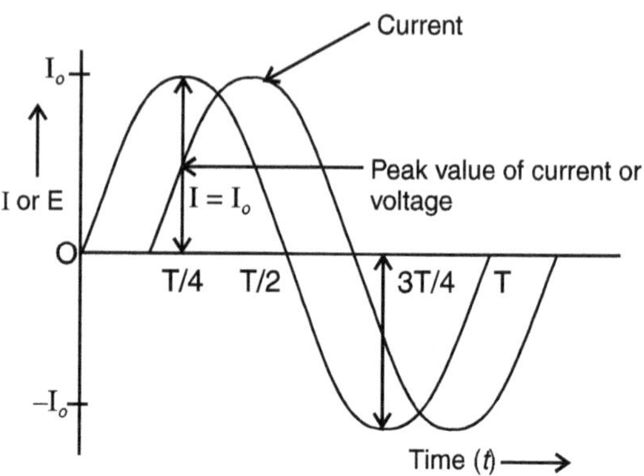

Fig. 6.3

***(ii)* Time period :** The time interval of one each complete cycle as shown in Fig. 6.3 is known as *time period* (T)

$$\therefore \qquad T = 1/f$$

***(iii)* Frequency :** The number of cycles per second is called *frequency*. It is denoted by symbol '*f*' and its unit is cycles/sec (c/s) or Hz/sec.

$$f = \omega/2\pi$$

The frequency depends upon

(a) number of poles and *(b)* speed of the conductor/sec.

$f = \dfrac{P \times N}{2 \times 60}$ where P = no. of poles; N = rev. per min. (r.p.m).

***(iv)* Amplitude :** The maximum value of the cycles is called *amplitude* as shown in Fig. 6.3

***(v)* Phase difference:** The angle difference between their two zero values of e.m.f. and current is called *phase difference* and is denoted by symbol ϕ.

***(vi)* A.C. series circuits :** In d.c. circuits, there is a relationship between the applied voltage and current flowing throgh the circuits. The expression of current is I = V/R where R is the resistance of the circuit. But in a.c. circuits, this relation does not hold good because of magnetic and electrostatic effects.

In an a.c. circuits, the current I is given by the expression

I = V/Z where V = voltage and Z = impedance of circuit.

The following are the types of series circuit.

(a) Pure resistive circuit

(b) Pure inductive circuit

(c) Pure capacitive circuit

(d) R.L.C. series circuits.

***(vii)* Pure resistive circuits :** A circuit which has neither magnetic effect nor electrostatic effect but only resistive effect is called *pure resistive circuit.* All heating elements come under the heading of pure resistive circuit such as ordinary lamps, heaters, electric-iron etc.

***(viii)* Inductance :** The product of flux per amp. and number of turns of the coil is called *inductance*. It is denoted by symbol L and its unit is henry.

***(ix)* Inductive Reactance :** The effect of inductance in an a.c. circuit is called inductive reactance. It is denoted by symbol X_L and its unit is ohm. Its magnitude is given as

$X_L = 2\pi fL$ ohms where f = frequency and L = inductance of the coil in henry.

***(x)* Capacitive reactance :** The effect of capacitance in an a.c. circuit is called *capacitive reactance*. It is denoted by symbol X_C & its unit is also ohm.

Its magnitude is given as

$$X_C = \frac{1}{2\pi fC} \text{ ohms}$$

where f is the frequency and c is the capacitance of the capacitor in Farad.

***(xi)* Power Factor :** The average power of an a.c. circuit is

$$P = V_{eff} \cdot I_{eff.} \cos \phi.$$

This power is also called *true power.* The product $V_{eff} \cdot I_{eff}$ is called *apparent power* which gives true power only when it is multiplied by factor cos ϕ. So the factor cos ϕ is called *power factor* of A.C. circuit. The value of power factor varies from *zero to one*.

***(xii)* Resonance circuit :** The circuit in which $X_L = X_C$ is called resonance circuit.

$$\therefore \qquad 2\pi fL = \frac{1}{2\pi fC} \text{ or } f^2 = \frac{1}{4\pi^2 LC}$$

or,

$$f = \frac{1}{2\pi\sqrt{LC}}$$

where L = inductance in Henry and
C = capacitance in Farad.

The frequency at which X_L becomes equal to X_C is known as resonance frequency and it is denoted by f_0. The resonance frequency can be calculated by the formula

$$f_0 = \frac{1}{2\pi\sqrt{LC}}$$

***(xiii)* A.C. parallel circuits :** When two or more branches are connected in parallel, the circuit is said to be parallel circuit.

Properties : The following are the properties of *parallel circuits :*

(i) The voltage across each branch is same.

(ii) The current in each branch is different and depends upon the value of impedance.

(ii) The angle between voltage and current of each branch will be different.

(iv) The total current will be the vector sum of branch currents.

(v) The total impedance will be

$$\frac{1}{Z} = \frac{1}{Z_1} + \frac{1}{Z_2} + \frac{1}{Z_3} + \ldots$$

or, $$Y = Y_1 + Y_2 + Y_3 + \ldots.$$

Since Admittance (Y) is the reciprocal of impedance, its unit is *mho* and its symbol is ℧.

***(xiv)* Susceptance :** The reciprocal of reactance is called susceptance, which is denoted by letter ℧ and its unit is *mho* and its symbol is ℧. It can be calculated by the formula

$$b = Y.\sin\phi = \frac{1}{Z}.\frac{X}{Z} = \frac{X}{Z^2}$$

***(xv)* Methods of Solving A.C. parallel circuits :** The following are the methods of solving A.C. parallel circuits

1. Vector method
2. Admittance method
3. J-method

***(xvi)* Q-Factor (Magnification factor) :** It is defined as the ratio of circulating current to the line current.

$\therefore$ $$\text{Q factor} = \frac{I_C}{I} = \frac{2\pi f_r L}{R}$$

where f_r = resonance frequency; L = Inductance, and R = Resistance.

6.1.6. Electrical Measurements

Meters which are used for measuring electrical quantities in an electrical circuit are called *Measuring Instruments.* The meters which measure current, voltage, power, energy are called Ammeters, Voltmeters, Wattmeter, Energymeter respectively.

1. Requirements of an Indicating Instrument : The following are requirements for a indicating instrument:

(i) Deflecting torque *(ii)* Controlling torque *(iii)* Damping torque.

2. Application of various effects : The various effects employed for the construction of the electrical instruments are:

(i)	Magnetic effect	For Voltmeter, Ammeter and Wattmeter
(ii)	Thermal effect	For Ammeters and Voltmeters
(iii)	Electrodynamic effect	For Ammeters, Voltmeters and Wattmeters
(iv)	Chemical effect	For D.C. Ampere hour meter
(v)	Electromagnetic Induction effect	For Ammeter, Voltmeter, Wattmeter and Energymeter
(vi)	Electrostatic effect	For Voltmeters only

3. Wattmeter and Energymeter : The instrument used for measuring power is called wattmeter and the instrument used for measuring electrical energy of the circuit, i.e., kilo watt hour (kWh) is called energy meter. It is also called as kWh metre.

Wattmeter : The most commonly used wattmeter for measuring power in a circuit is Dynamometer type wattmeter.

4. Mega-ohmmeter : It is an instrument for measuring resistance in mega ohm (MΩ). From the construction point of view, it is a combination of a hand driven d.c. generator with an automatic gear slip arrangement and an ohm-meter. The speed of the Megaohmmeter is 160 r.p.m. For testing the installaion resistance, the voltage of megaohmeter should be double than the voltage of the installation as per Indian Electricity (I.E.) rules. For example, if the installation is for 250 V supply, the *megger* must be of 500 volts.

5. Multimeter : It is a measuring instrument which can measure currents, voltages and resistances. It is also called an *Avometer.* It can be used for measuring a.c. as well as d.c. currents and voltage.

Principle : It consists of a moving coil galvanometer which works on the principle of motor, that is, when a current carrying conductor is placed in the magnetic field, a force is developed in the moving system and the pointer moves on the graduated scale.

Applications : The following are the applications of multimeter:

(i) It can be used as a voltmeter for measurement of A.C. and D.C. voltage.

(ii) It can be used as an ammeter for measuring A.C. and D.C. currents.

(iii) It can be used as an ohm meter for measuring resistances.

Advantages

(i) It is portable.

(ii) It has small size.

(iii) The accuracy is reasonably good.

(iv) It can measure currents, voltages and resistances.

6.2. MACHINES

6.2.1. D.C. Generators : The machine which converts mechanical energy into electrical energy of direct form is called *Generator.* It is usually driven by some source of mechanical power, which may be a diesel or petrol engine, a steam or gas turbine, etc. The electrical energy is generated following Faraday's law of electromagnetic induction according to which e.m.f. is induced whenever there is a relative movement of conductor with respect to the field.

Working Principle : The generator works on the principle when a conductor moves in a magnetic flux, e.m.f. is induced in the conductor due to change of flux. The e.m.f. thus produced is called dynamically induced e.m.f. The e.m.f. induced in the armature coil is proportional to the rate of change of flux linkage, i.e.,

$$e = N\frac{d\phi}{dt}$$

The e.m.f. generated depends upon

(i) the flux density,

(ii) the number of conductors,

(iii) the speed of rotation, and

(iv) the natural of armature winding

Parts of a D.C. Generator

The principle parts of a d.c. generator are:

1. Field magnets,
2. Yoke,
3. Armature,
4. Armature winding,
5. Commutator,
6. Brushes, and
7. Source of energy.

6.2.2. Types of Generators : The following are the types of generators:

1. Separately Excited Generator
2. Self Excited Generator

1. Separately Excited Generator : The generator in which the field winding is excited by the external source of supply is called *Separately Excited Generator.*

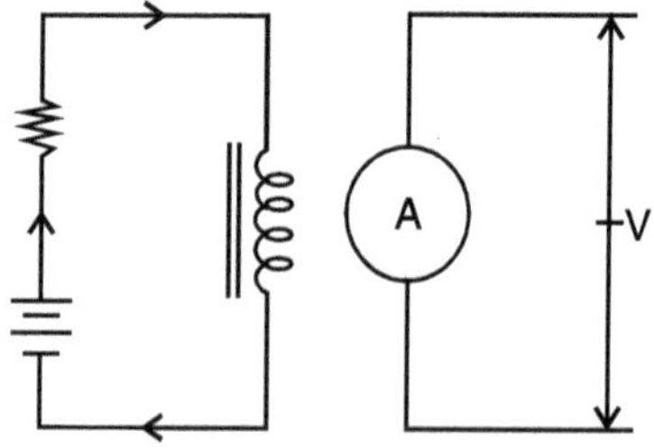

Fig. 6.4 : *Separately Excited Generator*

2. Self Excited Generator : The generator in which the field winding is excited by its own current is called *Self Excited Generator.* The different types of self excited generators are:

(*i*) Series Generator

(*ii*) Shunt Generator

(*iii*) Compound Generator; these are two types of Generators:

(*a*) Short Shunt Compound Generator

(*b*) Long Shunt Compound Generator.

***(i)* Series Generator :** In series generator, the field winding, the external load and the armature winding are all connected in series and the same current flows through each of them. In such generators, a diverter is used which is coil of a few turns of heavy copper wire which can carry the load current of the generator and is connected in parallel.

Series generators are unsuitable for constant voltage application. Such generators can be used as boosters to raise the voltage at the ends of long feeders

In Fig. 6.5, curve (1) represents the saturation curve, curve (2) shows the terminal voltage, load current variation and finally curve (3) represents the internal characteristic.

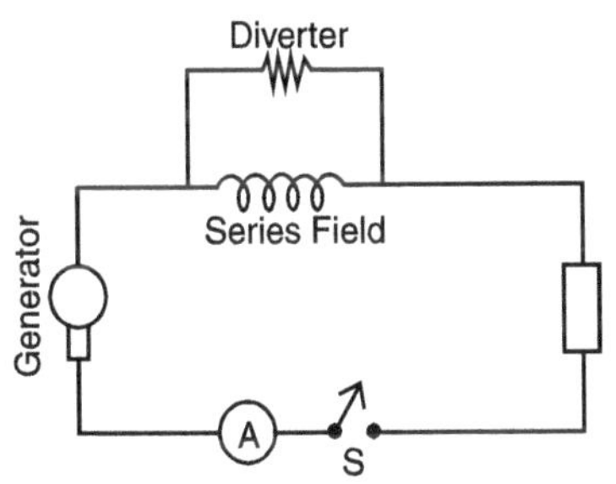

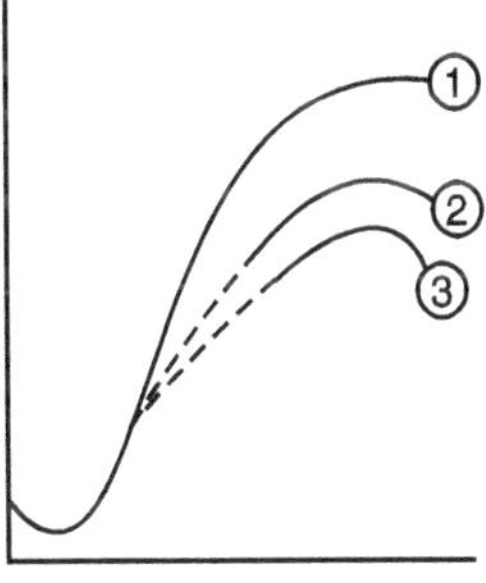

Fig. 6.5

***(ii)* Shunt Generator :** In this type of generator, the field winding is connected across the armature as shown in Fig. 6.6. The field winding is wound with a thin wire having more turns as it is to be connected in parallel. A shunt generator gives full voltage on no load and the voltage drops as the load on the generator increases. Thus voltage on load, $V = E - I_a R_a$

where $I_a R_a$ is armature drop. In these generators, when the load current reaches a certain value (much higher than full load value) the characteristic turns back, as shown in Fig. 6.6. In fact, there are two critical resistances in case of shunt generators.

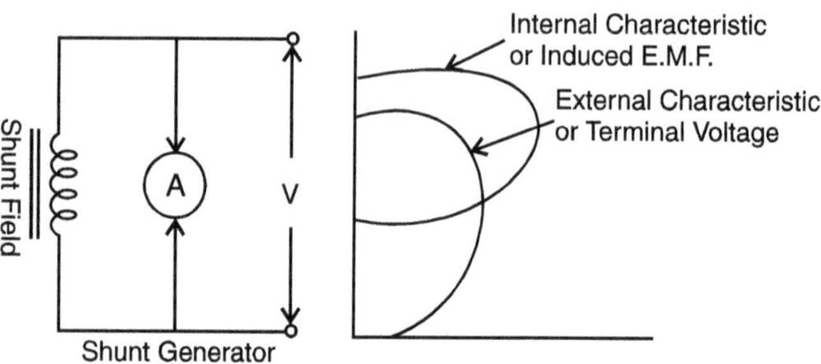

Fig. 6.6

E.M.F. of the Generator : The e.m.f. generated in the armature coil can be calculated by the following formula:

(i) $$E = \frac{P\phi ZN}{60a} \text{ volts}$$

(ii) $$E = (V_b + I_a R_a) \text{ volts}$$

where P = No. of poles of the machine, ϕ = Flux/pole in weber, Z = No. of conductor in the armature, N = r.p.m., a = No. of parallel path in the winding.

In case of lap winding, a = P. In case of wave winding, a = 2,

V_b = Voltage across brushes, I_a = Armature current, R_a = Resistance of the armature and E = e.m.f. generated in volts.

Lap Winding : It is used for generating large currents. In this coil connections are made from one segment, through the two sides of a coil and hence back to the next adjacent segment, from which similar connection is made to the next coil. In this

(i) pitch must be such that the opposite sides of a coil lie under unlike poles,

(ii) the winding includes each element once and only once, and

(iii) the winding closes on it self i.e., must be re-entrant.

Wave Winding : For a certain fixed number of poles and armature conductors, a wave winding gives higher e.m.f. It is useful for small generators. Wave winding also have the advantage that due to unbalancing of magnetic reluctances or flux densities, no circulatory currents are produced like lap winding.

Losses in the Generator : Various losses in d.c. generators are summarized below:

Types of loss	Formula for Estimation	Percentage of full load losses	Remarks
1. Copper Losses	$I_a R_a$	30% to 40%	Also, includes loss due to brush contact resistance
(a) Armature copper loss	R_a = resistance of armature, interpoles and series field winding		
(b) Field copper loss	$I_{sh}^2 R_{sh}$ for shunt generator and $I_{se}^2 R_{se}$ for series generators	20% to 30%	Practically constant in shunt generators R_{sc} is the resistance of series winding. Practically constant for shunt and compound generators
2. Magnetic Losses			
(a) Hysteresis loss	B_{max} 1.6 f		
(b) Eddy current loss	$B_{max}^2 f^2$ where f is the frequency of magnetic reversals	20% to 30%	
3. Mechanical Losses			
(a) Friction loss at bearing and commutator		10% to 20%	
(b) Air friction or windage loss of rotating armature			

Efficiency of Generator : The following are types of efficiencies:

(a) $\eta_{\text{over all}} = \dfrac{\text{Output}}{\text{Input}} \times 100 = \dfrac{\text{Out}}{\text{In}} \times 100\%$

(b) $\eta_{\text{Elect}} = \dfrac{\text{Output}}{\text{Elect. power developed}} \times 100 = \dfrac{\text{Out}}{\text{E}} \times 100\%$

(c) $\eta_{\text{Mech}} = \dfrac{\text{Elect. power developed}}{\text{Input}} \times 100 = \dfrac{\text{E}}{\text{In}} \times 100\%$

Characteristic of D.C. Generator : Following are the important characteristic of a d.c. generator :

1. Magnetisation Characteristic : This characteristic provides the relationship between the e.m.f. induced in the armature at no load and the excitation current at a given speed of rotation. This characteristic is also known as *no load saturation characteristic.*

2. Internal Characteristic : This characteristic gives the relation between the e.m.f. actually induced and the armature current I_a. This is known as *total characteristic.*

3. External Characteristic : This characteristic gives the relation between the terminal voltage and the load current. This characteristic takes into account the voltage drop over the armature circuit resistance. The characteristic is also known as *performance characteristic* as it can be used to judge the suitability of generator for a practical application.

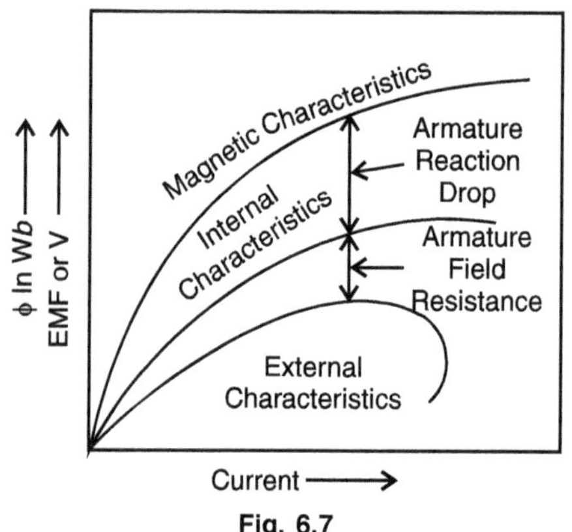

Fig. 6.7

Application of D.C. Generator: From the characteristic curve a series Generator can be suitable where variable voltage is required. It is generally used as a booster and for experimental purposes in the laboratories.

The shunt generator is used where constant voltage is required. It is generally used for lighting load or battery charging.

The compound generator is used where there is a great fluctuation in load and constant voltage is required, such for lighting load and for running high rating motors.

6.2.1.1. D.C. Motors

The machine which converts dielectric current electric energy into mechanical energy is called *Motor,* whereas generator converts mechanical energy into electrical energy.

Working Principle: The action of the motor is based on the principle that when a current carrying conductor is placed in a magnetic field, mechanical force is developed in the conductor which tends to rotate it. The direction of the force can be deetermined by *Fleming's Left Hand Rule* which is also known as *motor rule.*

Back E.M.F : The rotating conductors in a motor armature cut the flux from the poles, so an e.m.f is developed them. By Lenz's law, this e.m.f. opposes the applied e.m.f. It is known as *back e.m.f.*, E_b, and is given by

$$E_b = \frac{P\phi ZN}{60a} \text{ Volts}$$

where ϕ = flux per pole

Z = total number of armature conductors

P = number of Poles

a = number of parallel paths in armature and

N = speed of rotation

The Fundamental Motor Equation is expressed by

$$V = E_b + I_a R_a$$

where V = p.d. applied to the brushes in volts

I_a = armature current and

R_a = armature circuit resistance

E_b = is zero when the motor is at standstill.

The mechanical power of a motor is given by

$$P_m = VI_a - I_a^2 R_a$$

The condition for maximum power is $E_b = \frac{V}{2}$

Torque : The torque on motor armature,

$$T = 0.159 \frac{\phi ZPI_a}{A} \text{ Nm}$$

$$= 0.162 \frac{\phi ZPI_a}{A} \textit{ kg-m}$$

Types of D.C. Motors : The following are the types of d.c. motors :

(i) Series Motor;

(ii) Shunt Motor

(iii) Compound Motor :

Compound Motors are of two kind :

(a) Cumulative Compound Motor,

(b) Differential Compound Motor.

(i) Series Motor : In this type of motor, the field winding is connected in series with the armature as shown in Fig. 6.8. The series winding is wound with a thick enamelled wire and a few number of turns. The resistance of series winding is very less in comparison to shunt winding, generally less than 1 ohm.

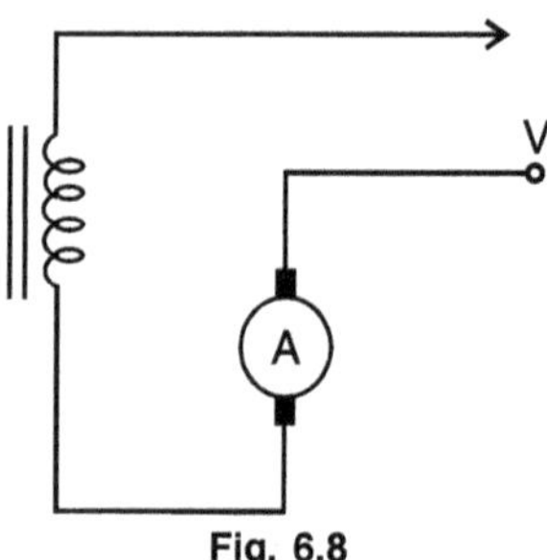

Fig. 6.8

(ii) Shunt Motor : In this type of motor, the field is connected in parallel with the armature as shown in Fig. 6.9. The shunt winding is wound with thin enamelled wire and more number of turns. The resistance of shunt winding is very high as compared to series and armature winding.

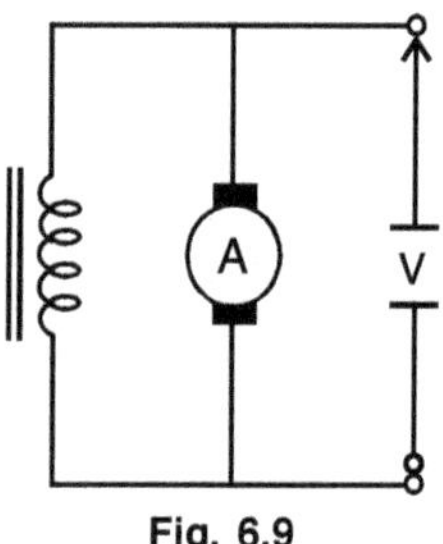

Fig. 6.9

(iii) Compound Motor : In this type of motor, there is shunt winding as well as series winding both. The shunt winding is connected across the armature and the series winding in series as shown in Fig. 6.10.

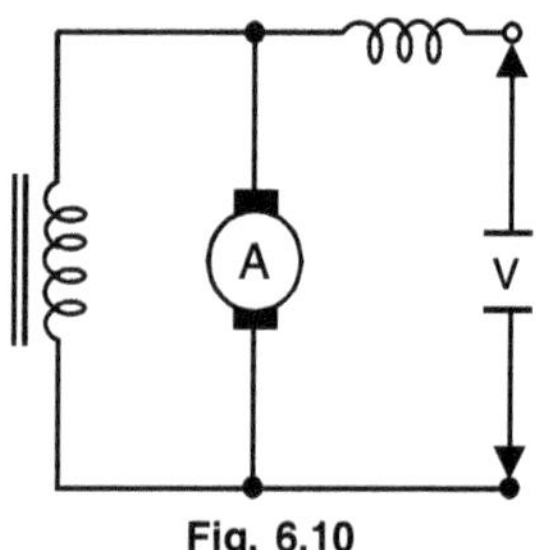

Fig. 6.10

The motor is either cumulative compound or differential compound depending upon the connection of the series winding.

(a) Cumulative Compound : In this case, if the series field flux has an additive effect with the shunt field flux, then the motor is called *Cumulative Compound.*

(b) Differential Compound : In this case, the series field flux opposes the shunt field flux, the motor is called *Differential Compound.*

Construction of D.C. Motor : The construction of D.C. motor is similar as that of d.c. generator. The only difference lies in the construction of the frame or enclourse. The frame of the generator is generally open type whereas the frame of the motor is either partly or totally enclosed depending upon the use.

Functions of D.C. Starter : The following are the function of D.C. starter.

(i) It limits the current in the armature circuit at the time of starting.

(ii) It protects the motor from being over-loaded.

(iii) In case of failure of supply, it trips the handle to *off*-position so that it is not directly connected with supply.

Characteristic of D.C. Motors : The following characteristic curves are drawn for studying the behaviour of D.C. motors,

(i) Torque and armature current characteristics : It is a curve between torque and armature. It is also known as *electric characteristic* shown in Fig. 6.11*(a).*

(ii) Speed and armature current chracteristics : It is a curve between speed and armature current (I_a) shown in Fig. 6.11 *(b)*

(iii) Speed - Torque characteristics : It is a curve between speed and torque. It is also known as *mechanical characteristic.*

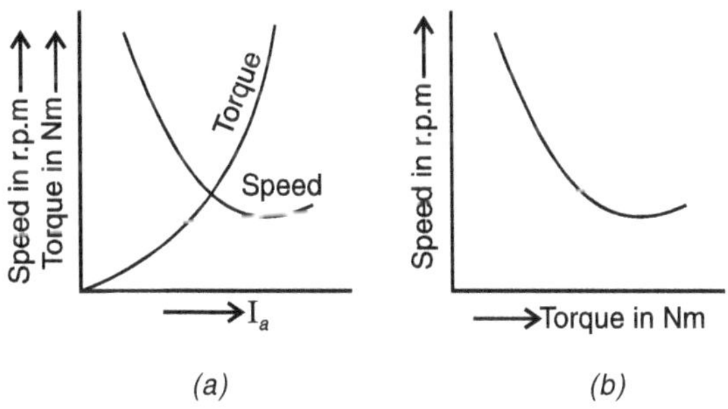

Fig. 6.11

Characteristic of Series Motor : From the above characteristics curves of d.c. series motor, it is clear that the motor is suitable for high starting torque and variable speed. At no load, the speed of the motor will become tremendously high that due to high speed either the bearing will be damaged or the motor may come off from the foundation due to virbration. It is always recommended that a series motor should not run without load.

Application of D.C. Motor

Types of Motor	*Characteristics*	*Applications*
(*a*) Series Motor	(*i*) High starting torque	(*i*) Lifts
	(*ii*) It has automatic adjustable speed according to the load current	(*ii*) Crane
	(*iii*) Speed can be varied by divertor.	(*iii*) Conveyors
		(*iv*) Trolley cars
		(*v*) Electric locomotives
(*b*) Shunt Motor	(*i*) Medium starting torque	(*i*) Pumps
	(*ii*) Almost constant speed	(*ii*) Lathes
	(*iii*) Speed can be regulated	(*iii*) Drills machines
		(*iv*) Blowers
		(*v*) Planners
		(*vi*) Driving line shaft
(*c*) Compound Motor	(*i*) High starting torque	(*i*) Rolling mills
	(*ii*) Variable speed.	(*ii*) Conveyors
		(*iii*) Shears and punches
		(*iv*) Elevators

Armature Reactions : When the armature flux and field flux react each other, certain effects are caused:

(*i*) Demagnetisation of flux

(*ii*) Cross magnetisation of flux

These effects are called *armature reaction.*

Due to these defects the magnetic natural axis changes with the change of load, which result in sparking.

6.2.2. A.C. Machines

Transformer : It is a device which transforms voltage from one level to another level. If it increases the input voltage, it is called *step-up transformer* and if it decreases the input voltage, it is called *step-down transformer.*

Working Principle : It is based on the principle of mutual induction, i.e., e.m.f. is induced in any coil which is linking with a changing flux.

Nature of Supply : From the working principle, it is clear that transformer will work only on a.c. supply. In case it is connected to d.c. supply, the flux produced will not vary but remain constant in magnitude and hence no e.m.f. is induced in secondary winding except at the time of switching on.

E.M.F. equation of a Transformer : The e.m.f. induced in primary or secondary winding depend upon

(*i*) Supply frequency (*f*)

(*ii*) Magnitude of flux(ϕ)

(*iii*) No. of turns in the winding (N_P or N_S)

The magnitude of e.m.f. can be found out by the following formula:

$$\frac{\epsilon_S}{\epsilon_P} = \frac{N_S}{N_P} = \frac{I_P}{I_S}$$

where ϵ_P = Voltage induced in primary winding,
ϵ_S = Voltange induced in secondary winding,
I_P = Current in primary,
I_S = Current in secondary,
N_P = No. of turns in primary winding, and
N_S = No. of turns in secondary winding

Auto Transformer : A single winding transformer is called an *Auto transformer.*

6.2.2.1. Alternator

It is a machine which converts mechanical energy into electrical energy. As this machine generates alternating currents, so it is called *Alternator.*

Working Principle: The alternator works on the principle of Faraday's law of electromagnetic induction, *i.e.,* when a conductor is rotated in a magnetic flux, e.m.f. is induced in that conductor due to change in flux. In larger size, alternators flux is kept revolving and conductors statinary.

Construction of Alternator : From the construction point of view, there are two types of alternators.

(*i*) Salient pole type

(*ii*) Cylinderical type.

E.M.F. Equation : The magnitude of the e.m.f. induced in the armature conductors depends on the following factor:

(*i*) Number of poles

(*ii*) Frequency

(*iii*) Number of turns in the winding

(*iv*) Coil span factor

(*v*) Distribution factor.

The magnitude of the e.m.f. can be determined by the formula

$$\text{E.M.F./phase} = 4.44\ K_c .\ K_d\ f.\ \phi.\ T \text{ volts}$$

where K_c = coil span factor
K_d = distribution factor
f = frequency
ϕ = flux per pole in webers

T = no. of turns per phase.

Distribution Factor (K_d) : It is the ratio of the vector sum of the e.m.f.'s induced in all coils distributed in a number of slots under one pole to the arithmetic sum of e.m.f's induced is known as distribution factor or breadth factor. It is denoted by the symbol K_d.

Its magnitude can be determined by the formula

$$K_d = \frac{\sin\frac{m\beta}{2}}{m\sin\frac{\beta}{2}}$$

where m = no. of slots/phase

B = 180/no. of slots/pole

Synchronising of Alternators : The process of connecting an alternator in parallel with another alternator is called *synchronising.* The various advantages of running alternators in parallel are:

(i) Better continuity of supply can be maintained than running a single unit;

(ii) Alternators give maximum efficiency because of running at full load.

(iii) Repairing of a unit is more convenient and economical.

(iv) The additional unit can be installed as and when required with the increase of load.

(v) The cost of stand by unit is less.

6.2.3. Induction Motor

Motors which run with 3 phase (ϕ) supply are called 3 phase induction motors. As the necessary voltage and current in the rotor circuit is produced by induction effect so they are called as *Induction motors.* In case of induction motors, supply is only given to the stator and no supply is given to the rotor.

Three Phase Induction Motor : Of all a.c. motors, three phase induction motor extensively used for various industrial applications. It offers the following advantages :

(i) It is extremely rugged in construction.

(ii) It has low cost and high reliability.

(iii) It requires least maintenance.

(iv) It has sufficiently high efficiency.

(v) It is self-starting and it needs simple arrangement for starting.

Limitation :

(i) Speed variation is difficult.

(ii) Its speed decrease with increasing load.

(iii) As compared to dc shunt motor, it has lower starting torque.

Types of Three Phase Induction Motor :

The most commonly used induction motors are :

(i) Squirrel cage induction motor

(ii) Slipring induction motor

Construction of 3 phase squirrel cage induction motor :

The induction motor consists of two parts :

(a) Stator

(b) Rotor

(a) Stator : Stator of the motor consists of stampings with slots to house the winding. As 3 phase motor has 3 phase winding and each winding is wound for a definite number of poles. The stator winding produces revolving magnetic field which induces e.m.f. in the rotor by mutual induction.

(b) Rotor : Two rotors are commonly used

(i) Squirrel-cage rotor

(ii) Phase wound or wounded-rotor

In squirrel cage, the rotor consists of longitudinal conductor bars shorted by circular connectors at the two ends while in wound-rotor motor, the rotor has a balanced three-phase distributed winding.

Speed : For p poles in the machine there would be $p/2$ pairs of poles and hence the magnetic field will rotate through $\frac{f}{p/2}$ or $\frac{2f}{p}$ rotations per second in f cycles of the current. Thus synchronous speed, N_s is given by

$$N_s = \frac{f}{p/2} = \frac{2f}{p} \text{ r.p.s.} = \frac{120f}{p} \text{ r.p.m.}$$

Slip : If the supply frequency is constant, the synchronous speed will also be constant. The rotor of the motor revolves at less than the synchronous speed, say N and the difference $(N_s - N)$ is called the *slip of the motor.* Thus

$$\% \text{ slip} = \frac{\text{Synchronous speed} - \text{actual speed}}{\text{Synchronous speed}} \times 100$$

$$s = \frac{N_s - N}{N_s} \times 100$$

The slip usually lies in the range 0 to 5%

Rotor Current : In an induction motor, the rotor current I_R is given by

$$I_R = \frac{\text{e.m.f. induced in the rotor phase}}{\text{rotor impedance per phase}}$$

Torque : In case of induction motor, the torque developed is proportional to the product of flux per stator pole and the rotor current. Thus

$$T \propto \phi \,.\, \cos \phi_2 \Rightarrow T = K.\, \phi.\, I_R \cos \phi_2$$

where K is a constant.

6.2.3.1. Single Phase Motors

Single phase motors are manufactured in a large number of types to perform a wide variety of useful services in home, offices, workshops etc. The selection of single phase motor for a particular application is governed by the following factors:

1. The ambient temperature at the point of installation and the presence of dust, moisture, explosive materials etc.
2. Starting torque requirement.
3. Starting current limitations.
4. Single and multi-speed operation.
5. Continuous and inermittent operation.
6. Efficiency and power factor.

For motors, the starting torque requirement depends upon the load characteristic of the driven machine, low starting torque motors may be used with any machine that starts unloaded. On the other hand, high starting torque motors must be used when the driven machine starts under load. Since the motors starting currents often exceed several times the fulll load of the motor, a low starting current characteristic is desirable in order to reduce the starting load on the connected equipment wiring, transformers etc.

Single phase motors may be classified on the basis of construction and the method of starting as :

1. *Induction motors : (i)* Split phase type *(ii)* Capacitor start motors *(iii)* Capacitor start and run motors *(iv)* Permanent capacitors motor *(v)* Shaded pole motors.

2. *Repulsion motors.*

3. *AC series motors.*

4. *Unexcited synchronous motors.*

6.2.4. Synchronous Motors : Synchronous motors are electrically identical to an alternator or A.C. generator. These motors have a three phase distributed a.c. winding on stator and D.C. excitation winding on rotor.

Construction : There is no difference in the construction of synchronous motor and an alternator. When two alternators are running in parallel, the prime-mover is disconnected from one, it will continue to rotate and will draw power to overcome the internal losses. In the synchronous motor, stator winding is energised with 3 phase supply and the rotor winding is excited with d.c. supply, i.e., it requires 3 phase supply as well as d.c. supply.

Characteristics : The following are the characteristics of synchronous motor.

1. It runs at constant speed.

2. It is not self starting. It has to be run upto synchronous speed or near to synchronous speed by some means before it can be synchronised with supply.

3. It can run under wide range of power factor both lagging and leading. When it operates at leading power factor it is also called *synchronous condenser.*

Comparision between Synchronous Motor and Induction Motor

Induction Motor	*Synchronous Motor*
1. These motors have wound rotor with slip ring or a squirrel cage rotor.	1. These motors have d.c. poles on rotor energised by excitation system.
2. Rotor current is a.c. and is induced by magnetic induction.	2. The field current can be changed to vary the power factors.
3. These motors run at less than synchronous speed. Full load slip is about 4%.	3. These motors always run at synchronous speed without slip.
4. These motors take lagging power factor current.	4. These motors take different p.f. currents depending upon the excitation level.
5. These motors have inherent starting torque.	5. These motors do not have any inherent starting torque.
6. These motors start unaided.	6. These motors have to be started by suitable means and brought to synchronous.
7. These motors are used for variable speed and variable load drives.	7. These motors are used for constant speed and constant load drives.
8. For the same size, these motors are cheaper.	8. These motors are costly due to additional cost of exitation system.

Torque Definition : *(i) Synchronous torque :* It is the steady state torque required to drive the motor and the load at synchronous speed.

(ii) Pull in torque : It is the maximum constant load torque under which the motor will pull into synchronous at the rated rotor supply voltage and rated frequency, when the rated field current is applied.

(iii) Normal pull in torque

(iv) Pull out torque

(v) Pull up torque

(vi) Reluctance torque

(vii) Locked rotor torque

Synchronizing Reactance : A synchronous machine can be represented as an e.m.f. source in series with internal impedance of the machine. The internal impedance, Z_s is called *synchronizing impedance.* The synchronizing reactance takes into account the effect of armature reactions and the flux produced by the armature current.

Open-circuit Characteristics : The open-circuit characteristics of a synchronous machine is a curve of armature terminal voltage on open-circuit as a a function of the field excitation, when the machine is running at synchronous speed.

Short-circuit ratio : The short-circuit ratio of a synchronous machine is the ratio of the field current $(I_f)_{oc}$ required for obtaining rated sustained short-circuit under rated speed conditions.

Example : A motor generates a 210-V back e.m.f. when the applied voltage is 220 V and the armature current is 5.7 A. Find *(a)* total mechanical power output, and *(b)* the power dissipated in the motor.

Solution : The back e.m.f. is less than the applied voltage because of dissipative loss

(a) $P_{mech.} = E_b I_a = (210)(5.7) = 1197$ W

(b) The dissipative power loss is $V_I I_a - P_{mech.}$.

$\therefore \quad P_{dis} = (220 - 210)\, 5.7 = 57$ W

6.3. HEATING

6.3.1. Resistance Heating

In this heating, heat is generated by passing current through the charge or current is passed through a highly resistive element which is either placed above or below the oven depending upon the nature of job to the performed.

Types of electric resistance furnaces : There are two types of electric resistance furnaces:

(i) Direct resistance heating furnaces.

(ii) Indirect resistance heating furnace.

***(i)* Direct resistance heating furnace :** In this method of heating, the material or charge is taken as resistance and current is passed through it. Two electrodes are immersed in the charged and placed at a distance. The electrodes are connected with a.c. supply or d.c. supply.

When metal pieces are to be heated, a powder of high resistive material is sprinkled over the surface for avoiding short-circuit and to have continuity. The current is passed through the electrodes which flows through the charge and heat is produced. This method is quite efficient as the heat is generated in charge itself.

***(ii)* Indirect resistance heating furnace :** In this method heat is produced by passing current through a highly resistive element which is either placed above or below the oven, depending upon the nature of job. The heat produced by the heating element is delivered either by radiation or by convection. This type of heating provides uniform heating and automatic temperature control can also be provided.

Advantages of Electric Heating Oven :

(i) Cleanliness
(ii) Absence of fume gases
(iii) Easy to control
(iv) Uniform heating
(v) High efficiency
(vi) Less attention and low maintenance cost
(vii) Better working conditions,
(viii) Automatic protection.

Properties of heating element material : The following are the properties of the material to be used for heating material.

(i) It must have high specific resistance
(ii) It should have high melting point
(iii) It should be free from oxidation at high temperature
(iv) It should have low temperature coefficient
(v) It should be mechanically strong.
(vi) High specific resistance.
(vii) should withstand vibrations.

Use of Electric Resistance Ovens : The electric resistance ovens are used for heat-treatment of metals like annealing and hardening, stoving of enamelled wires, drying and baking of pottery and in domestic cooking etc. These type of oven can produce temperature upto 1000°C. For producing high temperature, elements of graphite are used, which can produce temperature upto 3000°C.

Temperature Control of Electric Resistance Ovens : By following method, the temperature of electric resistance oven can be controlled:

1. By varying the number of elements.
2. By changing connections, making series parallel grouping.
3. By inserting variable resistance in the circuit.
4. By changining transformer tapping.
5. By making use of thermostat in the circuit.
6. By varying the ratio of 'ON' and 'OFF' times of supply.

2. Induction Heating : The furnaces in which the material itself is heated by electro-magnetic induction is called *induction heating*.

The induction furnace works on the principle of transformer. The value of induced current in the material depends upon

(i) The magnitude of primary current
(ii) Coefficient of magnetic coupling

(iii) The ratio of number of turns in primary and secondary winding.

Types of Induction Furnaces : The following are the types of induction furnaces:

(i) Direct core type
(ii) Indirect core type
(iii) Coreless type

(i) **Direct Core Type Furnace :** This is similar in construction of a transformer, with the difference that the material to be heated serves as a secondary winding as shown in Fig. 6.12

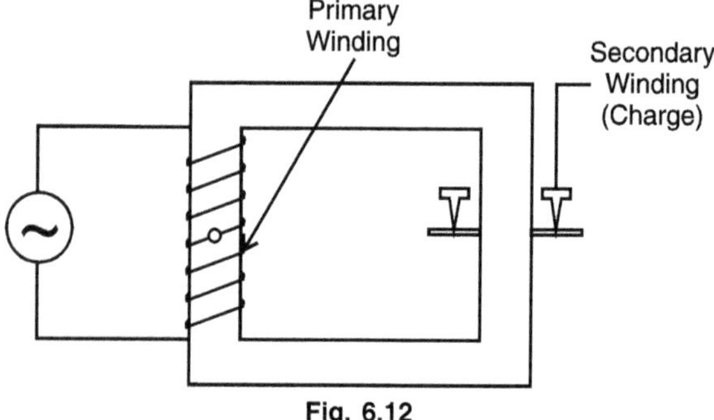

Fig. 6.12

The secondary winding is coupled magnetically. The charge to be heated is kept in a special shaped curcible.

The direct core type furnace has following drawbacks:

(i) Leakage of flux is high.
(ii) Power factor is low due to poor magnetic coupling.
(iii) The electro-magnetic forces produce great turbulance of molten metal.
(iv) High current density causes pinch effect in the molten metal due to which secondary circuit may be interrupted.
(v) Being the shape of the crucible very odd, it is not convenient.
(vi) At the time of starting, the presence of metallic ring in the crucible is must, otherwise the secondary circuit will remain open.
(vii) For minimising the leakage reactance and turbulance effect, the furnace is operated at low frequency, low frequency supply is required either from motor generator set or from a frequency convertor.

(ii) **Indirect Core Type Furnace :** The construction of an indirect core type induction furnace is similar to a transformer having primary and secondary winding. The furnace can work from 400°C to 1000°C.

Advantages :

(i) Leakage reactance is low.

(ii) Working power factor is high as compared to direct core type.
(iii) The shape of the crucible is convenient.
(iv) At the time of starting, presence of metallic ring is not required.
(v) It is simple and a fool-proof method of temperature control.

***(iii)* Coreless Type Furnace :** In the coreless type induction furnace no magnetic core is used to provide magnetic coupling, so the flux density is very low. The general construction of coreless induction furnance is shown in Fig 6.13.

This furnace has lining container which works as a secondary winding. The primary winding coils are wound around it. The coils are constructed in the form of hollow tubes through which cold water is circulated. The artificial cooling of primary coil is necessary because high amount of cooper losses exist.

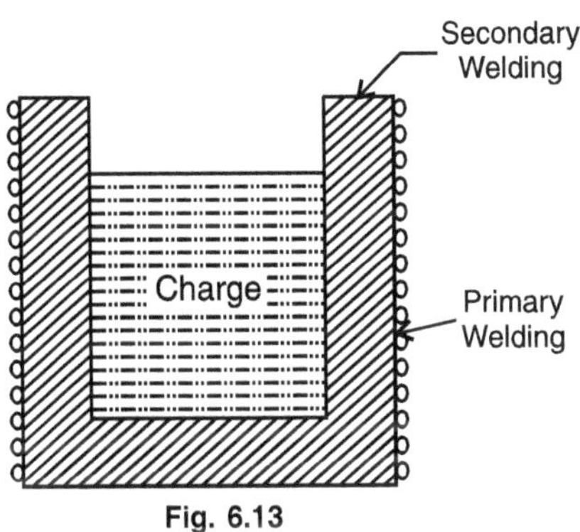

Fig. 6.13

When primary winding is connected with supply, flux at high frequency is set up. This flux produced by the primary winding sets up eddy currents in the charge. These eddy currents are sufficient to heat the metal to melting point and also set up electromagnetic forces which produce strirring action in the charge itself. The eddy currents thus produced are proportional to f^2. B^2, where f is the supply frequency and B is the flux density. As the furnace works at high frequency, stray magnetic field outside the primary coils is set up which causes serious eddy current loss in supporting structure.

Advantages : The following are the advantages of the coreless induction type furnace :

(i) Crucible is of the convenient shape.
(ii) Charging and pourting is simple.
(iii) Automatic stirring in the charge due to eddy currents.
(iv) The time taken to reach the melting temperature is low.
(v) Erection cost is low.
(vi) Operating cost is low.

3. Arc Heating : It works on the principle, when an air gap is subjected to high voltage, the air in the gap gets ionised due to electrostatic forces. The ionised air serves as a conducting material and the current begins to flow through the air gap in the form of continuous *spark* or *arc.* By making use of carbon electrodes, temperature between 3000°C to 3500°C can be obtained.

Type of Arc Furnaces : There are two types of arc furnaces :

(i) Direct arc furnace

(ii) Indirect arc furnace

***(i)* Direct Arc Furnace :** In this furnace, a direct arc is maintained between the electrodes and the charge. Here, because of arc and due to the flow of current through the change itself, heat is produced.

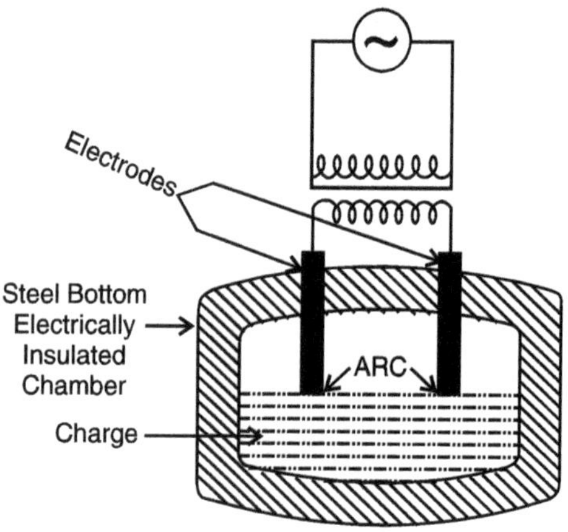

Fig. 6.14

The construction of this arc furnace is shown in Fig. 6.14. Here, the number of electrodes depends upon the nature of supply. In case of 1f supply furnace, two electrodes are fitted and in case of 3 f supply, three electrodes are fitted. This type of furnace is very suitable for attaining high temperature.

This type of furnace is commonly used for the production of steel.

Advantages : The advantages of direct arc furnace are :

(i) Very high temperature can be obtained,

(ii) It gives a very uniform product, and

(iii) Due to flow of current through the charge stirring action caused by electro-magnetic forces.

***(ii)* Indirect Arc Furnace :** In this furnace, arc is maintained between the two electrodes and the charge is heated up by radiation. There furnaces are usually cylinderical in shape.

Indirect Arc furnace (Rocking Arc Furnace)

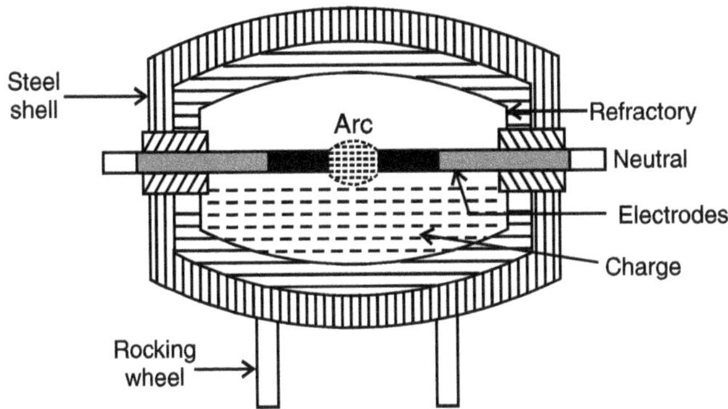

This type of furnace is generally used for melting of non-ferrous metals and sometimes it is also used in iron foundries where small quantities of metal is required intermittently.

Advantages : The advantages of indirect arc furnace are :

(i) High melting speed,

(ii) Small heat losses and low power consumption, and

(iii) Low metal losses

Disadvantages :

(i) It limits the number of electrodes only to two,

(ii) It limits the size of the chamber,

(iii) Extra arrangement of roller is required for providing rocking action, and

(iv) It will work on only 1 ϕ supply.

6.3.2. Welding

The process of joining two metal pieces of similar composition by electric heating to a suitable temperature with or without application of pressure and addition of filler material is called *Electric Welding.*

Fabrication by welding offers several advantages over other methods—saving in time and cost, strong joints, less consumption of material etc. In industries, like ship building and atomic energy, welding is now the pre-eminent method of fabrication. For welding of ferrous materials, flux coated electrodes are used. Non-ferrous materials can also be welded. Various methods used for welding are given as :

1. Arc welding
2. Resistance welding

1. Arc Welding : In this welding, an arc is produced between the electrodes and the material to be welded. In case of direct current for producing arc 30 to 50 volts are needed. However, in case of alternating currents 60 to 90 volts are necessary for striking the arc. A filler material is also applied to the weld as the local fusion takes place.

(i) **AC equipment :** Single operator type—Multiple type

(ii) **DC equipment :** Motor generator set—Rectifier supply

(iii) **Engine driven equipment :** When no main supply is available DC generator are used. These may be driven by internal combustion engines.

Welding Transformers : Welding transformers may be either of the air cooled types. In oil cooled transformers, the winding is immersed in the transformer oil, the set is enclosed in a steel tank and is protected from moisture, dirt etc. These transformers may be single operator type or multiple operator type.

The transformers for one welder have usually a simple double wound single phase winding. They are provided with tapping and a series-parallel arrangement of coils so that they can be connected to a supply mains of different voltages. Where three phase supply is available, single phase welding sets are connected across lines rather than from line to neutral.

Three Operator Transformer Equipment : Such equipment is used when three operators are to be provided individual welding facilities using signal transformer. Each welding station is provided with a current regulator which can be available resistance or inductance. The latter gives better efficiency and improved arc stability. The number of reactor and welder circuits on the three phase system must be a multiple of three, so that they can be distributed evenly on the secondary windings.

Direct Current Equipment : Commonly used equipment for d.c. welding is d.c. generator driven either by electric motor or internal combustion engines. Rectifiers can also be used for this purpose. Both d.c. generator as well as rectifiers have dropping voltage/current characteristics. Open circuit voltage is usually 40 to 80 volts DC generators may be differentially compound machines or series and cross field machines. Rectifier equipment may be operated on single phase or three phase supply. Selenium metal rectifiers are in common use for welding duty as they can better withstand current and voltages surges. Recently silicon crystal rectifiers have been introduced for better efficiency.

Types of Arc Welding : The electric arc welding are of following types :

(i) Carbon arc welding

(ii) Metallic arc welding

(i) **Carbon Arc Welding :** This welding method provides that electrode is made up of earbon and is kept negative and job to be welded is kept positive. An arc is maintained by passing a heavy current between the electrode and job from a source of d.c. supply. The heat of arc melts the parts of the job to be welded and filler material is provided by a separate electrode to make the weld.

Types of Supply : For carbon arc welding only d.c. supply is used as the carbon electrode is to be connected with the negative terminal and the job with the positive terminal whereas no fixed polarity can be maintained in the case of a.c. supply.

The idea of keeping electrodes at the negative potential is that the heat produced at the electrode tip is less than at the job, so the carbon contents of the electrode may not be carried over by the job and make it brittle. Thus, negative electrode prevents the carbon particles to go to the weld and make it brittle.

(ii) **Metallic Arc Welding :** In this type of welding, an arc is maintained by passing a current between a metallic electrode from a source of low voltage d.c. or a.c. supply. The heat of the arc melts the part of the job to be welded. The electrode used itself serves as a filler material. For this tye of welding d.c. supply 50 to 60 volts and a.c. supply 70 to volts 100 volts is used.

Bare wire rods, dipped of lightly covered electrodes and heavy-coated elertrodes are the three types of electrodes which are used for arc welding.

Advantages of Coated Electrodes : The advantages of using coated electrodes are as follows :

(i) It helps in shielding the molten material from oxidation.

(ii) It helps in maintaining the arc.

(iii) It prevents the weld from sudden cooling.

(iv) A slag of coating is formed which removes impurities along as it floats to the surface.

(v) The coating may be used for adding other material to the weld.

2. Resistance Welding : In this method of welding, a heavy current is passed through the joint to be welded. By passing current, heat is produced at the joint due to I^2 R losses which take place due to the current I flowing the resistance R offered by the joint.

The welding heat is given by

$$H = \int_0^{t_w} I^2 \, Rdt$$

where R is the resistance between the pieces to be welded and t_w, time during which weld current flows.

The major components of a resistance welding plant are :

(i) *Heating unit* consisting of transformer.

(ii) *Timing unit* which controls the length of time of weldng current flow.

(iii) *Mechanical unit* which provides the necesary electrode force.

Types of Resistance Welding : The following are the types of electric resistance welding :

(i) Butt-Welding

(ii) Spot Welding
(ii) Seam Welding
(iv) Projection Welding
(v) Flash Welding.

Here we give an outline of seam welding.

Seam Welding : In this type of welding, wheel or roller type electrodes are used and pressure between them remains constant. The seam welding is done to produce a continuous joint.

For operating seam welding machine the secondary winding of the transformer is connected with the wheels as shown in Fig. 6.15. The sheets which are to be welded are pushed together between the revolving electrodes. The metal between the electodes get heated to welding heat and welded continuously under a constant pressure. The speed of the revolving electrode generally varies 2 to 10 metres per minute. The seam welding is used for the fabrication of tanks and cylindrical pieces.

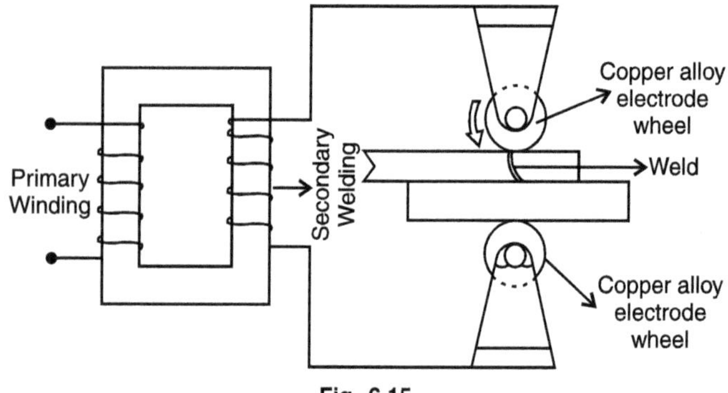

Fig. 6.15

Advantages of resistance welding :

(i) There is very little waste of the metal,
(ii) The welds are consistently uniform, and
(iii) It is a quick method of joining two pieces.

Comparison between Arc Welding and Resistance Welding

Arc Welding	*Resistance Welding*
1. Supply voltage can be A-C or D-C	1. A.C. supply is generally used.
2. No external pressure is required.	2. External pressure is required.
3. Suitable filler metal electrode is used.	3. No filler electrode is required.
4. Not suitable for mass production.	4. Suitable for mass production.
5. Heat is produced by the arc formed between electrode and the job.	5. Heat is produced by flow of current through the contact resistance.

Arc Welding	*Resistance Welding*
6. The temperature of the arc is very high.	6. The temperature is not very high.
7. The striking voltage is high.	7. Voltage required is low.
8. It is suitable for repair work.	8. Not suitable for repair work.

Comparison between A.C. and D.C. Welding

A.C. Welding	*D.C. Welding*
1. The equipment required is cheap.	1. The equipment required is costly.
2. The equipment used occupies less space.	2. The equipment used occupies more space.
3. Transformer is used for A.C. welding.	3. Motor-Generator set is used for D.C. welding.
4. The equipment has high efficiency.	4. The equipment used has low efficiency.
5. The heaing is not uniform.	5. The heat developed is uniform.
6. Electrical energy consumption is less.	6. Electrical energy consumption is more.
7. Maintenance of the equipment is less.	7. Maintenance of the equipment is more.
8. Running cost is low.	8. Running cost is more.
9. Power wastage is less.	9. Power wastage is more.
10. 1 $\phi \rightarrow$ phase transformer when used produces unbalancing, when conneted to 3 ϕ wire network.	10. Does not produce unbalancing.

6.3.3. Electroplating

The process of electro-deposition of metal upon metallic surfaces is called *Electroplating.*

Working Principle : The electroplating principle works on the principle of Faraday's laws of electrolysis.

We give two laws of electrolysis.

Faraday's First Law : The mass of a substance deposited or liberated at an electrode is directly proportional to the amount of electric charge passed through the electrolyte.

$$m \propto \text{It} \Rightarrow m = \text{zIt}$$

where Z is a constant of proportionality called electrochemical equivalent of a substance.

- *Electrochemical equivalent of a substance* may be defined as the mass of the substance deposited at the electrode when 1 amp. current is passed through the electrolyte for 1 second.

Faraday's Second Law : When the same amount of electric charge is passed through different electrolytes, the masses of the substances deposited at the electrodes are proportional to their chemical equivalents.

$$\frac{m_1}{m_2} = \frac{E_1}{E_2}$$

- *Chemical equivalent* is defined as the ratio of 1 mole of an atom to its valency.
- *One Faraday* is the amount of charge required to deposit 1 gram equivalent of the substance. It has the value 96,487 ($\simeq$ 96,500)C/mol.

Main Advantages of Electroplating : The following are the main advantages of electroplating :

(i) It protects the metallic surfaces from corrosion.
(ii) It gives shining appearance to the metallic articles.
(iii) It gives reflecting properties to the reflectors.
(iv) It replaces the worn out material.

Quality of Electroplating : The following are the factors on which the quality of electroplating depends:

(i) Current density
(ii) Electrolytic concentration
(iii) Addition agents
(iv) Nature of electrolyte and its temperature
(v) Throwing power
(vi) Polarisation.

Requirement of Electroplating : The various requirements involved in electroplating are as following :

(i) Cleaning operation
(ii) Deposition of metal
(iii) Polishing and Buffing.

(i) **Cleaning Operation :** The job of this operation is first to clean throughly the area to be electroplated. The cleaning of the job is of great importance before electroplating. The most common contaminants are as follows :

(a) Dirt
(b) Grease sticking to the surface
(c) Oxide and scale formed as a result of hot working or heat treatment.
(d) Sand of the mould sticking to the surface.

For removing dirt and grease, chemical means are employed. For removing oxide and scale from the surface, the job is given an acid bath.

Sometimes, sand blasting and hydraulic jet is also employed for cleanning the job depending upon the type of contaminant.

(ii) **Deposition of Metal :** In this operation, the metal is deposited on the surface of the job which is to be electroplated. The job to be electroplated is made cathode and the anode of the same metal which is to be deposited.

(iii) **Polishing and Buffing :** This operation is carried over after depositing the metal on the job to be electroplated. This operation consists of mops made of leather and canvas or felt is driven at high speed ranging from 2000 to 3000 r.p.m on the job. The high speed mops help in spreading the metal uniformly on the surface and give a smooth and shining surface after polishing.

Plating : We give below following plating :

(i) Copper *(ii)* Nickel *(iii)* Chromium

(i) **Copper Plating :** In this plating, the job is kept on the cathode and the anode made of pure copper. For the electrolyte, there are two types of copper plating baths :

(i) Acid bath *(ii)* Cynide bath

(ii) **Nickel Plating :** In this plating, anode of pure nickel is used and the job to be electroplating is kept on cathode. The electrolyte used is different for different metals. Nickel plating is done to the articles for giving shinning appearance.

(iii) **Chromium Plating :** In this plating, the anode is of antimonial lead and sometimes chromic acid is added as may be necessary. The job is kept on cathode. For chromium plating steel tank with lead lining is used and it requires arrangement for removing the fumes.

Chromium plating is employed where surface is to be protected from atmospheric corrosion. It gives highly polished and extremely hard coating.

Type of Electric Supply : The type of electric supply required for electroplating is d.c. low voltage 6 to 20 volts and heavy current. For getting the required supply the following sources are used.

(i) Motor Generator set

(ii) Metal Rectifier

(i) **Motor Generator Set :** In this system of electric supply, an induction motor is employed for driving a low voltage, heavy current d.c. generator. For getting good performance of the generator, the commutator of such type of generator is kept having considerable size and brushes used are of copper graphite. Because of high voltage regulation, self excited generator are not preferred as compared to separately excited generators.

(ii) **Metal Rectifier :** In this system of electric supply, selenium metal rectifier is mostly employed. The plates are immersed in oil along with transformer for protecting the plates from the corrosive fumes of the electrolyte. The metal rectifier has the following advantages as compared to motor generator set:

(*a*) It has a static running.
(*b*) It requires less space for installation.
(*c*) It has high operating efficiency.
(*d*) Its maintenance cost is less.
(*c*) Its output voltage can be controlled by use of auto transformer.

Equipments required for Electroplating : The following equipments are needed for electroplating shop :

(*i*) *Source :* d.c. low voltage and heavy current. It may be motor generator set or selenium metal rectifier.
(*ii*) Agitating plant.
(*iii*) Filter plant.
(*vi*) Steel vats (P.V.C. lining or lead lining).
(*v*) High speed buffing machine.
(*vi*) Silicon heaters for maintaining temperature.
(*vii*) Steel vats or P.V.C. buckets for washing the job.
(*viii*) Electric heater or stove.

6.4. POWER SYSTEMS

6.4.1. Electric Power

We have known about natural existence of electric energy. In most of the cases first step is to produce mechanical power which is utilized in driving a generator of electric energy. The practical ways of converting, on large scales, the natural energy resources into electrical energy are by thermal plants, nuclear plants, hydro-electric plants and diesel-engine plants. Corresponding sources of energy, i.e., fuels, nuclear materials, water power and diesel fuel are known as conventional sources of energy. Some conventional sources of energy are :

1. Solar energy
2. Wind power
3. Tidal power
4. Ocean wave power
5. Geothermal energy.

The sources of limited quantity of electrical energy are :

1. Fuel cells
2. Thermo-electric convertors
3. Thermoionic convertors.

(*i*) **Condenser :** Thermal efficiency of a steam power plant can be improved by reducing the turbine exhaust pressure. Low pressure at the exhaust can be maintained, by condensing the steam discharged from the turbine. There are two types of condensers: jet and surface type.

(*ii*) **Ash Handling :** Most of the plants have arrangements for quenching ash with water and then carrying it through pipe lines to distant places used as pumps.

(iii) **Power plant cycle :** The idealised cycle for a steam power plant is the Rankine cycle.

(iv) **Boilers :** High steaming rates at higher pressures steam call for careful designing of boilers. A power station has to operate continuously for longer periods of time, hence boiler must be available for longer period without need for shut downs on account of breakdowns or repairs.

6.4.2. Turbines

To obtain full benefit from high steam conditions, it is necessary to use, large turbines. Axial flow turbines are commonly used in power plants. Maximum permissible speed for alternator for expanding steam in alternator being 3000 r.p.m., reduction gear boxes are used whenever turbines rotor speed is higher. Turbines commonly used in hydro-power stations are Pelton wheel, Francis turbine and Kaplan turbine.

Gas Turbine Power Plants : A gas turbine power plant consists of rotatory multistage compressor, generally of axial flow type, in which air or working substance is compressed. Compressed air flows to the combustion chamber where fuel is burnt, thereby raising the temperature of the working substance. The high pressure, high temperature, working substance expand in a turbine producing mechanical power. Turbine in turn drives a generator for producing eletrical energy. A gas turbine works on Brayton cycle.

Nuclear Power Plants : A nuclear reactor is used as a source of heat energy. Thus biolet of a steam power plant may be replaced by nuclear reactor, taking adequate precautions and the plant may be operated as a steam power plant.

Reactors : The key on the release of energy in nuclear reactors is the *neutron.* The nuclear reactor using fission process may use fast or thermal neutrons. The fuel used in reactors may be *(i)* Natural or enriched Uranium *(ii)* Plutonium or Uranium^{233}.

The flowing functions are associated with the working of nuclear reactor:

(a) Producing a chain reacting or critical system.

(b) Controlling the level of power release from the system.

(c) Using spare neutrons to convert fertile into fissile material.

(d) Protecting personnel from harmful radiations emanating from the core.

Fast Breeder Reactors : These reactors use highly enriched uranium or plutonium as fuel. A small core of four cubic meters is sufficient to give a heat output of about 100 MW. The core is surrounded by a blanket of ordinary fertile uranium^{238} or thorium which can be converted to fissile plutonium or uranium-233. It is possible to get more new atoms of fissile material in the blanket than are destroyed by fission in the core. Such a reactor is known as *breeder type*. The terms associated with nuclear reactions are as follows:

(a) **Reflector :** In order to keep the size of the reactor small, and hence the amount of the fissionable material, it is necessary to conserve the neutrons. For this purpose the reactor core is surrounded by a material which reflects the escaping neutrons back into core. This material is known as *reflector.*

(b) **Shielding :** The intensity of gamma and neutron radiation coming from the reactor core is far greater than the human body can tolerate. Hence it is necessary to surround the reactor with a shielding material to reduce the radiation intensity to the levels which are not harmful to personnel.

All the electrical energy generated in a power station must be consumed immediately as it cannot be stored. So the electrical energy in a power station must be regulated according to the demand. Certain definitions related to power station practice are given as below:

Load curve : It is a plot of load in *kilowatts versus* time usually for a day or a year.

Base load : It is the minimum load over a given period of time.

Demand factor : It is the ratio of maximum demand to the connected load of consumer.

Load factor : It is the ratio of average load during a specified period to the maximum load occurring during the period.

Prime power : It is the maximum potential power constantly available for transformation into electrical power.

Station load factor : It is the ratio of net power generated to the net maximum demand on a power station.

Plant factor : It is the ratio of the average load on the plant for the period of time considered, to the rating of the machine.

Firm power : It is the power intended always to be available even under emergency conditions.

Peak load : Load on a power plant seldom remains constant. The load varies from season to season and also in a day from hour to hour. The period during which the demand on a power station is highest is known as *peak load.* Peak load on a plant may exist for small duration but still the plant has to devise ways and means for meeting with such demands.

6.4.3. Electrical Installation

The wiring done for the lighting load or power load in a residential house is called domestic installation.

Types of sub-circuit : There are two types of sub-circuits in a domestic installation:

1. Lighting load sub-circuit
2. Power-sub-circuit.

1. Lighting load sub-circuit : The sub-circuit which gives supply to lighting load points is called *lighting load sub-circuit*. This circuit includes lamps, fans, tubes etc. According to Indian Electricity Rules, the following rating should be assumed for the purpose of load estimation:

(i)	Filament lamp	60 W
(ii)	Ceiling fan	60 W
(iii)	Socket for radio, table fan etc.	60 W
(iv)	Fluorescent tube	40 W
(v)	Mercury vapour lamp	80 W

The following points must be observed for the lighting load sub-circuit :

(i) The number of points connected in one sub-circuit should not be more than 10 points or load exceeding 800 watts.

(ii) The switches used must be of rating 5 A, 250 V.

(iii) The sockets provided for radio, table fan etc, must of 3 pin type 5 A, 250 V.

(iv) The size of wire used must be 3/22 S.W.G. or 3/0.29" in copper and 1/1.5 mm^2 in aluminium.

(v) The size of earth wire must be 14 S.W.G. copper/G.I.

2. Power sub-circuit : The sub-circuit which gives power to power load like electrical iron, heater single phase motors of refrigerator, washing machine etc. is called *power sub-circuit*.

For the installation of power sub-circuits, the following points must be kept in view :

(i) The number of points in a power sub-circuit should not be more than two.

(ii) The load connected should not be more than 500 watts.

(iii) All switches and sockets used in the power sub-circuit must be of rating 15 A, 250 V.

(iv) The size of the wire used for the power sub-circuit must be 7/22 S.W.G. or 7/0.29" in copper or 1/2.5 mm^2 in aluminimum.

(v) The size of earth wire must be 14 S.W.G. copper/G.I.

Types of wiring : The systems of wiring are as following :

1. Cleat wiring
2. Wooden casing and capping wiring.
3. Lead sheathed wiring
4. C.T.S. (Cab. Tyre Sheathed) or T.R.S. (Tough Rubber Sheathed) or P.V.C. (Poly Vinyl Chloride) wiring.
5. Conduit wiring :

(i) Surface conduit wiring

(ii) Concealed conduit wiring.

1. Cleat wiring : In this system of wiring, V.I.R. or P.V.C. insulated wires are held to the walls and ceiling by means of procelain cleats which are fixed at a distance of 0.5 metre horizontally and 0.75 metres vertically above the walls. The cleats are made in two halves, one is known as *base* and the other is known as *cap*. In two way cleats there are two grooves and in three way cleats there are three grooves and finally tightened by tightening the screws in the wooden gutties fitted on the wall.

Applications : This type of wiring is suitable for temporary wiring purpose where the connector is sanctioned for a short period like barracks, factories etc.

Advantages :

(*i*) This is the cheapest type of wiring.
(*ii*) It requires little skill.
(*iii*) It can be quickly installed.
(*iv*) In this type of wiring, addition and alterations are easy.
(*v*) It is easy to locate faults.
(*vi*) It is easy to dismantle and the material can be used.

Disadvantages :

(*i*) Its appearance is not good.
(*ii*) There is no protection of conductors from mechanical injury.
(*iii*) There is no protection from dampness and atmospheric effect.
(*iv*) It can be easily tampered.

2. Wooden Casing and Capping Wiring : In this wiring, the casing is fitted on the walls and ceiling on the wooden gutties which are fixed first. For house wiring, the size of casing and capping generally used is 20 mm × 12 m.m. The casing is generally kept 3.2 mm away from the wall or ceiling by placing round procelain cleasts between the casing and the wall, for protecting the casing from dampness.

Applications :

(*i*) It is cheaper as compared to lead sheathed and conduit wiring.
(*ii*) It is easy to install.
(*iii*) It is easy to repair.
(*iv*) It is easy to inspect for detecting faults.
(*v*) Its appearance seems to be good.
(*vi*) The conductors are well protected.

Disadvantages :

(*i*) This type of wiring is not suitable for damp places.
(*ii*) There is a risk of fire.
(*iii*) It requires highly skilled labour.

3. Lead Sheathed wiring : In this system of wiring, the wiring procedure is same except the wire used is V.I.R. covered with an outer sheath made of lead aluminium alloy of 95% lead and 5% aluminium.

Application : It is used in house and indutrial wiring. Now it is totally out of date.

Advantages :

(i) Its life is long
(ii) It has good mechanical protection.
(iii) Possibility of fire is less.
(iv) Its protection from dampness is good.
(v) It can be used on the places exposed to sun and rain.
(vi) Its appearence is good.

Disadvantages :

(i) It requires skilled labour.
(ii) There is risk of shock in case lead sheath becomes alive.
(iii) Earth continuity is to be maintained throughout the wiring.
(iv) It is costly wiring.

4. C.T.S. or T.R.S. or P.V.C. wiring : In this system of wiring, we first fit Teak Wood batten on the walls and ceiling. The batten is tightened by drawing wooden screws in the gutties fitted in the walls and ceiling. The size of batten depends upon the number of wires to run on the batten.

Applications : This type of wiring is suitable for domestic installation, commercial or industrial building except where it is liable to mechanical injury.

Advantages :

(i) It gives good appearance.
(ii) It has long life.
(iii) It requires less skilled labour.
(iv) Its cost is medium.
(v) Its protection from dampness is good.

Disadvantages :

(i) It cannot be used where there is possibility of mechanical injury.
(ii) It cannot be used in places where it is open to sun or rain.

5. Conduit wiring : In this type of wiring system, V.I.R. or P.V.C. wires are carried through steel or P.V.C. tubes called as *conduit.* A number of inspection boxes are provided along the run of conduit to facilitate the drawing of wires.

Application of surface conduit wiring : It is mostly used in factories.

Application of concealed conduit wiring : It is mostly used for residential and public building, work-shops etc.

Advantages :

(i) It has very long life.
(ii) It has very good protection against mechanical injury.
(iii) It has protection from dampness.

(iv) The concealed wiring has a decorative look.

(v) The wiring can be made shock proof by suitable earthing.

(vi) Possibility of fire is very less.

Disadvantages :

(i) It is costly.

(ii) Its repair and replacement of defective conductor is difficult.

Choice of Wiring System : In selecting the type of wiring, the following points must be considered :

1. Voltage of the system
2. Mechanical protection
3. Safety of system
4. Durability of wiring system
5. Cost of wiring system
6. Possibility for extension and repair
7. Safety from chemical action
8. Appearance of wiring system.

Testing of Installation : The following tests are recommended as per Indian Electricity Rules, 1956 :

1. Insulation test *(i)* Conductor to conductor *(ii)* Conductor to earth
2. Continuity or open-circuit test
3. Short circuit test
4. Polarity test
5. Earth continuity test

6.4 ELECTRIC TRACTION

Electric traction systems may be broadly classified as those operating on:

1. Alternating current supply
2. Direct current supply

In general, following electric traction systems exist

(i) AC 3 phase 3.7 kV system

(ii) AC single phase $\frac{15}{16}$ kV.$\frac{16\frac{2}{3}}{25}$ Hz

(iii) AC single 20/25 kV – 50/60 Hz

(iv) DC 600 V

(v) DC 1200 V

(vi) DC 1.5 kV

(vii) DC 3 kV

AC Single Phase System : This supply is taken from a single overhead conductor with the running rails. A pantograph collector is used for this purpose.

The supply is transferred to primary of the transformer through an oil circuit braker. The secondary of the transformer is connected to the motor through switchgear connected to suitable tapping on the secondary winding of the transformer.

Direct Current System : The transformation and high voltage generation of d.c. is very inconvenient so the d.c. supply used is *at normally 600 V and this* voltage is almost universal for use in urban and sub-urban railways. For direct current equipment, the series motor is universally employed as its speed-torque characteristics are best suited to traction requirements. Generally, two or more motors are used in single equipment and these are coupled in series or in parallel to give the different running speeds required.

The motors are initially connected in series with starting rheostats across the contact line and rails, the rheostats are then cut out in steps, keeping roughly constant current unitl the motors are running in full series. After this the motors are rearranged in parallel, again with rheostats, the rheostats are cut out in steps, leaving the motors in full parallel. The power input remains approximately constant during the series notching, then jumps to twice this value during the parallel notching. Thus a 4 motor unit will have three economical speeds when the motors are running in series-parallel connections. The rheostats are operated electromagnetically or electropneu-matically.

Braking : When a locomotive is running at certain speed and if it is to be stopped within a short distance, brakes are to be applied. For this purpose brake shoes are provided which are pressed against the wheels for retardation. Steam and diesel locomotives have pneumatic braking system. Some electrical methods of braking have also been devised which are used mainly to stop electric motors. During electric braking, the kinetic energy of the motor and the coupled mechanism is steadily dissipated in some form or other and the speed of the machine goes on reducing. There are four methods of electric braking :

(*i*) Magnetic braking
(*ii*) Plugging
(*iii*) Resistance braking
(*iv*) Regenerative braking

Speed time curve : Fig. 6.20 shows the typical speed-time curve for a locomotive. The curve may be broadly split into the following periods :

1. Acceleration period : From starting to the stage when locomotive attains maximum speed, the period is known as *acceleration period,* as the vehicle is constantly accelerated. In Fig. 6.20, this period is represented by OA portion of the curve and here the time duration is t_1.

2. Free running : During this period the motor develops enough torque to overcome the friction and wind resistance. Hence, the locomotive runs at constant speed. In Fig. 6.20, this is shown by the portion AB of the curve.

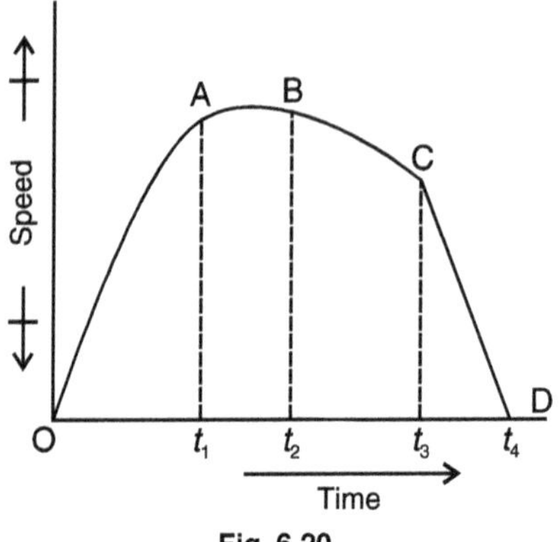

Fig. 6.20

3. Coasting : When the locomotive is running at certain speed, if the motor is switched off, due to inertia the vehicle will continue to run.

4. Braking : The locomotive is retarded to stop it within short distance and at a particular spot. The shape of the curve will change depending upon the distance between consecutive stations.

OBJECTIVE TYPE QUESTIONS

1. Energy consumed by a heater of rating 1000 watts by operating it for a period of 2 hours will be :

A. 3 units B. 5 units
C. 2 units D. 2.5 units

2 Horse power is the unit of:

A. work B. power
C. force D. electrical energy

3. Energy consumed by an electrical iron of rating 1000 watts as compared to 750 watts will be :

A. less B. half
C. more D. none of the above

4. In M.K.S. system, one kilo-watt is equal to :

A. 3.5×10^{-6} Joules B. 3.6×10^{6} Joules
C. 1.34 H.P. D. 3.6 H.P.

5. Power taken by a resistance of 20 ohms with a flow of 10 amp. current is:

A. 2 kW B. 2.3 kW
C. 7.5 kW D. 5.2 kW

6. The force tending to move the electricity is called :

A. potential difference B. e.m.f.

C. resistance D. current

7. With the increase of temperature, the insulating power of insulator:

A. gains B. losses

C. remains constant D. none of the above

8. With the increase of temperature, the resistance of carbon:

A. becomes zero B. increases

C. decreases D. none of the above

9. With the increase in length of conductor, the value of resistance

A. increases B. decreases

C. remains constant D. becomes zero

10. The meter which measure voltage is known as:

A. multimeter B. ampere-meter

C. voltmeter D. none of the above

11. Ohm's law is not applicable to:

A. small resistors B. semi-conductors

C. high currents D. d.c. circuits

12 Ampere-second could be the unit of :

A. charge B. power

C. energy D. conductance

13. The specific resistance of mica is:

A. very low B. very high

C. low D. high

14. The unit measuring resistance is:

A. volt B. ohm

C. ampere D. none of the above

15. The efficiency of the electric kettle is expressed in:

A. heat utilised over heat developed

B. heat developed over heat utilised

C. energy input in kWh over rating of kettle in kW

D. None of the above

16. How many different combinations may be obtained with three resistors, each having the resistance R?

A. 3 B. 5

C. 4 D. 7

17. A wire of resistance R has its length and cross-section both doubled. Its resistance will become:

A. 2R B. R

C. 3R D. R/3

18. Ohm's law is not applicable in all the following cases except:

A. vacuum ratio values B. insulator

C. electrolytes D. none of the above

19. The life of a lead acid battery is expected to be:

A. two to five years B. six months

C. one year D. two years

20. Which of the following is a dry storage cell?

A. Carbon-zinc cell B. Nickel-cadmium cell

C. Dry-cell D. Mercury-cell

21. The e.m.f. of a dry cell is:

A. 1.5 volts B. 1.2 volts

C. 2.5 volts D. 3.5 volts

22 Which medium has least dielectrical strength?

A. Glass B. Quartz

C. Air D. None of the above

23. Permittivity is expressed in terms of:

A. farad/m B. webers/m

C. N/m D. farad/sq. m

24. Dielectric strength of a material depends on:

A. temperature B. moisture content

C. thickness D. none of the above

25. Which of the following is a vector quantity?

A. Electric charge B. Electric potential

C. Electric field intensity D. None of the above

26. Relative permittivity of vacuum is:

A. zero B. unity

C. 7.532×13^{-12} D. 8.875

27. Static electricity is produced by:

A. friction B. induction

C. chemical reaction D. none of the above

28. The force between two charges 4 and 8 coulomb's which are placed at a distance of $2\sqrt{2}$ meters will be, $k = 2$:

A. 18×10^{-12} newton B. 8 newton

C. 9×10^{12} newton D. none of the above

29. The sure test of electrification is:

A. friction B. induction

C. repulsion D. lines of force

30. What will be the capacity of fair capacitors of equal capacity when connected in series:

A. C/4 B. 3/4 C

C. C D. 4C

31. The parctical unit of measuring capacity of a condenser is :

A. Joules
B. Ergs
C. Farad
D. Coulombs

32. Inside a hollow spherical conductor:

A. electrical field is constant
B. electrical field is zero
C. electric field is unity
D. none of the above

33. When a dielectric is placed in an electric field, the field strength :

A. reduces to zero
B. increases
C. decreases
D. none of the above

34. A circuit component that opposes the change in the circuit voltage is:

A. capacitance
B. resistance
C. inductance
D. none of the above

35. The power dissipated in a pure capacitor is :

A. minimum
B. zero
C. maximum
D. none of the above

36. The charge in a 4 μF capacitor charged to 100 V will be :

A. 400 μC
B. 100 μC
C. 4 μC
D. 20 μC

37. Paper condenser is a type of :

A. electrolytic condenser
B. fixed condenser
C. variable condenser
D. none of the above

38. The potential energy of a charged condenser is given by :

A. $\frac{2V}{Q}$ ergs
B. $\frac{1}{2}QV$ ergs
C. 3 QV ergs
D. QV ergs

39. A bank of condenser across the load of the factory is used:

A. for reducing the power factor
B. for improving the power factor
C. for quick starting of the motors
D. none of the above

40. Poles of a magnet :

A. can be used separately
B. can be separated
C. cannot be separated
D. none of the above

41. The unit of magnetic flux is:

A. newton
B. amp/turn
C. coulomb
D. weber

42 If the current flows in clockwise direction, then the polarity of the nearer pole will be:

A. no polarity
B. south pole
C. north pole
D. none of the above

43. The direction of magnetic field can be determined by:

A. thumb rule
B. end ule

C. right hand rule D. left hand rule

44. An electromagnet can be made by:

A. passing current through solenoid B. decreasing the number of turns

C. divided touch method D. single touch method

45. The law that the induced e.m.f. and current always oppose the cause producing them is propounded by:

A. Newton B. Lenz

C. Coulomb D. Faraday

46. The crack in the magnetic path of an inductor will result in:

A. zero inductance B. increased inductance

C. reduced inductance D. none of the above

47. Permanent magnets are not used in:

A. transformers B. loud-speakers

C. energy meters D. none of the above

48. Which of the following is not a ferromagnetic matrials?

A. Cobalt B. Copper

C. Nickel D. Iron

49. Substances having permeability less than the permeability of free space are known as:

A. bipolar B. diamagentic

C. paramagnetic D. ferromagnetic

50. Earths magnetic field always has a horizontal component except at:

A. the geographical poles B. the equator

C. the magnetic poles D. none of the above

51. Hard magnetic materials are used:

A. for making permanent magnets B. for relays

C. in circuit breakers D. in electric machines

52. A magnetic compass needle in a magnetic field will:

A. become dead

B. rotate uniformly

C. will assume position along the lines of magnetic flux

D. none of the above

53. All of the following are ferromagnetic material except:

A. cobalt B. nickel

C. iron D. silver

54. It is generally difficult to magnetise steel because:

A. it corrodes easily B. it has low permeability

C. it has high specific gravity D. none of the above

55. The unit of relative permeability:

A. Henry B. Henry/sq.m

C. it is dimensionless
D. Henry/m

56. Which of the following is a vector quantity?
A. Flux density
B. Magnetic field
C. Magnetic potential
D. None of the above

57. The unit of retentivity is :
A. weber
B. weber/sq.m
C. ampere turn
D. weber/m

58. Air gap in the iron core prevents:
A. core separation
B. induction effect
C. eddy current loss
D. hysteresis loss

59. The law that induced e.m.f. and current always oppose the cause which produces it, is discovered by:
A. Leonard
B. Newton
C. Lenz
D. Maxwell

60. The electromagnet is made of:
A. soft iron core with current passing around it
B. steel core
C. soft iron core
D. none of the above

61. Electromotive force (e.m.f.) can be produced by:
A. electromagnetic action
B. magnetic action
C. chemical action
D. heating thermo junction

62 The line joining the two poles of a magnet inside its body is called:
A. axis
B. magnetic axis
C. electro axis
D. electromagnetic axis

63. A soft iron core with a current passing around, it is called:
A. magnetic substances
B. reluctance
C. electromagnet
D. none of the above

64. When a coil is rotated in a magnetic field, e.m.f. is induced in coil due to change in:
A. electric current
B. linkage flux
C. residual magnetism
D. permeability

65. The magnetism left in an iron piece after removing the magnetising force is called:
A. low permeability
B. residual magnetism
C. high permeability
D. polarity of the poles

66. The angle between voltage and current is called:
A. form factor
B. power factor
C. phase difference
D. peak factor

67. If there is an angle between two alternating quantities, the two alternating

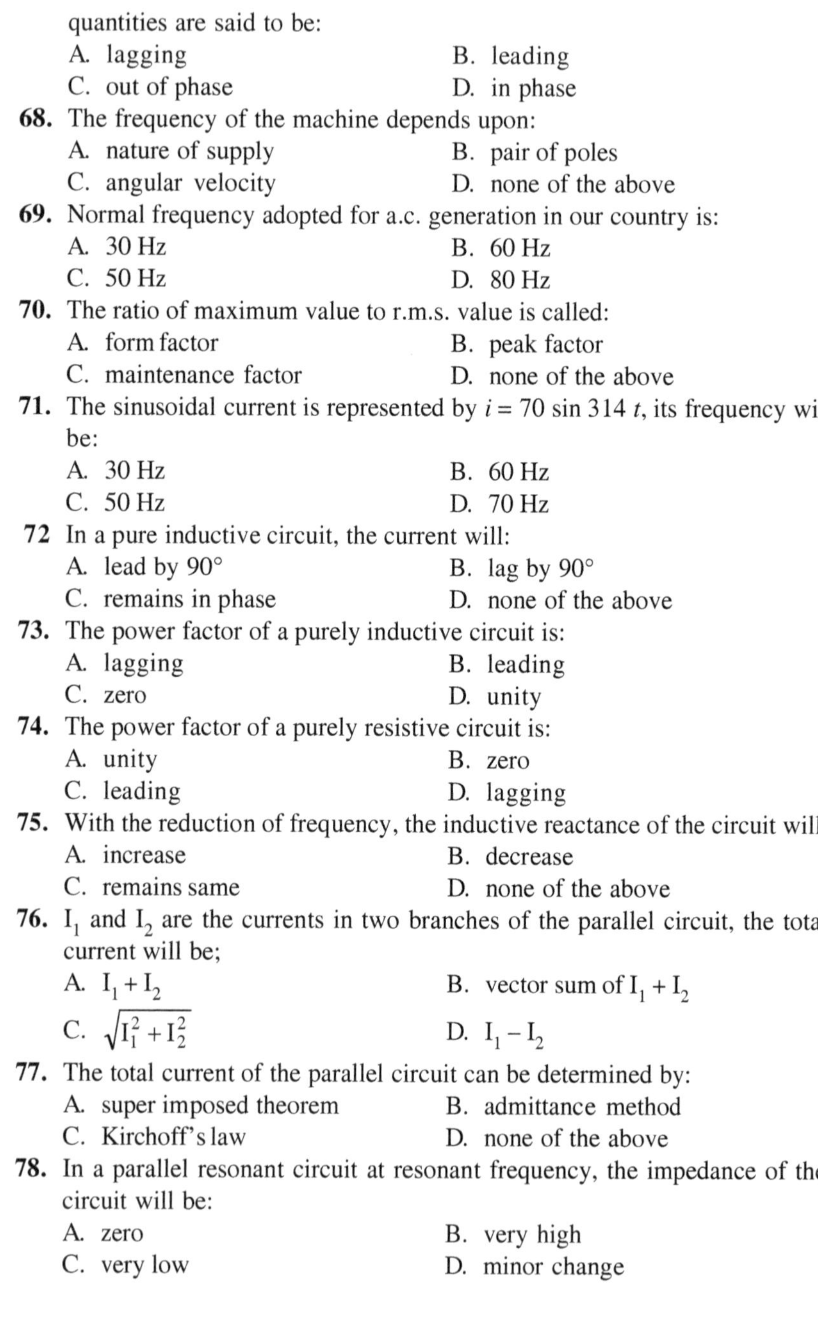

quantities are said to be:

A. lagging B. leading
C. out of phase D. in phase

68. The frequency of the machine depends upon:

A. nature of supply B. pair of poles
C. angular velocity D. none of the above

69. Normal frequency adopted for a.c. generation in our country is:

A. 30 Hz B. 60 Hz
C. 50 Hz D. 80 Hz

70. The ratio of maximum value to r.m.s. value is called:

A. form factor B. peak factor
C. maintenance factor D. none of the above

71. The sinusoidal current is represented by $i = 70 \sin 314\, t$, its frequency will be:

A. 30 Hz B. 60 Hz
C. 50 Hz D. 70 Hz

72 In a pure inductive circuit, the current will:

A. lead by 90° B. lag by 90°
C. remains in phase D. none of the above

73. The power factor of a purely inductive circuit is:

A. lagging B. leading
C. zero D. unity

74. The power factor of a purely resistive circuit is:

A. unity B. zero
C. leading D. lagging

75. With the reduction of frequency, the inductive reactance of the circuit will:

A. increase B. decrease
C. remains same D. none of the above

76. I_1 and I_2 are the currents in two branches of the parallel circuit, the total current will be;

A. $I_1 + I_2$ B. vector sum of $I_1 + I_2$
C. $\sqrt{I_1^2 + I_2^2}$ D. $I_1 - I_2$

77. The total current of the parallel circuit can be determined by:

A. super imposed theorem B. admittance method
C. Kirchoff's law D. none of the above

78. In a parallel resonant circuit at resonant frequency, the impedance of the circuit will be:

A. zero B. very high
C. very low D. minor change

79. Polyphase motors:
A. are self starting
B. require auxilary winding
C. do not require self starting
D. none of the above

80. In case of two phase supply the electrical displacement of the winding is:
A. 60°
B. 30°
C. 90°
D. 120°

81. In case of 3 phases supply, the electrical displacement of the winding is:
A. 90°
B. 120°
C. 180°
D. 135°

82 For the generation of 3 phase 4 wire supply, number of winding used on the armature are:
A. 2
B. 5
C. 3
D. 7

83. Three similar loads are connected in star connection. The current in the neutral will be:
A. zero
B. arithmetic sum
C. vector sum
D. unity

84. If the battery of the multimeter is weak, it will give:
A. more reading
B. less reading
C. accurate reading
D. no reading

85. For measuring the value of resistance which of the following meter will give accurate result?
A. Pointer type
B. Intergrated circuit type
C. Digital type
D. none of the above

86. The meter of multimete will work on:
A. a.c. supply
B. d.c. supply
C. half wave rectified a.c.
D. both A and B

87. The mass of a substance liberated during electrolysis in a given time depends upon
A. electric current
B. electric power
C. working temperature
D. resistance

88. Megaohm,meter is used for measuring:
A. very low resistance
B. medium resistance
C. low resistance
D. high resistance

89. Speed of the megger is kept at:
A. 120 r.p.m.
B. 80 r.p.m.
C. 50 r.p.m.
D. 160 r.p.m.

90. The megaohmmeter voltage for testing 250 V installation should be:
A. 300 V
B. 500 V
C. 1000 V
D. 250 V

91. Megaohmmeter is used for testing:

A. short-circuit B. open-circuit
C. both A and B D. high resistance circuit only

92 If the megaohmmeter terminals are connected to 230 V supply, megaohmmeter will:

A. burn B. work
C. not work D. none of the above

93. Which of the following frequencies has the longest period?

A. 10 kHz B. 1 Hz
C. 1 kHz D. 100 kHz

94. All the laws of d.c. circuit also apply to a.c. circuits without modifications in case the circuit contains:

A. inductance only B. resistance only
C. capacitance only D. none of the above

95. Power factor of an iductive circuit can be improved by connecting a capacitor to it in :

A. parallel
B. series
C. both A and B
D. depends on the value of the capacitor

96. Magnetic moment is a:

A. vector quantity B. scalar quantity
C. pole strength D. universal constant

97. If two ends of a circular uniform wire are joined to the terminals of a battery, the field at the centre of the circle:

A. will be zero
B. will be infinite
C. will depend on the radius of the circle
D. none of the above

98. Which capacitor is preferred in case of single phase motor?

A. Electrolytic capacitor B. Paper capacitor
C. Ceramic capacitor D. Mica capacitor

99. A circuit component that opposes the flow of curent is:

A. inductance B. capacitance
C. resistance D. none of the above

100. Which laws find application in electrolysis?

A. Ohm's law B. Faraday's laws
C. Newton's laws D.Coulomb's laws

101. The synchronous motor can be started by:

A. providing damper winder

B. coupling with d.c. compound motor
C. coupling with a.c. motor
D. A, B and C

102. The voltage supplied to the rotor of the synchronous motor is:
A. 300 V, a.c. B. 100 to 250 V, d.c.
C. 500 V, d.c. D. none of the above

103. 3 ϕ slipring induction motor can be started with:
A. Stator-rotor starter B. D.O.L. starter
C. Auto-transformer starter D. Star-delta starter

104. If the full load spead of a 4 pole, 3 ϕ induction motor is 1440 r.p.m., its speed at half load will be:
A. 1520 r.p.m. B. 1460 r.p.m.
C. 1000 r.p.m. D. 1250 r.p.m.

105. If a motor of lower speed is purchased in place of high speed motor, its cost will be:
A. more B. less
C. same D. slightly more

106. The speed of the squirrel cage induction motor can be controlled from:
A. rotor side B. stator side
C. supply voltage side D. none of the above

107. If a 3 ϕ induction motor run on 2 ϕ supply, it will:
A. blow off the fuses B. likely to burn
C. run with jerks D. none of the above

108. In case the starting resistance of a series motor is short-circuited, the motor will:
A. run at very high r.p.m. B. not start
C. burn out D. none of the above

109. The retardation test in case of shunt motors and generator is used to determine:
A. eddy current losses B. stray losses
C. friction losses D. copper losses

110. D.C. motors are commonly used in:
A. electric traction B. pump sets
C. driving compressors D. none of the above

111. A rotory convertor can also be run as a:
A. induction motor B. synchronous motor
C. D.C. series motor D. D.C. compound motor

112 The synchronous motors are not self-starting because:
A. the direction of instantaneous torque on the rotor reverses after half-cycle
B. there is no slip

C. both A and B

D. none of the above

113. The induced e.m.f. in a synchronous motor working on leading pf will be

A. less than the supply voltage

B. more than the supply voltage

C. equal to the supply voltage

D. none of the above

114. The imaginary or fictitious part of synchronous reactance takes care of:

A. inductive reactance

B. armature reaction

C. voltage regulation

D. none of the above

115. The frequency of voltage generated by an alternator having 8 poles and rotating at 250 r.p.m is:

A. 16.34 Hz

B. 20 Hz

C. 35 Hz

D. 15 Hz

116. The frequency of voltage generated in an alternator depends on:

A. rotative speed

B. number of poles, rotative speed and type of winding

C. number of poles

D. none of the above

117. The power factor of an alternator depends on:

A. speed of rotor

B. load

C. core losses

D. none of the above

118. The construction of d.c. motor :

A. similar but different in frame construction

B. similar as d.c. generator

C. different than d.c. generator

D. none of the above

119. If the direction of field and direction of current in the conductor is known, the direction of motion can be found out by:

A. Fleming's left hand rule

B. Crok screw rule

C. Lenz's law

D. Fleming's right hand rule

120. In series motor, the number of turns of field pole is:

A. less than shunt field

B. less than armature

C. more than shunt field

D. none of the above

121. The resistance of shunt winding is :

A. less than series only

B. less than armature only

C. both A and B

D. more than armature

122. Synchronous motor always runs at:

A. lagging power factor

B. leading power factor

C. unity power factor

D. any one of the above

123. Under running condition on load, the angle between induced voltage and supply voltage will be:

A. little more than 180° B. zero

C. 180° D. 60°

124. The angle between the rotor poles and stator poles is called:

A. angle of retardation B. torque angle

C. power factor angle D. none of the above

125. If one of the 3 phase of synchronous motor is short-circuited, more will:

A. not start B. start

C. over heated D. none of the above

126. When the supply voltage for an induction motor is reduced, which of the following will increase?

A. full load current

B. % slip

C. maximum temperature rise on full load

D. all the above

127. Which of the parameter for an induction moror varies as square of the supply voltage?

A. Synchronous speed B. Maximum running torque

C. Slip D. None of the above

128. Which of the following parameters of an induction motor varies inversely as the supply frequency?

A. Starting current B. Full load current

C. Slip D. None of the above

129. When supply frequency of an induction motor is reduced by 5%, which of the following will also decrease?

A. Maximum running torque B. Full load speed

C. Temperature rise on full load D. None of the above

130. For a three phase induction motor, if the supply frequency is increased, which of the following will also increase?

A. Temperature rise on Full load B. Synchronous speed

C. Full load current D. None of the above

131. A ceiling fan of 1400 mm sweep will have motor rating of:

A. 120 to 180 watts B. 200 to 250 watts

C. 175 to 200 watts D. 50 to 70 watts

132. Which of the following application would need the smallest size of motor?

A. Table fan B. Domestic mixi

C. Electric clock D. None of the above

133. Which capacitor is referred in case of single phase motor?

A. Electrolytic capacitor B. Mica capacitor

C. Ceramic capacitor D. Paper capacitor

134. A motor suitable for signalling device is :
A. reluctance motor
B. d.c. series motor
C. d.c. shunt motor
D. none of the above

135. The motor used in house-hold refrigeration is:
A. universal motor
B. single phase induction motor
C. d.c. shunt motor
D. d.c. series motor

136. A tap changer is used on a transformer for:
A. adjustments in secondary voltage
B. adjustments in power factor
C. adjustments in primary voltage
D. none of the above

137. An insulator material in a transformer may fail due to:
A. dust
B. moisture
C. voids in winding
D. any of the above

138. Burden of a current transformer is usually expressed in:
A. kilowatt
B. volt amperes
C. volts
D. none of the above

139. A current transformer can be used with which of the following instruments?
A. Watt hour meter
B. Wattmeter
C. Ammeter
D. Any of the bove

140. Transformer ratings are usually expressed in terms of:
A. kWh
B. kVA
C. Volts
D. kW

141. An auto transformer has:
A. two winding of the same gauge of wire
B. only one winding
C. more than two winding
D. none of the above

142. The essential condition for parallel operating of two single phase transformer is that they should have same:
A. polarity
B. capacity
C. voltage ratio
D. efficiency

143. Out of the following insulating materials which one can withstand the highest temperature safely?
A. Mica
B. Asbestos
C. Glass fibre
D. None of the above

144. The efficiency of two identical transformers under load conditions can be determined by :
A. open-circuit test
B. short-circuit test
C. back-to-back test
D. any of the above

145. Simple porcelain bushings are used for transformers upto:
A. 11 kV B. 13 kV
C. 18 kV D. 25 kV

146. Which of the following parts of a transformer is visible from outside?
A. core B. bushing
C. primary winding D. any of the above

147. Which of the following is the most inferior insulating material?
A. Asbestos B. Quartz
C. Cellulose D. None of the above

148. The noise produced by a transformer is termed as:
A. hum B. buzz
C. zoom D. ringing

149. The permittivity of transformer oil is about:
A. 2.2 B. 1.5
C. 2.5 D. 3.7

150. If a transformer is continuously operated the maximum temperature rise will occur in:
A. core B. winding
C. tank D. cooling

151. Transformer is a device which transforms the voltage:
A. from lower level to higher level B. from higher level to lower level
C. both A and B D. none of the above

152 Transformer works on the principle of:
A. mutual induction B. self induction
C. both A and B D. none of the above

153. Transformer works on:
A. D.C. B. A.C
C. both and B D. none of the above

154. Transformer is a:
A. magnetic device B. rotating device
C. static device D. none of the above

155. If D.C. supply is given to a transformer, it will:
A. burn the winding B. work
C. not work D. none of the above

156. If a lower voltage is given to the primary and higher voltage is taken from secondary of a transformer, it is called:
A. current transformer B. set up
C. step down D. voltage stabilizer

157. The e.m.f. induced in the secondary winding depends upon:
A. flux B. supply frequency

C. number of terms D. A, B and C

158. The efficiency of transformer is more because it has:

A. windage losses B. no friction

C. both A and B D. less iron losses

159. The transformer is commonly used, because :

A. the supply frequency remains constant

B. construction cost per kVA is less as compared to other machine

C. it has high efficiency

D. all the above

160. The efficiency of a transformer lies between:

A. 75 to 85% B. 95 to 98%

C. 85 to 90% D. 80 to 85%

161. The salient pole type rotors are:

A. larger in diameter and smaller in axial length

B. smaller in axial length

C. smaller in diameter

D. none of the above

162. The generator which gives D.C. supply to the rotor is called:

A. exciter B. invertor

C. convertor D. none of the above

163. The rotor of the alternator has:

A. two slip rings B. no slip rings

C. four slip rings D. none of the above

164. The rotor of the alternator requires:

A. A.C. B. D.C.

C. pulsating D.C. D. none of the above

165. Alternator works on the principle of :

A. self induction B. mutual induction

C. both A and B D. none of the above

166. Alternator generates:

A. pulsating D.C. B. D.C.

C. A.C. D. both A and B

167. When two alternators are running in parallel, primemover of one of the alternator is disconnected, the alternator will:

A. run as a synchronous motor B. stop running

C. run as a invertor D. none of the above

168. The condition for running two alternators in parallel will be:

A. voltage should be the same B. frequency should be same

C. phase sequence should be same D. A, B and C

169. When load of an alternator is thrown off, the terminal voltage:

A. decreases B. increases

C. remains same D. none of the above

170. No current flows between two charged bodies connected together when they have the same

A. Charge B. Potential

C. Capacitance D. Resistance

171. The e.m.f. generated in an alternator depends upon:

A. frequency B. coil span factor

C. flux per pole D. A, B and C

172. Out of the following losses in D.C. machines, which one has the highest proportions?

A. Hysteresis loss B. Armature copper loss

C. Eddy current loss D. None of the above

173. Which loss in a D.C. generator significantly varies with the load current?

A. Field copper loss B. Windage loss

C. Copper losses D. Armature copper loss

174. Out of the following losses in a D.C. generator, which one has the least proportional?

A. Windage losses B. Copper losses

C. Field copper losses D. None of the above

175. A brake test is usually restricted to:

A. variable speed motors B. high speed motors

C. small horse power motors D. none of the above

176. Hopkinson's test is conducted at:

A. part load B. no load

C. full load D. low load

177. A 200 V D.C. motor will be subjected to a high voltage test at:

A. 1300 V B. 1400 V

C. 800 V D. 1200 V

178. The rotor is:

A. keyed to the shaft B. bolted to the shaft

C. welded to the shaft D. none of the above

179. Which of the following loss of motor decreases with increase in load?

A. Core loss B. Brush contact loss

C. Both A and B D. None of the above

180. Small d.c. motors upto 5 HP usually have:

A. 4 poles B. 2 poles

C. 3 poles D. 5 poles

181. A d. c. generator can be termed as:

A. Power line B. Rotating amplifier

C. prime mover D. None of the above

182. Which of the following can be used for controlling the speed of a D.C. motor?

A. Thyristor
B. Thermister
C. Transistor
D. None of the above

183. Which of the following test can be conducted on all types of d.c. machines?

A. Field's test
B. Back-to-back test
C. Swinburne's test
D. None of the above

184. If a single phase motor is being heated, the probable cause may be:

A. worn out bearing
B. dry bearing
C. over loading
D. A, B and C

185. In a shaded pole type motor, the revolving field is produced by the use of:

A. shading coils
B. using damper winding
C. copper winding
D. none of the above

186. The 1 ϕ fractional horse power meters are generally fitted with:

A. sleep bearing
B. ball bearing
C. both A and B
D. roller bearing

187. The rotating part of a 1 ϕ motor is called:

A. rotor
B. armature
C. starting winding
D. none of the above

188. For high speed and high starting torque which of the following motor can be recommended:

A. universal motor
B. capacitor motor
C. shaded pole type motor
D. none of the above

189. Single phase universal motor can be used on:

A. D.C.
B. A.C.
C. both A and B
D. rectified A.C.

190. In a capacitor start, capacitor run motor, the type of capacitor used is:

A. paper spaced oil filled type
B. air capacitor
C. paper capacitor
D. none of the above

191. A single phase motor is:

A. self starting with the help of auxiliary winding
B. self starting
C. not self starting
D. none of the above

192. If a single phase motor runs hot, the probable cause may be:

A. low voltage
B. over load
C. high voltage
D. any of the above

193. A single phase capacitor start motor will take starting current nearly:

A. twice the full load current
B. same as full load current
C. three times the full load current
D. none of the above

194. If a single phase motor runs slow, the probable cause may be:

A. low frequency | B. low voltage
C. over load | D. any of the above

195. Which of the following does not change in an ordinary transformer?

A. Current | B. Frequency
C. Voltage | D. None of the above

196. The material used in the construction of core is usually:

A. aluminium | B. silicon steel
C. carbon | D. wood

197. In a transformer the chemical contained inside the breather is:

A. silica gel | B. salt
C. water | D. none of the above

198. The power factor in a transformer:

A. is always leading
B. depends on the power factor of the load
C. is always unity
D. none of the above

199. Which part of the transformer is subjected to maximum heating?

A. frame | B. oil
C. core | D. none of the above

200. Which motor will make least noise?

A. Universal motor | B. Hysteresis motor
C. Capacitor motor | D. Shaded pole motor

201. Mostly selenium metal rectifier is used for:

A. welding | B. heating
C. electroplating | D. none of the above

202. For copper plating, type of copper plating baths are:

A. copper sulphate bath | B. acid bath
C. cyanide bath | D. none of the above

203. A DC generator used for AC welding should have :

A. dropping characteristic | B. straight characteristic
C. rising chracteristic | D. none of the above

204. In arc welding the temperature of the arc is of the order of:

A. 350°C | B. 3500°C
C. 450°C | D. 4500°C

205. In arc welding by d.c. supply, the voltage required is:

A. 50 to 60 V | B. 200 to 250 V
C. 110 to 150 V | D. 300 to 350 V

206. Arc can be produced by:

A. DC current only | B. AC current only

C. Either A or B
D. none of the above

207. The welding electric circuit is:
A. never earthed
B. always earthed
C. through cables only
D. none of the above

208. A rectifier for welding has voltage/current characteristic in :
A. rising
B. drooping
C. variable
D. static

209. Gray iron is usually welded by:
A. gas welding
B. TIG welding
C. arc welding
D. MIG welding

210. Steel pipes are manufactured by:
A. resistance welding
B. arc welding
C. argon arc welding
D. none of the above

211. Electroplating is used for:
A. giving shining appearance to the surface
B. giving reflecting property to the reflector
C. replacing worn out material
D. A, B and C

212. The electrode at positive potential is called:
A. anode
B. cathode
C. positive terminal
D. none of the above

213. The amount of metal deposited on cathode depends upon:
A. time
B. electric chemical equivalent
C. current
D. A, B and C

214. Electroplating protects:
A. Corrosion at the surface of metal
B. oxidation at the surface of metal
C. direct at the surface of metal
D. none of the above

215. The electrolyte at negative potential is called:
A. anode
B. cathode
C. electrode
D. none of the above

216. The advantage of using coated electrode in metallic arc welding is that:
A. it helps in maintaining arc
B. it prevents the weld from sudden cooling
C. it prevents the weld for oxidation
D. A, B and C

217. In an arc welding, filter material is:
A. not essential
B. essential
C. sometimes essential
D. none of the above

218. In carbon arc welding, the electrode is kept at negative potential for:
A. making the weld brittle

B. preventing the carbon particles to go to the weld
C. making the weld soft
D. none of the above

219. In a carbon arc welding, the supply used is:
A. d.c. supply | B. a.c. 1 ϕ supply
C. A and B both | D. none of the above

220. In metallic arc welding, the supply voltage may be:
A. a.c. 1 ϕ supply | B. d.c. supply
C. both A and B | D. none of the above

221. High frequency for induction heating can be generated by:
A. spark gap oscillator | B. vacuum tube oscillator
C. motor generator set | D. none of the above

222. Which of the following is the ideal method of heating plastic?
A. Dielectric heating | B. Oil fired furnace
C. Coal fired furnace | D. None of the above

223. For heating of plywood, the frequency should be:
A. 1000 Hz | B. 1-2 MHz
C. 10-20 kHz | D. 120 Hz

224. Radiant heating is used for:
A. varnishes | B. drying of paints
C. both A and B | D. none of the above

225. If f be the frequency then dielectric loss is proportional to:
A. f^2 | B. f
C. $\sqrt{f}$ | D. f^3

226. Induction hardening is possible:
A. on a.c. supply only | B. on d.c. supply only
C. on ferrous material only | D. none of the above

227. In a domestic cake baking oven the temperature is controlled by:
A. voltage variation | B. thermostat
C. auto transformer | D. none of the above

228. Thermal conductivity is least for:
A. water | B. air
C. glass | D. copper

229. Which of the following heating element can give highest temperature in resistance?
A. silicon carbide | B. nickel copper
C. copper | D. nichrome

230. Which of the following element will have the least range of temperature?
A. Nichrome | B. Eureka

C. Kanthal D. Silicon carbon

231. Which of the following is of high value is case of induction heating:

A. frequency B. voltage

C. current D. none of these

232. The welding load is always:

A. intermittent B. continuous

C. constant D. both B and C

233. Which of the following automatic welding process is likely to give maximum rate of metal deposition?

A. Multiple power submerged arc B. Gas shielded bare wire

C. Submerged arc (single wire) D. None of the above

234. Argon is:

A. oxidising agent B. inactive gas

C. inert gas D. rare gas

235. Flux used in TIG welding is :

A. Ash B. Borax

C. Ammonium chloride D. None of the above

236. Electrode is not consumed in case of :

A. TIG welding B. Gas welding

C. AC arc welding D. None of the above

237. The danger of electric shock is maximum:

A. before welding

B. after welding

C. while inserting electrode into the holder

D. none of the above

238. Which of the following is not a welding accessory?

A. Cable B. Gloves

C. Hand screen D. Electrode holder

239. For welding duty the rectifier commonly used are:

A. Gelenium metal rectifiers B. Mercury arc rectifiers

C. Both A and B D. none of the above

240. Steel rails are welded by:

A. thermit welding B. gas welding

C. resistance welding D. none of the above

241. For welding lamp filaments with supporting wires, which welding machine is required?

A. Seam welding B. Spot welding

C. Butt welding D. Both A and C

242. For welding of sheets, which type of welding is recommended?

A. Seam welding B. Spot welding

C. Butt welding D. Projection welding

243. External pressure is required for:

A. spot welding B. atomic arc welding

C. arc welding D. hydrogen welding

244. The voltage required for resistance welding is:

A. very low B. low

C. high D. very high

245. Resistance welding can be used for:

A. repairing the light jobs B. repairing the high jobs

C. both A and B D. none of the above

246. Types of welding used for attaching nuts and bolts with the sheets is:

A. flash welding B. butt welding

C. projection welding D. spot welding

247. The most common contaminants are:

A. deposit of oxide B. dirt

C. grease slicking to the surface D. A, B and C

248. Which operation is necessary for electroplating a job:

A. deposition of metal B. polishing and buffing

C. cleaning D. A, B and C

249. Before starting electroplating which operation is necessary:

A. polishing B. cleaning

C. buffing D. none of the above

250. For removing oxide and scale from the surface of the job, the job is given:

A. acidic bath B. alkaline bath

C. pickling bath D. none of the above

251. In cynide bath, the copper deposited on the job is:

A. thin B. smooth

C. both A and B D. rough

252. The copper plating is mostly employed on iron articles for:

A. giving a shiny look B. preventing from rust

C. giving reflecting property D. none of the above

253. For nickel plating, anode is made of :

A. pure nickel B. nickel chrome

C. nickel iron D. none of the above

254. For chromium plating, anode is made of:

A. alloy of nickel and lead B. pure lead

C. antimonial lead D. none of the above

255. Chromium plating is employed on the metallic surfaces for:

A. giving shiny look

B. giving hard coating

C. protecting from atmospheric corrosion
D. A, B and C.

256. Buffing and polishing helps:
A. making the surface smooth
B. shining the surface
C. spreading the metal uniformly on the surface
D. A, B and C

257. The speed of the buffing machine used for electroplating chould:
A. high
B. low
C. medium
D. none of the above

258. In gas welding the gases used are:
A. acetylene
B. oxygen
C. both A and B
D. oxygen

259. The resistance of arc:
A. increases with increase of current
B. decreases with increase of current
C. does not depend upon current
D. none of the above

260. The eye of welding operator must be protected against:
A. infrared radiations
B. ultra-violet radiations
C. both A and B
D. none of the above

261. The load taken by a welding transformer is:
A. highly inductive
B. non-inductive
C. purely resistive
D. none of the above

262. The power factor of the load using welding transformer is usually:
A. very low of the order of 0.3 to 0.5 lagging
B. 1.0
C. nearly unity lagging
D. none of the above

263. The power factor of load using welding transformer least depends on:
A. type of electrolyte
B. arc length
C. material to be welded
D. none of the above

264. A plywood board is to be heated through 100°C. Which method will be suitable for this purpose?
A. Resistance heating
B. Induction heating
C. Arc heating
D. None of the above

265. Which method is appropriate for heating non-ferrous metals?
A. Indirect arc heating
B. Dielectric heating
C. Radiant heating
D. None of the above

266. For arc heating, the electodes are made of:

A. graphite
B. copper
C. nickel
D. aluminium

267. In an electric press mica is used:

A. for induction heating
B. as an insulator
C. for dielectric heating
D. none of the above

268. Which method of heating is likely to give leading power factor?

A. Dielectric heating
B. Resistance heating
C. Electric arc heating
D. None of the above

269. Nichrome wires can be safely used for heating upto:

A. 1600°C
B. 1400°C
C. 1435°C
D. none of the above

270. Furnaces used for cremation use:

A. arc heating
B. resistance heating
C. induction heating
D. none of the above

271. In dielectric heating current flows through:

A. dielectric
B. air
C. metallic conductor
D. none of the above

272 Which of the following method is suitable for the heating of conducting medium?

A. Eddy current heating
B. Induction heating
C. Radiant heating
D. None of the above

273. The highest value of thermal conductivity is for:

A. melting ice
B. solid ice
C. stem
D. water

274. Which insulating material is suitable for low temperature application?

A. Diatomaceous earth
B. 85% magnesia
C. Cork
D. Asbestos paper

275. When t is the thickness of the sheet, the tip diameter for spot welding is usually:

A. $\frac{1}{t}$
B. $\sqrt{t}$
C. $t^{3/2}$
D. $2t$

276. The efficiency of a welding motor generator is usually in the range of:

A. rising
B. droping
C. static
D. none of the above

277. In argon arc welding the electrode is made of:

A. steel
B. tungsten
C. carbon
D. nickel

278. The transformer used for a.c. welding sets is:

A. step down transformer
B. booster type
C. step up transformer
D. none of the above

279. Induction heating, the depth upto which the current will penetrate is proportional to:

A. $1/(\text{frequency})^{1/2}$
B. frequency
C. $(\text{frequency})^2$
D. none of the above

280. The metod of heating used in an electric room heat convector is:

A. induction heating
B. resistance heating
C. arc-heating
D. dielectric heating

281. The electric resistance ovens are used:

A. for hardening of metals
B. for drying and baking of pottery
C. for annealing of metals
D. A, B and C

282. In an indirect resistance heating furnace, heat is transferred to the change by:

A. radiation
B. convection
C. both A and B
D. radiation only

283. In a direct resistance heating furnace, a high resistance material is sprinkled over the surface for:

A. having better continuity
B. passing more current
C. controlling current
D. none of the above

284. Types of electric resistance furnaces are:

A. direct and indirect resistance heating furnace
B. direct resistance heating furnace
C. induction heating furnace
D. both B and C

285. Electric furnace requires:

A. less maintenance
B. more maintenance
C. no maintenance
D. none of the above

286. Electric heating is considered better as compared to ordinary core furnace because:

A. it gives uniform heating
B. easy to control temperature
C. it is more efficient
D. above three A, B and C

287. Coreless induction furnaces are operated on:

A. medium frequency
B. low frequency
C. supply frequency
D. none of the above

288. For minimizing the leakage reactance and turbulance effect, the furnace must operate:

A. at low frequency
B. at high frequency
C. at supply frequency
D. none of the above

289. In a core type furnace, the secondary winding has:

A. no turns
B. more number of turns
C. less number of turns
D. none of the above

290. An indirect furnace can be:

A. of small size
B. restricted to the size of electrodes
C. of any size
D. none of the above

291. Chemical equivalent weight is the ratio of:

A. electro chemical equivalent weight/valency
B. atomic weight/valency
C. valency/atomic weight
D. none of the above

292. For electroplating, the eletrolyte is prepared from:

A. different salt of metal to be deposited
B. salt of metal to be deposited
C. both A and B
D. none of the above

293. Under coating of copper is used for articles for:

A. nickel plating
B. chromium plating
C. silver plating
D. none of the above

294. For copper plating cynide bath is perferred, as it gives:

A. thin coating
B. smooth coating
C. both A and B
D. none of the above

295. The current density is different for:

A. different types of electroplating
B. similar type of electroplating
C. any types of electroplating
D. none of the above

296. The requirement for electroplating is/are:

A. D.C. low voltage
B. high current
C. both A and B
D. none of the above

297. Greater the quantity of electricity passed through the electrolyte, greater will be the mass of metal deposited on the:

A. anode
B. cathode
C. both A and B
D. none of the above

298. The solution of a salt when used for electrolytic process is called:

A. anode
B. cathode
C. electrolyte
D. none of the above

299. Energy efficiency is equal to:

A. theoretical energy required/actual enrrgy required
B. theoretical energy
C. actual energy
D. none of the above

300. Eddy currents produced in the coreless furnace are proportional to:
A. flux density square
B. frequency square
C. both A and B
D. none of the above

301. Long distance railways use:
A. 25 kV two phase AC
B. 200 V DC
C. 25 kV single phase AC
D. 25 kV three phase AC

302. The range of horsepower for diesel locomotives is:
A. 1500 to 2500
B. 500 to 1000
C. 1200 to 1500
D. 800 to 1200

303. Which motor is used in tramways:
A. DC series motor
B. DC shunt motor
C. AC three phase motor
D. none of the above

304. A submarine while moving under water, is provided driving power through
A. gas turbine
B. batteries
C. steam turbine
D. diesel engines

.305. Diesel locomotives are manufactured in India at:
A. Ajmer
B. Jabalpur
C. Varanasi
D. Bangalore

306. Maximum horse power of steam locomotive is:
A. 3000
B. 1500
C. 2000
D. 2500

307. In force-current analogy, capacitance is analogous to:
A. velocity
B. mass
C. displacement
D. none of the above

308. Under thermal and electrical system analogy, temperature is considered analogous to:
A. charge
B. current
C. voltage
D. none of the above

309. When analogy is drawn between electrical systems and thermal systems, current is considered analogous to:
A. temperature
B. heat flow rate
C. heat flow
D. none of the above

310. The transfer fuction of a system is used to calculate:
A. input for a given output
B. output for a given output
C. time constant
D. none of the above

311. The input which is established or varied by some means external to and independent of the feedback control system is known as:
A. command
B. disturbance
C. signal
D. none of the above

312 The transfer system is applicable to:
A. linear and time-invariant systems
B. linear and time variant systems
C. linear system only
D. non-linear system only

313. The advantage of transmitting power at high voltage is:
A. power loss will be less
B. magnitude of current will be small
C. both A and B
D. none of the above

314. The next lower voltage line feeding areas on either side of the main transmission line is called:
A. secondary transmission
B. primary transmission
C. secondary distribution
D. none of the above

315. The basic ingradients of an a.c. supply system consists of:
A. transmission
B. generation
C. distribution
D. all A, B and C

316. In case of high voltage transmission the control devices must have
A. faster controls
B. medium controls
C. slow controls
D. none of the above

317. In case of high voltage transmission, the conductors become heavier and costlier because they require:
A. less resistivity
B. more insulation
C. better conductivity
D. none of the above

318. The mass of a substance liberated during electrolysis in a given time depends upon
A. Electric current
B. Electric power
C. Working temp.
D. Resistance

319. Isogonic lines have
A. Same value of dip
B. Same value of declination
C. Same value of BH
D. None of these

320. The permeability of air is
A. 0.5
B. 1
C. 1.3
D. 2

321. The magnetic susceptibility of water is
A. directly proportional to T
B. inuersely proportional to T
C. independent of T
D. None of these

322. An electric motor
A. generates electric energy
B. converts electrical energy into mechanical energy
C. generates mechanical energy
D. converts mechanical energy into electrical energy

323. A rod of mild steel kept inside a coil carrying high frequency currents gets heated due to

A. Resistance heating B. Infrased heating
C. Dielectric heating D. Induction heating

324. In metting chamber of direct are Furnace is made usuelly

A. cylindrical B. spherical
C. cubical D. rectanguler

325. The total timing of the time cycle in a resistance welding process is called the timing of

A. holding B. squeezing
C. hardening D. heat control

326. The system will be underdamped system when the gain of critically damped system is:

A. increased B. decreased
C. remain constant D. none of the above

327. The electrical inductor is analogous to:

A. spring B. inertia
C. viscous damper D. none of the above

328. In the system design the differentiators are not used because:

A. they develop the noise and will saturate the amplifier.
B. of smaller size
C. of larger size
D. medium size

329. The electrical resistance is analogous to:

A. fluid capacity B. spring
C. fluid restance D. none of the above

330. The Bode diagram approach is applied to:

A. minimum phase network B. any network of control system
C. both A and B D. none of the above

331. The size of transformer:

A. decreases with rise of transmitting voltage
B. increases with rise of transmitting voltage
C. remains constant with voltage
D. none of the above

332. Maintenance and protection becomes costlier:

A. with increase of voltage B. with decrease of voltage
C. with decrease of kVA D. none of the above

333. Minimum arcing voltage will be least in case of:

A. silver B. tungsten
C. carbon D. graphite

334. Piezoelectric materials serve as a source of:
A. resonant waves
B. musical waves
C. ultrasonic waves
D. none of the above

335. A system in which the control action is dependent upon the output is known as:
A. closed loop system
B. open loop system
C. both A and B
D. none of the above

336. Which system has tendency to oscillate:
A. closed loop system
B. open loop system
C. both A and B
D. none of the above

337. Human eye can be considered as:
A. a closed loop system
B. an open loop system
C. both A and B
D. none of the above

338. Under electrical system and pneumatic system analogy, current is considered analogous to:
A. air flow rate
B. pressure
C. velocity
D. none of the above

339. Under electrical and pneumatic system analogy, pressure is considered analogous to:
A. resistance
B. current
C. charge
D. none of the above

340. In an open loop system the control action:
A. is independent of the output
B. depends on the input signal
C. depends on the output signal
D. none of the above

341. The size of wire used for power sub-circuit is copper conductor is:
A. 7/22 S.W.G.
B. 7/15 S.W.G.
C. 3/25 S.W.G.
D. 3/15 S.W.G.

342. The size of wire used for lighting sub-circuit is:
A. 1/2 mm^2
B. 1/1.5 mm^2
C. 1/1.2 mm^2
D. 1/35 mm^2

343. In a power sub-circuit, the maximum current allowed:
A. 5 A
B. 17 A
C. 15 A
D. 17 A

344. In a lighting sub-circuit, the maximum current allowed:
A. 5 A
B. 7 A
C. 15 A
D. 17 A

345. Screw type lamp holders are used for lamps whose wattage exceeds:
A. 150 watts
B. 250 watts
C. 100 watts
D. 200 watts

346. The type of main switch used in small domestic installation is:
A. double pole type
B. triple pole type

C. single pole type D. none of the above

347. The potential barrier acts as barrier against the flow of:
A. holes only B. electrons only
C. both A and B D. none of the above

348. The acceptor type of impurity is:
A. boron B. freon
C. phosphorus D. none of the above

349. The majority charge carriers in an N-type semiconductors are:
A. electrons B. neutrons
C. holes D. none of the above

350. The addition of impurity atoms to a pure semiconductor makes it an:
A. intrinsic semiconductor B. extrinsic semiconductor
C. both A and B D. none of the above

351. The work function of metal is generally expressed in:
A. electron volt B. joules
C. volts D. none of the above

352. Ideally a constant voltage source should have:
A. infinite capacitance B. infinite resistance
C. both A and B D. zero resistance

353. Carbon arc welding is suitable particularly for
A. Non-ferrous metals B. Ferrous metals
C. Insulators D. None of these

354. The number of diodes required in a bridge rectifier circuit is:
A. three B. four
C. two D. one

355. The ripple factor in case of a full wave rectifier is:
A. 0.48 B. 0.25
C. 0.35 D. 0.75

356. In a full wave rectifier the diode conduct for:
A. full cycle B. alternate half cycle
C. one half cycle D. none of the above

357. Multimeter is used for measuring:
A. current B. resistance
C. voltage D. all the above

358. Feedback regulators are used to provide:
A. low load current B. high load current
C. very low load current D. none of the above

359. To eliminate the cross over distortion, the transistors are given at their bases:
A. self bias B. smallest current
C. larger current D. small forward bias

360. The plate current in a triode can be controlled by controlling:
A. grid voltage
B. plate voltage
C. both A and B
D. none of the above

361. The efficiency of diesel locomotives is nearly:
A. 10-15 percentage
B. 20-25 percentage
C. 30-35 percentage
D. 25-30 percentage

362. The advantage of electric braking is:
A. more heat is generated during braking
B. it avoids wear of track
C. it is instantaneous
D. none of the above

363. A drive suitable for mines where explosive gas exist, is:
A. battery engine
B. steam engine
C. diesel engine
D. none of the above

364. Overload capacity of diesel engines is usually restricted to
A. 10%
B. 5%
C. 15%
D. 20%

365. Which locomotive has the highest operational availability
A. steam
B. diesel
C. electric
D. None of the above

366. Overhead lines for power supply to tram cars are at a minimum height of:
A. 5 m
B. 10 m
C. 15 m
D. 20 m

367. For tramways, the return circuit is:
A. through rails
B. through cables
C. through common earthing
D. none of the above

368. Which city of India was first to adopt electric traction?
A. Calcutta
B. Chennai
C. Mumbai
D. Delhi

369. Locomotives with manometer bogie have:
A. low coefficient of adhesion
B. lot of skidding
C. suitability for passenger and freight service
D. none of the above

370. Specific energy consumption is least in:
A. sub-urban service
B. main-line service
C. urban service
D. none of the above

371. A load versus is a plot of:
A. load versus current
B. load versus time
C. load versus cost of power
D. none of the above

372 The load of a consumer is generally measured in terms of:
A. kW B. amperes
C. volts D. none of the above

373. Which domestic utility item has highest power rating?
A. Ceiling fan B. Electric iron
C. Mixi D. Refrigerator

374. Fuel transportation cost is least in:
A. nuclear power plant B. steam power stations
C. diesel generating plant D. none of the above

375. Which plant can never have 100% load factor?
A. Base load plant B. Peak load plant
C. Nuclear power plant D. Hydro electric plant

376. A gas turbine power plant usually suits for:
A. base load operation B. peak load operation
C. casual run D. none of the above

377. A diesel power plant is best suited as:
A. stand by plant B. peak load plant
C. base load plant D. none of the above

378. The maximum load on the station will occur at:
A. 6 hr B. 0 hr
C. 12 hr D. 9 hr

379. The life of underground cables is taken as:
A. 5 years B. 2 years
C. 1 year D. none of the above

380. Diesel engine power plants usually run on:
A. kerosene B. light diesel oil
C. high speed diesel engine D. none of the above

381. A nuclear plant is invariably used as a:
A. peak load plant B. base load plant
C. stand-by plant D. none of the above

382 Copper conductors are generally used for transmission line because it:
A. requires more support
B. requires more insulators
C. has longer life and high conductivity
D. none of the above

383. The steel towers are employed because they have:
A. better workability B. longer life
C. more mechanical strength D. all the above A, B and C.

384. The most important components required for tansmission lines are:
A. pooles B. towers

C. conductors and insulators D. all the above A, B and C.

385. Different types of insulators used for transmission lines are:

A. suspension type B. pin type

C. schackle type D. all A, B and C

386. Which of the following industries will consume maximum power per tonne of product?

A. aluminium B. cement

C. zinc D. alloy steel

387. A steam power station will run with maximum efficiency when it is run:

A. near full load B. at low steam pressures

C. at highest speeds D. none of the above

388. The useful life of a diesel engine is a power plant is expected to be:

A. 50 years B. 15 years

C. 30 years D. 20 years

389. Anything having some heat value can be sed as fuel in case of:

A. closed cycle gas turbines B. diesel engines

C. petrol engines D. both B and C

390. Ships are generally powered by:

A. hydraulic turbines B. diesel engines

C. steam accumulators D. nuclear power plants

391. For the same cylinder dimensions and speed, which engine will produce least power?

A. Diesel engine B. Petrol engine

C. Super charged engine D. None of the above

392. Load shedding is possible through:

A. switching off the loads B. voltage reduction

C. frequency reduction D. any of the above

393. The acceleration rate of trains on suburban services is:

A. 0.4 to 6.5 km/h^2 B. 0.1 to 0.3 km/h^2

C. 10 to 26 km/h^2 D. none of the above

394. The maximum number of passenger coaches that can be attached to diesel locomotives on broad gauge is:

A. 36 to 40 B. 25 to 35

C. 25 to 30 D. 35 to 45

395. The coasting retradation on trains is approximately:

A. 1.6 km/h^2 B. 0.16 km/h^2

C. 18 km/h^2 D. 25 km/h^2

396. Maintenance requirements are least in case of:

A. steam locomotives B. electric locomotives

C. diesel locomotives D. none of the above

397. Free running and coasting periods are generally long in case of:

A. main line service B. sub-urban service

C. urban service D. none of the above

398. Electrification of railway track in India was done or the first time in:

A. 1925-1932 B. 1940-1947

C. 1887-1893 D. 1857-1865

399. At an average, the coal consumption per km in case of steam engine is nearly:

A. 30 kg to 45 kg B. 28 kg to 30 kg

C. 45 kg to 65 kg D. 50 kg to 70 kg

400. When a locomotive for Indian Railways is designated as WAM_1, in this the letter W indicates that:

A. the locomotive is for shuting duty

B. the locomotive is to run on broad gauge track

C. the locomotive is for goods trains only

D. the locomotive is to run on metre gauge track

ANSWERS

1	**2**	**3**	**4**	**5**	**6**	**7**	**8**	**9**	**10**
C	B	C	B	A	B	B	C	A	C
11	**12**	**13**	**14**	**15**	**16**	**17**	**18**	**19**	**20**
B	A	A	B	A	C	B	C	A	B
21	**22**	**23**	**24**	**25**	**26**	**27**	**28**	**29**	**30**
A	C	A	B	C	B	A	B	B	A
31	**32**	**33**	**34**	**35**	**36**	**37**	**38**	**39**	**40**
C	B	C	A	B	A	B	B	B	C
41	**42**	**43**	**44**	**45**	**46**	**47**	**48**	**49**	**50**
D	B	C	A	B	C	A	B	B	C
51	**52**	**53**	**54**	**55**	**56**	**57**	**58**	**59**	**60**
A	C	D	B	B	B	B	A	C	A
61	**62**	**63**	**64**	**65**	**66**	**67**	**68**	**69**	**70**
A	B	C	B	B	B	C	B	C	B
71	**72**	**73**	**74**	**75**	**76**	**77**	**78**	**79**	**80**
C	B	C	A	B	B	C	C	A	C
81	**82**	**83**	**84**	**85**	**86**	**87**	**88**	**89**	**90**
B	C	A	A	D	D	A	B	A	B
91	**92**	**93**	**94**	**95**	**96**	**97**	**98**	**99**	**100**
D	C	B	B	B	A	C	A	C	B
101	**102**	**103**	**104**	**105**	**106**	**107**	**108**	**109**	**110**
D	B	A	B	A	B	B	A	B	A

111	**112**	**113**	**114**	**115**	**116**	**117**	**118**	**119**	**120**
B	A	B	B	A	B	B	A	A	B
121	**122**	**123**	**124**	**125**	**126**	**127**	**128**	**129**	**130**
C	D	A	B	A	A	B	A	B	B
131	**132**	**133**	**134**	**135**	**136**	**137**	**138**	**139**	**140**
A	C	A	A	B	A	D	B	D	B
141	**142**	**143**	**144**	**145**	**146**	**147**	**148**	**149**	**150**
B	A	A	C	A	B	C	A	A	B
151	**152**	**153**	**154**	**155**	**156**	**157**	**158**	**159**	**160**
C	A	B	C	A	A	D	C	D	B
161	**162**	**163**	**164**	**165**	**166**	**167**	**168**	**169**	**170**
A	A	A	B	B	C	A	D	B	B
171	**172**	**173**	**174**	**175**	**176**	**177**	**178**	**179**	**180**
D	B	D	A	B	C	B	A	D	B
181	**182**	**183**	**184**	**185**	**186**	**187**	**188**	**189**	**190**
B	A	C	D	A	D	A	A	B	A
191	**192**	**193**	**194**	**195**	**196**	**197**	**198**	**199**	**200**
A	D	A	D	B	B	A	B	D	B
201	**202**	**203**	**204**	**205**	**206**	**207**	**208**	**209**	**210**
C	D	A	B	A	C	B	B	A	A
211	**212**	**213**	**214**	**215**	**216**	**217**	**218**	**219**	**220**
D	A	D	A	B	D	B	B	A	C
221	**222**	**223**	**224**	**225**	**226**	**227**	**228**	**229**	**230**
A	A	B	C	B	A	B	B	A	B
231	**232**	**233**	**234**	**235**	**236**	**237**	**238**	**239**	**240**
A	A	A	C	D	A	C	A	A	A
241	**242**	**243**	**244**	**245**	**246**	**247**	**248**	**249**	**250**
B	A	A	B	D	C	D	D	B	A
251	**252**	**253**	**254**	**255**	**256**	**257**	**258**	**259**	**260**
C	B	A	C	D	D	A	C	B	C
261	**262**	**263**	**264**	**265**	**266**	**267**	**268**	**269**	**270**
A	A	C	B	A	A	B	A	D	B
271	**272**	**273**	**274**	**275**	**276**	**277**	**278**	**279**	**280**
A	B	B	A	B	D	B	A	A	B
281	**282**	**283**	**284**	**285**	**286**	**287**	**288**	**289**	**290**
D	C	A	A	A	D	D	A	A	B
291	**292**	**293**	**294**	**295**	**296**	**297**	**298**	**299**	**300**
B	B	C	C	A	C	B	C	A	C
301	**302**	**303**	**304**	**305**	**306**	**307**	**308**	**309**	**310**
C	A	A	B	C	B	B	C	B	B

311	**312**	**313**	**314**	**315**	**316**	**317**	**318**	**319**	**320**
A	B	C	A	D	A	B	A	A	B
321	**322**	**323**	**324**	**325**	**326**	**327**	**328**	**329**	**330**
C	B	D	B	D	A	A	A	D	A
331	**332**	**333**	**334**	**335**	**336**	**337**	**338**	**339**	**340**
B	A	A	C	A	D	D	A	D	A
341	**342**	**343**	**344**	**345**	**346**	**347**	**348**	**349**	**350**
A	B	C	A	A	A	C	A	A	B
351	**352**	**353**	**354**	**355**	**356**	**357**	**358**	**359**	**360**
A	D	A	B	A	B	D	B	D	C
361	**362**	**363**	**364**	**365**	**366**	**367**	**368**	**369**	**370**
B	B	A	A	C	B	A	C	C	B
371	**372**	**373**	**374**	**375**	**376**	**377**	**378**	**379**	**380**
B	A	B	A	B	B	A	A	D	B
381	**382**	**383**	**384**	**385**	**386**	**387**	**388**	**389**	**390**
B	C	D	D	D	A	A	B	A	B
391	**392**	**393**	**394**	**395**	**396**	**397**	**398**	**399**	**400**
B	D	A	C	B	B	A	A	B	B

3

ELECTRONICS

Units—Thermionic Tubes-Semiconductors-PN-Junction-Rectifiers-Transistors-Amplifiers-Oscillators-Integrated circuits

7.1 ELECTRONICS

The branch of engineering which deals with flow of electrons, gas, vacuum and semiconductor is called electronics.

The mechanism of electron emission is classified into the following categories:

(i) **Thermionic emission :** Here electrons are emitted from the metal surface with the help of thermal energy.

(ii) **Field emission:** Here electrons are emitted from the metal surface by subjecting it to a very high electric field.

(iii) **Photoelectric emission :** Here electrons are emitted from the metal surface with the help of suitable e.m. radiations.

(iv) **Secondary emission :** Here the electrons are ejected from the metal surface by striking over it fast moving electrons.

7.2 THERMIONIC TUBES

These tubes play an important part in the operation of electronic equipments. There development has facilitated advances in the field of power and transposition.

In radio circuits, vaccum tubes are used as voltage amplifiers, power amplifiers, detectors, frequency convertors, rectifiers, regulators, oscillators and modulators etc. These tubes are used to generate high power radio waves as transistors cannot handle high power required in a radio transmitting station.

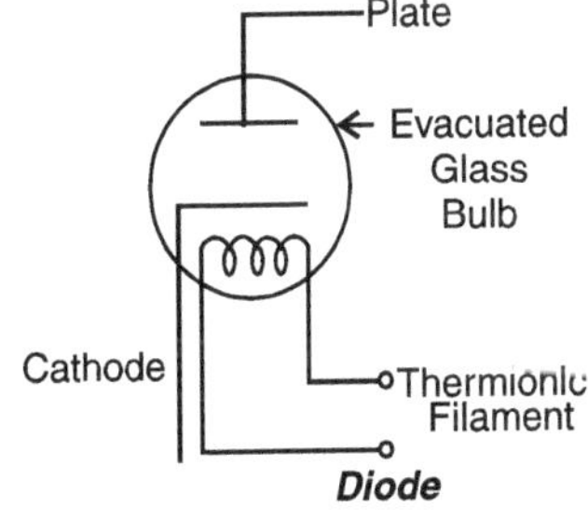

Diode

1. Vacuum Diode : It is an evacuated glass bulb with two electrodes fused in it, viz, the cathode and the plate. Below the cathode a thermionic filament attached to an auxiliary heating circuit is available. The current flows through the diode only when the plate is positive and current flows only in one direction through the diode. It is for unidirectional flow of current through a diode, so it is called a valve and hence the name *diode valve*.

Characteristic curves of a vacuum diode

In figure, there are two regions,

(i) the raising part where anode current I_B increases with the anode voltage E_B, called space-charge limited region, and

(ii) the flat portion where current is essentially independent of the anode potential, called temperature limited region.

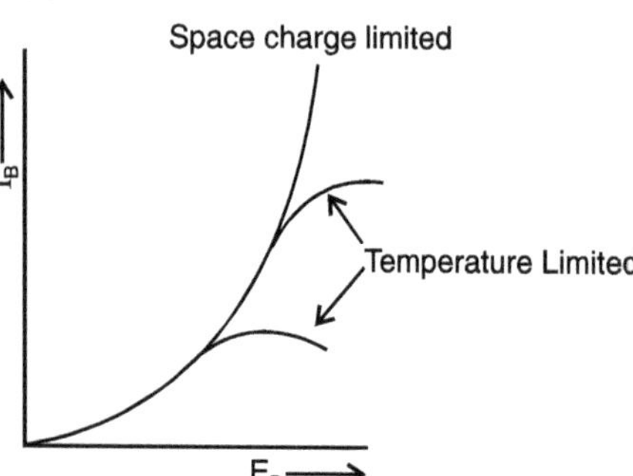

2. Vacuum Triode : Besides all that we have in a diode, a triode additionally has one more electrode called grid. Grid is perforated and so allows electrons to pass through it. It is placed quite close to the cathode compared to the plate. This grid controls the plate current. The control grid is in the form of a mesh of fine wire.

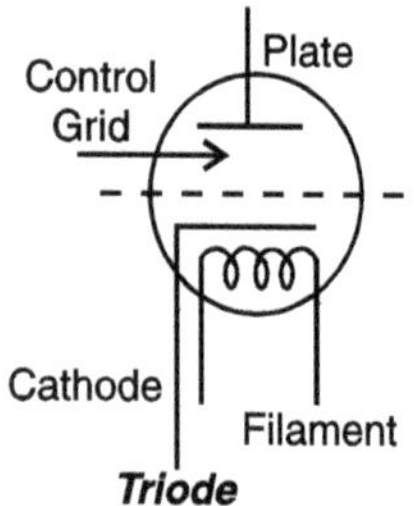

Triode

Triode constants

(a) Plate resistance, R_P $= \left[\dfrac{\partial V_P}{\partial I_P}\right]_{V_G}$ = constant

(b) Transconductance, $g_m = \left[\dfrac{\partial I_P}{\partial V_G}\right]_{V_P}$ = constant

(c) Amplification factor, $\mu = \left[\dfrac{\partial V_P}{\partial V_G}\right]_{I_P}$ = constant

Generally, $\mu = g_m \times R_P$

Triode are used as an amplifier, oscillator, demodulator and modulator.

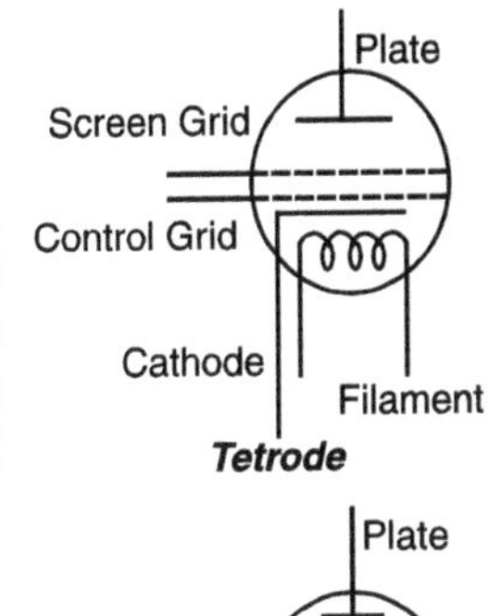

Tetrode

3. Vacuum Tetrode : It is a four-element vacuum tube. The elements are cathode, control grid, screen grid and plate. The additional grid known as screen grid, is similar in construction to the control grid except that it is usually somewhat more loosely wound. It is operated at a fixed positive potential which is ordinarily somewhat lower than the plate voltage.

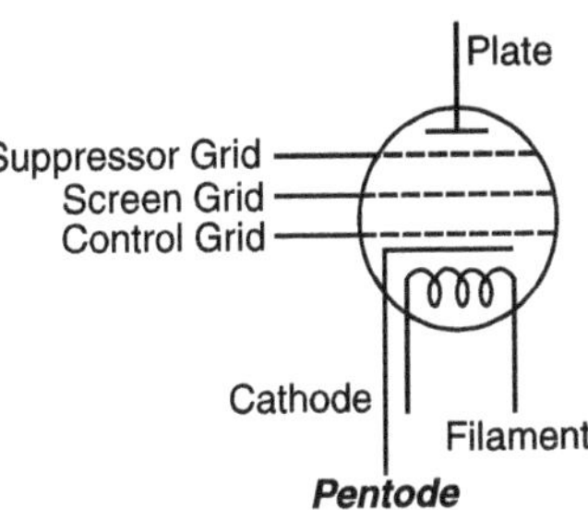

Pentode

4. Pentode : The valve having cathode, control grid, screen grid, suppressor grid and the plate is known as *pentode* (having five elctrodes). Suppressor grid is placed between the screen grid and the plate, to increase the operating range of the tube.

7.3 SEMICONDUCTORS

Semiconductors are the fourth group elements like silicon and germanium which ordinarily do have some conductivity less than those of conductors but whose conductivity, unlike the conductors, increase with rise in temperature. The gap between the valence and conduction bands is quite small and both bands are partly filled.

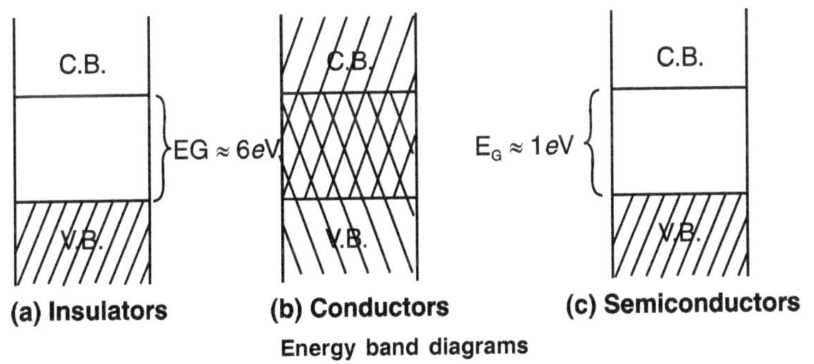

Energy band diagrams

At room temperature, their resistivity lies in the range 10^2 to 10^9 ohm cm. At very low temperatures, a semiconductor behaves as an insulator.

A pure semiconductor has negative temperature coefficient of resistance.

7.3.1 Types of Semiconductors

1. Intrinsic Semiconductors : The pure semiconductors in which the electrical conductivity is totally governed by the electrons excited from the valence band to the conduction band and in which no impurity atoms are added to increase their conductivity are called intrinsic semiconductors. In an intrinsic semiconductor,

$$n_e = n_h = n_i$$

where n_e, n_h and n_i are free electron density in conduction band, the hole density in valence band and intrinsic carrier concentration.

Doping : It is the process of adding a desirable impurity to a pure semiconductor. The impurity atoms added are called dopants and the semiconductor doped with impurity atoms is called an extrinsic semiconductor. The methods of doping are:

(a) by adding the impurity atoms to an extremely pure sample of a molten semiconductor.

(b) by bombarding the semiconductor with the ions of dopant atoms, the dopant atoms can be implanted into the semiconductor.

2. Extrinsic Semiconductors : It is a semiconductor doped with suitable impurity atoms so as to increase its conductivity. These semiconductors are of two types:

***(a)* N-type Semiconductors :** These are extrinsic semiconductors obtained by doping Ge or Si with pentavalent impurity atoms of Sb, As etc. Each impurity atom provides a free electron and is called a *donor.*

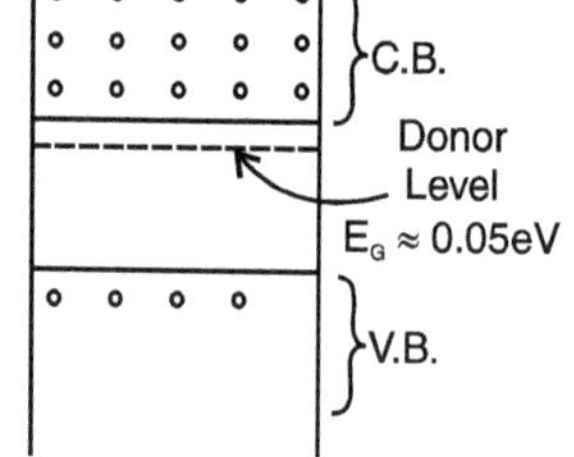

N-type semiconductor

Electrons are majority carriers and holes are minority carriers. The number density of free electrons is nearly equal to that of donor atoms and is much greater than that of holes i.e.

$$n_e \simeq n_d >> n_h$$

***(b)* P-type Semiconductors :** These are extrinsic semiconductors obtained by doping Ge or Si with trivalent impurity atoms of Al, In or B.

Each impurity atom creates a vacancy or hole in the crystal and is called an *acceptor.*

Holes are majority carriers and electrons are minority carriers. The number density of holes is nearly equal to that of acceptor atoms and is much greater than that of the free electrons, i.e.

P-type Semiconductor

$$n_h \simeq n_a >> n_e$$

7.4 P-N JUNCTION

A P-N Junction is a combination of N-type and P-type semiconductors in intimate contact. There are two main techniques of fabricating a P-N-Junction:

(a) Grown Junction technique and

(b) Fused Junction technique

Symbolic Representation : In figure, the direction of arrow is from P-region to N-region. The P-side is known as an *anode* and N-side is known as *cathode*.

7.4.1 Depletion Region

At thin layer on both sides of the junction is devoid of the charge carriers. It is called *depletion layer*. Its thickness is about 10^{-6} metre.

7.4.2 Forward Bias and Reverse Bias

The P-N-junction diode is said to be forward biased if the positive terminal of the external source of e.m.f. is connected to the P-type semiconductor and the negative terminal is connected to the N-type semiconductor.

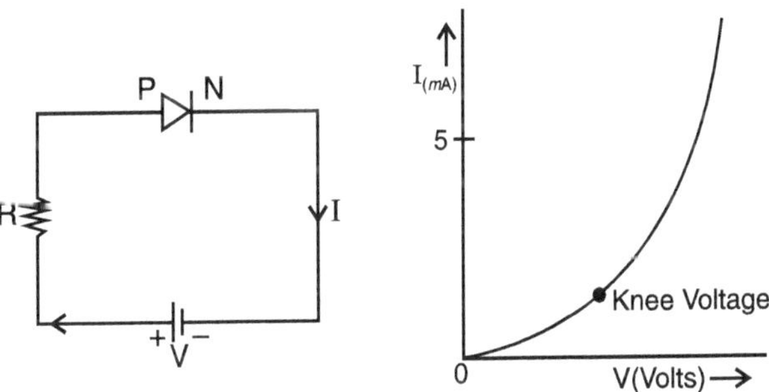

The P-N junction diode is said to be reverse biased if the positive terminal of the external source of e.m.f. is connected to the N-type semiconductor and the negative terminal is connected to the P-type semiconductor.

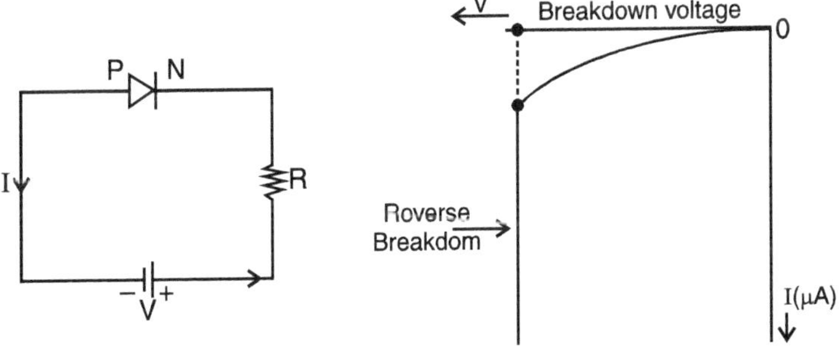

7.4.3 Dynamic resistance of the diode

The ratio of the change in junction voltage ΔV to that in junction current ΔI is called *dynamic resistance* (r_d) of the diode.

7.4.4 Some important points about depletion region and potential barrier

(i) The depletion region becomes thin during forward bias and so it offers less resistance.

(ii) The depletion region becomes thick during reverse bias and so it offers high resistance.

(iii) The value of potential barrier depends on the doping of the semiconductor.

(iv) The electric field set up across the potential barrier is of the order of 3×10^5 V/m for Ge and 7×10^5 V/m for Si.

(v) The potential barrier in Ge-diode is about 0.3 V and that in Si-diode is about 0.7 V.

7.4.5 Different types of diodes

(i) **Zener Diode :** It is a junction diode specially designed to work only in the reverse breakdown region continuously (without getting damaged).

The voltage drop across such a diode is practically independent of the current through it. So this diode acts as a *voltage regulator*. The voltage rating can be increased by using multiple diodes.

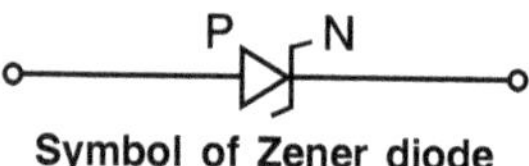

Symbol of Zener diode

(ii) **Varactor Diode :** The voltage-variable capacitance of a P-N junction biased in the reverse direction is useful in a number of circuits. Diodes made for such applications are called varactors.

The reverse current saturation is of the order of 10^{-9} ampere. The avalanche breakdown is at a bias of – 70 volts approximately.

Symbol of varactor diode

(iii) **Solar Cell :** It is a junction diode used to convert solar energy into electrical energy. Solar cells are used in light meters, in photography, some wrist watches and hand calculators etc.

Light(Photon)

P N

Symbol of Solar cell

(iv) **Photo Diode :** It is a P-N junction made from a photosensitive semiconducting material in such a way that light can fall on its junction.

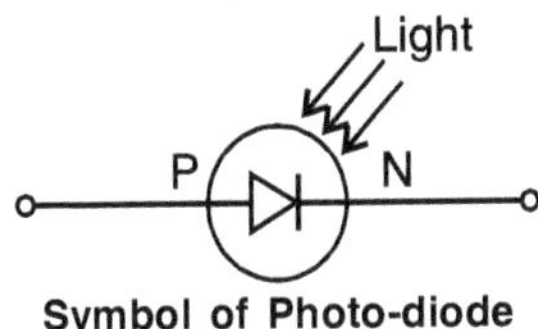

Symbol of Photo-diode

These diodes are used in many light controlling devices.

(v) **Light Emitting Diode (LED) :** The PN-junction can radiate light, as energy is released by the recombination of charges.

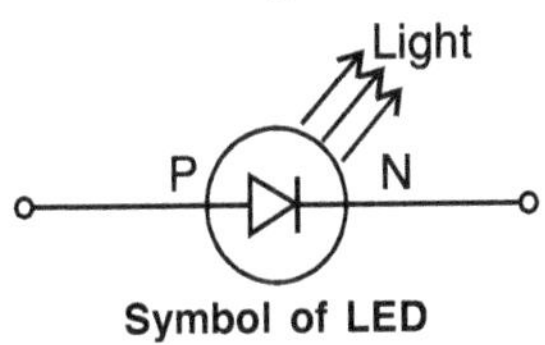

Symbol of LED

For better efficiency, gallium compounds are used. The light is emitted, when forward voltage is applied, the radiation is in the wavelengths of red, green and yellow light.

7.5 RECTIFIER

Rectification is the process of coverting a.c. into d.c. and a device used for this purpose is called a *rectifier*.

We give below some of the following four classes of rectifiers :

(i) Half-wave Vacuum Tube and Semiconductor Diode Rectifiers,

(ii) Full-wave Vacuum Tube and Semiconductor Diode Rectifiers,

(iii) Hot Cathode Gas Diode Rectifier, and

(iv) Cold Cathode Gas Diode Rectifier.

7.5.1 Some points about rectifiers

(i) A half-wave rectifier conducts during one half cycle of the applied voltage, while in full wave rectifier, the rectification is in operation for the full wave of the applied a.c. voltage.

(ii) The vacuum tube rectifiers are used for low voltage, low power requirements, while gas diode rectifiers are used for high power applications.

(iii) The main disadvantage of hot cathode mercury vapour rectifier is that it has a tendency towards are back and produces r.f. transients as the tube ionises. Due to all these defects, and since momentary overload causes damage to cathode, it is not used in home receivery.

7.5.2 Power supply

The power supply system includes the following sections :

(a) Rectifier,

(b) Filter

(c) Regulation system and

(d) Bleeder Resistor

The rectifier section consists of two vacuum diodes (if full wave rectifier) along with a transformer. We give below some important points of filter section:

(i) Ripple Factor,

(ii) Output Voltage, and

(iii) Voltage Regulation.

The effect of output resistor on the above points will also be considered. The output of a rectifier contains a.c. component of a considerable magnitude. The effect of this a.c component is to vary the output d.c. voltage. The filter system is used to reduce the magnitude of this ripple and to provide a regulated and constant voltage.

Different types of filters are series inductor filter, capacitor filter, choke input filter, (i.e. L-section filter) and capacitor input filter (i.e π section filter).

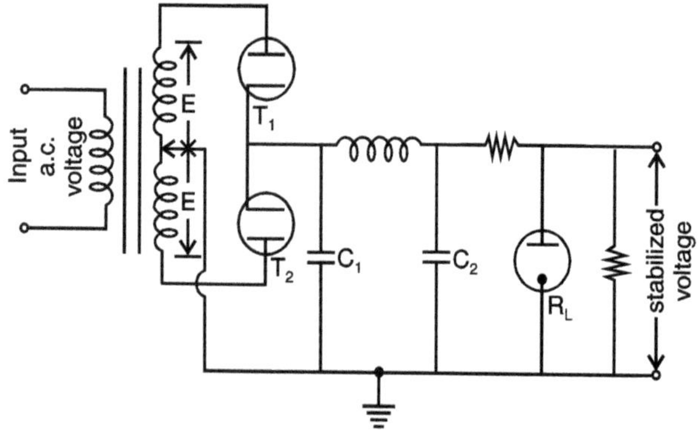

Power Supply Unit

7.5.3 Silicon Controlled Rectifier (SCR)

It consists of three junctions J_1, J_2 and J_3 (J_1 and J_3 operate in forward direction while middle junction J_2 operates in reverse direction) and three terminals known as anode A, cathode K and gate G respectively as shown in figure. In order to consider the operation of a silicon controlled rectifier, it can be regarded as consisting of one NPN transistor and other PNP transistor interconnected.

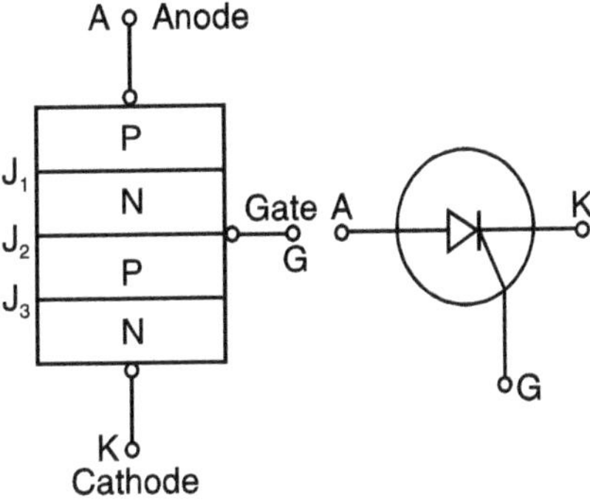

Structure and Symbol of SCR

7.6 Transistor

Transistors are prepared by sandwitch diffusion of either one N-type piece between two other P-types or *vice-versa*. Accordingly, we have PNP and NPN transistors. Just as PN-junction is comparable to a diode valve, transistor is comparable to a triode and so transistors can replace triode valves in different circuits.

The end of the transistor which is forward biased has the emitter while the one which is reversed bias has the collector. The central part is called the base. The basic difference between the two types of transistors is that the polarities of the potentials used in the two cases are just opposite.

Some of the advantages offered by transistors are :

(i) Smaller size,

(ii) Light in weight,

(iii) No heater or filament needed,

(iv) Usually operates on low voltages,

(v) Consume little power,

(vi) Improved circuit efficiency, and

(vii) Long life and shock proof

Transistor Symbols : The two types of transistors are symbolised in circuit diagrams as shown below :

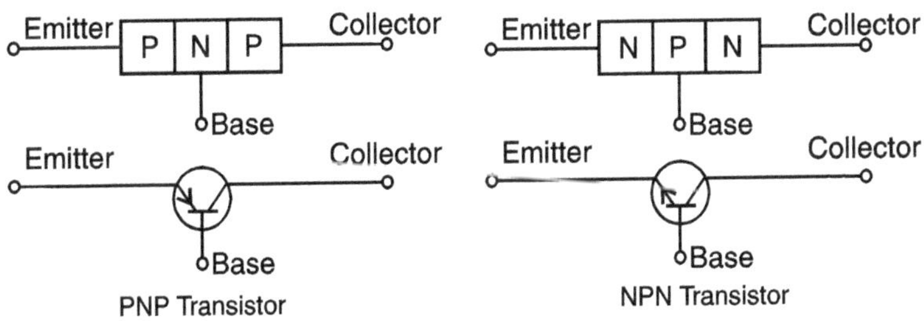

PNP Transistor

NPN Transistor

The distinguishing factor between the emitter and collector is that emitter is represented with an arrow on it in the direction of flow of current (positive charge) through the transistor.

7.6.1 Some important points about transistors

(i) The collector region is made physically larger than the emitter region as it is required to dissipate more heat.

(ii) The emitter is heavily doped.

(iii) The base is lightly doped and is thin.

(iv) The emitter emits electrons in case of NPN transistor (holes in case of PNP transistor) into the base.

(v) The collector collects these electrons in NPN transistor (holes in PNP transistor).

(vi) A PNP transistor is a complement of NPN transistor.

(vii) The junction of a transistor may be forward biased or reverse biased.

(viii) Emitter current is equal to the sum of base current and collector current, i.e. $I_E = I_B + I_C$

(ix) The *d.c. current gain* is defined as the ratio of collector current to the emitter current, i.e.

$$\alpha_{d.c.} = \frac{I_C}{I_E}$$

Its value lies between 0.95 to 0.98.

(x) The *a.c. current gain* is defined as the ratio of change in collector current to the change in emitter current at constant collector-base voltage, i.e.

$$\alpha_{a.c} = \left[\frac{\Delta I_C}{\Delta I_E}\right]_{V_{CB}\text{ constant}}$$

(xi) The *a.c. voltage gain* is defined as the ratio of the change in collector-base voltage to that in emitter-base voltage, i.e.

$$A_V = \frac{\Delta V_{CB}}{\Delta V_{EB}} = \alpha \frac{R_{out}}{R_{in}}$$

(xii) *Common-base current amplification factor* (α) is defined as

$$\alpha = \left[\frac{\Delta I_C}{\Delta I_E}\right]_{V_{CB}\text{ constant}}$$

(xiii) *Common-emitter current amplification factor* (β) is defined as

$$\beta = \left[\frac{\Delta I_C}{\Delta I_B}\right]_{V_{CE}\text{ constant}}$$

(xiv) α and β are related as follows:

$$\alpha = \frac{\beta}{1+\beta} \text{ and } \beta = \frac{\alpha}{1-\alpha}$$

7.7 AMPLIFIER

An amplifier is a circuit which is used for increasing the voltage, current or power of alternating form. A transistor can be used as an amplifier.

We may classify the amplifiers in the following way:

(i) **Frequency Range**
- *(a)* DC Amplifiers (From 0 Hz to 10 Hz)
- *(b)* Audio Amplifiers (From 30 Hz to 15 kHz)
- *(c)* Video Amplifiers (Upto a few MHz)
- *(d)* Radio Frequency Amplifiers (Few kHz to hundreds of MHz)

(ii) **Coupling**
- *(a)* Direct Couple Amplifier
- *(b)* R-C Coupled Amplifiers
- *(c)* Transistor Coupled Amplifiers
- *(d)* L-C Coupled Amplifier

(iii) **Applications**
- *(a)* Voltage or Small Signal Amplifiers
- *(b)* Power or Large Signal Amplifiers

(iv) **On the basis of operation**
- *(a)* Class A Amplifier
- *(b)* Class B Amplifier
- *(c)* Class C Amplifier
- *(d)* Class AB Amplifier

Amplifiers can also be classified on the basis of comparison between range of frequencies amplified and central frequencies as:

(i) **Narrow Band Amplifier :** This amplifier is one in which the band of frequencies amplified is small in comparison with the central frequency. Most of the radio frequency tunned amplifiers are narrow band amplifiers.

(ii) **Wide Band Amplifier :** This amplifier is one in which the band of frequencies amplified is large compared with the central frequency RC-Coupled amplifiers come under this type of category.

7.7.1 Different types of amplifications

(i) **Voltage Amplification :** It is defined as the ratio of the signal voltage available at the output terminals of an amplifier, transformer or other four terminal network, to the signal voltage impressed at the input terminals.

(ii) **Current Amplification :** It is defined as the ratio of the signal current

produced in the output circuit of an amplifier to the signal current supplied to its input circuit.

(iii) **Power Amplification :** It is defined as the ratio of the power delivered to the output circuit of an amplifier to the power supplied to the input circuit.

(iv) **Power Sensitivity:** It is defined as the ratio of the signal frequency power, delivered by the output circuit of an amplifier, to the square of the effective value of the signal voltage impressed at the input terminals.

7.7.2 Distortion in Amplifiers

One of the main objectives of an amplifier is to reproduce an exact replica of the input signal. However, the output waveform is not an exact replica. This is due to many factors, inherent non-linearity in the characteristics, or from the influence of the associated circuits.

Any deviation present in the output waveform from the input waveform is called *distortion*. The distortions are of three types, non-linear distortion, frequency distortion and delay (or phase) distortion. These may be present either separately or simultaneously.

(i) **Non-linear distortion :** A distortion is said to be non-linear distortion when in the output new frequencies are produced which are not present in the input signal. The new frequencies appear in the output due to the operation of the tube over non-linear characteristic curve.

(ii) **Frequency distortion :** A signal is composed of many frequencies. Ideally each frequency should be amplified by the same amount. The frequency distortion is said to exist when various frequencies are amplified by different amounts. This distortion is caused by the internal capacitances or may arises due to the circuit associated with the tubes.

(iii) **Delay/Phase distortion :** This distortion results from unequal phase shifts of signals of different frequencies. This distortion is not important in audio frequency amplifiers because ear cannot distinguish small delay between different frequency components. It is objectionable in systems that depend on waveshape for operation like television etc.

7.8 Oscillator

An oscillator is an electronic device which produces electric oscillations of constant frequency and amplitude. The basic principle of an oscillator is that one kind of energy is converted into another kind. The conversion of energy from one form to other and vice-versa goes on forever if no energy is dissipated in the system. The system is called *oscillator* because energy goes back and forth from one form to other. In a mechanical oscillator, like pendulum energy changes from kinetic to potential.

An *electrical oscillator* is one in which electrostatic energy is converted into electromagnetic energy and *vice-versa.*

An LC-circuit is the basic oscillatory circuit. But its oscillations are damped. A transistor can be used as an oscillator. Here the oscillations are set up in the LC-circuit (i.e. tank circuit) and feedback energy is supplied in the correct phase by an inductance L' which is inductively coupled with the inductance L of the tank circuit.

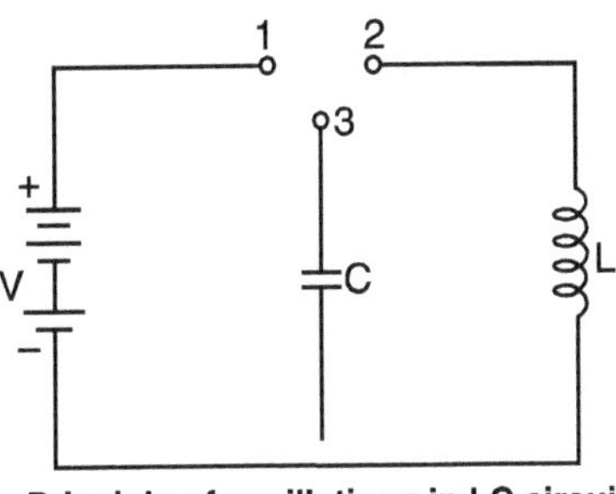

Principle of oscillations in LC circuit

The frequency of the oscillations in the tank circuit is

$$f = \frac{1}{2\pi\sqrt{LC}}$$

7.8.1 Barkhausan Criterion for sustained oscillations

In an amplifier, when the feedback is positive, the overall gain of the amplifier can be written as

$$A_f = \frac{A}{1 - A_\beta}$$

When $A_\beta = 1$, then $A_f = \infty$. The infinite gain means that there is output without any input. Thus an amplifier will become an oscillator when $A_\beta = 1$.

7.8.2 Classification of Oscillators

Vacuum tube oscillator circuit may be broadly divided into following two groups :

(i) *Those circuits which produce non-sinusoidal waves [i.e. relaxation oscillators]*

(a) Venderpol, *(b)* Multivibrator,
(c) Glow tube discharge, *(d)* Arc tube discharge,
(e) Saw tooth wave generator, and *(f)* Square wave generator.

(ii) *Those circuits which produce sinusoidal waves*

(a) Negative Resistance oscillators : Dynatron; Transitron; Push-pull circuit; and Resistance-capacitance circuit.

(b) Feedback oscillators : Tuned grid; Tuned plate; Colpitt; and complex types using more than one tuned circuits are, tuned grid-tuned plate, meissner and electron coupled.

(c) Crystal oscillators

(d) Magnetostriction oscillators

7.8.3 Applications of oscillators

(i) In transmitters to generate the radio frequency carrier waves.
(ii) In signal generators to supply test signals.
(iii) In digital circuits as multivibrator clock generator.
(iv) In superheterodyne receivers as frequency convertor for infra-red signals.

7.9 INTEGRATED CIRCUITS (ICs)

In a conventional electronic circuit, we find many passive components like resistance and capacitance, active devices like diode and transistor all interconnected by a number of wires connections. Such circuits are bulky and large in size.

An entire conventional electronic circuit fabricated on a small single semiconductor chip is known as Integrated Circuit (IC). Integrated circuit is light, low cost, more reliable, small device which requires lesser power to operate.

7.9.1 Classification of ICs

Depending upon the number of circuit components or logic gates, ICs are classified as

(i) Small Scale Integration SSI (Logic Gates ≤ 10)
(ii) Medium Scale Integration MSI (Logic Gates ≤ 100)
(iii) Large Scale Integration LSI (Logic Gates ≤ 1000)
(iv) Very Large Scale Integration VLSI (Logic Gates > 1000)

Integrated circuits are extensively used in television, computers and other electronic circuits.

MULTIPLE CHOICE QUESTIONS

1. Mobile electrons of P-side of the P-N junction diode constitute
   A. depending upon voltage
   B. majority current carriers
   C. minority current carriers
   D. both (A) and (B)
2. Which of the following element belongs to the same group of periodic table as that of Germanium and Silicon?
   A. Sulphur
   B. Carbon
   C. Gold
   D. Copper
3. Forbidden energy gap is highest for
   A. Gallium
   B. Germanium
   C. Silicon
   D. None of the above
4. Which of the following is not electro-magnetic in nature?
   A. γ-rays
   B. Cathode rays
   C. X-rays
   D. None of the above

5. The crystal structure of silicon is

A. Diamond | B. Face centred cubic
C. Simple cubic | D. None of the above

6. The work function of a photo-surface whose threshold wavelength is 1,200 A, will be

A. 1.27 eV | B. 1.03 eV
C. 1.54 eV | D. 2.27 eV

7. The difference between a hole and electron is that a hole

A. has no momentum
B. has no mass
C. always remains in the valance band
D. none of the above

8. Which photo-conductor is commonly used?

A. CdS | B. AsBr
C. GaAs | D. None of the above

9. Which of the following doping will produce P-type semiconductor?

A. Germanium with Phosphorous | B. Germanium with Indium
C. Silicon with Indium | D. None of the above

10. Thermionic emission of electrons is due to

A. high temperature | B. low temperature
C. electromagnetic field | D. both (B) and (C)

11. A transistor amplifier with 85% efficiency is likely to be

A. Class B | B. Class C
C. Class A | D. None of the above

12. In case of amplifiers which coupling gives highest gain?

A. Capacitance coupling | B. Transformer coupling
C. Resistance coupling | D. None of the above

13. Which class of amplifier has the lowest efficiency?

A. Class AB | B. Class B
C. Class A | D. None of the above

14. In general, the gain of amplifier is

A. Complex | B. real
C. imaginary | D. zero

15. Which class of amplifier has the least distortion?

A. B | B. C
C. A | D. AB

16. A transistor that can be used in enhancement mode is

A. MOSFET | B. JFET
C. N-P-N transistor | D. None of the above

17. Audio frequency range extends from 20 Hz to

A. 15 kHz | B. 12 kHz

C. 13 kHz D. 18 kHz

18. Class B amplifier has less efficiency compared to
A. Class AB B. Class A
C. Class C D. None of the above

19. In high frequency region, an amplifier behaves like a
A. low pass filter B. band pass filter
C. both (A) and (B) D. none of the above

20. Logarithmic amplifiers are used in
A. dividers B. adders
C. Both (A) and (B) D. none of the above

21. In a pentode, the suppressor grid is placd between
A. plate B. screen grid
C. both (A) and (B) D. none of the above

22. The material conductance of a triode is usually in the range of
A. 60 to 300 ms B. 1 to 10 ms
C. 1 to 50 ms D. 100 to 500 ms

23. Vacuum tubes can be used in
A. rectifiers B. amplifiers
C. oscillators D. all (A), (B) and (C)

24. The phenomenon of secondary emission is common in
A. tetrodes B. diodes
C. triodes D. None of the above

25. Which of the following vacuum tube cannot be used as an amplifier?
A. Pentode B. Diode
C. Tetrode D. Both (A) and (B)

26. In a triode parasitic capacitance may exist between
A. plate and cathode B. grid and cathode
C. plate and grid D. all (A), (B) and (C)

27. The mutual conductance of triode is usually expressed in terms of
A. milli-siemens B. pico-siemens
C. siemens D. none of the above

28. The units of amplification factor are
A. it is dimensionless B. V
C. mA D. none of the above

29. In a pentode the suppressor grid is used to
A. suppress secondary emission B. dissipate heat
C. limit anode voltage D. none of the above

30. When a tube is required to handle 100 kW, the emitter material will be
A. copper B. pure tungsten
C. tungsten D. none of the above

31. The heat sink disposes off heat mainly by
A. conduction
B. radiation
C. natural convention
D. none of the above

32. The transistor is usually encapsuled in
A. epoxy resin
B. enamel paint
C. graphite
D. none of the above

33. Aging effect exists in
A. transistors only
B. vacuum tubes only
C. both (A) and (B)
D. none of the above

34. The encapsulation of transistor is necessary for
A. avoiding less of free electrons
B. mechanical ruggedness
C. preventing radio interference
D. none of the above

35. Power transistors are invariably provided with
A. heat sink
B. metallic casing
C. both (A) and (B)
D. none of the above

36. In a resistance loaded, RC coupled amplifier the dc component is blocked by
A. R_c
B. R_s
C. transistor
D. C_c

37. The input and output signals for CE amplifier are always
A. out of phase
B. in phase
C. equal
D. none of the above

38. In a transistor leakage current mainly depends on
A. temperature
B. size of emitter
C. doping of base
D. none of the above

39. Which of the following is the point of reference in JFET?
A. Source
B. Gate
C. Drain
D. None of the above

40. Which of the following is the fastest switching device?
A. Triode
B. MOSFET
C. JFET
D. None of the above

41. A D.C. amplifiers
A. ac only
B. dc only
C. both *(a)* and *(b)*
D. none of the above

42. Complementary symmetry use two transistors that are
A. both P-N-P
B. both N-P-N
C. (A) and (B)
D. none of the above

43. Three cascaded stages have gains of 10, 20 and 25. The overall gain will be
A. 5000
B. 4000
C. 3000
D. 2500

44. In oscillators, class C-operation is preferred because it
A. has frequency stability
B. is most efficient
C. produces nearly square waves
D. none of the above

45. Each of two cascaded stages has a voltage gain of 30. The overall gain is
A. 800
B. 900
C. 1200
D. 1500

46. Which one of the following is a unipolar device?
A. PN diode
B. FET
C. Zener diode
D. None of the above

47. Which of the following statement is not true in case of FET?
A. It has large : gain × bandwidth
B. It has high input impedance
C. It is less noisy than bipolar transistor
D. None of the above

48. Highest operating frequency can be expected in case of
A. JFET
B. Bipolar transistor
C. MOSFET
D. None of the above

49. The input gate current of FET is closer to
A. few microamperes
B. negligibly smaller value
C. few amperes
D. none of the above

50. The properties of JFET resemble those of
A. N-P-N transistors
B. P-N-P transistors
C. Unijunction transistor
D. None of the above

51. An open heater, results zero in
A. plate
B. current
C. plate current
D. none of the above

52. In a diode, plate current can flow in only
A. two directions
B. one direction
C. three directions
D. an infinite direction

53. The anode has a positive potential with respect to the cathode to
A. remain electrons
B. attract electrons
C. emit electrons
D. none of the above

54. A thermionic cathode is heated to
A. attract electrons
B. emit electrons
C. remain electrons
D. none of the above

55. Oxide coated cathodes are generally used for
A. power tubes
B. high power tubes
C. low power tubes
D. none of the above

56. Typical the amplification factor of a triode is about
A. 50
B. 30

C. 70 D. 90

57. In a cathode ray tube, the anode voltage ranges from 2 kV to

A. 70 kV B. 50 kV

C. 80 kV D. 95 kV

58. Typical resistance for the cold heater of a vacuum tube is 1 to

A. 30 ohms B. 40 ohms

C. 60 ohms D. 50 ohms

59. Triode usually produce more noise as compared to

A. diodes B. pentodes

C. both (A) and (B) D. none of the above

60. With an indirectly heated cathode, a separate heater makes the insulated cathode to

A. electrons B. emit electrons

C. far any electrons D. none of the above

61. SCR is a .... layer device used as a silicon rectifier.

A. 3 B. 2

C. 4 D. 5

62. The .... is a silicon power rectifier to control the start of current between anode and cathode.

A. electron B. thyristor

C. SCR D. LED's

63. A bridge rectifier uses

A. 3 diodes B. 4 diodes

C. 7 diodes D. 2 diodes

64. A full wave rectifier uses atleast

A. 4 diodes B. 3 diodes

C. 5 diodes D. 2 diodes

65. A varactor diode in parallel with an indicator gives a resonant

A. circuit B. tank circuit

C. both (A) and (B) D. none of the above

66. LED's are sensitive to

A. vibrations B. mechanical vibrations

C. forced vibrations D. none of the above

67. LED's have long life around ... years.

A. 10 B. 15

C. 20 D. 25

68. Major portion of the V-I characteristic of a gas diode represents ... characteristics.

A. voltage B. constant voltage

C. gas D. none of the above

69. A zener diode is operated with

A. bias | B. reverse bias
C. both (A) and (B) | D. none of the above

70. The injection of a gas current reduces the break over voltage of a

A. diode | B. circuit
C. thyristor | D. SCR

71. The gain of an amplifier when there is feedback, is given by $A_f = A/1 - ...$

A. β | B. A/β
C. $A\beta$ | D. β/A

72. When feedback is negative, the amplifier gain is

A. zero | B. reduced
C. increased | D. constant

73. Every transmitter needs an oscillator to generate RF

A. waves | B. mechanical waves
C. carrier waves | D. both (B) and (C)

74. A signal generator is essentially an oscillator used to supply

A. signals | B. test signals
C. waves | D. electrons

75. An audio signal generator is meant to produce sinusoidal voltages of frequencies varying from 20 kHz to

A. 25 Hz | B. 40 Hz
C. 20 kHz | D. 50 kHz

76. An oscillator circuit is basically dc to ac

A. current | B. converter
C. voltage | D. none of the above

77. A signal generator supplies both RF and

A. signals | B. AF signals
C. voltage | D. none of the above

78. In RC feedback oscillators, the frequency depends on the values of R and

A. C | B. L
C. I | D. None of the above

79. The Wein-bridge oscillators, uses RC feedback in a balanced

A. circuit | B. bridge circuit
C. manner | D. none of the above

80. All the oscillator make use of active ... in conjuction with the passive circuit elements.

A. circuit | B. devices
C. current | D. voltage

81. The colpitts oscillator circuit uses a capacitive voltage divider for

A. a current | B. feedback

C. voltage D. none of the above

82. With an FM signal, the carrier and its frequency deviation are

A. added B. divided

C. multiplied D. none of the above

83. In FM, the change from the centre is known as the

A. deviation B. frequency deviation

C. both (A) and (B) D. none of the above

84. In FM, the modulating voltage produces proportional changes in

A. velocities B. frequencies

C. carrier frequencies D. none of the above

85. Any state amplifying an AM wave must operate class A to preserve the

A. modulation B. modulation envelope

C. both (A) and (B) D. none of the above

86. The RF amplifiers in transmitters generally operate class C for

A. minimum efficiency B. efficiency

C. maximum efficiency D. none of the above

87. AM results in RF sideband frequencies above and below the carrier by an amount equal to the

A frequency B. velocity

C. modulating frequency D. none of the above

88. In amplitude modulation the value of modulation index lies between

A. 1 to 2 B. 0 to 1

C. 3 to 2 D. 4 to 5

89. In AM, increased depth of modulation increases the sideband power and therefore the total

A. power B. transmitted power

C. current D. none of the above

90. In amplitude modulation, the modulated wave contains less power than the

A. carrier B. current

C. velocity D. none of the above

91. At eigen-values of the modulation index the carrier component of the frequency modulated wave

A. exists B. decreases

C. disappears completely D. none of the above

92. A modulated signal combines the RF carrier wave with a lower frequency signal that has the

A. any information B. desired information

C. both (A) and (B) D. none of the above

93. The modulating intelligence is the base

A. signal B. band signal

C. both (A) and (B) D. none of the above

94. There are ... main types of modulations.

A. four B. three
C. two D. five

95. The carrier is suppressed in a ... signal.

A. SSBC B. SSSC
C. SSBSC D. SBC

96. In PM, special signals called ...... are injected to detect errors.

A. bits B. parity bits
C. circuit D. none of the above

97. A subcarrier has a lower frequency than the

A. velocity B. mechanical velocity
C. main carrier D. both (A) and (B)

98. The inductance of connecting leads can be a source of ...... parasitics.

A. frequency B. low frequency
C. high frequency D. none of the above

99. Blocked grid keying as similar to frequency

A. keying B. shift keying
C. signal D. none of the above

100. The purpose of a balanced modulator circuit is to eliminate

A. lower sideband B. the carrier
C. baseband signal D. none of the above

101. LED's find application in

A. intercoms B. panel indicators
C. instrument displays D. all the above

102. LED's normally work on a voltage of

A. 3 to 5V B. 1 to 2V
C. 30 to 50 V D. 40-50 V

103. Which of the following device has characteristic close to that an ideal current source?

A. Crystal diode B. Zener diode
C. Transistor in CB mode D. None of the above

104. The power consumption of LED's may be of the order of

A. 5 to 10 milliamperes B. 5 to 10 amperes
C. 5 to 10 microamperes D. none of the above

105. Which of the following material is used for infrared LED's?

A. Silicon B. Gallium arsenide
C. Both (A) and (B) D. none of the above

106. A thyristor is often used in

A. speed control of motors B. digital multimeter

C. both (A) and (B) D. none of the above

107. For a SCR typical gate trigger voltage is

A. 1 mV B. 600 V

C. 100 mV D. 500 mV

108. The voltage drop across a triac in conduction is about

A. 1 V B. 5 V

C. 1 mV D. 5 mV

109. P-N junction is heavily doped in case of

A. Gun diodes B. PIN diodes

C. Tunnel diodes D. None of the above

110. The internal voltage drop in case of silicon diodes is around

A. 3 to 4 volts B. 1 to 2 volts

C. 4 to 5 volts D. 2 to 3 volts

111. Oscillators are widely used in

A. radio and television receivers B. television broadcasting

C. both (A) and (B) D. none of the above

112. A multivibrator produces

A. square waves B. pure sine waves

C. distorted sine wave D. none of the above

113. Which of following oscillator will be preferred for generating 1-MHz frequency?

A. Phase shift oscillator B. Colpitts oscillator

C. Both (A) and (B) D. None of the above

114. The main advantage of using crystal oscillators is

A. high efficiency B. constant frequency of oscillations

C. high output voltage D. none of the above

115. An oscillator circuit is mainly

A. a.c. to d.c. convertor B. d.c. to d.c.convertor

C. d.c. to a.c. convertor D. none of the above

116. LC oscillators can be used to produce frequencies as high as

A. 400 MHz B. 500 MHz

C. 300 MHz D. 200 MHz

117. Oscillators have

A. negative feedback B. positive feedback

C. no feedback D. none of the above

118. Surface Acoustic wave oscillators are suitable for

A. I-C applications B. low-power oscillations

C. low frequency oscillations D. none of the above

119. Parasitic oscillations can be suppressed by using a

A. separate tank circuit B. low value capacitor

C. both (A) and (B) D. none of the above

120. Spot the odd one out

A. satellite B. quartz
C. both (A) and (B) D. none of the above

121. Which of the following oscillator will be suitable for generating a 1 kHz frequency?

A. Colpitts oscillator B. Weinbridge oscillator
C. Both (A) and (B) D. None of the above

122. The crystal oscillator frequency is very stable due to

A. high Q of the crystal B. structure of crystal
C. rigidity of crystal D. none of the above

123. Parasitic oscillations

A. are unwanted oscillations created due to stray capacitances and inductances
B. are free from distortion
C. both (A) and (B)
D. none of the above

124. An oscillator that uses a tapped coil in the LC tunned circuit is the

A. Hartley oscillator B. Colpitts oscillator
C. Pierce oscillator D. None of the above

125. Positive feedback is the same as

A. regeneration B. negative feedback
C. positive feedback D. none of the above

126. When L is doubled and C is halved, the frequency is

A. unchanged B. halved
C. doubled D. none of the above

127. In PM, without any modulation, all the transmitted pulses have the same

A. spacing and width B. amplitude
C. Both (A) and (B) D. none of the above

128. All the output pulses are at full tansmitter power for a strong signal in all of the following except

A. PAM B. PCM
C. PWM D. PFM

129. In AM, the modulation envelope has a peak value double the unmodulated carrier level, when the modulation is

A. 100% B. 95%
C. 80% D. 75%

130. Pulse modulation is often used in

A. FL band B. microwave band
C. telegraphy D. none of the above

131. Pluse modulation is used in

A. data communications
B. radio navigation
C. automatic landing equipment
D. none of the above

132. Which of the following frequency is likely to be associated with FM radio broadcasting

A. 90 MHz
B. 70 MHz
C. 50 MHz
D. 30 MHz

133. A frequency multiplier stage should operate as

A. Class B
B. Class C
C. Class A
D. No Class

134. A broadcast radio transmitter radiate 20 kW when the modulation percentage is 60. The carrier power will be

A. 16.94 kW
B. 20 kW
C. 1.45 kW
D. 1.25 kW

135. A 200 W carrier is modulated to a depth of 75%. The power of the modulated wave will be

A. 512.5 W
B. 890.5 W
C. 375.5 W
D. 280.4 W

136. FM broadcast band generally lies in

A. SHF
B. VHF
C. LF
D. HF

137. Which of the following receiver does not have amplitude limiter stage?

A. FM
B. AM
C. Both (A) and (B)
D. None of the above

138. In case of wideband FM signal, the modulation index may be expected to be

A. more than 1
B. less than 1
C. two
D. more than two

139. Which of the following will carry the same information as the AM wave itself?

A. VSB only
B. VSB and SSB
C. Both (A) and (B)
D. None of the above

140. In AM receiver the following frequency is

A. always higher than signal frequency
B. always qual to 450 kHz
C. always equal to signal frequency
D. none of the above

141. A FM signal has modulating frequency f_m and maximum frequency deviation of S. The bandwidth will be approximately

A. 28
B. 8
C. 38
D. 58

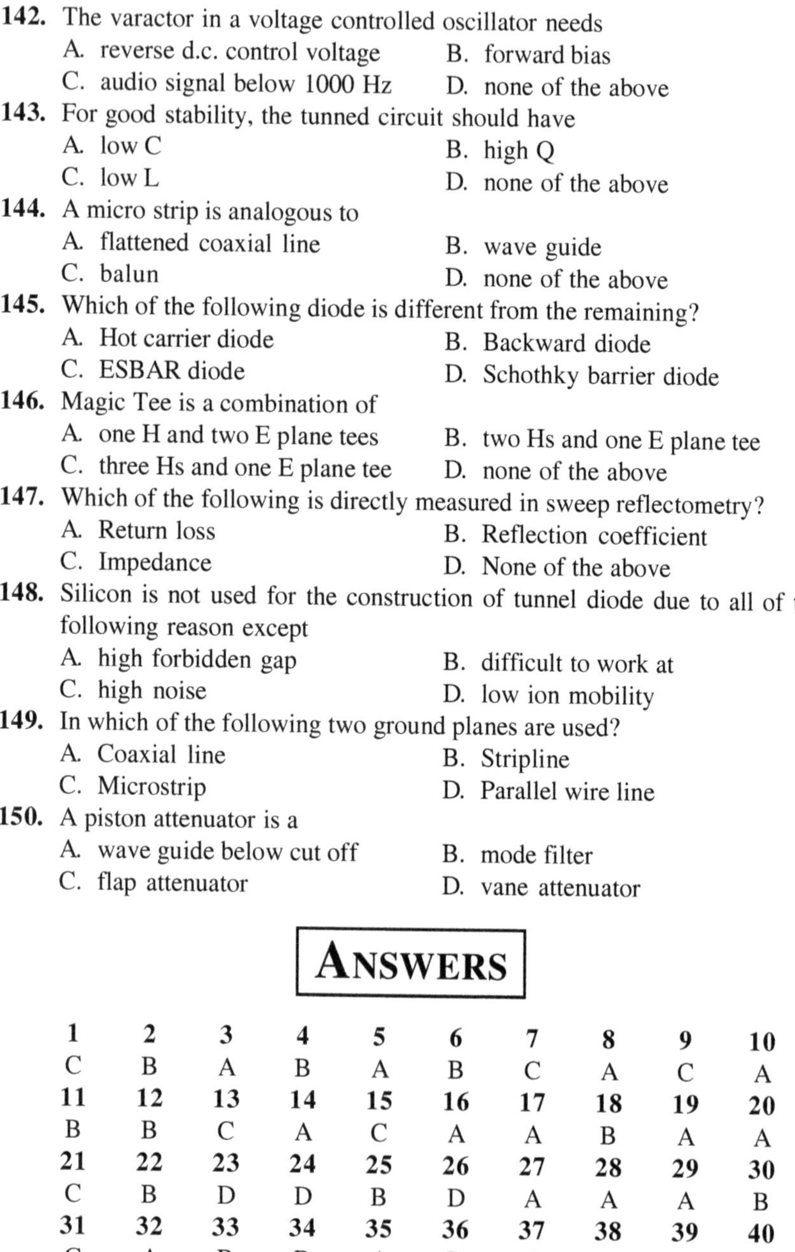

142. The varactor in a voltage controlled oscillator needs

A. reverse d.c. control voltage B. forward bias
C. audio signal below 1000 Hz D. none of the above

143. For good stability, the tunned circuit should have

A. low C B. high Q
C. low L D. none of the above

144. A micro strip is analogous to

A. flattened coaxial line B. wave guide
C. balun D. none of the above

145. Which of the following diode is different from the remaining?

A. Hot carrier diode B. Backward diode
C. ESBAR diode D. Schothky barrier diode

146. Magic Tee is a combination of

A. one H and two E plane tees B. two Hs and one E plane tee
C. three Hs and one E plane tee D. none of the above

147. Which of the following is directly measured in sweep reflectometry?

A. Return loss B. Reflection coefficient
C. Impedance D. None of the above

148. Silicon is not used for the construction of tunnel diode due to all of the following reason except

A. high forbidden gap B. difficult to work at
C. high noise D. low ion mobility

149. In which of the following two ground planes are used?

A. Coaxial line B. Stripline
C. Microstrip D. Parallel wire line

150. A piston attenuator is a

A. wave guide below cut off B. mode filter
C. flap attenuator D. vane attenuator

ANSWERS

1	**2**	**3**	**4**	**5**	**6**	**7**	**8**	**9**	**10**
C	B	A	B	A	B	C	A	C	A
11	**12**	**13**	**14**	**15**	**16**	**17**	**18**	**19**	**20**
B	B	C	A	C	A	A	B	A	A
21	**22**	**23**	**24**	**25**	**26**	**27**	**28**	**29**	**30**
C	B	D	D	B	D	A	A	A	B
31	**32**	**33**	**34**	**35**	**36**	**37**	**38**	**39**	**40**
C	A	B	B	A	D	A	A	A	B

41	42	43	44	45	46	47	48	49	50
C	C	A	B	B	B	A	B	B	A
51	**52**	**53**	**54**	**55**	**56**	**57**	**58**	**59**	**60**
C	B	B	B	C	B	C	D	B	B
61	**62**	**63**	**64**	**65**	**66**	**67**	**68**	**69**	**70**
C	C	B	D	B	B	C	B	B	C
71	**72**	**73**	**74**	**75**	**76**	**77**	**78**	**79**	**80**
C	B	C	B	C	B	B	A	B	B
81	**82**	**83**	**84**	**85**	**86**	**87**	**88**	**89**	**90**
B	C	B	C	B	C	C	B	B	A
91	**92**	**93**	**94**	**95**	**96**	**97**	**98**	**99**	**100**
C	B	B	B	C	B	C	C	B	B
101	**102**	**103**	**104**	**105**	**106**	**107**	**108**	**109**	**110**
D	B	C	A	B	A	B	A	C	B
111	**112**	**113**	**114**	**115**	**116**	**117**	**118**	**119**	**120**
C	A	B	B	C	B	B	A	B	A
121	**122**	**123**	**124**	**125**	**126**	**127**	**128**	**129**	**130**
B	A	A	A	A	A	C	A	A	B
131	**132**	**133**	**134**	**135**	**136**	**137**	**138**	**139**	**140**
B	A	B	A	A	B	B	A	C	A
141	**142**	**143**	**144**	**145**	**146**	**147**	**148**	**149**	**150**
A	A	B	D	B	B	A	B	B	A

4

COMMUNICATIONS

Units— Communication System– Control System– Feedback– Modulation – Transmission line – Wave propagation – Satellite Communication – Antenna – Television – Telegraphy – Telegraph – Instruments and Relays – Multiplexed Telegraphy – Fax Telegraphy and e-mail – Telegraph Circuits – Baudot System – Teleprinter – Telephone Links

8.1 COMMUNICATION SYSTEM

A set up that transfers information implicitly from one point to another is called communication system. It may be electrical, electronic and optical. Major constituents of communication system are:

(i) Transmitter, *(ii)* Communication channel, and *(iii)* Receiver.

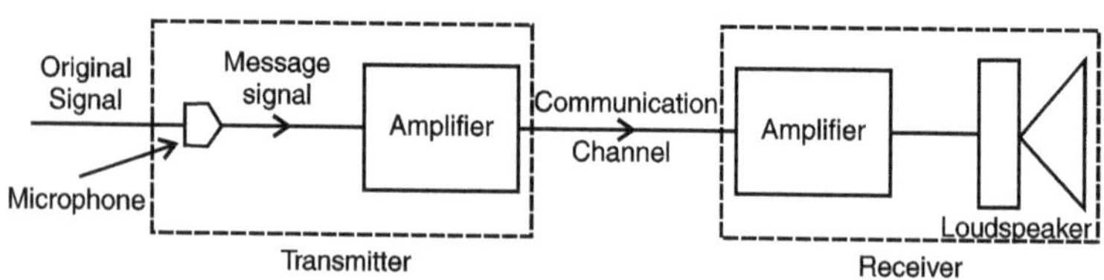

Block Diagram of communication system

8.2 Control Systems

Control system is the thing which is operated upon to produce some desired result of outcome. The initial stimulus is called the *input* and that which is produced is called the *output*. The operating entity which produces the output from the input stimulus is the control system.

We can say, thus, a control system is an arrangement of physical components connected or related in such a manner as to command, direct or regulate itself or another system.

There are three basic types of control systems:

(i) Man-made control system,

(ii) Natural, including biological control systems, and

(iii) Control systems whose components are both man-made and natural

8.2.1 Classification of control system :

(i) **Open-loop Control System :** An open-loop control system is one in which the control action is independent of the output.

(ii) **Closed-loop Control System :** A closed-loop control system is one in which the control action is somehow dependent on the output.

Comparison between open-loop system and closed-loop system

Open-loop System	*Closed-loop System*
1. Input command is the sole factor responsible for providing the control system.	The control action is provided by the difference between the input command and the corresponding output.
2. Inability to perform accurately is determined by its calibration.	It produces the input owing to feedback.
3. Generally easier build.	Generally complicated and costly.
4. Presence of non-linearities causes malfunctioning.	It usually performs accurately even in the presence of non-linearities.
5. Generally not troubled with problems of instability.	Due to feedback action, the system has tendency to oscillate.

8.3 FEEDBACK

It is that characteristic of closed-loop control systems which distinguish them from open-loop system. Feedback permits the output to be compared with the input to the system so that the appropriate control action may be formed as some function of the output and input.

8.3.1 Basic terminology

Command : It is the input which is established or varied by some means external to and independent of the feedback control system under consideration.

Control element : It consists of the feedback control system that is required to produce the manipulated variable from the actuating signal.

Disturbance : It is a signal, other than the reference input that tends to affect the value of the controlled variable.

Primary feedback : It is a signal, function of the controlled variable and that is compared with the reference input to obtain the actuating signal.

Servomechanism : It is a power-amplifying feedback control system in which the controlled variable C is mechanical positioned or a time derivative of position such as velocity or acceleration.

Regulator : It is a feedback control system in which the reference input or command is constant for long periods of time, often for the entire time interval during which the system is operational.

Stability : A system is said to be stable if its impulse response approaches zero as time approaches infinity. Alternatively, a system is stable if every bounded input produces a bounded output.

Routh Stability Criterion : It is a method for determining system stability that can be applied to an nth order characteristic equation of the form

$$a_n x^n + a_{n-1} x^{n-1} + \dots\dots\dots + a_1, x + a_o = 0$$

Transfer functions : An open loop system shown in figure has direct transfer function G, such that when it is multiplied by the input E yields the output C. Thus,

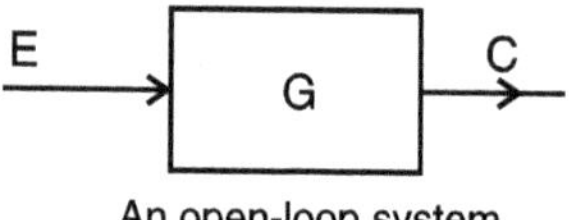

An open-loop system

$$G = \frac{C}{E}$$

where G is characterized entirely by the components that make up the system. In general, in addition to gain factor, it also contains operations of differentiation and integration.

In case of closed loop system, the actuating signal E is dependent upon a portion of the output signal HC, as well as reference input R, such that

$$E = R - HC$$

where H is the feedback function.

Closed-loop system

The feed back signal is opposite in sign from the reference input.

But $\quad C = G(R - HC)$

Hence, $\quad C = \dfrac{G}{1 + HG} . R$

Thus, transfer function of a closed-loop system is,

$$T = \frac{C}{R} = \frac{G}{1 + HG}$$

In general,

$$\text{Closed-loop transfer function} = \frac{\text{Direct transfer function}}{1 + \text{loop - transfer function}}$$

8.3.2. Characteristics of feedback :

(i) It increases accuracy.s
(ii) It reduces sensitivity of the ratio of output to input to variations in system characteristics.
(iii) It increases bandwidth.
(iv) It has tendency towards oscillation or instability.
(v) It reduces effects of non-linearities and distortion.

8.3.3 Signal flow graph

For complicated systems, the block diagram reduction process becomes tedious and time consuming. For this purpose, signal flow graphs, developed by S.J. Mason are used.

In other words, it represents a system variable which is equal to the sum of all incoming signals at the node.

8.3.3.1 Branch

A signal travels along a branch from one node to another in the direction indicated by the branch arrow, as shown in figure, and in the process gets multiplied by the gain or transmittance of the branch. For example, EC is a branch where G is the gain.

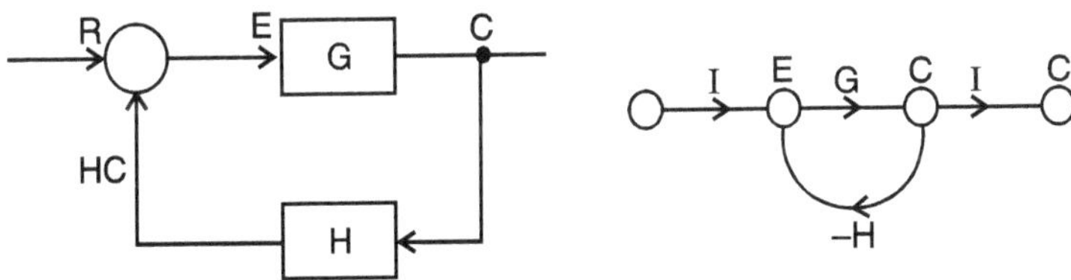

8.3.3.2 Methods of analysis

The following are the methods of analysis :

(i) Nyquist analysis
(ii) Root locus analysis
(iii) Bode analysis
(iv) Nichols chart analysis.

8.3.3.3 Properties of signal flow graph

(i) Signal flow graph applies only to linear systems.

(ii) The branch is a joining representation between two nodes.

(iii) Signals travel along branches only in the marked direction.

(iv) Branch directing from node y_k to y_j represents the dependence of variables y_k, but not the reverse.

(v) A signal travelling along a branch between nodes y_k and y_j is multiplied by the gain of branch a_{kj} so that a signal a_{kj} , y_k is delivered at node y_j.

(vi) The equations desired from drawing signal flow graph must be algebric in the form of cause and effect relationship.

(vii) Nodes are used to represent variables.

(viii) Nodes are arranged from left to right, following as sequence of cause and effect through the system.

8.4 MODULATION

Modulation is a process in which the characteristics of the waves varies as a function of the instantaneous value of the another wave.

The wave which is transmitted or carries the information, is called '*Carrier wave*'. It is an electromagnetic wave having frequencies in the range of that of radio waves (> 10^6 Hz). The wave which is superimposed on the electromagnetic wave is called the '*modulating wave*' or '*signal frequency*'.

During modulation, the basic sine waves in the radio frequency carrier are converted into a complex waveform. The waveform is still a radio frequency signal, but it contains the variations of the modulating signal. It is possible to allow transmission over long distances with the help of radio frequency. The lower frequency signal that modulates the radio frequency carrier is called the *baseband signal,* a general term that includes all types of modulating information. These may be

(i) Audio-signal modulation for voice or music information.

(ii) Video-signal modulation for picture information.

(iii) Pulse data for numerical information.

8.4.1 Grid Bias Modulation

In this modulation, modulating voltage corresponding to the signal that is to be modulated on the RF wave, is superimposed on a fixed bias in grid circuit of a class-C amplifier.

Advantages

(i) Due to low power requirement of modulating signal, this type of modulation is especially suitable for TV transmitters.

(ii) Grid modulated class-C amplifier has the advantage of requiring very little modulating signal power for complete modulation as compared to plate modulated class C amplifier. The reason being that only a small amount of energy is drawn from the modulating source to compensate for power losses in the grid circuit. This greatly reduces the size and cost of modulating system.

Disadvantages

(i) It has much lower plate circuit efficiency and it is also varies throughout the modulation cycle. At zero modulation index, plate circuit efficiency is about 34% (at the positive peak of modulation cycle) which is only about one-half of the plate circuit efficiency of class C amplifier.
At 100% modulation, plate circuit efficiency is about 51%.

(ii) It is somewhat more typical in adjustment than plate modulated class C amplifier because circuit adjustments are more sensitive to plate supply voltage and load impedance.
Also due to wide variations in grid voltage during operation, the modulation tends to be somewhat non-linear. It has higher *amplitude distortion.*

8.4.2. Types of Modulation

(i) **Amplitude Modulation :** It is a process in which original signal is superimposed over a carrier wave in such a way that amplitude of the modulated wave varies with the amplitude of the modulating signal whereas its frequency is same as that of the carrier wave.

Suppose the carrier wave and modulating wave are represented by

$$e_c = E_c \cos \omega_c t$$

and $$e_m = E_m \cos \omega_m t$$

respectively. An amplitude modulated wave is represented as

$$e = (E_c + K_a E_m \cos \omega_m t) \cos \omega_c t$$

where K_a is a constant.

$$\Rightarrow \qquad e = E_c \left[1 + \frac{K_a E_m}{E_c} \cos \omega_m t\right] \cos \omega_c t$$

$$\Rightarrow \qquad e = E_c (1 + m_a \cos \omega_m t) \cos \omega_c t$$

where $m_a \left(= \frac{K_a E_m}{E_c} \right)$ is a constant known as *modulation index.* 100 m_a is the *percentage modulation.*

Methods of Amplitude Modulation : There are two main categories of amplitude modulation methods. *(i)* Linear Modulation, and *(ii)* Square Law Modulation.

(ii) **Angular Modulation :** When phase angle θ, of the carrier wave is varied

according to the baseband signal and amplitude of the carrier wave is kept constant, the mode of modulation is called *angular modulation*.

Angular modulation has two forms :

(a) **Frequency Modulation :** In this mode, frequency of the modulated wave varies with the frequency of the modulating signal whereas its amplitude is same as that of the carrier wave.

(b) **Phase Modulation :** In this mode, frequency of the phase-modulated wave follow the phase of the modulating signal, the amplitude of carrier wave being kept fixed.

(iii) **Pulse Modulation :** It is the process of transmitting signals in the form of short pulses of radio-frequency carrier at periodic intervals.

Pulse modulation has two types:

(a) **Analog Pulse Modulation :** In this mode, sampling of the information signal is done at periodic intervals, usually about twice the maximum frequency present.

It is further of three types :

1. Pulse-Amplitude Modulation (PAM)
2. Pulse-Position Modulation (PPM)
3. Pulse-Duration Modulation (PDM)

(b) **Digital Pulse Modulation :** In this mode, sample amplitudes are coded according to a system (usually a binary system).

It is further of two types:

1. Pulse-Code Modulation (PCM)
2. Delta-Modulation (DM)

Pulse modulation allows high transmitter efficiency and good signal to noise ratio, but it requires appreciable bandwidth.

8.5 Transmission Line

Radio communication requires the transference of energy between the transmitter and the receiver. During this transmission, three main intermediate phenomena are involved as stated below :

(i) A device with minimum energy losses, used for the transference of radio-frequency energy to some radiator is called '*transmission line*'.

(ii) The second step is the release of this RF energy into space for the communication of intelligence. For this energy release, transmission line is terminated by a radiating element transferred RF energy affected by the intelligence, is applied to this radiator, which sets up high frequency currents along its length. The electromagnetic waves are

produced into the space due to the escape of electrical energy from this radiating element, which then travel with the velocity of light. The radiating element is usually known as '*antenna*'.

(iii) The third step is the mechanism of the '*propagation of e.m. waves*'. Generally these waves are propagated as ground waves, sky waves or space waves.

Transmission line is a device to transmit RF power from one place to another. In order to avoid the disturbance which would occur if the transmitter and antenna are located at the same place, a transmission line with minimum loss of energy is applied between the transmitter and antenna.

The most usual form of transmission lines are :

(i) a pair of conducting lines in the form of parallel wires, and

(ii) a pair of concentric tubular conductors, *i.e.*, coaxial cables.

The line consists of resistance, inductance and capacitance which are distributed along the length of the line.

As the purpose of transmission line is to transmit power from generator to load, therefore its study should include the following is :

(i) In order to have an idea of power at different points on the line, it is essential to know the magnitudes, and phase relationships of voltage and current at different line lengths. This requires the derivation of a relation which connects voltage or current with line length.

(ii) It is very important to study that how the termination of the line affects the power transmission by the line on account of changes in the magnitude and phase of voltages and currents on the line.

(iii) In order that maximum of energy received by the line be transferred to the load, it is essential to obtain the conditions under which lossess and distortion on the line be minimum.

8.6 WAVE PROPAGATION

Radio waves are electromagnetic waves of frequency ranging from a few kHz to about a few hundred MHz. Wavelength of such waves is about 0.3 m and above.

Ground wave, sky wave and space wave propagations are as follows :

8.6.1.1 Ground Wave or Surface Wave Propagation

Radio waves of frequency upto 1500 kHz (wavelength more then 200 m) travel directly along the surface of the earth. So signals can be sent via ground waves using radio waves of frequencies upto 1500 kHz as carrier waves. At higher frequency, the transmission becomes weaker.

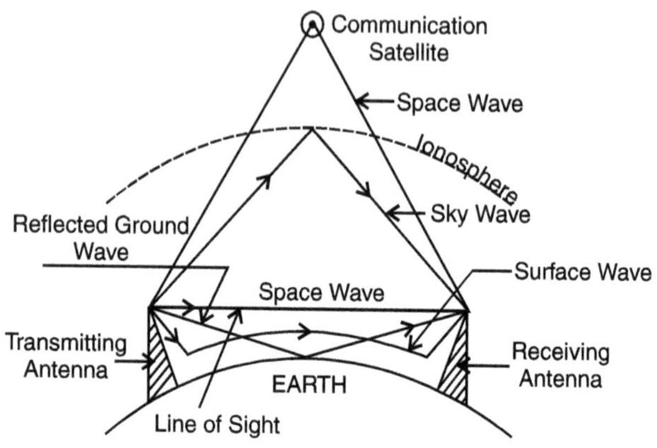

8.6.1.2 Sky Wave Propagation

Carrier waves of frequencies ranging between 1500 kHz and 40 MHz can be used for sky wave communication. In this mode, the waves are directed towards the ionosphere which reflects them back to earth. This way larger distances on earth can be covered.

Use of High Antenna and Artificial Satellites : TV transmission is done with the help of radio waves of frequencies ranging between 80 MHz and 200 MHz. Transmission of such signal is not possible via sky wave because the ionosphere does not reflect these waves back to earth. Therefore, either the receiving antenna must directly intercept the signals from the transmitting antenna, or the signal to be transmitted must be first sent to an orbiting satellite and the satellite in turn, may direct it to earth.

In the case of an antenna, the height h of the antenna decides the distance d upto which its signals can be intercepted on earth and is given as

$$d = \sqrt{2hR}$$

where R be the radius of earth.

8.6.1.3 Space Wave Propagation

When the frequency of the radio wave exceeds 40 MHz, propagation due to ground waves and sky wave is almost impossible. This is because of high attenuation of these waves by the ground and inability of the ionosphere to reflect them back. The television frequencies lie in the 100-220 MHz range. For the transmission of TV signals, the only method is space wave propagation, in which the wave travels directly from a high transmitting antenna to the receiving antenna.

8.6.2 Critical frequency

The critical frequency of an ionised layer of the ionosphere is defined as the highest frequency which can be reflected by a particular layer at vertical incident. This highest frequency is called critical frequency for that particular layer and it is different for different layer.

Critical frequency, $f_c = 9\sqrt{N_{max}}$

where N_{max} is the maximum electron density expressed in electrons per cubic metre.

8.6.3 Fading

It is defined as the fluctuation in the received signal strength at the receiver or a random variation in the received signals.

Types of fading

(i) **Selective fading :** It is produced by serious distortion of modulated signals.

(ii) **Interference fading :** It is produced by the interference between upper and lower rays of a sky wave and also between sky waves reaching the receiver by different paths.

8.7 SATELLITE COMMUNICATION

A communication satellite is a space craft placed in orbit around the earth which carries transmitting and receiving equipments. The transmitting signal is uplink and received by satellite station which downlinks it with ground station. Both uplink and downlink frequencies lie in UHF/Microwave region. They can cross the ionosphere and reach the

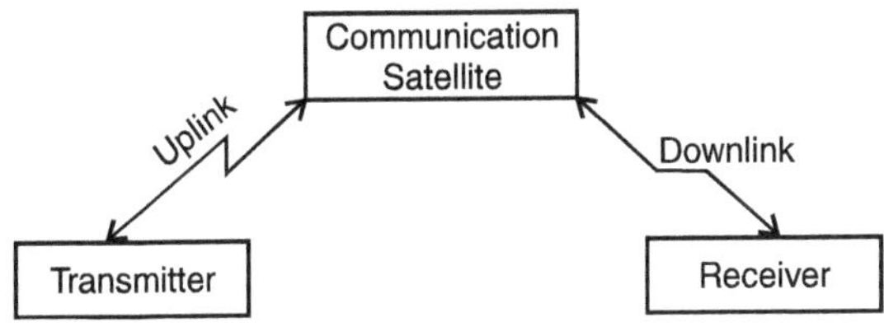

Satellite Communication

satellite located well above atmosphere. In fact, it is at the height of geostationary satellite, *i.e.*, 36,000 km.

8.8 ANTENNA

An antenna is a length of conductor which radiates or picks up electromagnetic wave carrying signals. Basic function of antenna is to convert high frequency signals into electromagnetic waves and vice-versa.

In most cases, length of an antenna is given as

$$L = \frac{\lambda}{2},$$

where λ is the wavelength of *r.f.* signal applied.

8.8.1 Isotropic Radiator

It is the radiator which radiates uniformly in all directions. Also, it is known as omni-directional radiator or simply, *unipole*. This is also used as reference antenna.

8.8.2 Radiation Pattern

It is a graphical representation which shows the variation in actual field strength of elctromagnetic field at all points which are at equal distance from the antenna. It should be a three-dimensional path.

8.8.3 Radiation Intensity

It is defined as the ratio of power and solid angle, *i.e.*

$$\text{Radiation intensity} = \frac{\text{Power (measured in watt)}}{\text{solid angle (measured in steradian)}}$$

unit : watt/steradian

8.8.4 Direction Gain

It is defined as the ratio of radiation intensity in a direction to the average radiated power of some standard antenna.

8.8.5 Power Gain

Power gain in a given direction is defined as the ratio of the radiation intensity in that direction to the average total input power.

8.8.6 Directivity

Directivity of an antenna is defined as the maximum directive gain, and is given as

$$D = \frac{\text{Maximum Radiation Intensity of Test Antenna}}{\text{Average Radiation Intensity of Test Antenna}}$$

Directivity and gain are related as

$$G = KD$$

where K is the efficiency factor.

8.8.7 Antenna Efficiency

It is defined as the ratio of power radiated to the total input power.

The loss resistances in an antenna may be as follows:

(i) Ohmic loss in the antenna conductor,

(ii) Dielectric loss,

(iii) Loss in earth connection,

(iv) Leakage loss in insulation, and

(v) I^2R loss in antenna and ground system

8.8.8 Effective length of an antenna

It represent the effectiveness of an antenna as radiator or collector of electro-magnetic wave energy. It can be expressed as

$$\text{Effective length} = \frac{\text{Open circuit voltage}}{\text{Incident field strength (electric)}}$$

8.8.9 Front-to-Back Ratio

It is defined as the ratio of the power radiated in desired direction to the power radiated in the opposite direction.

8.8.10 Antenna Bandwidth

It is defined as the range of frequency over which the antenna maintains certain required characteristics like gain, front-to-back ratio or SWR pattern polarization and impedance.

8.8.11 Antenna Arrays

It is defined as an arrangement of several individual antennas so spaced and phased that their individual contributions combine in one preferred direction and cancel in all other directive gain or directivity.

8.9 TELEVISION

It is the electrical transmission of transient visual images. This system can transmit sound synchronously with visual images.

8.9.1 Pick-up Instrument

The instrument which responds to the light intensities reaching it from the illuminated object and converts the fluctuations in brightness of light. It receives into corresponding electrical variations, can serve the purpose of image transmission. Such a device is called pick-up instrument.

8.9.2 Sound and Picture Transmission

A separate transmitter is used for sound connected to the same antenna as the picture transmitter.

8.9.3 Reception of signals

At the television receiver, both audio and video signals are picked up by the receiving antenna and then subjected to heterodyne action by the conventional superheterodyne receiving circuits. After suitable amplification by the radio frequency amplifier, both signals are applied to video detector. This detector separates audio I.F. signal from video I.F. signal, and then demodulates video signal. Audio I.F. signal after separation is sent to frequency demodulation circuit.

Video signal is applied to a cathode ray tube (C.R.T.) for the image reproduction. The synchronising pulses are applied to beam deflecting circuits of the tube to keep picture scanning at the screen in step with that at the transmitting camera tube.

The television system can be discussed in the following steps.

(i) Pick-up instrument,

(ii) Image scanning sequence,

(iii) Scanning synchronisation

(iv) Television Transmitter,

(v) Television Receiver, and

(vi) Vestigal Sideband Transmission

8.9.4 Cathode-Ray Tube (CRT)

CRT is a special type of tube among vacuum tubes which makes used of the geometrical form rather than the intensity of its electron stream and converts the energy of its electron stream into a visual indication.

8.9.4.1 Dimensions

The ordinary cathode ray tube ranges from 3 to 5 inches in diameter. The tubes operate with a beam accelerating potential between 800 to 10,000 volts. The tube is evacuated to a pressure of about 10^{-5} mm or 10^{-7} mm of mercury.

8.9.4.2 Components

CRT consists of three basic components:

(i) **Electron Gun :** The electron gun produces, accelerates and focusses the emitted into a narrow beam.

(ii) **Deflecting System :** This deflects the electron beam either electrically or magnetically in accordance with the phenomenon (V or I waveform) to be displayed.

(iii) **Fluorescent screen :** A fluorescent screen is the screen upon which the beam of electrons impinges to produce a spot of visible light. With the help of power supply, system, suitable voltages are applied to the different cathode ray tubes. The input signal to be examined is fed to the input of vertical amplifier.

8.9.4.3 Uses of Cathode Ray Oscilloscope (CRO)

(i) Study of waveforms,
(ii) Measurement of phase angle,
(iii) In television,
(iv) In Radar, (Radio Detection and Ranging),
(v) Measurement of direct or alternating voltage, and
(vi) Measurement of direct or alternating current.

8.10 TELEGRAPHY

The word *telegraphy* was originally introduced by a French chappa from the greek letter *tele* means *far* and *graphs* means *writing*, thus we can say that telegraph means writing information at far off distances. In 1844, Morse invented telegraphy.

Telegraph information consists of letters, figures and punctuations marks such as full stop, comma etc. Each of these is called a *character*. The complete set of these characters is called a *signal code*. Thus a *code* is defined as a coherent system of rules serving some particular object or purpose.

The *time interval feature* is the basis of telegraph transmission technique and various factors of signelling speed, distortion and reception margin are all defined in relation to the basic time intervals on which the signals are built up.

8.10.1 Secondary Constants

In transmission line, characteristic impedance indicated by Z_o and propagation constant indicated by P are called *secondary constants*.

Characteristic impedance of a uniform transmission may be defined as the steady state vector ratio of the voltage to the current at the input of an infinite line. It is generally devoted by Z_o. Alternately, it can also be defined simply as the impedance looking into an infinite length of the line. Its units is ohm and is also known as *surge impedance*. Characteristic impedance is a fine and useful constant of transmission line.

Propagation constant is usually a complex quantity that can be expressed as

$$P = \alpha + j\beta$$

where α is called *attenuation constant* and, it determines the variation in phase position of the voltage and current along the line. Unit of α is radian per km.

Generally, α and β both are functions of frequency and therefore, they are also referred as attenuation function and phase function.

8.10.2 Loading

The best practicable solution for achieving distortionless and minimum condition is increasing inductance by *inserting inductance in series with line* which is termed as *loading* and such transmission line and cable are called *loaded lines* or *cables.*

8.10.2.1 Morse Code : It is used for hand signalling. In this code, all letters, figures, punctuation mark etc. are different combination of two basic elements dot (.) and dash (—).

The difference between a dot and dash is usually of times duration, a dash being three times as long in duration as dot. The time duration is equivalent to the length of the character. These dots and dashes making up a character are separated from one another by an interval equal in duration to one dot. These characters in a word are separated by an interval equal to three dots. The words of a message are separated by an interval equal to seven dots.

The dot/dash condition is called *marking* and the interval between them is called *spacing*.

8.10.2.2 Cable Code : This code is the special form of morse code which is employed in submarine cable telegraphy. In these days, two types of codes are used:

(i) **Normal cable code :** In this type of cable code, the dots and dashes are not distinguished by their length (time interval). As the dash is made of the same length similar to dash, with an appreciable and considerable saving in time. The difference between them is affected by a change in the signalling and considerable saving in time. Thus, the dots can be represented by positive voltage to line, dashes by positive voltage and the space between the letters and words by no voltage in the line being earthed at the transmitter for the duration of spacing signal of cable code requires three signalling conditions.

(ii) **Double current cable code :** In this code, only two conditions are possible, either positive current or negative current conditions. Thus, it is also called as *two condition code*. In this code, dot is represented by a positive current followed by a negative one of some duration and a dash is represented by a negative current followed by a positive one of some duration.

8.10.2.3 Five Unit Code : This code is of uniform length as the name implies. Each character consists of five elements.

8.10.2.4 Binary Code : In this code, only two conditions, one possible during the transmission.

8.10.2.5 Hellscriber Code : This code is related to printing telegraph system, and was invented by *Dr. Hell,* a *German Scientist* and is often referred as *Hell System.*

8.10.2.6 More than Five Unit Codes : When a code is so constructed that multiplication of five units can result in a combination which does not represent a character. It is said to be *possess redundancy.*

8.10.2.7 Error Detecting and Correcting Codes : Errors in the received message can be detected and also corrected by using some additional impulses, or the bits along with those of the code. The codes in which such precautions are taken are called *error detecting* or *error correcting codes* normally abbreviated as EDC or ECC respectively.

One way of ensuring error-free transmission is to perfect the medium and instruments through which the pulses pass, so as to reduce the probability of error. This is, however, not possible due to certain limitations lying the system.

8.11 TELEGRAPH INSTRUMENTS AND RELAYS

In ordinary telegraph system, the first part is the *telegraph key* (called *Morse key* after the name of Morse who invented it), the second is the *landlines* and the third one *telegraph sounder* or *telegraph relay.*

8.11.1 Telegraph Keys

There are two types of telegraph keys:

(i) Morse key and double current working known as *SC key,* and

(ii) Double current working known as *D.C. Key.*

8.11.2 Morse Sounders and Telegraph Relays

The *Morse Sounders* produce sound by the striking of armature levers against some fixed stops when received currents are passed through their coils, whereas telegraph makes some contacts only under the same conditions. These instruments may be of *non-polarised* or *polarised types.*

The important features of telegraph relays are :

(i) Differential winding,

(ii) Operate and release relays, and

(iii) Symbols of relays

8.12 MULTIPLEXED TELEGRAPHY

Multiplexing is the process of transmitting more than one message over a given channel by use of same transmitting equipment. There are two accepted methods of multiplexing.

(i) Frequency division multiplexing by modulating sub-carrier, and

(ii) Time division multiplexing

8.13 FACSIMILE TELEGRAPHY AND ELECTRONIC MAIL

By Facsimile, we mean an exact reproduction and the object which transmitted in such a way that the received copy is an exact reproduction or image of the original one.

Bandwidth of 2000 Hz is required for facsimile communication while only 120 Hz is sufficient for ordinary telegraphy.

8.13.1 FAX Machine : Facsimile (FAX) machine are the latest high-tech products of 1988-89. Fax machines work by scanning documents and converting them into an electronic format than can be sent over normal telephone lines. The fax machine that receive the message converts the electronic information back into a document. The basic steps involved in FAX operations are scanning, encoding, modulation, transmission, decoding and printing.

Facsimile devices are capable of handling computer signals as well as signals created by another facsimile.

8.13.2 Electronic Mail : E-mail is the term that could be applied to any electronic transfer of information.

Basic function involved in *e*-mail system are message creation, message transfer and post delivery processing.

8.14 Telegraph Circuits

This is a way to convey the signals over a transmission line. Telegraph transmission may use either a *d.c.* or an *a.c.* It depends very much on the distance between the transmitter and receiver.

8.14.1 Types of Telegraph Circuits :

(i) **Direct Current Telegraph Circuits :** Direct current circuits can be operated in many ways :
   (a) Simplex telegraph circuits,
   (b) Duplex telegraph circuits, and
   (c) Quadruplex telegraph circuits.

(ii) **Alternating Current Telegraph Circuits :** Alternating current circuits may be operated in many ways, some of them are:
   (a) Auto frequency telegraph circuits,
   (b) Multi-channel voice frequency telegraph circuits,
   (c) Sub-audio telegraph circuits, and
   (d) Super-auto telegraph circuits.

8.14.2 Duplex Balance Network

The duplex balance should have a resistance equal to the resistance of the line and the apparatus. But due to the capacitance of the line, the current goes through transit condition before reaching the steady value. So, if the duplex balance consists of a resistance simply, there is a possibility of rich being produced in the relay during transient period. In order to overcome this undesirable effect of rich, the duplex balance also contains capacitances in addition to resistances.

(S + 4DX) System : This is the short form of speeds plus four frequency modulated duplex system. It provides for establishing a speech channel in addition to two-way telegraph channels of 240 Hz spacing over a four wire circuit. The way of equipment is wired for two systems but can be sure equipped to cater for one system if so required.

8.14.3 Repeater

Telegraph signals may get distorted in shape and attenuated in amplitude during long distance transmission. As a result of which, a relay operated by such a signal produces erroneous reception. Therefore, a repeater station is necessary at an intermediate point where distortion and attenuation are not very much pronounced.

8.15 BAUDOT SYSTEM

This system uses 5-unit CCITT Code No. 1. Thus each character is represented by a combination of five positive and negative impulses and this combination impulses is sent and received by means of brush arms moving over metallic arcs or quadrants each divided into five segments as shown in figure below.

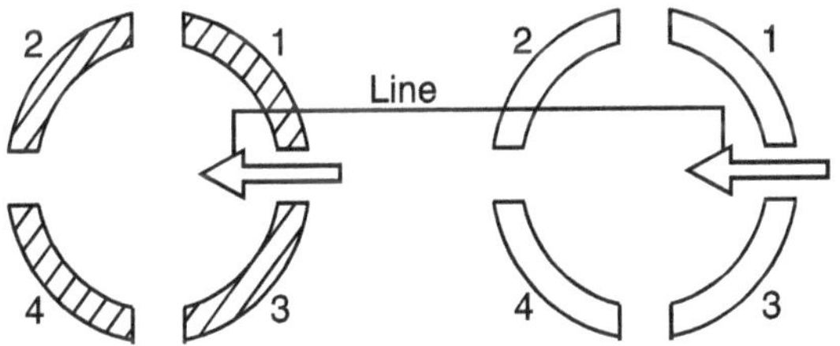

Principle of Baudot System

8.15.1 Baudot Code

This is known as a 5-unit synchronious code and is used in Baudot multiplex system, *i.e.,* this code is used to send several messages over a single line. The first practical system of this kind wave discovered by *Emile Baudot* in 1874. This system of code is internationally is referred as CCITT Code No.1.

8.15.2 Baudot Distributor

It consists of three set of segmented rings and three sets of continuous rings. In Quad-Baudot system, there are four quadrants in each segment ring, each quadrant having five segments insulations from one another.

8.15.3 Baudot Receiver

Baudot receiver points the character received on a paper tape. The type wheel W of the receiver containing all the characters on the periphery is rotated by means of a separate motor which is run from batteries.

When a negative pulse is received, the polarized relay is operated and the corresponding electromagnet is received.

When a positive pulse is received, the polarized relay is not operated and the corresponding electromagnet is not received.

8.15.4 Baudot Governor

It is used with weight-driven distributors and is attached to a very fast running axle. It revolves in a ground ring. It has a sleeve which fits to the distributor axle and is clamped by a screw.

8.15.5 Phase Correction in Baudot System

The time taken by the signal to be transmitted from station A to B is zero. In actual practice, a finite time, however small is elapsed before the signal from A arriver at B.

Thus the brushes at B lags the brush at A by an amount equivalent to this time of transmission.

8.15.6 Distortion

A modulation/restitution suffers from telegraph signal distortion when all the significant intervals do not have exactly their theoretical duration. Distortion resulting from the displacement of either of the significant instant from its ideal position is referred as *individual distortion.*

There are three distinct sources of distortion which have been recognised *characteristic, bias* and *fortuitous*. The combination of characteristic and bias distortion is often referred as the *system distortion*, and that due to all three causes is referred as *total distortion.*

8.16 TELEPRINTER

By teleprinter, we mean a electromechanical device by means of which messages can be sent and received on a piece of paper in typical forms as in an ordinary typewriter machine.

In an actual teleprinter, the rotating burst and metal rings are replaced by *cam* and *levers*.

Keyboard, transmitter, receiver and printer are the essential components of a teleprinter.

8.16.1 Teleprinter Code

This code is also known as five-unit start/stop code. Thus, teleprinter system is called start/stop telegraphy. In earlier times, this code is termed as *Murray code* and is internationally referred as CCITT Code No. 2.

8.16.2 Special functions in Teleprinter

For a page printer, carriage return, line feed, space, letter shift, figure shift, bell and answer to the 'who are you signal' are the special functions. For a tape printer, as the tape advances continuously the signal carriage return and line feed are not required. When the receiver of a teleprinter receives the code elements for these special functions, it stores and transfers it to the code bar or code rings in the same way as it does for a character to be printed.

8.16.3 Teleprinter Speed and Margin

The speed of the signal of teleprinter is expressed either in *bauds* or in *words per minute*. The usual speed of signalling in India is 50 bauds corresponding to 66.6 words per minute.

The *margin of the teleprinter* is defined as the ratio of the highest distortion acceptable to the teleprinter to the undistorted.

8.16.4 Electronic Teleprinter

Telegraph interface makes possible to connect the teleprinter in point to point mode or in switched telegraph network according to type A or B signalling, singled or doubled, connect in half duplex or full duplex. It can be divided into two parts, *i.e.*, transmission and reception.

A typical ETP Model SAGEM TX-30 manufactured by M/S Hindustan Teleprinter, Chennai in collaboration with SAGEM Paris, France, has maximum 97 messages can be stored into memory and memory recall facility of stored messages is possible. Prepared, transmitted and received messages can be stored into the memory and they are automatically numbered. Duplication, deletion and correction of stored messages is possible by manipulating suitable keys ETP is equipped with *battery back-up facility* for taking care of the loss of information in the memory due to power failure.

8.17 TELEPHONE LINKS

Now-a-days even a kid would know what a telephone is. Telephone is a combination of apparatus for converting speech into electrical waves, transmitting the electrical energy to a distant point, and there reconverting the electrical energy into audible sounds.

A telephone set is an assembly of apparatus that includes a suitable handset containing the transmitter and receiver, and usually a switch hook and the immediately associated wiring. A telephone set connected to a telephone system is a *telephone station*; One that has access to the public telephone network is a *subscriber station*. It is mainly large organization that have a *private exchange* to interconnected telephone stations. Usually such an exchange is also connected to the public telephone system and is known as a *private branch exchange*. It is either a *private automatic branch exchange* (PABX) or *private manual branch exchange* (PMBX).

There have been basically three generations of exchanges:

(i) Stowger type

(ii) Cross bar type and

(iii) Processor controlled type

MULTIPLE CHOICE QUESTIONS

1. A positive feedback signal improves the performance of

A. a system
B. control system
C. automatic control system
D. both (A) and (B)

2. VSWR is minimum when

A. line is terminated with load equal to the characteristic impedance of the load
B. line is terminated with full load
C. line is short-circuited
D. both (A) and (B)

3. The unit of polarization is the same as that of

A. Charge
B. E
C. D
D. None of the above

4. Pick out the odd :

A. ASK
B. FET
C. FSK
D. PSK

5. The M.K.S. unit of magnetic flux density is

A. Tesla
B. Webers
C. Amperes/metre
D. None of the above

6. When electric field is parallel to the plane of incident, the electromagnetic wave is said to be

A. elliptically polarised
B. parallely polarized
C. both (A) and (B)
D. none of the above

7. The value of VSWR is taken as ∞ when the line is

A. short-circuited
B. open-circuited
C. terminated with full load
D. none of the above

8. For which of the following range of frequencies, tropospheric scatter is used?

A. UHF B. SHF
C. VHF D. None of the above

9. The relative permeability is taken as unity for

A. vacuum B. cobalt
C. bismuth D. none of the above

10. The relative permeability for iron may be around

A. 4000 B. 5000
C. 7000 D. 9000

11. Which of the following material will have the least value of relative permeability?

A. Iron B. Palladium
C. Silver D. Cobalt

12. Current density is the ratio of the current to the surface area whose plane is..........to the direction of the charge motion.

A. parallel B. normal
C. perpendicular D. none of the above

13. The electric intensity at any point is the..........of the potential gradient at that point.

A. positive B. zero
C. negative D. infinite

14. Electric field intensity is the force per unit charge exerted on a test charge in the

A. infinite field B. field
C. magnetic field D. none of the above

15. The closed loop frequency response can be obtained from.......... loop frequency plot.

A. any B. closed
C. open D. both (A) and (B)

16. The polar plot and nicholas plot can be obtained from .... plot and vice-versa.

A. frequency B. bode
C. open D. none of the above

17. Audio amplifiers are often compared on the basis of their

A. frequency B. wavelengths
C. bandwidth D. none of the above

18. Source nodes represent independent variables and have only .... branches.

A. a few B. five
C. six D. outgoing

19. Gain margin is a measure of relative stability of a

A. control system B. system

C. circuit D. none of the above

20. The Bode plot is a plot relating log ω with magnitude in decibel and

A. any angle B. right angle

C. phase angle D. none of the above

21. A magnetic amplifier has dropping .... characteristics.

A. type of B. load

C. of poor D. none of the above

22. Simultaneous equations can be solved using

A. any technique B. a very few techniques

C. SFG technique D. none of the above

23. The integral error control produces lesser steady state error as compared to the derivative

A. control B. error control

C. of any control D. none of the above

24. The steady state error control for unit step input is always zero for system larger than type

A. two systems B. three systems

C. one system D. none of the above

25. The type 1 system has constant steady state output velocity for constant steady

A. error B. state error

C. velocity D. none of the above

26. A typical signal strength received from a geostationary satellite is of the order of a few

A. watts B. picowatts

C. microwatts D. both (A) and (B)

27. A passive satellite

A. reflects the signal B. absorbs the signal

C. amplifies the signal D. none of the above

28. The source of energy for a satellite is

A. fuel cell B. battery

C. solar cell D. none of the above

29. Apple was launched from

A. Newyork B. Ahmedabad

C. French Guyana D. Trivandrum

30. Apple was put in

A. medium circular orbit B. lower circular orbit

C. geostationary orbit D. none of the above

31. For a tracking satellite in low orbit normally the antenna used is
A. circularly polarized helical antenna
B. dicone
C. both (A) and (B)
D. none of the above

32. A satellite used for international communication is known as
A. Intelsat B. Cosmat
C. Domsat D. None of the above

33. A geostationary satellite completes one orbit in
A. 24 hours B. 28 days
C. two hours D. one hour

34. The master control facility for INSAT-1B is located at
A. Trivandrum B. Hasan
C. New Delhi D. Ahmedabad

35. The lowest limit of frequency for satellite communication is
A. 120 GHz B. 250 GHz
C. 10 MHz D. 50 MHz

36. In satellite transmission, analog signals may be converted into digital form using
A. codec B. compander
C. modem D. none of the above

37. For global communication the number of satellite needed is
A. 3 B. 4
C. 7 D. 9

38. INSAT-1A was launched in
A. 1984 B. 1987
C. 1982 D. 1983

39. 'Apple' was launched in
A. 1981 B. 1985
C. 1975 D. 1987

40. The first Indian communication satellite was
A. INSAT-1B B. Aryabhatta
C. Apple D. INSAT-1A

41. Wave guides are generally used above
A. 1000 MHz B. 100 MHz
C. 200 MHz D. 500 MHz

42. The frequencies used in radio communication range from 15 kHz to
A. 3000 kHz B. 30,000 MHz
C. 1000 MHz D. 500 MHz

43. According to Siegel and Labus, antenna can be treated as
A. earth transmission line B. closed transmission line

C. opened-out transmission line D. none of the above

44. A wavelength of 1 mm could be expected in

A. EHF B. VHF

C. HF D. VLF

45. For a frequency of 300 MHz, the wavelength will be

A. 1 m B. 0.01 m

C. 0.25 m D. 0.75 m

46. An antenna is synonymous to a

A. reflector B. generator

C. transformer D. regulator

47. The frequency of micro-waves is

A. more than 2000 B. more than 5000

C. less than 2000 D. 1000 constant

48. A log periodic antenna is a

A. directional antenna B. frequency independent antenna

C. frequency dependent antenna D. none of the above

49. In case of antenna, the ratio of the power radiated in the desired direction to the power radiated in the opposite direction is known as

A. front to back ratio B. loss coefficient

C. transmission efficiency D. none of the above

50. A unipole is also known as

A. line radiator B. unidirectional radiator

C. omni directional radiator D. none of the above

51. Front to back ratio can be increased by

A. using material of high conductivity

B. sacrificing gain

C. increasing size of conductor

D. none of the above

52. The material having directional properties are known as

A. oriental B. anisotropic

C. isotropic D. none of the above

53. Which of the following constitute the loss resistance of an antenna?

A. Loss in insulation B. Dielectric loss

C. Leakage loss in insulation D. (A), (B) and (C)

54. Magnesium is alloyed with conducting materials for antenna primarily with the purpose of

A. reducing weight B. increasing density

C. increasing efficiency D. none of the above

55. VFL is generally used for

A. satellite communication B. telegraphy

C. both (A) and (B) D. none of the above

56. The binomial arrays the elimination of secondary lobes takes place

A. at the cost of gain B. at the cost of directivity

C. both (A) and (B) D. none of the above

57. A balun is virtually

A. flying resistor B. an impedance transformer

C. frequency compensator D. none of the above

58. Reflectors and lens antenna are commonly used

A. above 1000 MHz B. less 1000 MHz

C. in LF communication system D. none of the above

59. The power gain of a half-wave dipole with respect to an isotropic radiator is

A. 1.75 db B. 2.15 db

C. 6 db D. 3.5 db

60. The null of a loop antenna occurs with

A. a signal off the ends B. a broad side signal

C. both (A) and (B) D. none of the above

61. The night effect is most prominent in

A. loop antenna B. vertical antenna

C. adcock antenna D. none of the above

62. A T.V. signal from the antenna is processed by

A. RF amplifier B. RF tuner

C. local transmission line D. none of the above

63. Equalizing pulses in TV are sent during

A. vertical blanking B. the horizontal retrace

C. horizontal blanking D. none of the above

64. The aspect ratio in TV receiver is

A. 5 : 2 B. 4 : 3

C. 3 : 2 D. 1 : 2

65. The antenna often used with TV receivers is

A. multimeter B. marconi antenna

C. dipole antenna D. none of the above

66. In India, the width of one channel is

A. 5 MHz B. 3 MHz

C. 7 MHz D. 9 MHz

67. The line frequency of TV system in India is

A. 15,750 Hz B. 15,625 Hz

C. 18,235 Hz D. 25,625 Hz

68. In India, first TV station was established in

A. 1962 B. 1960

C. 1959 D. 1975

69. Another name for the horizontal retrace in a TV receiver is the
A. burst B. flyback
C. ringing D. none of the above

70. The demodulation of the sound signals in a TV receiver is accomplished by
A. discriminator B. linear detector
C. product detector D. none of the above

71. The fine tuning control in television receiver is
A. a variable inductor B. a potentiometer
C. a variable capacitor D. none of the above

72. A primary colour differs from its complementary by a phase angle of
A. 180° B. 90°
C. 0° D. 45°

73. The signal sent by the TV transmitter to ensure correct scanning in the receiver are called
A. chroma B. video
C. sync D. none of the above

74. The three primary colours are
A. red, orange and blue B. red, blue and green
C. red, yellow and blue D. none of the above

75. In TV receivers, the electron beam is deflected by
A. electromagnetic technique B. electrostatic technique
C. both (A) and (B) D. none of the above

76. The height of a TV picture tube of 20" size is
A. 12" B. 15"
C. 25" D. 16"

77. The gain of a simple half-wave dipole over an isotropic radiator is of the order of
A. 7 dB B. 5 dB
C. 2 dB D. 3 dB

78. In a TV receiver which stage is not necessary for producing horizontal output?
A. Horizontal oscillator B. Horizontal AFC
C. Damper D. None of the above

79. In India, the method of modulation of sound in TV system is
A. frequency modulation B. phase modulation
C. amplitude modulation D. none of the above

80. For 51 cm size TV, the voltage required for picture tube of the order of
A. 1 kV B. 15 kV
C. 13 kV D. 25 kV

81. The sound signal in video composite signal of TV is
A. FSK B. AM

C. FM D. PPM

82. Under force-voltage analogy, mass is analogous to
A. resistance B. current
C. inductance D. none of the above

83. Under force-voltage analogy, viscous friction coefficient is analogous to
A. resistance B. current
C. reciprocal of resistance D. none of the above

84. Which of the following represents an analogous pair between electrical systems and pneumatic systems?
A. Voltage-air flow rate B. Charge-air flow
C. Resistance-pressure D. none of the above

85. Which system is most sensitive to the presence of non-linearities?
A. Closed loop system B. Open loop system
C. Both (A) and (B) D. None of the above

86. Which system has tendency to oscillate?
A. Closed loop system B. Open loop system
C. Both (A) and (B) D. None of the above

87. Which of the following generally finds application in computer printers, tape drives and capstan drives?
A. AC servo motor B. Stepper motor
C. Synchros D. None of the above

88. If this system is viewed as a processor of sinusoidal input signal to generate the frequency response, it would be
A. unstable filter B. low pass filter
C. band pass filter D. none of the above

89. Zero initial condition means that the system is
A. at rest and no energy is stored in any of its components
B. working with zero stored energy
C. both (A) and (B)
D. none of the above

90. The system response can be tested better with
A. ramp input signal B. sinusoidal input signal
C. unit in pulse input signal D. none of the above

91. Microwave signals follow the curvature of the earth and the phenomenon is known as
A. duct propagation B. Faraday effect
C. both (A) and (B) D. none of the above

92. Long distance short-wave radio broadcasting uses
A. ionospherical wave B. direct wave
C. ground wave D. none of the above

93. The ground waves eventually disappear as one moves away from the transmitter because of

A. interference from the sky waves B. tilting

C. both (A) and (B) D. none of the above

94. Which of the following is a non-resonant antenna?

A. Surface wave B. The end-fire array

C. The broad side array D. None of the above

95. The fluctuation in the received signal strength at the receiver or a random variation in the received signal is known as

A. fading B. fluctuation

C. cycling D. none of the above

96. By telecommunication, we mean only the electrical signals of

A. any distance B. long distances

C. a few distances D. none of the above

97. If the channel is in the form of a transmission line, the whole system is called

A. Radio B. Wireless communication

C. Either (A) or (B) D. None of the above

98. Fading is the fluctuation in the received signal strength at the receiver or a random variation in

A. any signal B. the received signal

C. both (A) and (B) D. none of the above

99. The absorption of radio waves by the atmosphere depends on

A. frequency of the wave

B. the polarization of the waves

C. the polarization of the atmosphere

D. none of the above

100. A loop antenna is a commonly used for

A. satellite communication B. radar

C. direction finding D. none of the above

101. Which type of speaker is used in telephone receivers?

A. Coaxial type B. Fixed coil type

C. Moving coil type D. None of the above

102. In telephone system the number un-attainable tone has a frequency of

A. 400 Hz B. 100 Hz

C. 320 Hz D. 550 Hz

103. A telegraph sounder is basically a

A. electrostatic device B. mechanical device

C. electromagnetic device D. none of the above

104. Telex is the abbreviated name for

A. telegraph exchange B. teleprinter exchange

C. telephone exchange D. none of the above

105. The function of a telephone exchange is to interconnect

A. three-wire line B. four-wire line
C. two-wire line D. none of the above

106. Microphone used in an ordinary telephone is

A. crystal microphone B. carbon microphone
C. pressure microphone D. none of the above

107. Baudot system uses .... CCITT Code No. 1.

A. 4 B. 3
C. 5 D. 2

108. ..... is a most important part of Baudot system.

A. Governor B. Baudot station
C. Distributor D. Quad-Baudot system

109. Baudot receiver points the character received on a

A. sheet B. paper tape
C. operator D. none of the above

110. The time taken by the signal to be transmitted from station X to Y is

A. one B. two
C. three D. zero

111. Telegraph signals are formed by making changes in the electrical condition of a

A. wire B. circuit
C. traffic D. none of the above

112. Fax machines work by scanning documents and converting them into an

A. format B. mechanical format
C. electronic format D. none of the above

113. Facsimile machine abbreviated as Fax machine are latest high-tech products of

A. 1987-88 B. 1988-89
C. 1965-66 D. 1974-75

114. In the fax device can recognise the computer's signal, it can be used like a

A. printer B. facsimile
C. computer printer D. none of the above

115. Transmission of pictures imposes more stringent requirements upon the

A. circuit B. telephone
C. channel D. none of the above

116. Good quality facsimile transmission requires the use of high-grade 4-wire

A. system B. telephone circuit
C. telephone line D. none of the above

117. AM is the normal mode of transmission on
A. circuits B. line
C. landline circuits D. none of the above

118. Synchronism is essential between the scanning at
A. sender B. receiver
C. both (A) and (B) D. none of the above

119. The process of transmitting more than one message over a given channel by use of same transmitting equipment is termed as
A. Facsimile B. a typical facsimile
C. multiplexing D. none of the above

120. Information rate is proportional to
A. bandwith B. wavelength
C. both (A) and (B) D. none of the above

121. At the transmitter, telegraph signals are
A. equal to wavelength B. square in wavelength
C. square root of wavelength D. none of the above

122 A 4-wire telephone circuit is allocated for telegraph use and is then referred to as
A. circuit B. ordinary circuit
C. bearer circuit D. none of the above

123. Signal processing with the electronic teleprinter is faster than
A. ordinary teleprinter B. electro-mechanical printer
C. network D. none of the above

124. In EMPT printing is done by type bars with mechanical setting of
A. combination B. code combination
C. circuits D. network

125. Working of Electronic Teleprinter can be divided into
A. three parts B. four parts
C. two parts D. five parts

126. ETP has .... printing styles.
A. four B. two
C. five D. three

127. Management unit is main processing unit of ETP built around a
A. network B. microprocessor
C. circuit D. none of the above

128. Basically an electronic teleprinter consists of
A. two units B. three units
C. four units D. several units

129. The distorted signal is given a shape in the
A. shaper B. signal shaper

C. circuit D. none of the above

130. An ordinary telegraph repeater is not adequate when a telegraph signal has to travel

A. a small distance B. a long distance

C. nil distance D. none of the above

131. The individual code pulse arriving early or late is the deviation of the transmitting shaft from its

A. speed B. standard speed

C. zero speed D. none of the above

132 The cause of distortion is that the space-to-mark transition or mark-to-space transition .... in time.

A. occurs B. do not occur

C. exists D. none of the above

133. To connect the output of a data source to a telephone line, it is necesary to have

A. a lease for the line B. an MVFT system

C. phase shift keying D. none of the above

134. An online real time data transmission system is most likely to require a connection that is

A. simplex B. duplex

C. semi-duplex D. none of the above

135. The most common modulation system used for telegraphy is

A. frequency-shift keying B. pulse code modulation

C. two-tone modulation D. none of the above

136. Which of the following is not a binary code?

A. CCITT-2 B. Baudot

C. Morse D. None of the above

137. Quantizing noise occurs in

A. pulse-width modulation B. pulse code modulation

C. time-division multiplex D. none of the above

138. The modulation system inherently most noise resistance is

A. pulse-width modulation B. SSB supressed carrier

C. pulse-code modulation D. none of the above

139. Which of the following pulse-modulation system is analog?

A. Differential PCM B. Delta

C. PWM D. None of the above

140. In order to separate channels in a frequency division multiplex receiver, it is necessary to use

A. integration B. AND gates

C. differentiation D. band pass filters

141. Broad band long distance communications were originally made possible by the advent of

A. repeater amplifiers
B. HF radio
C. telegraph cables
D. none of the above

142. Telephones in India are managed by

A. public sector
B. government department
C. private sector
D. joint sector

143. In order to separate channels in a time division multiplex receiver, it is necessary to use

A. band pass filter
B. AND gates
C. integration
D. differentiation

144. Identical telephone numbers under different exchanges are distinguished by

A. area code
B. access digits
C. language digits
D. none of the above

145. A scheme in which several channels are interleaved and then transmitted together is known as

A. a sub-group
B. a frequency division multiplex
C. both (A) and (B)
D. none of the above

146. Which public sector unit in India is engaged in the munufacture of telephone?

A. ITI
B. HAL
C. ECIL
D. BEL

147. Bridge duplex works on the principle

A. potential balance
B. resistance balance
C. current balance
D. none of the above

148. The modulation system used for telegraphy is

A. PCM
B. FSK
C. PSK
D. None of the above

149. In Morse code the spacing between the element is

A. 3 dots
B. one dot
C. two dots
D. 7 dots

150. Code used in teleprinter is

A. Five unit start-stop code
B. Five unit code
C. Morse code
D. None of the above

151. The Morse Code is of ....

A. equal length
B. unequal length
C. same character
D. different character

152. Another name of Baudot code is

A. 3 unit synchronous
B. 2 unit synchronous
C. 5 unit synchronous
D. 4 unit synchronous

153. 5-unit code is of

A. different length
B. uniform length
C. zero length
D. none of the above

154. In double current cable code only ..... are possible.

A. four conditions
B. two conditions
C. three conditions
D. five conditions

155. In binary code uses signals of positive

A. current
B. and negative current
C. ions only
D. none of the above

156. A bridge duplex works on the principle of

A. power balance
B. potential balance
C. current balance
D. none of the above

157. Telephone traffic is measured in terms of

A. daubs
B. erlangs
C. numbers
D. none of the above

158. When most of the traffic fails to get the circuit, is results in

A. break down
B. congestion
C. over population
D. none of the above

159. During the period of no occupancy the traffic was

A. 1 erlangs
B. 0 erlang
C. two erlangs
D. none of the above

160. The grade of service is measured in

A. number
B. percentage
C. fractional number
D. none of the above

161. Cross fire is

A. distortion in adjacent telegraphy lines
B. distortion in demodulated signal
C. both (A) and (B)
D. none of the above

162. Time division multiplex

A. combines five groups into a supergroup
B. can be used with PCM only
C. both (A) and (B)
D. none of the above

163. Which of the following was the first generation of telephone exchanges?

A. Cross bar exchange
B. Strowger type exchange
C. Both (A) and (B)
D. None of the above

164. Reduce (R) will decrease the attenuation but will require

A. little conductors
B. a conductor
C. large conductors
D. no conductor

165. Lumped inductors known as .... are placed with suitable intervals along the line.

A. coils
B. circuits
C. loading coils
D. none of the above

166. There are .... ways in which energy impressed at the sending end of a transmission line may become dissipated before reaching the load.

A. four
B. five
C. three
D. six

167. Dielectric heating loss increases with

A. wavelength
B. frequency
C. voltage
D. none of the above

168. VSMR is always greater than

A. one
B. two
C. three
D. four

169. Reflection coefficient is defined as the ratio of the reflected voltage to the

A. voltage
B. incident voltage
C. current
D. none of the above

170. The ratio of the maximum to minimum magnitudes of current or voltage on line having

A. wave ratio
B. no ratio
C. standing wave ratio
D. none of the above

171. The cut off frequency may be raised by decreasing the inductance

A. by two coils
B. per coil
C. by three coils
D. none of the above

172. Which dealing with ratio voltage only, the standing wave ratio is abbreviated as

A VWR
B. SWR
C. VSWR
D. RSW

173. High frequency transmission line may have appreciable ohmic and

A. losses
B. dielectric losses
C. Both (A) and (B)
D. none of the above

174. Any communication system requires .... essential parts.

A. four
B. three
C. two
D. five

175. Morse keys is used for single current working known as

A. SA keys
B. CS keys
C. SC keys
D. none of the above

176. Alternating current telegraph circuits can be operated into

A. two parts
B. three parts
C. many ways
D. none of the above

177. Single current simplex circuit can also be arranged for

A. any circuit operation
B. open circuit operation
C. closed circuit operation
D. none of the above

178. Single current simplex circuits are

A. three types
B. two types
C. four types
D. five types

179. In duplex circuit two messages are sent in

A. one direction
B. two same directions
C. opposite directions
D. none of the above

180. Bridge duplex works on the principle of potential balance of the

A. ammeter
B. voltmeter
C. Wheatstone bridge
D. none of the above

181. In Half-Duplex circuit, two messages can be transmitted in the

A. three directions
B. two directions
C. four directions
D. none of the above

182. Which of the following statement is false?
In order to combat noise

A. The signalling rate may be used
B. The channel bandwidth may be increased
C. Redundancy may be used
D. None of the above

183. A telephone relay armature is made of material with

A. negligible electrical conductivity
B. high electrical conductivity
C. low electrical conductivity
D. none of the above

184. Which of the following circuit can transmit two messages simultaneous in one direction?

A. Duplex circuit
B. Simplex circuit
C. Diplex circuit
D. None of the above

185. The unit of erlang is

A. number
B. minute
C. second
D. dimensionless

186. When a route carries no subscriber dialed traffic, the internationally accepted worst grade of service is

A. 3%
B. 2%
C. 1%
D. 4%

187. Which of the following telephone exchange makes use of computer?

A. Cross bar exchange
B. Processor controlled exchange
C. Strowger type exchange
D. None of the above

188. Frequency frogging is used in carrier system to

A. reduce cross talk
B. reduce distortion
C. converse frequencies
D. none of the above

189. Which of the following system is digital?

A. Pulse-frequency modulation
B. Pulse-tone modulation
C. Pulse-code modulation
D. None of the above

190. Which of the following code is not a telegraphic code?

A. Gray code
B. Cable code
C. Five unit code
D. 7-5 unit code

191. The number of pulses generated in 7½ code is

A. 14
B. 15
C. 1
D. 7

192. Telex is an abbreviation of the system known as

A. teleprinter
B. telephone
C. teleprinter exchange
D. system

193. In telex system, a carrier frequency of ...... is used.

A. 1400 Hz
B. 1500 Hz
C. 1200 Hz
D. 1300 Hz

194. In telex apparatus, there is a source of producing signals of .... frequency.

A. 1400 Hz
B. 1300 Hz
C. 1500 Hz
D. 1200 Hz

195. By operating the local key, the teleprinter is cut off from

A. source
B. circuit
C. exchange
D. none of the above

196. The teleprinter automatic switching normally abbreviated as

A. TSA system
B. TAS system
C. AST system
D. STA system

197. The TAS network was based upon a number of fully .... zone.

A. any communicated
B. intercommunicated
C. switching centres
D. area centre

198. To avoid establishing a third telegraph network, ... is operated over the telex network.

A. telex
B. gentex service
C. communication service
D. any service of the above

199. Facsimile devices are capable of handling .... signals as well as signals created by another facsimile device.

A. two
B. three
C. computer
D. five

200. If the fax images are to be sent over a public phone network, the .... generated must be modulated.

A. circuit
B. network

C. signals
D. none of the above

201. For an antenna of given aperture size, the beam width

A. has no relationship with wavelength
B. increases with decrease in wavelength
C. increases with increase in wavelength
D. none of the above

202. In a radar, in case the return echo arrives after the allocated pulse interval, then

A. the target will appear closer than it really is
B. it will not be received
C. the receiver will get overloaded
D. none of the above

203. In case the target cross-section is changing the best system for accurate tracking is

A. sequential lobing
B. monopulse
C. lobe switching
D. none of the above

204. Radar detection is limited to line-of sight because

A. long wave lengths are used
B. of curvature of the earth
C. short wavelengths are used
D. none of the above

205. *Second time around,* echoes are caused by

A. echoes that arrive after transmission of the next pulse
B. extreme ends of bandwidth
C. second time reflction from target
D. none of the above

206. In case the antenna diameter in a radar system in increased to four times, the maximum range will increase by

A. 2 times
B. 4 times
C. 3 times
D. 5 times

207. An MTI radar operator at 10 GHz with PRF of 3000 ppps. The lowest blind will be

A. 162 km/hr
B. 152 km/hr
C. 140 km/hr
D. none of the above

208. The maximum range of a radar depends on all of the following except

A. direction of movement of target
B. target area
C. capture area of antenna
D. none of the above

209. Radar range primarily depends upon

A. average transmitted power
B. peak transmitted power

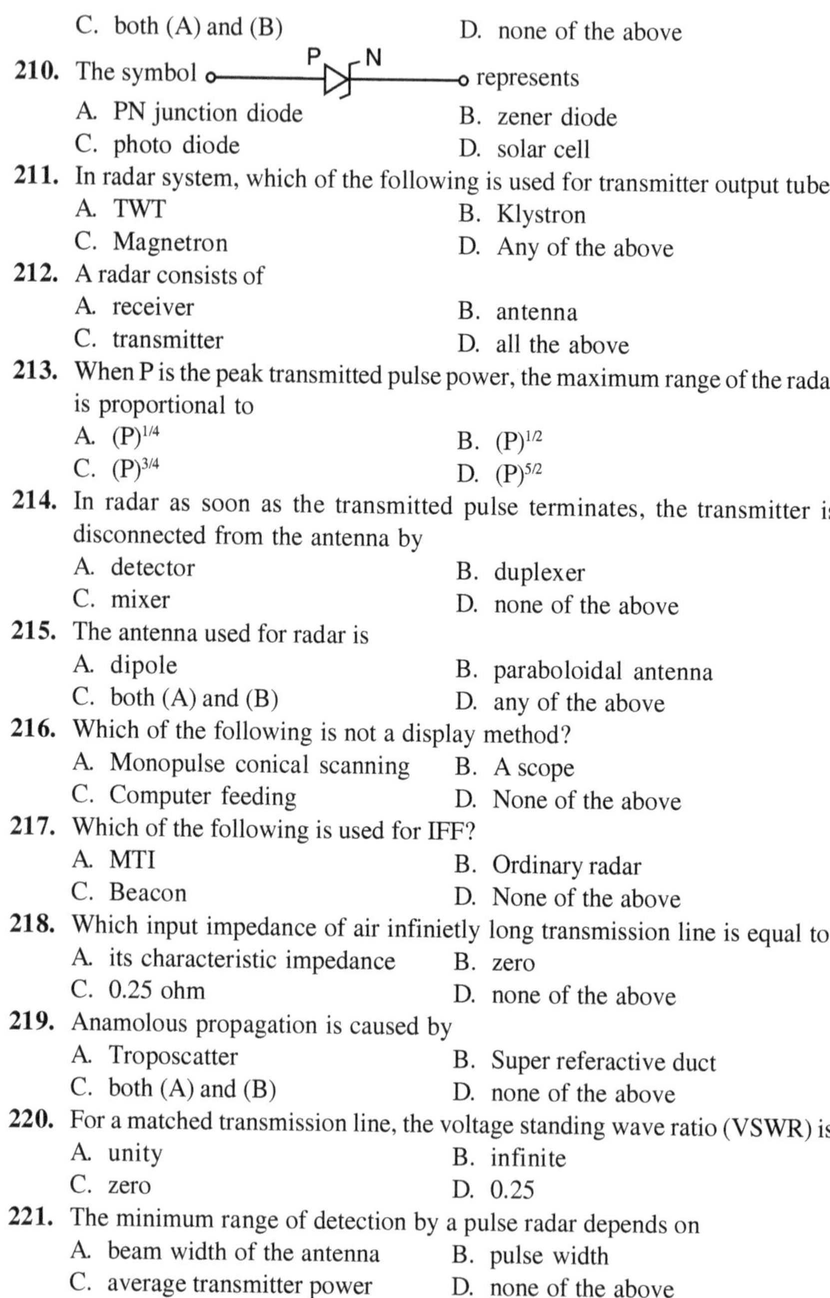

C. both (A) and (B)
D. none of the above

210. The symbol P N represents

A. PN junction diode
B. zener diode
C. photo diode
D. solar cell

211. In radar system, which of the following is used for transmitter output tubes

A. TWT
B. Klystron
C. Magnetron
D. Any of the above

212. A radar consists of

A. receiver
B. antenna
C. transmitter
D. all the above

213. When P is the peak transmitted pulse power, the maximum range of the radar is proportional to

A. $(P)^{1/4}$
B. $(P)^{1/2}$
C. $(P)^{3/4}$
D. $(P)^{5/2}$

214. In radar as soon as the transmitted pulse terminates, the transmitter is disconnected from the antenna by

A. detector
B. duplexer
C. mixer
D. none of the above

215. The antenna used for radar is

A. dipole
B. paraboloidal antenna
C. both (A) and (B)
D. any of the above

216. Which of the following is not a display method?

A. Monopulse conical scanning
B. A scope
C. Computer feeding
D. None of the above

217. Which of the following is used for IFF?

A. MTI
B. Ordinary radar
C. Beacon
D. None of the above

218. Which input impedance of air infinietly long transmission line is equal to

A. its characteristic impedance
B. zero
C. 0.25 ohm
D. none of the above

219. Anamolous propagation is caused by

A. Troposcatter
B. Super referactive duct
C. both (A) and (B)
D. none of the above

220. For a matched transmission line, the voltage standing wave ratio (VSWR) is

A. unity
B. infinite
C. zero
D. 0.25

221. The minimum range of detection by a pulse radar depends on

A. beam width of the antenna
B. pulse width
C. average transmitter power
D. none of the above

222. Most of the aircraft surveillance radars operate in

A. C band
B. X band
C. L band
D. none of the above

223. The term "rat-race" in a radar is associated with

A. Modulator
B. Duplexer
C. Receiver bandwith
D. None of the above

224. A CW radar cannot give information about

A. direction
B. past track
C. range
D. none of the above

225. For precise target location and tracking, retards operate in

A. D-band
B. S-band
C. L-band
D. None of the above

226. In a receiver which stage contains the primary of the first IF transformer?

A. Detector
B. Mixer
C. Both (A) and (B)
D. None of the above

227. What will be the beat frequency between two waves at 2.76 MHz if they are 180° out of phase?

A. zero Hz
B. 10 Hz
C. 15 Hz
D. 150 Hz

228. The standard IF value for FM receivers is

A. 10.7 MHz
B. 10.5 kHz
C. 15.20 MHz
D. 14.9 kHz

229. The best frequency between 1500 kHz and 1955 kHz will be

A. 455 kHz
B. 155 kHz
C. 375 kHz
D. 475 kHz

230. Transistors are generally free from which of the following type of noise?

A. Ficker noise
B. Partition noise
C. Shot noise
D. None of the above

231. A receiver having poor IF selectivity may be expected to have poor

A. sensitivity
B. bandwidth
C. blocking
D. none of the above

232. Neper is

A. smaller than decibel
B. equal to decibel
C. both (A) and (B)
D. none of the above

233. The ionosphere consists of

A. positive charge layer
B. neutral
C. negative charge layer
D. none of the above

234. During heterodyne process in a receiver the modulation of the signal

A. increases
B. remains unaffected
C. decreases
D. none of the above

235. In communication receivers the fidelity is provided by

A. audio stage
B. mixer stage
C. detector range
D. none of the above

236. Which of the following noise is of great importance at high frequency?

A. Transit noise
B. Flicker noise
C. Shot noise
D. None of the above

237. Channel capacity is equal to

A. amount of information per second
B. noise rate
C. average frequency
D. none of the above

238. In troposcatter which of the following antenna is preferred?

A. Conical antenna
B. Lens antenna
C. Both (A) and (B)
D. None of the above

239. In a radio receiver padders are provided

A. to improve tracking
B. for fine tuning
C. both (A) and (B)
D. none of the above

240. The effect of transist-time noise is significant in

A. MF
B. HF
C. LF
D. None of the above

241. When power ratios are expressed in dBm, the reference power is

A. 1 mW
B. 1 μW
C. 0.1 W
D. 0.25 W

242. The beat frequency between 1500 kHz and 1940 kHz is

A. 455 kHz
B. 455 Hz
C. 355 kHz
D. none of the above

243. Which stage contains the primary of the first IF transformer?

A. Detector
B. Mixer
C. Oscillator
D. None of the above

244. Three-point tracking is achieved with

A. the padder capacitor
B. variable selectivity
C. double spotting
D. none of the above

245. The disadvantage of tunned radio frequency receiver is

A. instability
B. bandwidth variation
C. insufficient adjacent-frequency rejection
D. all the above

246. The value of a resistor creating thermal noise is doubled. The noise power generated will be

A. doubled
B. unchanged

C. halved
D. none of the above

247. A device with minimum energy losses, used for the transference of r.f. energy to some radiator is called

A. line
B. current line
C. transmission line
D. none of the above

248. The radiating element is usually known as

A. antenna
B. device
C. conductor
D. none of the above

249. Radio communication requires the transference of energy between the transmitter and

A. frequency
B. receiver
C. communication
D. none of the above

250. The ratio of '*time on*' to '*time off*' is called the

A. cycle
B. duty cycle
C. PCM
D. none of the above

ANSWERS

1	**2**	**3**	**4**	**5**	**6**	**7**	**8**	**9**	**10**
C	A	C	B	A	B	B	A	A	B
11	**12**	**13**	**14**	**15**	**16**	**17**	**18**	**19**	**20**
C	B	C	B	C	B	C	D	B	C
21	**22**	**23**	**24**	**25**	**26**	**27**	**28**	**29**	**30**
B	C	B	C	B	B	A	C	C	C
31	**32**	**33**	**34**	**35**	**36**	**37**	**38**	**39**	**40**
A	A	A	B	C	A	A	C	A	C
41	**42**	**43**	**44**	**45**	**46**	**47**	**48**	**49**	**50**
A	B	C	B	A	C	A	B	A	C
51	**52**	**53**	**54**	**55**	**56**	**57**	**58**	**59**	**60**
A	B	D	A	B	B	B	A	B	B
61	**62**	**63**	**64**	**65**	**66**	**67**	**68**	**69**	**70**
A	B	A	B	A	C	B	C	B	A
71	**72**	**73**	**74**	**75**	**76**	**77**	**78**	**79**	**80**
B	A	C	B	B	A	C	B	A	B
81	**82**	**83**	**84**	**85**	**86**	**87**	**88**	**89**	**90**
C	C	A	B	B	A	B	B	A	C
91	**92**	**93**	**94**	**95**	**96**	**97**	**98**	**99**	**100**
A	A	B	B	A	B	C	B	A	C
101	**102**	**103**	**104**	**105**	**106**	**107**	**108**	**109**	**110**
B	A	C	B	B	B	C	C	B	D

111	**112**	**113**	**114**	**115**	**116**	**117**	**118**	**119**	**120**
B	C	B	C	C	B	C	C	C	A
121	**122**	**123**	**124**	**125**	**126**	**127**	**128**	**129**	**130**
B	C	B	B	C	D	B	D	B	B
131	**132**	**133**	**134**	**135**	**136**	**137**	**138**	**139**	**140**
B	B	D	B	A	C	B	C	C	D
141	**142**	**143**	**144**	**145**	**146**	**147**	**148**	**149**	**150**
A	B	B	A	B	A	A	B	B	A
151	**152**	**153**	**154**	**155**	**156**	**157**	**158**	**159**	**160**
B	C	B	B	B	B	B	B	B	B
161	**162**	**163**	**164**	**165**	**166**	**167**	**168**	**169**	**170**
A	B	B	C	C	C	B	A	B	C
171	**172**	**173**	**174**	**175**	**176**	**177**	**178**	**179**	**180**
B	C	B	B	C	C	B	B	C	C
181	**182**	**183**	**184**	**185**	**186**	**187**	**188**	**189**	**190**
B	B	A	C	D	A	B	A	D	A
191	**192**	**193**	**194**	**195**	**196**	**197**	**198**	**199**	**200**
B	C	B	C	C	B	B	B	C	C
201	**202**	**203**	**204**	**205**	**206**	**207**	**208**	**209**	**210**
C	A	B	B	A	B	A	A	B	B
211	**212**	**213**	**214**	**215**	**216**	**217**	**218**	**219**	**220**
D	D	A	B	D	A	C	A	B	A
221	**222**	**223**	**224**	**225**	**226**	**227**	**228**	**229**	**230**
B	C	B	C	B	B	A	A	A	B
231	**232**	**233**	**234**	**235**	**236**	**237**	**238**	**239**	**240**
C	D	C	B	A	D	A	D	A	B
241	**242**	**243**	**244**	**245**	**246**	**247**	**248**	**249**	**250**
A	D	B	A	D	B	C	A	B	B

GENERAL INTELLIGENCE

VERBAL TEST

SERIES

In questions on series, a series of four numbers is given. The numbers of the series bear some relationship among themselves. You will have to find out the relationship that obtains among the numbers. Then, on the basis of the knowledge of that relationship you can find out the next number(s) in the series.

Series questions may contain a series of letters as well as alphabets.

To begin with, we give some questions on series, each with four options, of which only one is correct. You have to mark the correct answer. Then follow the *Questions for Practice* without options. Detailed answers to questions are given at the end.

Directions: *In each of the following questions on series, a series of numbers or letters is given with one space blank. Choose the correct option out of the four options given under each question.*

These questions are based on the samples of questions set for the examination.

1. 1, 3, 7, 15, ...

A. 25 B. 31
C. 33 D. 35

2. 4, 9, 16, 25, ...

A. 36 B. 38
C. 40 D. 42

3. 1, 13, 25, 37, ...

A. 41 B. 45
C. 49 D. 53

4. 64, 32, 16, 8, ...

A. 1 B. 2
C. 4 D. 6

5. AZ, DW, GT, ...

A. CX B. TG
C. JQ D. EV

6. A, D, G, ...

A. I B. K
C. H D. J

7. Z, A, Y, B, ...

A. X B. C
C. D D. W

8. If 3 + 2 = 25 and 3 + 4 = 49, then 2 + 3 = ?

A. 6 B. 15
C. 25 D. 18

9. 2, 4, 8, 16, ...

A. 20 B. 24
C. 32 D. 28

10. 20, 15, 11, 8, ...

A. 3 B. 4
C. 5 D. 6

QUESTIONS FOR PRACTICE

11. 76, 63, 50, 37, ...

12. 5, 10, 17, 26, ...

13. 2, 6, 12, 20, ...

14. 3, 6, 9, 12, ...

15. 3, 7, 11, 13, ...

16. 1, 4, 9, 16, ...

17. 0, 3, 8, 15, ...

18. 3, 6, 12, 24, ...

19. 1, 4, 8, 13, ...

20. 1, 3, 6, 10, ...

21. 1, 5, 17, 53, ...

22. 3, 8, 15, 24, ...

23. 25, 19, 14, 10, ...
24. 3, 7, 15, 31, ...
25. 80, 40, 20, 10, ...
26. 1, 6, 11, 16, ...
27. 59, 52, 45, 38, ...
28. 2, 5, 11, 23, ...
29. 13, 17, 19, 23, ...
30. 13, 23, 33, 43, ...
31. 1, 4, 10, 22, ...
32. 1, 4, 9, 16, ...
33. 96, 48, 24, 12, ...
34. 14, 10, 13, 9, 12, 8, ...
35. 4, 7, 14, 17, 34, 37, ...
36. 32, 16, 20, 10, 14, ...
37. 2, 3, 3, 5, 4, 7, ...
38. 5, 6, 8, 11, 15, 20, ...
39. 2, 9, 28, 65, ...
40. 0, 2, 6, 12, 20, ...
41. 2, 5, 10, 17, 26, ...
42. 1, 5, 11, 19, 29, ...
43. $\frac{11}{12}, \frac{10}{11}, \frac{9}{10}, \frac{8}{9}$.....
44. 4, 5, 9, 14, 23, ...
45. 5, 10, 15, 25, 40, ...
46. 360, 180, 60, 15, ...
47. 4, 9, 16, 25, 36, ...
48. 4, 8, 3, 6, 2, 4, ...
49. 1, 8, 27, 64, ...
50. 4, 8, 16, 28, ...
51. 1, 2, 5, 10, 17, ...
52. 720, 120, 24, 6, ...
53. 1, 2, 4, 8, 16, ...
54. 1, 3, 6, 10, 15, ...
55. 0, 1, 4, 9, 16, ...
56. 810, 270, 90, 30, ...
57. 9, 16, 25, 36, ...
58. 6, 9, 12, 15, ...
59. 4, 8, 13, 19, ...
60. 3, 7, 15, 31, ...
61. 89, 79, 70, 72, ...
62. 2, 3, 4, 6, 8, ...
63. 3, 4, 9, 16, 27, ...
64. 45, 35, 26, 18, ...
65. 2, 9, 16, 23, ...
66. 40, 32, 26, 22, ...
67. 1, 3, 6, 10, ...
68. 66, 47, 28, ...
69. 5, 7, 11, 19, ...
70. 12, 6, 3, 1½, ...
71. 2, 3, 4, 6, 6, 9, ...
72. 5, 36, 10, 18, 20, ...
73. 5, 7, 11, 13, ...
74. 2, 4, 8, 16, ...
75. 45, 36, 27, ...
76. 1, 7, 13, 19, ...
77. 1, 4, 9, 16, ...
78. 54, 63, 72, ...
79. 42, 53, 63, 72, ...
80. 20, 8, 10, 4, 5, ...
81. 5, 11, 23, ...
82. 10, 22, 46, ...
83. 37, 41, 47, ...
84. 3, 2, 9, 6, 27, ...
85. 3, 6, 10, 15, ...
86. 2, 6, 12, 20, ...
87. 1, 8, 27, 64, ...

88. 125, 64, 27, 8, ...

89. 36, 49, 64, 81, ...

90. 64, 49, 36, 25, ...

91. If 3 + 4 = 25 and 4 + 5 = 41, then 5 + 6 = ?

92. If 2 + 3 = 25 and 3 + 4 = 49, then 4 + 5 = ?

93. If 6 – 4 = 20 and 5 – 3 = 16, then 4 – 3 = ?

94. If 8 – 6 = 4 and 7 – 4 = 9, then 5 – 2 = ?

95. If 7 + 9 = 32 and 3 + 6 = 18, then 5 + 4 = ?

96. If 3 + 2 = 25 and 3 + 4 = 49, then 3 + 5 = ?

97. If 9 – 5 = 2 and 25 – 15 = 5, then 12 – 6 = ?

98. If 2 × 3 = 12 and 3 × 4 = 25, then 4 × 5 = ?

99. If 2 + 3 = 13 and 3 + 4 = 25, then 2 + 5 = ?

100. If 6 – 3 = 9 and 7 – 2 = 25, then 8 – 4 = ?

101. If 5 + 2 = 19 and 2 + 3 = 13, then 3 + 5 = ?

102. If 6 – 3 = 27 and 5 – 4 = 9, then 6 – 4 = ?

103. 4 – 2 = 4 and 6 – 4 = 4, then 5 – 3 = ?

104. If 3 + 5 = 64 and 2 + 3 = 25, then 4 + 6 = ?

105. If 1 + 4 = 10 and 2 + 5 = 14, then 3 + 6 = ?

106. If 3 + 2 = 60 and 3 + 3 = 90, then 3 + 4 = ?

107. If 5 × 3 = 2 and 17 × 6 = 11, then 18 × 5 = ?

108. If 4 × 5 = 60 and 2 × 8 = 48, then 3 × 6 = ?

109. If 9 – 5 = 2 and 25 – 15 = 5, then 12 – 6 = ?

110. If 5 × 8 = 13 and 7 × 9 = 16, then 3 × 7 = ?

111. If $\frac{3}{4}+\frac{5}{6}=\frac{8}{10}$ and $\frac{6}{7}+\frac{2}{3}=\frac{8}{10}$, then $\frac{3}{4}+\frac{2}{3}=?$

112. If 4 × 7 = 11 and 11 × 4 = 15, then 7 × 9 = ?

113. If $\frac{5}{7}=12$ and $\frac{1}{10}=11$, then $\frac{3}{5}=?$

114. If 25 + 12 = 13 and 9 × 3 = 6, then 17 × 4 = ?

115. If 5 ÷ 2 = 7 and 11 ÷ 2 = 13, then 8 ÷ 3 = ?

116. BCD, CDE, DEF, ...

117. XYZ, WXY, VWX, ...

118. AZ, BY, CX, DW, ...

119. ACE, BDF, CEG, DFH, ...

120. ZX, YW, XV, WU, ...

121. AE, BF, CG, DH, ...

122. ABD, BCE, CDF, DEG, ...

123. AN, BO, CP, DQ, ...

124. ABZ, BCY, CDX, DEW, ...

125. ZA, YB, XC, WD, ...

126. A, D, G, J, ...

127. Z, W, T, Q, ...

128. AZY, BYX, CXW, ...

129. BA, DC, FE, HG, ...

130. ZYX, WVU, TSR, ...

FINDING THE WRONG OR SUPERFLUOUS NUMBER

Directions: *Below are given some series, each of which has a wrong or superfluous number. Find it out; that is your answer.*

1. 1, 4, 9, 16, 24, 36

2. 11, 12, 22, 24, 32, 36

3. 13, 17, 22, 28, 35, 41

4. 100, 81, 64, 49, 37, 25

5. 101, 110, 119, 125, 137, 146

6. 23, 33, 44, 56, 70

7. 40, 28, 19, 10, 2

8. 24, 21, 18, 15, 10, 9

9. 17, 15, 12, 13, 11, 9

10. 7, 10, 13, 17, 16, 19

11. 1, 3, 9, 25, 81

12. 2, 7, 12, 17, 19, 22

13. 4, 9, 16, 24, 25, 36, 49

14. 5, 11, 17, 23, 26, 29, 35

15. 3, 7, 8, 18, 33, 53

16. 1, 7, 27, 64, 125

17. 20, 10, 15, 11, 6, 0

18. 80, 90, 100, 111, 123, 136

19. 16, 24, 36, 49, 64, 81

20. 100, 93, 86, 76, 66

21. 11, 22, 32, 44, 55, 66

22. 216, 121, 64, 27, 8

23. 4, 9, 16, 25, 35, 49

24. 50, 39, 27, 17, 6

25. 23, 33, 44, 56, 70

26. 80, 71, 62, 52, 44

27. 4, 11, 18, 24, 32

28. 2, 4, 9, 16, 32

29. 1, 4, 8, 12, 19

30. 5, 7, 9, 13, 13, 20

31. 3, 4, 8, 16, 33, 58

32. 6, 13, 21, 27, 34

33. 6, 18, 30, 42, 48

34. 1, 8, 26, 64, 125

35. 6, 18, 28, 42, 54

36. 63, 56, 49, 43, 35

37. 91, 80, 65, 58, 47, 36

38. 2, 5, 18, 17, 26

39. 21, 25, 30, 39, 43, 51

40. 176, 88, 40, 22, 11

41. 8, 21, 34, 45, 60

42. 15, 21, 27, 34, 39

43. 17, 15, 13, 12, 9

44. 100, 90, 81, 71, 64, 52

45. 1, 4, 9, 15, 25, 36

ANALOGY

In analogy questions, three words are given. The first two words to the left of sign : : are related in some way. The same relationship holds between the third word to the right of the sign : : and one of the four responses A, B, C and D given thereunder. You have to choose the correct response, that is your answer.

Here is an example:

Student : Teacher : : Patient : ?

A. Hospital B. Medicine
C. Doctor D. Disease

In this case the correct response is C because a Doctor is related to a Patient in the same way as a Teacher is related to a Student.

QUESTIONS FOR PRACTICE

1. Milk : Curd : : Water : ?
A. River B. Thirst
C. Ice D. Vapour

2. Girl : Beautiful : : Gold : ?
A. Valuable B. Bright
C. Ornament D. Ring

3. Desert : Sand : : Sea : ?
A. Water B. Tide
C. Fish D. Crocodile

4. Beautiful : Ugly : : Healthy : ?
A. Sick B. Weak
C. Strong D. Fat

5. Cheese : Milk : : Sugar : ?
A. Molasses B. Palm
C. Sugarcane D. Syrup

6. Daughter : Mother : : Son : ?
A. Mother B. Sister
C. Father D. Brother

7. Book : Paper : : Table : ?
A. School B. Student
C. Wood D. Chair

8. Player : Team : : Ship : ?
A. Port B. Fleet
C. Ocean D. Captain

9. Kilogram : Weight : : Metre : ?
A. Journey B. Road
C. Cloth D. Length

10. Lid : Box : : Cork : ?
A. Seal B. Bottle
C. Drug D. Carton

11. Circle : Circumference : : Square : ?
A. Angle B. Area
C. Diagonal D. Perimeter

12. Advocate : Law : : Cook : ?
A. Cookery B. Kitchen
C. Food D. Dishes

13. Wardrobe : Clothes : : Purse : ?
A. Pocket B. Zip
C. Money D. Fare

14. Temperature : Heat : : Humidity : ?
A. Rain B. Weather
C. Night D. Moisture

15. Shakespeare : Drama : : Ghalib : ?
A. Urdu B. Literature
C. Ghazal D. Stories

16. Grass : Green : : Sky : ?
A. Endless B. Stars
C. Blue D. Bright

17. Monday : Week : : January : ?
A. Winter B. Month
C. Year D. Season

18. Thermometer : Temperature : : Barometer : ?
A. Atmosphere
B. Wind

C. Atmospheric Pressure
D. Velocity

19. Poverty : Riches : : Glory : ?
A. Penuary B. Happiness
C. Shame D. Suffering

20. Table : Chair : : Coat : ?
A. Pajama B. Shirt
C. Tie D. Pant

21. Hand : Elbow : : Leg : ?
A. Thigh B. Knee
C. Ankle D. Claw

22. Coal : Black : : Snow : ?
A. Water B. Mountain
C. Cold D. White

23. Precaution : Accident : : Cleanliness : ?
A. Disease B. Treatment
C. Filth D. Garbage

24. January : April : : Sunday : ?
A. Thursday B. Tuesday
C. Monday D. Wednesday

25. Soldier : Rifle : : Writer : ?
A. Book B. Paper
C. Pen D. Ink

26. Plate : Crockery : : Spoon : ?
A. Knife B. Fork
C. Chinaware D. Cultery

27. Night : Evening : : Day : ?
A. Morning B. Sun
C. Sunlight D. Daylight

28. Uncle : Aunt : : Father : ?
A. Daughter B. Mother
C. Brother D. Sister

29. Lotus : Water : : Fish : ?
A. Creature B. Food
C. Breath D. Water

30. Metre : Length : : Litre : ?
A. Weight B. Number
C. Volume D. Quantity

31. Heaven : Hell : : Drought : ?
A. Famine B. Water
C. Flood D. Crop

32. Sun : Planet : : Earth : ?
A. Satellite B. Sun
C. Moon D. Light

33. French : France : : Dutch : ?
A. Hungary B. Holland
C. Sea D. Hiroshima

34. Sri Lanka : Colombo : : Japan : ?
A. Island B. Tokyo
C. Hiroshima D. Bomb

35. Pen : Write : : Carpenter's Plane : ?
A. Tear B. Repair
C. Pierce D. Shave off

36. Thick : Thin : : Inferior : ?
A. Rough B. Spurious
C. Beautiful D. Superior

37. Table : Wood : : Book : ?
A. Pages B. Paper
C. Teach D. Student

38. Fan : Air : : Bulb : ?
A. Brightness B. Electricity
C. Switch D. Light

39. Seven : Number : : Green : ?
A. Colour B. Forest
C. Field D. Red

40. Stage : Drama : : Stadium : ?
A. Sports B. Circus
C. Wedding D. Convention

41. Fruit : Mango : : Serpent : ?
A. Cobra
B. Poison
C. Creature
D. Hood of a Cobra

42. Rain : Centimeter : : Tempera- ture : ?
A. Celsius B. Weather
C. Sun D. Heat

43. Road : Lane : : City : ?
A. Town B. Metropolis
C. Highway D. Capital

44. Aspirin : Headache : : Quinine : ?
A. Hepatitis B. Malaria
C. Influenza D. Cough

45. Hunger : Food : : Thirst : ?
A. Tap B. River
C. Water D. Sweat

46. Cat : Kitten : : Hen : ?
A. Bird B. Cock
C. Feed D. Chicken

47. Fruit : Banana : : Mammal : ?
A. Cow B. Heron
C. Fly D. Plant

48. Radio : Listener : : Film : ?
A. Camera B. Actor
C. Viewer D. Talky

49. Money : Exchange : : Language : ?
A. Write
B. Communication
C. Knowledge
D. Book

50. Friend : Enemy : : Kind : ?
A. Diety B. Demon
C. Anger D. Cruel

51. Train : Platform : : Ship : ?
A. Anchor B. Harbour
C. Ocean D. Island

52. 1st April : Fool : : 1st May : ?
A. Teacher B. Doctor
C. Labour D. Disabled

53. Time : Clock : : Rain : ?
A. Cloud B. Raingauge
C. Centimeter D. Barometer

54. Lion : Den : : Horse : ?
A. Stable B. *Tonga*
C. Chariot D. Stake

55. Book : Pages : : Flower : ?
A. Bouquet B. Buds
C. Colour D. Petals

56. Tea : Leaves : : Coffee : ?
A. Roots B. Flowers
C. Bark D. Seeds

57. Horse : Neigh : : Donkey : ?
A. Trumpet B. Roar
C. Bray D. Snarl

58. Car : Garage : : Aircraft : ?
A. Sky B. Hanger
C. Aerodrome D. Engine

59. Radius : Circle : : Spokes : ?
A. Wheel B. Table
C. Bus D. Matchbox

60. Stool : Carpenter : : Shoes : ?
A. Cobbler B. Foot
C. Leather D. Polish

61. Bus : Workshop : : Ship : ?
A. Harbour B. Yard
C. Dockyard D. Hanger

62. Ring : Finger : : Tie : ?
A. Coat B. Neck
C. Collar D. Waist

63. Sew : Needle : : Paint : ?
A. Colour B. Brush
C. Canvas D. Landscape

64. Nose : Smell : : Tongue : ?
A. Lick B. Taste
C. Speak D. Mouth

65. Pencil : Stationery : : Chair : ?
A. Carpenter B. Wood
C. Table D. Furniture

66. Cat : Dog : : Cow : ?
A. Goat B. Lion
C. Tiger D. Wolf

67. Snake : Lizard : : Fish : ?
A. Cow B. Dog
C. Cat D. Crocodile

68. Honour : Dishonour : : Fame : ?
A. Respected B. Glorious
C. Infamy D. Glory

69. Light : Rays : : Sound : ?
A. Ear B. Wave
C. Velocity D. Echo

70. Clock : Hand : : Thermometer : ?
A. Temperature B. Fever
C. Mercury D. Patient

71. Tractor : Diesel : : Scooter : ?
A. Wheel B. Petrol
C. Power D. Engine

72. Cuckoo : Cackle : : Horse : ?
A. Bray B. Neigh
C. Hiss D. Roar

73. Pitch : Cricket : : Ring : ?
A. Wrestling B. Boxing
C. Hockey D. Badminton

74. Car : Run : : Snake : ?
A. Run B. Bite
C. Creep D. Hiss

75. Urge : Deter : : Honest : ?
A. Dishonest B. *Thug*
C. Robber D. Cheat

76. Lion : Den : : Bird : ?
A. Tree B. Chrip
C. Nest D. Ruins

77. Calf : Cow : : Lamb : ?
A. Wolf B. Flesh
C. Goat D. Sheep

78. Obedience : Disobedience : : Life : ?
A. Salvation B. Death
C. Heaven D. Universe

79. Tailor : Cloth : : Carpenter : ?
A. Machine B. Wood
C. Saw D. Table

80. Cat : Rat : : Tiger : ?
A. Lamb B. Lizard
C. Crow D. Fish

81. Bakery : Bread : : Mint : ?
A. Cheque B. Coin
C. Note D. Cake

82. Studio : Film : : Shipyard : ?
A. Ship B. Trawler
C. Boat D. Net

83. Month : Year : : Hour : ?
A. Day B. Week
C. Minute D. Second

84. Food : Hunger : : Water : ?
A. Bath B. Irrigation
C. Thirst D. Rain

85. Revolver : Bullet : : Bow : ?
A. Sword B. Club
C. Arrow D. Pistol

86. Honey : Bee : : Wool : ?
A. Goat B. Horse
C. Hare D. Sheep

FINDING THE ODD ONE OUT

In these questions four pairs of words or four words are given and one of them is odd or does not belong to the class. You have to find out that odd pair/word. Two examples are given below:

Example 1.

A. Wood-Chair
B. Water-Ice
C. Milk-Cheese
D. Teacher-Student

Solution: Chair is made of Wood, Ice is made of Water, Cheese is made of Milk. But Student is never made of Teacher. Therefore, the odd pair is D. That is your answer.

Example 2.

A. Bihar
B. Gujarat
C. West Bengal
D. Calcutta

Solution: A, B and C are names of States. D is the name of a city. Therefore, D is odd. That is your answer.

QUESTIONS FOR PRACTICE

Directions: *In the following questions, find the odd one out.*

1. A. Man-Woman
B. Brother-Sister
C. Father-Son
D. Father-Mother

2. A. Fish-Water
B. Water-River
C. Coal-Mine
D. Bird-Tree

3. A. Hospital-Doctor
B. Court-Advocate
C. Thief-Robber
D. School-Teacher

4. A. Milk-Curd
B. Brick-House
C. Paper-Book
D. Horse-Stable

5. A. Milk-White
B. Leaf-Green
C. Sky-Blue
D. Blood-Red

6. A. Victory-Defeat
B. Carrot-Radish
C. North-South
D. Up-Down

7. A. Mouse-Hole
B. Bird-Nest
C. Horse-Stable
D. Tiger-Forest

8. A. Blue-Sky
B. Red-Kite
C. Blue-*Saree*
D. Black-Horse

9. A. Father-Son
B. Needle-Thread
C. Cup-Plate
D. Chair-Table

10. A. Well-Canal
B. River-Mountain
C. Lake-Sea
D. Gulf-Desert

11. A. Book-Note Book
B. Rubber-Pencil
C. Nose-Ear
D. Leg-Bone

12. A. Friend-Foe
B. Rich-Poor
C. Kind-Cruel
D. Games-Sports

13. A. Fire-Smoke
B. Sun-Heat
C. Moonlight-Cool
D. Paper-White

14. A. Mars B. Jupiter
C. Venus D. Moon

15. A. Grape B. Raisin
C. Apple D. Mango

16. A. Wolf B. Jackal
C. Goat D. Bear

17. A. *Riksha* B. Bus
C. Car D. Scooter

18. A. Tiger B. Horse
C. Elephant D. Camel

19. A. Monkey
B. Mongoose
C. Snake
D. Cat

20. A. Kanpur B. Lucknow
C. Patna D. Allahabad

21. A. Yen B. Dollar
C. Coin D. Pound

22. A. Diamond B. Mercury
C. Iron D. Copper

23. A. Legs B. Hands
C. Ankles D. Lungs

24. A. Steamer B. Boat
C. Ship D. Harbour

25. A. Rose B. Lotus
C. Dahlia D. Jasmin

26. A. Proteins
B. Carbohydrates
C. Copper
D. Vitamins

27. A. Piano B. Tabla
C. Flute D. Banjo

28. A. Metre
B. Kilometre
C. Centimetre
D. Square Kilometre

29. A. Cat B. Dog
C. Monkey D. Snake

30. A. Snake B. Lizard
C. Crocodile D. Frog

31. A. Mercury B. Earth
C. Moon D. Jupiter

32. A. Pencil
B. Rubber
C. Ink
D. Sketch Map

33. A. The Statesman
B. India Today
C. The Hindu
D. The Amrit Bazar Patrika

34. A. Ashoka
B. Chanakya
C. Chandra Gupta
D. Harsh Vardhana

35. A. Tangent
B. Arc
C. Radius
D. Hypotenuse

36. A. Delhi B. Patna
C. Mumbai D. Calcutta

37. A. Bicycle B. Scooter
C. Car D. Bus

38. A. Wheat B. Gram
C. Ragi D. Rice

39. A. Iron B. Copper
C. Steel D. Tin

40. A. Cancer B. Hepatitis
C. Bile D. Diabetes

41. A. Water B. Wind
C. Gasoline D. Soil

42. A. Cotton B. Rice
C. Tea D. Jute

43. A. Apple B. Banana
C. Sugarcane D. Mango

44. A. Dhaka B. Colombo
C. Karachi D. Rangoon

45. A. May B. March
C. April D. July

46. A. Rouble B. Diet
C. Dollar D. Taka

47. A. Libra B. Uranus
C. Pluto D. Neptune

48. A. Temple
B. Monastery
C. Mosque
D. Church

49. A. Ounce B. Shilling
C. Gram D. Pound

50. A. Shield B. Armour
C. Sword D. Helmet

51. A. Ganga B. Godavari
C. Krishna D. Narmada

52. A. Cataract B. Cornea
C. Retina D. Iris

53. A. Bigger B. Greater
C. Faster D. Larger

54. A. Fox B. Cow
C. Dog D. Horse

55. A. Jackal B. Fox
C. Stag D. Wolf

56. A. Father B. Teacher
C. Brother D. Sister

57. A. Shore B. Sea
C. River D. Pond

58. A. Moan B. Wail
C. Weep D. Sorrow

59. A. Eagle B. Crow
C. Vulture D. Cock

60. A. Dwarf B. Slender
C. Fat D. Lame

61. A. Mother B. Daughter
C. Son D. Aunt

62. A. Eye B. Ear
C. Neck D. Tooth

63. A. Tamil Nadu
B. Kerala
C. Karnataka
D. Pondicherry

64. A. Wing Commander
B. Pilot Officer
C. Colonel
D. Flight Lieutenant

65. A. Veena
B. Sitar
C. Sarod
D. Mridangam

66. A. Africa B. Asia
C. Arabia D. America

67. A. Shark B. Seal
C. Whale D. Crocodile

68. A. Square
B. Trapezium
C. Rectangle
D. Diagonal

69. A. Cat B. Dog
C. Fox D. Monkey

71. A. Potatoes
B. Tomatoes
C. Groundnuts
D. Onions

72. A. Influenza
B. Tuberculosis
C. Smallpox
D. Malaria

73. A. Bunglow B. Office
C. Hut D. House

74. A. Fly B. Sweets
C. *Kheer* D. *Gur*

75. A. Root B. Trunk
C. Stem D. Leaves

76. A. Brinjal
B. Potato
C. Beans
D. Lady Finger

77. A. Dog B. Crow
C. Cow D. Goat

78. A. C.V. Raman
B. Meghnad Saha
C. Kalidas
D. Dr. Bhabha

79. A. Pant B. Shirt
C. Shoes D. *Pajama*

80. A. Hydrogen B. Nitrogen
C. Oxygen D. Mercury

QUESTIONS RELATING TO CLOCKS AND CALENDARS

These questions are related to students' knowledge of Clock and days of week. They also involve their knowledge of directions of the hands of the clocks at various times as well as the angle between the two hands of the clock.

CLOCKS

Example: When it is 15 minutes past 12,

(*i*) What is the angle between the two hands of the clock?

(*ii*) What is the direction of the hour hand of the clock at that time?

Solution: 15 minutes past 12, is the time when the minute hand is pointing at 3 while the hour hand has just crossed 12. See the illustration below:

Therefore,

(i) The angle between the two hands of the clock is 90°.

(ii) The hour hand is pointed upwards toward 12, *i.e.,* towards north.

Remember:

(i) The sum total of all the angles at the centre of the clock is 360°.

(ii) The dial of the clock is divided into 12 equal parts.

$\therefore \frac{360^\circ}{12} = 30^\circ$

That the angle formed between each and every two numbers on the dial is always 30°.

(iii) The direction of the hands of the clock is indicated in the following manner:

(a) upside (where 12 is written) is always the north.

(b) down below (where 6 is written) is always the south.

(c) The right side (where 3 is written) is always the east.

(d) The left side (where 9 is written) is always west.

Another Example: When it is 5 o'clock, what is the angle between the two hands of the clock.

Solution: At 5 o'clock:

(i) the hour hand will point at 5

(ii) the minute hand will point at 12.

See the illustration below:

The two hands are 5 numbers apart

$\therefore 30^\circ \times 5 = 150^\circ$

$\therefore$ The angle between the two hands of the clock will be 150°.

Remember that in every hour:

(i) both the hands meet **once**.

(ii) The hands are straight pointing in opposite directions only **once**.

(iii) the hand make right angles **twice**.

(iv) the minute hand moves through an angle of 6° in **one minute**.

CALENDAR

Questions based on calendars are easy to solve.

Example 1: In a particular month, 17th was Friday. Then:

(i) What will be the date on the next Friday?

(ii) What was the date on the previous Friday?

Solution: We know that there are seven days in a week. If 17th of the month was Friday, then the day falling after 7 days (*i.e.,* 17 + 7 = 24), *i.e.,* the 24th will be Friday. Similarly, 17th being Friday, therefore the day falling 7 days before (*i.e.,* 17 – 7 = 10) *i.e.,* 10th should have been Friday.

Example 2: In a particular year, 20th August was Monday. On which day 3rd September will fall in that year?

Solution: August has 31 days. If 20th August was Monday, the next Monday will fall on 27th August. So, 31st August will be on Friday and accordingly, 1st September on Saturday and 3rd September will fall on Monday.

Months which have only 30 days: April, June, September and November

Months which have 31 days: January, March, May, July, August, October and December.

February has only 28 days. Every four years February has 28 + 1 = 29 days. Such a year is called Leap Year.

QUESTIONS FOR PRACTICE

1. If yesterday was Sunday, after how many days the next Sunday will come?

A. 7 B. 6
C. 5 D. 8

2. In a particular month, two days after Monday was the 5th (date), on which day will the 19th (date) of the same month fall?

A. Tuesday B. Monday
C. Sunday D. Friday

3. How many times between 4 o'clock afternoon and 10 o'clock night, the two hands of a clock are at right angles?

A. 14 B. 10
C. 12 D. 8

4. If 14th April in a particular year was Thursday. The first Thursday in May of that very year will fall on which date?

A. 3rd May B. 4th May
C. 5th May D. 6th May

5. If two days before January 11 was Monday, then the next Monday in the same month will fall on:

A. January 16 B. January 18
C. January 17 D. January 15

6. If February 28 was Tuesday in a particular year, the 5th February in that very year was on:

A. Friday B. Sunday
C. Saturday D. Monday

7. If 3 days after Monday was 11th (date) of the month, what day was there on the 22nd (date) of the same month?

A. Friday B. Monday
C. Sunday D. Saturday

8. In a particular year the 31st March was Tuesday. On which date was the first Sunday of March in that very year?

A. 1st March B. 3rd March
C. 2nd March D. 4th March

9. February 3 was Friday in a particular year. The last Sunday of February in that year will fall on?

A. February 25 B. February 26
C. February 27 D. February 28

10. If July 19 is Tuesday in a particular year, on what day will August 15 fall in that very year?

A. Friday B. Monday
C. Sunday D. Saturday

11. At 2 PM, the hands of a clock will make an angle of:

A. 60° B. 45°
C. 30° D. 80°

12. During a period of 12 hours, how many times the hands of a clock are at right angles?

A. 22 B. 24
C. 23 D. 25

13. During a day (24 hours), on how many occasions, both the hands of a clock are in a straight line?

A. 23 B. 12
C. 24 D. 22

14. At 4 AM, the hands of the clock will make an angle of:

A. 90° B. 110°
C. 120° D. 130°

15. At 25 minutes past 3, the hands of the clock will make an angle of:

A. 90° B. 60°
C. 30° D. 45°

16. At 5 minutes past 3, the hands of a clock will make an angle of:

A. 60° B. 30°
C. 90° D. 45°

17. At 9 o'clock, the hour hand of the clock will be facing towards:

A. East B. West
C. North D. South

18. At 10 minutes past 9, the hands of a clock will make an angle of:

A. 120° B. 150°
C. 180° D. 100°

19. A boy looks at the clock and tells the time as 15 minutes past 5. In doing so, he committed the mistake of treating the hour hand as minute hand and vice-versa. What was the correct time in the clock?

A. 15 minutes past 3
B. 20 minutes past 3
C. 25 minutes past 3
D. 10 minutes past 3

20. What will be the time when both the hands of the clock coincide (one over the other) and face towards the west?

A. 9 o'clock
B. 30 minutes past 8
C. 45 minutes past 8
D. 15 minutes past 8

CODING AND DECODING

In a code language the coded letters or numbers are not what they appear but they represent some other pre-determined letter or number. Coding implies use of some letter or number in a systematic way to represent another letter or number.

Decoding means resolving the system involved in a code. In other words decoding means finding out the original letter or number for which coded letters or numbers have been used.

Coding is done on a systematic way. If we are able to discover this system, we can decode.

To explain it further, we shall take some examples.

Suppose MARKET is coded as NBSLFU. In this case, for each alphabet in MARKET, certain other alphabets namely NBSLFU have been used.

Now if you are asked to find out the code for TEAM (on the basis of MARKET coded as NBSLFU), you can do it without much difficulty. You will find that all the letters in TEAM, *i.e.,* T, E, A and M occur in MARKET. To find out the code for TEAM arrange MARKET with its code in the following manner

M A R K E T

N B S L F U

You can find that N is for M, B is for A, S is for R and so on.

You also find that U is for T, F is for E, B is for A and N is for M.

∴ UFBN is for TEAM

∴ Code for TEAM is UFBN.

Similarly, you can find the code for RAT, TEA, MARK, TAKE, EAT, ARM etc. Codes for these will be as under:

RAT = SBU

TEA = UFB

MARK = NBSL

TAKE = UBLF

EAT = FBU

ARM = BSN

Now, we take another example. If EIGHT is coded as CGEFR, then SPOT will be coded as?

For finding out the code for SPOT, we shall follow the following method:

1 3 4 2

A B Ⓒ D Ⓔ Ⓕ Ⓖ H I J K L Ⓜ

5

Ⓝ O P Ⓠ Ⓡ S T U V W X Y Z

3 2 1 4

1 2 3 4 5

EIGHT are marked E I G H T, and C G E F R an marked Ⓒ Ⓖ Ⓔ Ⓕ Ⓡ

The pattern above makes clear that one letter has been skipped anti-clockwise at each step while coding.

Therefore, now apply the same formula to find out the code for SPOT.

Mark SPOT as S P O T. Skip one
1 2 3 4
letter anti-clockwise at each step to find

Ⓠ Ⓝ Ⓜ Ⓡ or Q N M R

∴ SPOT will be coded as QNMR.

In such questions, mark the expression and its code (as given in the question) in the alphabets (as shown above) to find the clue. Then apply the clue to find the code (as directed in the question).

QUESTIONS FOR PRACTICE

Directions: *In each of the following questions a coded expression is given. Then another expression is given, the code for which is to be found from*

amongst the four choices suggested below.

1. If COME is coded as BNLD, then CARE will be coded as:

A. BBQD B. BZQD
C. BZPD D. BZSD

2. If HIGH is coded as IJHI, then TURN will be coded as:

A. UVQO B. UVTO
C. UVSO D. UVSP

3. If LOAD is coded as MPBE, then PORT will be coded as:

A. QRSU B. QPRU
C. QPUS D. QPSU

4. If GOLD is coded as IQNF, then WIND will be coded as:

A. YKOF B. YLPF
C. YKPE D. YKPF

5. If SHIRT is coded as RGHQS, then ROUND will be coded as:

A. QNTMC B. QNUMC
C. QNTME D. QNTOC

6. If DEAR is coded as FGCT, then READ will be coded as:

A. FGCF B. TGFC
C. TCGF D. TGCF

7. If EASE is coded as HDVH, then SEE will be coded as:

A. DHH B. VHV
C. VHH D. VVH

8. If SERPENT is coded as TNEPRES, then PLAGUE will be coded as:

A. EUAGLP B. EUGLAP
C. EUGALP D. EULAGP

9. If DEFENCE is coded as CDEDMBD, then NEED will be coded as:

A. MCDC B. MCCD
C. MDDC D. DMMC

10. If CHAIR is coded as FKDLU, then RAID will be coded as:

A. ULGD B. ULKG
C. ULDG D. UDLG

11. If CONDEMN is coded as CNODMEN, then TEACHER will be coded as:

A. TAECHER B. TAEECHR
C. TCAEEHR D. TAECEHR

12. In a code language COME is written as 'XLNV' and ABLE as ZYOV, how would you write MOLLY in that code?

A. NLOBO B. NLBOO
C. LNOOB D. NLOOB

13. If CIGARETTE is coded as GICERAETT, then the word DEMONSTRATION is coded as:

A. MEDNSOARTOITN
B. MEDSNOATROITN
C. MEDSNOARTIOTN
D. MEDSNOARTOITN

14. If CENTURION is coded as 325791465, and RANK is coded as 18510, what will the figures 78510 represent?

A. BANK B. SANK
C. TANK D. TALK

15. In a certain code MAHESH is written as NCIGTJ. In that code NEELAM will be written as:

A. OGGNCO B. OGFNBN
C. OGFNBO D. OGHBNO

16. In a certain code FLOWER is written as SEXOMF. How will garden be written in that code?

A. OEERBH B. OFESBH
C. OEESBG D. OEERBG

17. If in a code SCRIPT is written as TCQIQT, how will DIGEST be written in that code?

A. EIGHTT B. TIHETT
C. EIFETT D. EIFERT

18. If RAM is coded as SBN, then FEW will be coded as:

A. GFX B. GHX
C. EFX D. GEX

19. If RUBBER is coded as REBBUR, then DEAD will be coded as:

A. DEAD B. DAED
C. DADE D. DDEA

20. If KANPUR is coded as LBOQVS, then NAGPUR will be coded as:

A. OHBQVS B. HBOQVS
C. OBHQVS D. BOHQVS

21. If DELHI is coded as IDHEL, then TUFAN will be coded as:

A. TNAUF B. NATUF
C. NTUAF D. NTAUF

22. If ANOTHER is coded as 7309521, then THORN will be coded as:

A. 95103 B. 95313
C. 95013 D. 95113

23. If SURENDRA is coded as DHTNPATI, then UNDER will be coded as:

A. PHANT B. HPANT
C. HPNAT D. HNPAT

24. If EFFICIENT is coded as DEEHBHDMS, then FIET will be coded as:

A. DHES B. EHSD
C. EHDS D. EDHS

25. If FACE is coded as GBDF, then BADE will be coded as:

A. CBEF B. CEBF
C. CFBE D. CBFE

26. If REST is coded as TGUV, then SETS will be coded as:

A. GUVU B. UVGU
C. UGVU D. VGUV

27. If DECADE is coded as 453145, then DEED will be coded as:

A. 5544 B. 4545
C. 4554 D. 4555

28. If BAD is coded as YZW, then MAD will be coded as:

A. MZW B. NZW
C. OZW D. LZW

29. If DIRT is coded as TDIR, then TRIM will be coded as:

A. MRTI B. MIRT
C. MTRI D. MTIR

30. If PIT is coded as QJU, then HUT will be coded as:

A. KXU B. KVU
C. IVU D. GVU

31. If DECEMBER is coded as ERMBCEDE, then NOVEMBER will be coded as:

A. ERBMVENO
B. REMBVENO
C. ERMBVENO
D. EMRBVENO

32. If ROUGH is coded as ORRJE, how will SMOOTH be coded?

A. PPLLOK B. PPLRQK

C. PJLLOK D. PPRRKK

33. If MOTHER is coded as PQWJHT, then SISTER will be coded as:

A. VKUVHT B. VKVVHU

C. VKVVHT D. VKVWHT

34. If LOFTY is coded as LPFUY, then DWARF will be coded as:

A. DXASF B. DXBSG

C. DXATF D. DWBSG

35. If PRICE is coded as SVNIL, then COST will be coded as:

A. FSXY B. FSWY

C. FTWZ D. FSXZ

36. If JAILAPPAS is coded as AIJAPLASP, then ECONOMICS will be coded as:

A. COEMONCSI

B. COEOMNCSI

C. OECMONSCI

D. COEMONCSI

37. If in a certain code CLOCK is written as KCOLC, then STEPS will be written as:

A. SPEST B. SPSET

C. SEPST D. SPETS

38. If in a certain code SPIDER is written as PSDIRE, then COMMON will be written as:

A. OCMMON B. OCMOMN

C. OCMMNO D. OCOMMO

39. In a certain code RECOMMENDATION is written as COMMENDATIONER, then REMUNERATION will be written as:

A. MUNERATION

B. MUNERATIONRE

C. MUNERATIONER

D. MUNERATIOENR

40. If in a certain code TRIPPLE is written as SQHOOKD, then DISPOSE will be written as:

A. CHRONRD B. CHROORD

C. CHROMRD D. CHROMSD

QUESTIONS BASED ON RELATIONSHIP

In these questions, one is required to find out relationship between/among persons such as whose father is A, who is A's father, or what is the relationship between A and B etc. These questions are not very difficult but somewhat involoved.

We shall take some examples to explain how to solve such questions.

Example 1. A is father of both B and C. B is not the brother of C. What relationship exists between B and C?

Solution: When both B and C are children of A, and B is not the brother of C, then only possible relationship between B and C is that one of them is the sister of the other.

Example 2. C is nephew of B. A is husband of B. How is A related to C?

Solution: C is nephew of B. A and B are husband and wife. Therefore, C must be nephew of both A and B.

∴ C is nephew of A too.

And, A is uncle of C.

QUESTIONS FOR PRACTICE

1. Ajit is brother of grandson of Mohan. What is Ajit in relation to Mohan?

A. grandfather B. grandson
C. son D. nephew

2. B is A's son. B is my son's uncle. Then A is my:

A. uncle B. grandfather
C. father D. brother

3. F is A's brother; C is A's daughter; K is F's sister and G is C's brother. Who is uncle of G?

A. A B. C
C. K D. F

4. The brother-in-law of the nephew of my wife will be my:

A. son-in-law B. nephew
C. cousin D. brother-in-law

5. Ramesh is Bihari's brother. Indira is Ramesh's wife and her son Devendra is brother of Yogendra. Bihari is Yogendra's:

A. father B. uncle
C. brother D. maternal uncle

6. Both A and B are C's children. C is A's father but B is not C's son. Then B is C's:

A. brother B. sister
C. daughter D. son

7. My maternal uncle is A and his son is B. C is B's son. Then I am C's:

A. grandfather B. uncle
C. brother D. nephew

8. Ram Bihari had three sons–Ram, Pratap and Kripa. Vijai is Ram's son and Veena is Pratap's daughter. Then Vijai is Veena's:

A. uncle B. cousin brother
C. nephew

9. K is P's sister's daughter. S is K's son. Then P is S's:

A. maternal uncle
B. maternal grandfather
C. father's sister's husband
D. grandfather

10. A is C's father. B is C's wife. Then A is B's:

A. husband's elder brother
B. husband's younger brother
C. father-in-law
D. son

QUESTIONS RELATED TO DIRECTIONS

These questions are related to directions. They are easy for solutions. Students are advised to pin-point on a piece of paper the starting-point. Then they should draw lines as directed (indicated) in the question. Thus, they will have a diagram (figure) of the movement. It will thus be easy to find the direction from the starting-point.

Example. Ramesh starts from his house and goes to the east. After covering 4 km, he turns to right and covers 2 km. Then he turns to right again and covers 4 km. In which direction now Ramesh is from his house?

Solution:

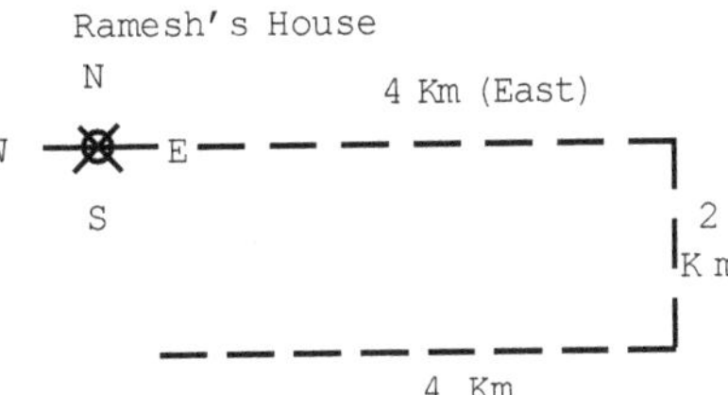

The above diagram indicates that he is now in the south from his house.

QUESTIONS FOR PRACTICE

1. Deepa starts from her house and goes 1 km towards north; then she turns to right and walks 1 km. She turns again to right and walks 1 km to reach her school. In which direction from her house is her school situated?

A. North B. East
C. South D. West

2. My house is situated to the east of your house. My friend's house is situated to the south-east of your house. To which direction should I go to reach my friend's house through the shortest route?

A. South B. South-West
C. South-East D. West

3. A person starts walking towards north. After sometime he turns to right and after walking some distance he turns to left. Then after walking the distance of 1 km, he turns again to left. To which direction is he walking now?

A. North B. East
C. South D. West

4. A person goes 200 m towards west from his house. Then he goes 500 m towards south. To which direction should he now walk for returning to the place from where he started his journey?

A. North-East B. North
C. South-East D. North-West

5. A person went towards west from his house and covered a distance of 5 km. Then he turned to left and covered 5 km. He, then, turned to right and covered 9 km. And finally he covered 5 km towards north. In which direction is he now from his starting-point?

A. South-West B. South
C. West D. East

6. A police van drove 5 km towards the east. Then it turned to right and travelled 3 km. After that it turned towards the west and covered a distance of 1 km. How many kms away is the van from its starting point?

A. 3 km B. 4 km
C. 5 km D. 6 km

7. Standing at the door of a room a policeman saw a wall-clock on the wall facing him, a sofa set near the wall on his right and a TV set near the wall on his left. He also saw rays on his left. He also saw rays of the setting sun falling on the wall-clock. The sofa set was near the:

A. eastern wall
B. western wall
C. northern wall
D. southern wall

8. On a straight road a police van chased a car upto 4 km towards the east. The car turned to right and was chased by the police van for 2 km. The car again turned to right and was caught by the police van after a 2 km chase. In which direction was the police van now from its starting point?

A. North-East B. North-West
C. South-East D. South-West

9. Dara is to the east of Vorli at a distance of 10 km. Towards the north is Madu situated at a distance of about 7 km from the above mentioned two places. A police van on patrol duty was proceeding towards Vorli from Dara. While on midway it was instructed to intercept a car that was speeding away from Dara to Madu. To which direction thte patrol van turn to intercept the speeding car?

A. East B. West
C. North D. South

10. A person travelled 12 km towards the north. Then he turned to left and travelled 5 km. How many kms is he away from his starting-point?

A. 14 km B. 13 km
C. 12 km D. 13.5 km

11. Shyam starts from his house and goes 5 km towards the east. He then turns to right and covers a distance of 5 km. He again turns to right and covers a distance of 5 km. In which direction is he now from his house?

A. East B. West
C. North D. South

12. A person started from his house and travelled 1 km towards the north. Then he turned to right and travelled 2 km. He again turned to right and travelled 1 km. How far is he from his house?

A. 1 km B. 2 km
C. 3 km D. 4 km

13. Ramesh starts from his house and goes 4 km towards the east. Then he turns to left and goes 3 km. He further turns to right and goes 1 km. He, then turns to left and goes 2 km and again turns to left and goes 5 km. In which direction is he now from his house?

A. East B. West
C. North D. South

ARRANGING THE LETTERS TO MAKE MEANINGFUL WORDS

In these questions, some letters are given in a haphazard manner. The students are required to rearrange those letters to make a meaningful word.

Example. Arrange the letters KOBO in such a way as to make a meaningful word.

Solution: These letters may be arranged in various forms such as KOOB, KBOO, OBOK, OKBO, BOKO and BOOK. Of these only BOOK is a meaningful word. Therefore, it is the correct answer.

In some questions, a particular direction may be included, such as arrange the letters in such a way as to make the name of an animal, fruit, vehicle, city, etc.

Example. Arrange the letters EORHS to make the name of an animal.

Solution: When arranged in right order, it will be HORSE.

QUESTIONS FOR PRACTICE

1. Arrange the letters EBUL in such a way as to make the name of a colour.

2. Arrange the letters CINHOC in such a way as to make the name of a city.

3. Arrange the letters UDUR in such a way as to make the name of an Indian language.

4. Arrange the letters NIOR in such a way as to make the name of a metal.

5. Arrange the letters CEAOCPK in such a way as to make the name of a bird.

6. Arrange the letters MANRADA in such a way as to make the name of a river.

7. Arrange the letters RHATE in such a way as to make the name of a planet.

8. Arrange the letters NIPELC in such a way as to make the name of an item of stationery.

9. Arrange the letters IRTEG in such a way as to make the name of a wild animal.

10. Arrange the letters COHYKE in such a way as to make the name of a sport.

11. Arrange the letters RISHT in such a way as to make the name of a wear.

12. Arrange the letters GNMAO in such a way as to make the name of a fruit.

13. Arrange the letters IERC in such a way as to make the name of a foodgrain.

14. Arrange the letters RAGA in such a way as to make the name of a city.

15. Arrange the letters AIRHC in such a way as to make the name of an item of furniture.

16. Arrange the letters NADH in such a way as to make the name of a part of human body.

17. Arrange the letters GIRN in such a way as to make the name of an ornament.

18. Arrange the letters LITMA in such a way as to make the name of the language of a State in India.

19. Arrange the letters MENE in such a way as to make the name of tree.

20. Arrange the letters IRATN in such a way as to make the name of a vehicle (transport).

21. Arrange the letters APUBJN in such a way as to make the name of a State in India.

22. Arrange the letters TCKEICR in such a way as to make the name of a sport.

23. Arrange the letters TERLPO in such a way as to make the name of a fuel.

24. Arrange the letters RIGOUT in such a way as to make the name of a musical instrument.

25. Arrange the letters BYBA in such a way as to make the name of a word representing infants.

26. Arrange the letters DEKYIN in such a way as to make the name of a part of body.

27. Arrange the letters UGOENT in such a way as to make the name of a part of the mouth.

28. Arrange the letters NKODYE in such a way as to make the name of an animal.

29. Arrange the letters ARINHSK in such a way as to make the name of a river.

30. Arrange the letters IDASLAK in such a way as to make the name of a classical Sanskrit poet.

31. Arrange the letters HAIKS in such a way as to make the name of a place of pilgrimage.

32. Arrange the letters RAISP in such a way as to make the name of capital of an European country.

33. Arrange the letters ROPEPC in such a way as to make the name of a metal.

34. Arrange the letters PRAEG in such a way as to make the name of a fruit.

35. Arrange the letters ARNAYMA in such a way as to make the name of an Indian epic.

36. Arrange the letters BRAAK in such a way as to make the name of a Mughal ruler of India.

37. Arrange the letters ABMUR in such a way as to make the name of a neighbour country of India.

38. Arrange the letters TACWH in such a way as to make the name of a machine that tells time.

39. Arrange the letters JNALRIB in such a way as to make the name of a vegetable.

40. Arrange the letters GOEYNX in such a way as to make the name of a gas.

ARRANGING WORDS IN THEIR NATURAL ORDER

In these questions, some words are given. They are to be arranged in their natural order. The arrangement may be, as required in the ascending order, descending order or alphabetical order (as used in dictionary). Sometimes the arrangement has to be made in such order as the things, activities happen in nature or in one's life, *i.e.*, brushing the teeth, breakfast, bath, lunch.

We shall have some examples.

Example 1. Which one of the following words will come in the first place if they are arranged in the manner as in a dictionary.

CAT, CAME, CAR, CAN

A. CAT B. CAN

C. CAME D. CAR

Solution: If arranged as required these words (given in the above example) will appear in the following order:

CAME, CAN, CAR, CAT.

Example 2. Which one of the following will come at the end in the natural order:

A. Printing B. Book
C. Binding D. Paper

In the natural order these items will appear as: Paper, Printing, Binding and Book.

QUESTIONS FOR PRACTICE

1. Which one is the smallest?

A. Lane B. Caste
C. Family D. Town

2. Which one of the followoing came into existence before others?

A. Caste B. Community
C. Family D. Clan

3. Which one of the following came into existence first?

A. Wood B. Chair
C. Seed D. Tree

4. Which one will come first in the natural order?

A. Shirt B. Stitching
C. Cloth D. Cutting

5. Which one will come first in the natural order?

A. Sugar B. *Khand*
C. Jaggery D. Sugarcane

6. Which one of the following will come last in the ascending order?

A. Adolscence B. Adulthood
C. Old age D. Childhood

7. Which will come in the third place from the top?

A. Eyes B. Waist
C. Knees D. Legs

8. Which one of the following will come first in the regular order?

A. College B. University
C. School D. Nursery

9. Which one of the following is the first vital requirement for life?

A. Food B. Water
C. Vitamins D. Air

10. The first thing while crossing the road is:

A. look around B. stop
C. go D. speed up

MISCELLANEOUS

1. Vipin is taller than Ram Lal. Ram Lal is not as tall as Ahmad. Mahendra is taller than Sheikh, but not as tall as Ram Lal. Ahmad is not as tall as Vipin is. Who is the shortest among them?

A. Vipin B. Ahmad
C. Ram Lal D. Sheikh
E. Mahendra

2. School is situated to the west of the hospital which is south to the police post. The court is to the north of the school. If the four places are at the equal distance from each other, the police post is situated to the:

A. East of the court

B. West of the court

C. North of the court

D. South of the court

3. Roads from the north, south, east and west directions meet near a police post. A constable coming on the road from the east finds that the road in front of him leads to a park and the road towards his right leads to the railway station and none of those roads lead to the police post. For reaching the police post, to which direction should the policeman turn?

A. East B. West

C. North D. South

4. While standing at the bus stop in the morning I saw a policeman riding a cycle on the other side of the road. With his left hand he was protecting his face from the sun rays and his right hand was towards me. In which direction from the policeman was I standing?

A. East B. West

C. North D. South

Directions (Qs. 5-7): *Six students A, B, C, D, E and F are sitting in a park. A and B belong to Nehru House while the rest belong to Gandhi House. D and F are tallish while the others are short-sized. A, C and D put on spectacles but others do not. On the basis of the above information, answer questions 5 to 7.*

5. Two short-sized students who do not put an spectacles are:

A. A and F B. C and E

C. B and E D. E and F

6. The tallish Gandhi House student who does not put on spectacles is:

A. B B. C

C. E D. F

7. The short-sized Gandhi House student who does not put on spectacles is:

A. B B. F

C. E D. A

8. Some boys are standing in a row. Kamal is sixth from the left and Appu is fourth from the right. When Kamal and Appu exchange their places, Appu becomes 17th from the right. What will be the position of Kamal from the left?

A. 20th B. 19th

C. 21st D. 4th

9. In the letters of English alphabet from A to Z are written in reverse order, *i.e.*, ZYX.....CBA, the 8th letter to the right of the 10th letter from the left will be:

A. Y B. I

C. J D. X

Directions: *Read carefully the following statements and then answer questions 10 to 12.*

Ramesh, Mohan and Edward play cricket.

Mohan, Rahman and Edward play hockey.

Rahman, Ramesh and Mohan play volleyball.

10. Who plays all the three sports?

A. Ramesh B. Mohan

C. Edward D. Rahman

11. Who plays cricket and volleyball but does not play hockey?

A. Ramesh B. Mohan

C. Edward D. Rahman

12. Who plays hockey and volleyball but does not play cricket?

A. Ramesh B. Mohan

C. Edward D. Rahman

Directions: *A cube is painted red on all sides and then it is cut into 64 small cubes of equal sizes.*

Based on the above given information, answer questions 13 and 14.

13. How many small cubes have only one side painted?

A. 4 B. 8

C. 16 D. 24

14. How many small cubes are such as to have none of their sides painted?

A. 8 B. 6

C. 4 D. 1

15. Five boys were climbing a hillock. Hari was ahead of all of them. Ram was ahead of Govind. Krishna was behind Hari and in between Jayant and Ram. All of them were climbing up in a column. Who was in the second position?

A. Jayant B. Hari

C. Ram D. Govind

E. Krishna

16. Of the six towns, Dhulia is bigger than Alamner and Sri Rampur is bigger than Nasik; Jalgaon is not equal to Sri Rampur but bigger than Alamner. Alamner is smaller than Nasik but bigger than Manmad. The smallest of them is:

A. Alamner B. Nasik

C. Jalgaon D. Manmad

E. Sri Rampur

17. Geeta is more beautiful than Rupa but not as beautiful as Neeta.

Choose the correct statement in the light of the above statements.

A. Rupa is more beautiful than Neeta

B. Neeta is more beautiful than Rupa

C. Neeta is not more beautiful than Geeta

D. None of the above statements is correct

18. All the faces of a cube are painted with different colours. Red and blue colours are on the opposite faces while the blue colour is in between the yellow and green colours. The colour on the face opposite the green colour is:

A. Red B. Blue

C. Yellow D. Violet

19. I was alone in the park. After a short while an old man and an old woman came there. They were followed by two couples, each of which was accompanied with a child. Now how many persons were there in the park?

A. 8 B. 9

C. 10 D. 11

20. Sitting on a bench are Girija, Ishan, Francis and Hema. Hema is to the left of Francis. Ishan is flanked by Francis and Girija. Who is at the extreme right?

A. Girija B. Hema
C. Ishan D. Francis

21. Shyam is elder than Pradip. Pravin is of same age as Anjan. Amrit is younger than Suresh and Suresh is of the same age as Anjan. Pradip is elder than Pravin. Who among them is the eldest?

A. Pradip B. Pravin
C. Suresh D. Shyam

Directions: *A toy cube has pictures of different fruits on its six faces. The top face has the picture of orange. Banana is adjacent to melon and orange. Apple is not at the bottom of the cube and melon is opposite the peace.*

Answer questions 22, 23 and 24 on the basis of the above information.

22. The neighbouring faces of the sixth fruit mango, do not have the picture of:

A. Apple B. Orange
C. Peach D. Banana

23. Which fruit is opposite the face having the picture of apple?

A. Banana B. Peach
C. Orange D. Mango

24. Which one of the following does not represent the correct pair of fruits on the opposite faces?

A. Orange-Mango
B. Apple-Banana
C. Apple-Mango
D. All the above

25. Manisha is the 11th from either end of the row of girls. How many girls are there in that row?

A. 19 B. 10
C. 21 D. 22
E. 23

26. Is it possible to make a meaningful word with the second, fourth, sixth, seventh, eighth and ninth letters of the word 'LEUTENANT'. If so, write the first letter of the word thus formed.

A. T B. E
C. N D. A
E. X

27. A is 3 years elder than B and 3 years younger than C; B and D are twins. How many years elder is C than D?

A. 3 B. 6
C. 2 D. equal in age
E. 12

DETAILED ANSWERS

SERIES

1. B: Multiply the number by 2 and add one to the product to obtain the subsequent number.

2. A: The numbers are 2^2, 3^2, 4^2 and 5^2 respectively. Therefore, the next number will be $6^2 = 36$.

3. C: Add 12 to each number to obtain the subsequent number.

4. C: The numbers are divided by 2 to obtain the subsequent number.

5. C: Two letters are skipped from the beginning (A, D, G) of the alphabets in the first units and two letters are skipped from the end (Z, W, T) of the alphabet in the second units respectively.

6. D: Skip two letters respectively from the beginning of the alphabets.

7. A: The letters in the series are first letter of the alphabet from the end, first letter of the alphabet from the beginning, the second letter of the alphabet from the end and the second letter of alphabet from the beginning respectively. Proceed further on the same pattern.

8. C: $3 + 2 = 5; 5^2 = 25$ and $3 + 4 = 7; 7^2 = 49$. Similarly $2 + 3 = 5; 5^2 = 25$.

9. C: Subsequent numbers are obtained by doubling the number.

10. D: Subsequent numbers are obtained by subtracting 5, 4, 3, etc. from the numbers respectively.

11. 24: Subsequent numbers have been obtained by subtracting 13 from the numbers.
$76 - 13 = 63; 63 - 13 = 50; 50 - 13 = 37$.
$\therefore$ Next number $= 37 - 13 = 24$.

12. 37: The numbers in the series are $2^1 + 1, 3^2 + 1, 4^2 + 1$ and $5^2 + 1$. Therefore, the next number will be $6^2 + 1 = 37$.

13. 30: The numbers in the series are $2^2 - 2, 3^2 - 3, 4^2 - 4, 5^2 - 5$. Therefore, the next number will be $6^2 - 6 = 30$.

14. 15: The numbers in the series increase by 3 at each step. $3 + 3 = 6; 6 + 3 = 9; 9 + 3 = 12$. Therefore, the next number will be $12 + 3 = 15$.

15. 17: The numbers in the series are consecutive prime numbers 3, 7, 11 and 13. Therefore, the next prime number will be 17.

16. 25: The numbers in the series are $1^2, 2^2, 3^2, 4^2$. Therefore, the next number will be $5^2 = 25$.

17. 24: The numbers in the series are $1^2 - 1; 2^2 - 1; 3^2 - 1$ and $4^2 - 1$. Therefore, the next number will be $5^2 - 1 = 24$.

18. 48: Multiply each number by 2 to find the next number. Therefore, the next number in the series will be $24 \times 2 = 48$.

19. 19: 3, 4 and 5 have been added respectively to find the next numbers in the series. Therefore, $13 + 6 = 19$ will be the next number.

20. 15: 2, 3 and 4 have been added respectively to find the next numbers in the series. Therefore, $10 + 5 = 15$ will be the next number.

21. 161: Multiply the number by 3 and then add 2 to the product to find the next number. Therefore, $53 \times 3 + 2 = 161$ will be the next number in the series.

22. 35: The numbers in the series are $2^2 - 1$, $3^2 - 1$, $4^2 - 1$ and $5^2 - 1$. Therefore, the next number will be $6^2 - 1 = 35$.

23. 7: The numbers in the series are reduced by 6, 5, 4 respectively to find the next numbers. Therefore, the next number will be 10 – 3 = 7.

24. 63: The numbers in the series are doubled and then 1 is added to the product to obtain the next numbers. Therefore, the next number will be 31 x 2 = 62 + 1 = 63.

25. 5: The numbers are reduced to half to get the next numbers. Therefore, the next number will be 10 ÷ 2 = 5.

26. 21: Add 5 to each number to find the subsequent number. Therefore, 16 + 5 = 21.

27. 31: Subtract 7 from each number to find the subsequent number. Therefore, 38 – 7 = 31.

28. 47: Double the number and then add 1 to the product to obtain the next number. Therefore, 23 x 2 + 1 = 47.

29. 29: The numbers in the series are consecutive prime numbers. The next prime number will be 29.

30. 53: Add 10 to obtain each subsequent number. Therefore, the next number will be 43 + 10 = 53.

31. 46: Multiply the number by 2 and then add 2 to the product to obtain the next number. Therefore, the required number will be 22 x 2 + 2 = 46.

32. 25: The number in the series are 1^2, 2^2, 3^2 and 4^2.
∴ The next number will be $5^2 = 25$.

33. 6: The numbers in the series have been divided by 2 to obtain the next number. Therefore, the next number will be 12 ÷ 2 = 6.

34. 11: Alternate numbers are reduced by 1.
For example 14, 13, 12 ...(*i*)
and 10, 9, 8 ...(*ii*)
The next number will be in series (*i*) above.
∴ The required number will be 12 – 1 = 11.

35. 74: In this question, the relationship among the numbers of the series is as under:

(*i*) add 3 to get the second number.
(*ii*) double the second number to get the third number.
(*iii*) again add 3 to get the 4th number.
(*iv*) again double the 4th number to get the 5th number.
(*v*) again add 3 to get the 6th number.

∴ Double the 6th number (37) to get the 7th number, 37 x 2 = 74.

36. 7: In this series, divide the first number by 2 to get the second number; now add 4 to the second number to get the third number. This pattern is repeated.

$\therefore$ $32 \div 2 = 16$; $16 + 4 = 20$; $20 \div 2 = 10$; $10 + 4 = 14$;

Now divide 14 by 2. You get 7. This is your answer.

37. 5: There are two series:

(i) 2, 3, 4

(ii) 3, 5, 7

In series *(i)* numbers increase by 1 at each step.

In series *(ii)* numbers increase by 2 at each step.

The next number will be in series *(i)* add 1 to 4 to get 5. This is the required number.

38. 26: Subsequent numbers have been obtained by adding 1, 2, 3, 4 and 5 respectively to the numbers.

$\therefore$ The next number will be $20 + 6 = 26$.

39. 126: The numbers in the series have been obtained by adding 1 to the cubes of 1, 2, 3 and 4 respectively such as $(1^3 + 1) = 2$; $(2^3 + 1) = 9$; $(3^3 + 1) = 28$; $(4^3 + 1) = 65$.

$\therefore$ The next number will be $5^3 + 1 = 126$.

40. 30: The numbers in the series are obtained as under:

$(1^2 - 1) = 0$; $(2^2 - 2) = 2$; $(3^2 - 3) = 6$; $(4^2 - 4) = 12$ and $(5^2 - 5) = 20$.

$\therefore$ The next number will be $(6^2 - 6) = 30$.

41. 37: Subsequent numbers in the series have been obtained by adding 3, 5, 6 and 9 to the given numbers. The numbers added, *i.e.,* 3, 5, 7, 9 are consecutive odd numbers. The next odd number will be 11. Therefore, the next number in the series will be obtained by adding 11 to 26. $26 + 11 = 37$.

42. 41: Subsequent numbers in the series have been obtained by adding 4, 6, 8 and 10 to the given numbers. The numbers added, *i.e.,* 4, 6, 8 and 10 are consecutive even numbers. The next even number is 12. Therefore, the next number in the series will be $29 + 12 = 41$.

43. $\frac{7}{8}$: The numerators and denominators of each fraction in the series have been reduced by 1 to obtain the numerators and denominators of the subsequent fractions in the series. For example, the numerators when reduced by 1 become $11 - 1 = 10$, $10 - 1 = 9$ and $9 - 1 = 8$, and the denominators 11, 10 and 9 when reduced by 1. Now to obtain the next unknown fraction in the series, take the last fraction *i.e.* $\frac{8}{9}$ and reduce both the numerator and the denominator by 1.

$\therefore \frac{8-1}{9-1} = \frac{7}{8}.$

44. 37: In this series the third number, *i.e.*, 9 has been obtained by adding the first number (4) to the second number (5), *i.e.*, 4 + 5 = 9. The fourth number, *i.e.*, 14 has been obtained by adding the second and the third number *i.e.*, 5 + 9 = 14, and so on. Therefore the sixth number in the series may be obtained by adding together the fourth and the fifth numbers, *i.e.*, 14 + 23 = 37.

45. 65: In this question also the method is the same as applied in Q. No. 44. First number + second number = third number; second number + third number = fourth number; and third number + fourth number = fifth number. To obtain subsequent number, apply same method.

∴ Sixth number will be = fourth number (25) + fifth number (40).

∴ 25 + 40 = 65.

46. 3: In this series, subsequent numbers have been obtained by dividing the numbers by 2, 3 and 4 respectively. Therefore, to obtain the next number, divide the fifth number by 5.

∴ 15 ÷ 5 = 3.

47. 49: The numbers in the series are squares of 2, 3, 4, 5 and 6. Therefore the next number will be square of 7 = 49.

48. 1: There are two series. *(i)* 4, 3, 2 and

(ii) 8, 6, 4

The numbers in *(i)* are reduced by 1 at each step.

Similarly, the numbers in *(ii)* are reduced by 2 at each step.

On the same analogy the next number in *(i)* will be 2 – 1 = 1.

49. 125: The numbers in the series are cubes of 1, 2, 3 and 4 respectively.

∴ The next number in the series will be cube of 5 = 125.

50. 44: In this series, the numbers increase by 4, 8 and 12 respectively.

∴ Add 16 to obtain the next number: 28 + 16 = 44.

51. 26: Subsequent numbers have been obtained by adding 1, 3, 5 and 7 to the numbers. These numbers, *i.e.*, 1, 3, 5 and 7 are consecutive odd numbers. The next odd number is 9.

∴ Add 9 to 17 to obtain the next number in the series.

∴ 17 + 9 = 26.

52. 2: The numbers in the series have been divided by 6, 5 and 4 respectively to obtain the subsequent numbers.

∴ Divide the last number in the series, *i.e.*, 6 by 3 to obtain the next number. ∴ 6 ÷ 3 = 2.

53. 32: Each subsequent number is double of the previous number, as $1 \times 2 = 2$; $2 \times 2 = 4$; $4 \times 2 = 8$ and $8 \times 2 = 16$.
Now multiply 16 by 2 to obtain the next number in the series.
$\therefore 16 \times 2 = 32$.

54. 21: Subsequent numbers in the series increase by 2, 3, 4 and 5. On the same analogy add 6 to the last number to find the next number in the series.
$\therefore 15 + 6 = 21$.

55. 25: The numbers in the series are squares of 0, 1, 2, 3 and 4.
$\therefore$ The next number will be $5^2 = 25$.

56. 10: Subsequent numbers have been obtained by dividing the numbers by 3.
$\therefore$ The next number will be $30 \div 3 = 10$.

57. 49: The numbers in the series are 3^2, 4^2, 5^2 and 6^2 respectively. Therefore, the next number will be $7^2 = 49$.

58. 18: The subsequent numbers have been obtained by adding 3 to each number. Therefore, the next number will be $15 + 3 = 18$.

59. 26: The subsequent numbers are obtained by adding 4, 5, 6. Therefore, the next number will be $19 + 7 = 26$.

60. 63: Double the number and add 1 to obtain the next number. Therefore, the next number will be $31 \times 2 + 1 = 63$.

61. 65: The numbers are reduced by 10, 9, 8 etc. respectively. Therefore, the next number will be $72 - 7 = 65$.

62. 12: There are two series—*(i)* 2, 4, 8 and *(ii)* 3, 6, 12. In both the series the numbers are doubled to obtain the subsequent numbers. Therefore, the next number will be $6 \times 2 = 12$.

63. 64: There are two series—*(i)* 3, 9, 27 and *(ii)* 4, 16, ... In series *(i)* the numbers are multiplied by 3. In series *(ii)* the numbers are multiplied by 4. Therefore, the next number will be $16 \times 4 = 64$.

64. 11: The numbers in the series are reduced by 10, 9, 8 to obtain the next numbers. Therefore, the next number will be $18 - 7 = 11$.

65. 30: Add 7 to each number to obtain subsequent numbers. Therefore, the next number will be $23 + 7 = 30$.

66. 20: The numbers have been reduced by 8, 6, 4 respectively. Hence the next number will be $22 - 2 = 20$.

67. 15: Add 2, 3 and 4 to the numbers respectively to obtain the next number. The next number will be $10 + 5 = 15$.

68. 9: Reduce each number by 19 to get the subsequent number. The next number will be $28 - 19 = 9$.

69. 35: The subsequent numbers have been obtained by adding 2, 4, 8 respectively. Therefore, the next number will be $19 + 16 = 35$.

70. $\frac{3}{4}$: The subsequent numbers have been obtained by dividing the number by 2. $1\frac{1}{2} \div 2 = \frac{3}{4}$.

71. 8: There are two series–*(i)* 2, 4, 6 and *(ii)* 3, 6, 9. In series *(i)* the next number will be 8.

72. 9: There are two series–*(i)* 5, 10, 20 and *(ii)* 36, 18, ... In series *(ii)* the next number will be 9.

73. 17: The numbers in the series are prime numbers. The prime number after 13 will be 17.

74. 32: Each number has been doubled to obtain the next number $16 \times 2 = 32$.

75. 18: Subtract 9 to obtain the next number $27 - 9 = 18$.

76. 25: Add 6 to obtain the next number $19 + 6 = 25$.

77. 25: The numbers in the series are 1^2, 2^2, 3^2 and 4^2. The next number will be $5^2 = 25$.

78. 81: Add 9 to obtain the next number. The next number will be $72 + 9 = 81$.

79. 80: The numbers in the series have been increased by 11, 10 and 9 respectively to obtain the next numbers. Therefore, the next number will be $72 + 8 = 80$.

80. 2: There are two series–*(i)* 20, 10, 5 and *(ii)* 8, 4, ... The next number in series *(ii)* will be 2.

81. 47: Double the number and add 1 to the product to obtain the next number. Therefore, the next number will be $23 \times 2 + 1 = 47$.

82. 94: Double the number and add 2 to the product to obtain the next number. Therefore, the next number will be $46 \times 2 + 2 = 94$.

83. 53: The numbers in the series are prime numbers. The next prime number after 37 will be 53.

84. 18: There are two series–*(i)* 3, 9, 27 and *(ii)* 2, 6, ... In series *(ii)*, the next number will be 18.

85. 21: The next numbers in the series have been obtained by adding 3, 4, 5 etc. Therefore, the next number in the series will be $15 + 6 = 21$.

86. 30: The numbers in the series are $2^2 - 2$; $3^2 - 3$; $4^2 - 4$ and $5^2 - 5$. Therefore, the next number will be $6^2 - 6 = 30$.

87. 125: The numbers in the series are 1^3, 2^3, 3^3, 4^3. Therefore, the next number will be $5^3 = 125$.

88. 1: The numbers in the series are 5^3, 4^3, 3^3, 2^3. Therefore, the next number will be $1^3 = 1$.

89. 100: The numbers in the series are 6^2, 7^2, 8^2 and 9^2. Therefore, the next number will be $10^2 = 100$.

90. 16: The numbers in the series are 8^2, 7^2, 6^2 and 5^2. Therefore, the next number will be $4^2 = 16$.

91. 61: $3^2 + 4^2 = 25$ and $4^2 + 5^2 = 41$. Therefore, $5^2 + 6^2 = 61$.

92. 81: $2 + 3 = 5$; $5^2 = 25$ and $3 + 4 = 7$; $7^2 = 49$. Therefore, $4 + 5 = 9$; $9^2 = 81$.

93. 7: $6^2 - 4^2 = 20$ and $5^2 - 3^2 = 16$. Therefore, $4^2 - 3^2 = 7$.

94. 9: $8 - 6 = 2$; $2^2 = 4$ and $7 - 4 = 3$; $3^2 = 9$. Therefore, $5 - 2 = 3$; $3^2 = 9$.

95. 18: $7 + 9 = 16$; $16 \times 2 = 32$ and $3 + 6 = 9$; $9 \times 2 = 18$. Therefore, $5 + 4 = 9$; $9 \times 2 = 18$.

96. 64: $(3 + 2)^2 = 25$ and $(3 + 4)^2 = 49$. Therefore, $(3 + 5)^2 = 64$.

97. 3: $\frac{9-5}{2} = 2$ and $\frac{25-15}{2} = 5$. Therefore, $\frac{12-6}{2} = 3$.

98. 41: $2^2 + 3^2 = 13$ and $3^2 + 4^2 = 25$. Therefore, $4^2 + 5^2 = 41$.

99. 29: $2^2 + 3^2 = 13$ and $3^2 + 4^2 = 25$. Therefore, $2^2 + 5^2 = 29$.

100. 16: $6 - 3 = 3$; $3^2 = 9$ and $7 - 2 = 5$; $5^2 = 25$. Therefore, $8 - 4 = 4$; $4^2 = 16$.

101. 34: $5^2 + 2^2 = 29$ and $2^2 + 3^2 = 13$. Therefore, $3^2 + 5^2 = 34$.

102. 20: $6^2 - 3^2 = 27$ and $5^2 - 4^2 = 9$. Therefore, $6^2 - 4^2 = 20$.

103. 4: $4 - 2 = 2$; $2^2 = 4$ and $6 - 4 = 2$; $2^2 = 4$. Therefore $5 - 3 = 2$; $2^2 = 4$.

104. 100: $3 + 5 = 8$; $8^2 = 64$ and $2 + 3 = 5$; $5^2 = 25$. Therefore $4 + 6 = 10$; $10^2 = 100$.

105. 18: $1 + 4 = 5$; $5 \times 2 = 10$ and $2 + 5 = 7$; $7 \times 2 = 14$. Therefore, $3 + 6 = 9$; $9 \times 2 = 18$.

106. 120: $3 \times 2 = 60$ and $3 \times 3 = 90$. Therefore, $3 \times 4 = 120$.

107. 13: $5 - 3 = 2$ and $17 - 6 = 11$. Therefore, $18 - 5 = 13$.

108. 54: $4 \times 5 = 20$; $20 \times 3 = 60$ and $2 \times 8 = 16$; $16 \times 3 = 48$. Therefore, $3 \times 6 = 18$; $18 \times 3 = 54$.

109. 3: $9 - 5 = 4$; $\frac{4}{2} = 2$ and $25 - 15 = 10$; $\frac{10}{2} = 5$. Therefore, $12 - 6 = 6$;

$\frac{6}{2} = 3$.

110. 10: $5 + 8 = 13$ and $7 + 9 = 16$. Therefore, $3 + 7 = 10$.

111. $\frac{5}{7}$: Add the numerator and denominators:

$\frac{3}{4} + \frac{5}{6} = \frac{8}{10}$ and $\frac{6}{7} + \frac{2}{3} = \frac{8}{10}$

$\therefore \frac{3}{4} + \frac{2}{3} = \frac{5}{7}$

112. 16: Add the two numbers: $4 + 7 = 11$ and $11 + 4 = 15$. Therefore, $7 + 9 = 16$.

113. 8: Add the numerator to the denominator: $5 + 7 = 12$; and $1 + 10 = 11$. Therefore, $3 + 5 = 8$.

114. 13: Subtract $25 - 12 = 13$ and $9 - 3 = 6$. Therefore, $17 - 4 = 13$.

115. 11: Add the two numbers. $5 + 2 = 7$ and $11 + 2 = 13$. Therefore, $8 + 3 = 11$.

116. EFG: These are two successive letters.

117. UVW: U after X, W, V; V after Y, X, W and W after Z, Y, X.

118. EV: One letter from the beginning and one letter from the end in the same order.

119. EGI: Next successive letters are taken.

120. VT: From the end, the letter just before the letter W, *i.e.,* the letter V, and the letter just before the letter U, *i.e.,* the letter T.

121. EI: Skip three continuous letters in the same order.

122. EFH: One letter is skipped after two letters in their natural sequence.

123. ER: The letters are the first letter and 14th letter; the second letter and the 15th letter; the third letter and 16th letter and so on.

124. EFV: From the beginning, the first two successive letters and one letter from the end.

125. VE: The last letter of the alphabet and the first letter of the alphabet are taken. It is repeated.

126. M: Two letters have been skipped at each step.

127. N: From the end, two letters have been skipped at each step.

128. DWV: One letter from the beginning and two letters from the end have been taken. The same process is repeated.

129. JI: Two successive letters have been transposed. Their order is second-first, fourth-third, sixth-fifth.

130. QPO: From the end, three letters in the reverse order.

FINDING THE WRONG OR SUPERFLUOUS NUMBER

1. 24: It should be 25 as the numbers in the series are 1^2, 2^2, 3^2, 4^2, 5^2 and 6^2.

2. 32: It should be 33 because there are two series—*(i)* 11, 22, 33 and *(ii)* 12, 24, 36.

3. 41: It should be 43 as the numbers increase by 4, 5, 6, 7 and 8 respectively.

4. 37: It should be 36 as the numbers in the series are 10^2, 9^2, 8^2, 7^2, 6^2 and 5^2.

5. 125: It should be 128 as the numbers increase by 9 at each step.

6. 70: It should be 69 as the subsequent numbers are obtained by adding 10, 11, 12 and 13 respectively.

7. 28: It should be 29 as the subsequent numbers are obtained by subtracting 11, 10, 9 and 8 respectively.

8. 10: It should be 12 as the subsequent numbers are obtained by subtracting 3 successively.

9. 12: 12 is superfluous as the numbers are reduced by 2 successively.

10. 17: 17 is superfluous as the numbers increase by 3 successively.

11. 25: 25 is wrong; it should be 27. The numbers are multiplied by 3 to obtain the subsequent number.

12. 19: 19 is superfluous. 5 is added to each number to obtain subsequent number.

13. 24: 24 is superfluous. The numbers in the series are 2^2, 3^2, 4^2, 5^2, 6^2 and 7^2 respectively.

14. 26: 26 is superfluous. The numbers increase by 6 at each step.

15. 7: 7 is superfluous. The numbers increase by 5, 10, 15 and 20 at each step.

16. 7: It should be 8 as the numbers are 1^3, 2^3, 3^3, 4^3 and 5^3.

17. 10: It should be 18 as the numbers decrease by 2, 3, 4, 5 and 6 at each step.

18. 80: It should be 81 as the numbers increase by 9, 10, 11, 12 and 13 respectively.

19. 24: It should be 25 as the numbers are 4^2, 5^2, 6^2, 7^2, 8^2 and 9^2 respectively.

20. 86: It should be 85 as the numbers decrease by 7, 8, 9 and 10 respectively.

21. 32: It should be 33 as the numbers increase by 11 at each step.

22. 121: It should be 125 as the numbers are 6^3, 5^3, 4^3, 3^3 and 2^3 respectively.

23. 35: It should be 36 as the numbers are 2^2, 3^2, 4^2, 5^2, 6^2 and 7^2 respectively.

24. 27: It should be 28 as the subsequent numbers are obtained by subtracting 11 at each step.

25. 70: It should be 69 as the subsequent numbers are obtained by adding 10, 11, 12 and 13 respectively.

26. 52: It should be 53 as the subsequent numbers are obtained by subtracting 9 at each step.

27. 24: It should be 25 as the subsequent numbers are obtained by adding 7 at each step.

28. 9: It should be 8 as the numbers are doubled at each step.

29. 12: It should be 13 as the subsequent numbers increase by 3, 4, 5 and 6 respectively.

30. 20: It should be 19 as there are two series—*(i)* 5, 9, 13 and *(ii)* 7, 13, 20. In series *(ii)*, the numbers increase by 6 at each step.

31. 16: It should be 17 as the subsequent numbers are obtained by adding 1^2, 2^2, 3^2, 4^2 and 5^2 respectively to them.

32. 21: It should be 20 as the numbers are increased by 7 at each step.

33. 48: It should be 54 as the numbers are increased by 12 at each step.

34. 26: It should be 27 as the numbers are 1^3, 2^3, 3^3, 4^3, 5^3 respectively.

35. 28: It should be 30 as the numbers are 6×1; 6×3; 6×5; 6×7; 6×9 respectively.

36. 43: It should be 42 as the subsequent numbers are obtained by subtracting 7 at each step.

37. 65: It should be 69 as the numbers decrease by 11 at each step.

38. 18: It should be 10 as the numbers are $1 + 1^2$; $1 + 2^2$; $1 + 3^2$; $1 + 4^2$ and $1 + 5^2$ respectively.

39. 39: It should be 36 as the number increase by 4, 5, 6, 7 and 8 respectively.

40. 40: It should be 44 as the numbers are reduced by half at each step.

41. 45: It should be 47 as the numbers are increased by 13 at each step.

42. 34: It should be 33 as the numbers are increased by 6 at each step.

43. 12: It should be 11 as the numbers are reduced by 2 at each step.

44. 64: It should be 62 as the numbers are reduced by 10 and 9, 10 and 9 and 10 and 9 respectively.

45. 15: It should be 16 as the numbers increase by 3, 5, 7, 9 and 11 respectively.

ANALOGY

1. C: We get curd from milk: similarly we get ice from water.

2. B: Girl is beautiful (quality): similarly gold is bright.

3. A: In desert we find sand: similarly in sea we find water.

4. A: Beautiful is to ugly (opposite): similarly healthy is to sick (opposite).

5. C: Cheese is made from milk. Similarly sugar is made from sugarcane.

6. C: Daughter is to mother as son is to father.

7. C: Book is made of paper: similarly table is made of wood.

8. B: A group of players is a team: similarly a group of ships is a fleet.

9. D: Kilogram is to weight as metre is to length.

10. B: Lid is to box as cork is to bottle.

11. D: Circle has a circumference as square has a perimeter.

12. A: Advocate knows law as cook knows cookery.

13. C: Wardrobe is meant for clothes: similarly purse is meant for money.

14. D: Temperature indicates level of heat: similarly humidity indicates level of moisture.

15. C: Shakespeare is known for his dramas: similarly Ghalib is known for his *ghazals*.

16. C: Grass is green (colour): similarly sky is blue.

17. C: Monday is a day in a week: similarly January is a month in a year.

18. C: Thermometer measures temperature: similarly barometer measures atmospheric pressure.

19. C: Poverty is to riches (opposite): similarly glory is to shame (opposite).

20. D: Table is to chair (pair): similarly coat is to pant (pair).

21. B: Hand is to elbow (relation): similarly leg is to knee (relation).

22. D: Coal is to black (colour): similarly snow is to white (colour).

23. A: Precaution prevents accident: similarly cleanliness prevents disease.

24. D: January is to April (4th month): similarly Sunday is to Wednesday (4th day).

25. C: Soldier is associated with rifle: similarly writer is associated with pen.

26. D: Plate is an item of crockery: similarly spoon is an item of cultery.

27. A: Night comes after evening: similarly day comes after morning.

28. B: Uncle is to aunt: similarly father is to mother.

29. D: Lotus grows in water: similarly fish lives in water.

30. C: Metre is to length (measure): similarly litre is to volume.

31. C: Heaven is to hell (opposite): similarly drought is to flood.

32. C: Planet revolves round the sun as moon revolves round the earth.

33. B: French is the language of the people of France: similarly Dutch is the language of the people of Holland.

34. B: Colombo is capital of Sri Lanka: similarly Tokyo is capital of Japan.

35. D: Pen writes: similarly carpenters' plane shaves off.

36. D: Thick is to thin (opposite): similarly inferior is to superior.

37. B: Table is made of wood: similarly book is made of paper.

38. D: Fan gives air: similarly bulb gives light.

39. A: Seven is a number (class): similarly green is a colour (class).

40. A: Stage is associated to drama as stadium is associated to sports.

41. A: Mango is a variety of fruit: similarly cobra is a variety of serpent.

42. A: Rain is measured in centimeter: similarly temperature is measured in celsius.

43. A: Lane is a smaller road: similarly town is a smaller city.

44. B: Aspirin cures headache: similarly quinine cures malaria.

45. C: Food satisfies hunger: similarly water satisfies thirst.

46. D: Young one of a cat is kitten: similarly young one of a hen is chicken.

47. A: Banana is one of the fruits: similarly cow is one of the mammals.

48. C: One listens to radio: similarly one views film.

49. B: Money, a medium of exchange: similarly language, a medium of communication.

50. D: Friend is to enemy (opposite): similarly kind is to cruel.

51. B: Train stops at platform: similarly ship stops at harbour.

52. C: 1st April is called Fools Day: similarly 1st May is called Labour Day.

53. B: Clock measures time: similarly rainguage measures rain.

54. A: Lion lives in den: similarly horse lives in stable.

55. D: Book is made up of pages: similarly flower is made up of petals.

56. D: Tea is made from leaves: similarly coffee is made from seeds.

57. C: Horse neighs: similarly donkey brays.

58. B: Garage is the place where car is kept when not in use: similarly hanger is the place where aircraft is kept when not in use.

59. A: Radius is to a circle as spoke is to a wheel.

60. A: Carpenters mends stool: similarly cobbler mends shoes.

61. C: Bus is repaired in the workshop: similarly ship is repaired in the dockyard.

62. B: Ring is put on the finger: similarly tie is put on the neck.

63. B: Needle is used for sewing: similarly brush is used for painting.

64. B: We smell through nose: similarly we taste through tongue.

65. D: Pencil is an item of stationery: similarly chair is an item of furniture.

66. A: Both cat and dog are carnivorous: similarly both cow and goat are harbivorous.

67. D: Both snake and lizard are reptile: similarly both fish and crocodile live in water.

68. C: Honour is to dishonour (opposite) as fame is to infamy.

69. B: Light travels through rays: similarly sound travels through waves.

70. C: In a clock hands tell time: similarly in a thermometer mercury indicates temperature.

71. B: Tractor runs on diesel: similarly scooter runs on petrol.

72. B: Cuckoo cackles: similarly horse neighs.

73. B: Pitch is a term associated with cricket: similarly ring is a term associated with boxing.

74. C: Car runs: similarly snake creeps.

75. A: Urge is to deter (opposite): similarly honest is to dishonest.

76. C: Lion lives in den: similarly bird lives in nest.

77. D: Calf is young one of a cow: similarly lamb is young one of a sheep.

78. B: Obedience is to disobedience (opposite): similarly life is to death.

79. B: Tailor uses cloth to make garments: similarly carpenter uses wood to make furniture.

80. A: Cat kills rat: similarly tiger kills lamb.

81. B: Bakery is the place where bread is prepared: similarly mint is the place where coins are produced.

82. A: Studio is associated with film: similarly shipyard is associated with ship.

83. A: Months make a year: similarly hours make a day.

84. C: Food satisfies hunger: similarly water satisfies thirst.

85. C: Revolver is associated with bullet: similarly bow is associated with arrow.

86. D: Bees give honey: similarly sheep give wool.

FINDING ODD ONE OUT

1. C: In this pair both the items are males while in other pairs one item is male and the other item is female.

2. D: Bird and tree are not related in the same way as coal and mine, water and river and fishes and water.

3. C: Thief and robber are not related to each other as hospital and doctor, court and advocate, and school and teacher are.

4. D: Curd is made from milk, house is made from brick, book is made from paper, but stable is not made from horses.

5. B: Milk is always white, sky is always blue and blood is always red, but leaf may be brown and yellow as well.

6. B: Carrot and radish are not opposite to each other whereas victory and defeat, north and south, and up and down are opposite to each other.

7. D: Tiger lives in den.

8. A: Sky is always blue whereas kite, saree and horse may be of different colours.

9. A: Items in pair A are living beings, whereas items in other pairs are non-living beings.

10. A: Items in pair A are man-made whereas items in all other pairs are nature-made (natural).

11. D: It is not a pair. Others are pairs.

12. D: The two items in the pair are not opposites whereas the two items in other pairs are opposite to each other.

13. D: Paper may be of other colours than white, whereas smoke, heat and cool are essential elements of fire, sun and moonlight respectively.

14. D: Moon is a satellite while others are planets.

15. B: Raisin is a dryfruit while others are fresh fruits.

16. C: Goat is a domestic cattle while others are wild animals.

17. A: Riksha is man driven while others are power driven.

18. A: Tiger is a wild animal while others are draught animals.

19. C: Snake does not have legs while all others have legs.

20. C: Patna is in Bihar while all others are in UP.

21. C: Coin is a general name while all others are names of currencies of various countries.

22. A: Diamond is not a metal while all others are names of metals (minerals).

23. D: Legs, Hands and Ankles are external parts of body, while Lungs are inside the body.

24. D: Steamer, Boat and Ship are means of transport, while Harbour is a place of shelter for ship.

25. B: Lotus is a flower that grows in water. Rose, Dahlia and Jasmin grow on land.

26. C: Protein, Carbohydrates and Vitamins are needed by human body as parts of balanced diet, while copper is not needed.

27. C: Piano, Tabla and Banjo are musical instruments that require the help of hands and fingers in playing, whereas Flute is a wind instrument.

28. D: Metre, Kilometre and Centimetre are units of linear distances whereas Square Kilometre is a unit of area.

29. D: Snake is a reptile, while others are not.

30. D: Snake, Lizard and Crocodile are reptile, whereas Frog is not a reptile.

31. C: Moon is a satellite, whereas others are planets.

32. D: Sketch Map is not an item of stationery. Others are items of stationery.

33. B: India Today is a forgnightly magazine whereas all others are daily newspapers.

34. B: Chanakya was a statesman and not a ruler or king whereas others were kings or rulers.

35. D: Tangent, Arc and Radius are associated with circle. Hypotenuse is related to right-angled triangle.

36. A: Delhi is capital of Delhi (of a country) whereas Patna (Bihar), Mumbai (Maharashtra) and Calcutta (West Bengal) are state capitals.

37. A: Scooter, Car and Bus are engine driven vehicles whereas bicycle is pedal driven.

38. B: Wheat, Ragi and Rice are cereals where Gram is a pulse.

39. C: Iron, Copper and Tin are not alloys whereas steel is an alloy.

40. C: Bile is a fluid secreted by liver and helps in the digestion, whereas Cancer, Hepatitis and Diabetes are names of diseases.

41. D: Soil cannot be used as a source of energy whereas all others can be used as a source of energy.

42. B: All other except B are commercial or cash crops.

43. C: Sugarcane is not a fruit whereas all others are fruits.

44. C: Karachi is not a capital town. All others are capital towns.

45. C: April has 30 days whereas May, March and July have 31 days each.

46. B: Diet is the name of the Japanese Parliament whereas Rouble, Dollar and Taka are currencies of different countries.

47. A: Libra is a constellation, whereas Uranus, Pluto and Neptune are planets.

48. B: Monastery is a building where monks live whereas Temple, Mosque and Church are places of worship.

49. B: Shilling is a currency whereas others are units of measurements.

50. C: Sword is a weapon of offence whereas others are defensive coverings.

51. D: Ganga, Godavari and Krishna, all flow from west to east whereas Narmada flows from east to west.

52. A: Cataract is a disease of eye whereas others are parts of eye.

53. C: Faster indicates speed, whereas all the other three words Bigger, Greater and Larger indicate size.

54. A: Cow, Dog and Horse are domesticated but not the Fox.

55. C: Jackal, Fox and Wolf, all are flesh eaters, but stag does not eat flesh.

56. B: Father, Brother and Sister are blood relations whereas Teacher is not.

57. A: Shore is the land that skirts any large body of water, whereas Sea, River and Pond are large body of water.

58. D: Sorrow is a state of sadness. Other words Moan, Wail and Weep are results of state of sadness.

59. D: Cock is a domestic or farmyard fowl, whereas others are not.

60. D: Lameness is the result of some or other accident or disease whereas Dwarfness, Slenderness and Fatness need not be associated with any accident or disease.

61. C: It is different because son is the only male member among females.

62. C: The word Neck has only one vowel, all other words have two vowels each.

63. D: Pondicherry is a Union Territory whereas others are states of Indian Union.

64. C: Colonel is a rank in the Army whereas the other three are ranks in the Air Force.

65. D: Mridangam is a percussion instrument whereas the other three are string instruments.

66. C: Arabia is the name of a country whereas others are names of continents.

67. D: Crocodile is not a fish, whereas others are names of fish.

68. D: Diagonal is a line that connects one angle to the opposite one, whereas Square, Trapezium and Rectangle are quadrilaterals.

69. D: Monkey does not eat flesh whereas Cat, Dog and Fox eat flesh.

70. D: Penicillin is an antibiotic drug whereas the other three are analgesic (pain reliever).

71. B: The other three grow under the earth.

72. D: Malaria is not an infectious disease, whereas the other three are infectious diseases.

73. B: Office is not a place for living, whereas Bunglow, Hut and House are places for living.

74. A: Fly is an insect, all others are non-living things.

75. A: Root is not visible because it is underground; other parts of a tree are visible.

76. B: Potato grows underground; other vegetables grow under land.

77. B: Crow is a bird; all others are animals.

78. C: Kalidas was a poet; all others are scientists.

79. C: All others except shoes are items of garments.

80. D: Except Mercury all others are gases.

QUESTIONS RELATING TO CLOCKS AND CALENDARS

1	**2**	**3**	**4**	**5**	**6**	**7**	**8**	**9**	**10**
B	B	C	C	A	B	D	A	B	B
11	**12**	**13**	**14**	**15**	**16**	**17**	**18**	**19**	**20**
A	A	A	C	B	A	B	B	C	C

CODING AND DECODING

1. B: The letters just preceding the letters C, O, M and E are B, N, L and D. On the same pattern, the letters just preceding the letters C, A, R and E will be B, Z, Q and D.

Hence CARE will be coded as BZQD.

2. C: The letters succeeding H, I, G and H are I, J, H and I. On the same pattern the letters succeeding T, U, R and N will be U, V, S and O. Therefore, TURN will be coded as UVSO.

3. D: The letters just succeeding L, O, A and D are letters M, P, B and E. On the same pattern, the letter just succeeding P, O, R and T will be Q, P, S and U. Therefore, PORT will be coded as QPSU.

4. D: Skip one letter clockwise at each step to find the coded letters for G, O, L and D. These letters are I, Q, N and F. On the same pattern skip one letter at each step to find the codes for W, I, N and D. You will find such letters Y, K, P and F.
Hence, the code for WIND will be YKPF.

5. A: SHIRT has been coded as RGHQS. You will find that just preceding letters have been used as codes, *i.e.,* R for S, G for S, H for I; Q for R and S for T. On the same pattern, the just preceding letters R, O, U, N and D will make the code. These letters are Q, N, T, M and C.
Therefore, code for ROUND is QNTMC.

6. D: DEAR is coded as FGCT. It means one letter has been skipped at each step to find the code letters, *i.e.,* F for D, G for E, C for A and T for R. On the same pattern, skip one letter at each step to find the code for R, E, A and D. These letters will be T, G, C and F.
Therefore, code for READ will be TGCF.

7. C: You will find that two letters have been skipped to find the codes for E, A, S and E. The coded letters are H, D, V and H. On the same pattern skip two letters at each step to find the codes for S, E and E. Code for S will be V, and code for E will be H.
Therefore, code for SEE will be VHH.

8. C: The letters have been written in reverse order as is evident from SERPENT and TNEPRES. On the same pattern, letters of PLAGUE will be written in reverse order to find the code. PLAGUE written in reverse order will be EUGALP.

9. C: The letters just preceding the letters D, E, F, E, N, C and E are C, D, E, F, M, B and D. On the same pattern, the letters just preceding the letters N, E, E and D will be M, D, D and C.
Therefore, code for NEED will be MDDC.

10. D: CHAIR has been coded as FKDLU. It shows that two letters have been skipped clockwise at each step to find the code letters F for C, K for H, D for A, L for I and U for R. On the same pattern, skip two letters to find the code for R, A, I and D. These letters will be U, D, L and G.
Therefore, code for RAID will be UDLG.

11. D: A close look will reveal that letters have exchanged their places to make the coded expression. Your will find that the second and the third letters have exchanged their places; similarly the fifth and the sixth letters have exchanged their places. On the same pattern, in finding out the code for TEACHER, exchange the position of the second and the third letters, *i.e.,* make them AE instead of EA; also exchange the position of the fifth and the sixth letters, *i.e.,* make them EH instead of HE.

Thus the code for TEACHER will be TAECEHR.

12. D: COME = XLNV

[C = 3rd alphabet from the beginning
X = 3rd alphabet from the end

[O = 15th alphabet from the beginning
L = 15th alphabet from the end

[M = 13th alphabet from the beginning
N = 13th alphabet from the end

[E = 5th alphabet from the beginning
V = 5th alphabet from the end

Similarly, A, B, L and E are 1st, 2nd, 12th and 5th alphabets from the beginning and Z, Y, O and V are the 1st, 2nd, 12th and 15th alphabets from the end.

Therefore, on the same pattern M, O, L, L, Y will be coded as NLOOB.

13. D: CIG ARE TTE. Make groups of three alphabets each from the left. Write letters in each group in reverse order, and you will get GIC ERA ETT. On the same pattern, make groups of three alphabets each in DEM ONS TRA TION.

Write letters in each group in reverse order as under MED SNO ART OIT N.

14. C:

8		3		2				4		10		
A	B	C	D	E	F	G	H	I	J	K	L	M
5, 5	6	5		1, 1		7	9					
N	O	P	Q	R	S	T	U	V	W	X	Y	Z

CENTURION = 325791465]
RANK = 18510] Mark the position assigned in the alphabets above.

It means 7 = T
8 = A
5 = N
10 = K, ∴ 78510 = TANK

15. C: The first, third and fifth letters, *i.e.,* M, H and S are replaced by letters just following them, *i.e.,* N, I and T. Similarly, the second, fourth and sixth letters, *i.e.,* A, E and H are replaced by letters obtained by skipping one letter at each step, *i.e.,* C, G and J.
Therefore NEELAM, the first, third and fifth letters, *i.e.,* N, E and A will be replaced by letters just following them, *i.e.,* O, F and B; while the 2nd, 4th and 6th letters, *i.e.,* E, L and M will be replaced by letters obtained by skipping one letter at each step, *i.e.,* G, N and O.
Thus NEELAM will be OGFNBO.

16. D: In FLOWER and SEXOMF, you will find that the second, fourth and sixth letters in F L O W E R are replaced by letters just following these letters, *i.e.,* M, X and S written in reverse order that is S, X and M. The order of the other three letters, *i.e.,* F, O and E is also reversed to make it E, O and F.
Now in G A R D E N, the 2nd, 4th and 6th letters will be placed by letters just following these letters, *i.e.,* B, E and O, but in reverse order, *i.e.,* O, E and B. The other three letters, *i.e.,* G, R and E will also be written in the reverse order.
Thus GARDEN will be OEERBG.

17. C: Compare SCRIPT and TCQIQT. You will find that the 2nd, 4th and 6th letters remain unchanged. The other three letters, *i.e.,* 1st, 3rd and 5th (S, R and P) have changed to T, Q and Q. Here you will notice that T is the letter just following letter S in the alphabet, Q is the letter just preceding letter R in the alphabet and Q is the letter just following letter P in the alphabet.
Now in DIGEST, the 2nd, 4th and 6th letters, *i.e.,* I, E and T will remain unchanged. The first, third and fifth letters, *i.e.,* D, G and S will change to the just following letter E, just preceding letter F and just following letter T.
Thus DIGEST will be coded as EIFETT.

18. A: Compare RAM and SBN. You will find that letter just following in the alphabet have been taken in code. S for R, B for A and N for M are just on the above pattern.
Now for FEW, take the letters just following these letters in the alphabets, *i.e.,* G for F, F for E and X for W.
∴ FEW will be coded as GFX.

19. B: Compare RUBBER and REBBUR. You will find that the letters in RUBBER have been written in just reverse order as REBBUR.
On the same pattern, to find the code for DEAD, write these letters in reverse order as DAED.

20. C: You will find that the letters as coded (LBOQVS) are the letters just following the letters KANPUR.
On the same pattern, the letters just following the letters N, A, G, P, U and R will be O, B, H, Q, V and S.
Therefore NAGPUR = OBHQVS.

21. D: Compare DELHI with IDHEL. You will find that the same letters have been arranged in a different order. The order is last, first, last but one, second and then the third letter at the end.
On the same pattern, change the order of the letters in TUFAN. It will become NTAUF.

22. C: ANOTHER is coded as 7309521

	7	3	0	9	5	2	1
∴	A	N	O	T	H	E	R

∴ THORN = 95013.

23. B: Surendra is coded as DHTNPATI

	↑	↑	↑	↑	↑		
S	U	R	E	N	D	R	A
D	H	T	N	P	A	T	I

∴ UNDER = HPANT

24. C: Compare EFFICIENT with DEEHBHDMS.

E	F	F	I	C	I	E	N	T
D	E	E	H	B	H	D	M	S

∴ FIET = EHDS.

25. A: G, B, D and F are letters just following the letters FACE. On the same pattern, B, A, D, E will be coded as (just the following letters *i.e.*) C, B, E, F. Therefore, BADE will be coded as CBEF.

26. C: All the letters of SETS are contained in REST
REST = TGUV
∴ SETS = UGVU

27. D: DECADE = 453145

D	E	C	A	D	E
4	5	3	1	4	5

∴ DEED = 4554.

28. B: AD is common to BAD and MAD. So it will be coded as ZW. Now B is the 2nd alphabet from the beginning and Y is the 2nd alphabet from the end. On the same pattern, M in MAD is the 13th alphabet from the beginning; it will be coded by the 13th alphabet from the end, *i.e.*, N.
∴ MAD will be coded as NZW.

29. C: DIRT is coded as TDIR. You will find that the same alphabets appear

in the coded expression but the order of the alphabets is changed. The pattern of change in the order of the alphabets is:
The first becomes the second,
The second becomes the third,
The third becomes the fourth, and
The fourth becomes the first.
Now, change the order of alphabets in TRIM as shown above.
Thus TRIM will be MTRI.

30. C: PIT is coded as QJU. You will find that the letters just following PIT are QJU. On the same pattern the letters just following HUT will be IVU.

31. C: DE CE MB ER = ER MB CE DE

∴ NO VE MB ER = ER MB VE NO

32. B: ROUGH is coded as ORRJE. You will find that alternately 2 letters are skipped backward and forward to find the letters in the code.
R = O (2 letters skipped backward)
O = R (2 letters skipped forward)
U = R (2 letters skipped backward)
G = J (2 letters skipped forward)
H = E (2 letters skipped backward)
On the same pattern, the code for SMOOTH will be PPLRQK.

33. C: MOTHER is coded as PQWJHT. You will find that alternately 2, 1, 2, 1, 2 letters are skipped forward in writing the coded letters, as:
M = P (2 letters NO skipped)
O = Q (1 letter P skipped)
T = W (2 letters UV skipped)
H = J (1 letter I skipped), and so on.
On the same pattern
S = V (2 letters TU skipped)
I = K (1 letter J skipped)
S = V (2 letters TU skipped)
T = V (1 letter U skipped)
E = H (2 letters FG skipped)
R = T (1 letter S skipped)
SISTER = VKVVHT

34. A: LOFTY = LPFUY. You will find that the first, third and fifth letters remain unchanged, while the second and the fourth letters are replacd by the next letters in the alphabets, *i.e.,* P for O and U for T.

On the same pattern in DWARF, the first, third and fifth letters will remain unchanged. The second and the fourth letters, *i.e.,* W and R will be replacd by the just following letters, *i.e.,* X and S.

Thus D W A R F

– X – S –

∴ DXASF.

35. D: PRICE = SVNIL.

You will find that 2, 3, 4, 5 and 6 letters are skipped in writing the code.

P = S (2 letters, *i.e.,* QR are skipped)

R = V (3 letters, *i.e.,* STU are skipped)

I = N (4 letters, *i.e.,* JKLM are skipped)

C = I (5 letters, *i.e.,* DEFGH are skipped)

E = L (6 letters, *i.e.,* FGHIJK are skipped)

On the same pattern, to find the code for COST, skip 2, 3, 4 and 5 letters.

C = F (2 letters DE skipped)

O = S (3 letters PQR skipped)

S = X (4 letters TUVWskipped)

T = Z (5 letters UVWXY skipped)

∴ COST = FSXZ

36. B: The letters in JAILAPPAS are divided into groups of three letters each as JAI, LAP and PAS. In each group the first letter is made the third letter as JAI becomes AIJ, LAP becomes APL and PAS becomes ASP. Thus JAILAPPAS becomes AIJALASP.

On the same pattern divide the expression ECONOMICS into groups of three letters each as ECO, NOM and ICS. Now, in each group make the first letter as third letter. They will becme COE, OMN and CSI.

∴ ECONOMICS will be coded as COEOMNCSI.

37. D: CLOCK is written as KCOLC. You will see that the letters have been written in reverse order beginning from the last letter

C L O C K = K C O L C

On the same pattern STEPS will be SPETS.

38. C: SPIDER is written as PSDIRE. The expression SPIDER is divided into groups of two letters each as SP, ID, ER. You will find the letters in each group exchange their place, *i.e.,* SP becomes PS, ID becomes DI and RE becomes ER. Thus SPIDER is written as PSDIRE.

On the same pattern divide the expression COMMON into groups of two letters each, *i.e.,* CO, MM and ON. When letters in each group exchange their places, the group will become OC, MM and NO.

Thus COMMON will become OCMMNO.

39. C: Compare RECOMMENDATION and COMNENDATIONER

RE COMMENDATION

COMMENDATION ER

You will find that the first two letters RE exchange their position and occupy the last, position in the expression.

On the same pattern, when RENUMERATION will be written in the code, the first two letters, *i.e.,* RE will exchange their position to become ER and will occupy the last position. Thus the coded expression will become—MUNERATIONER.

40. A: TRIPPLE is coded as SQHOOKD. You will find that the coded letters are just the preceding letters of the letters in the expression. For example, S for T, Q for R, H for I, O for P again O for P, K for L and D for E.

On the same pattern use the just preceding letters to obtain the code for DISPOSE.

D = C

I = H

S = R

P = O

O = N

S = R

E = D

∴ DISPOSE will be coded as CHRONRD.

QUESTIONS BASED ON RELATIONSHIP

1. B: Ajit is brother of Mohan's son. Therefore, Mohan is father of Ajit and his brother. Therefore, Ajit is Mohan's grandson.

2. C: B is A's son.

B is my son's uncle.

∴ A is my father.

3. D: G's uncle is A's brother.

4. A: son-in-law.

5. B: Bihari is Yogendra's uncle.

6. C: C has two children A and B. A is his son while B is his daughter.

7. B: The son of my maternal uncle's son will be my nephew and I will be his uncle.

8. B: Children of Ram, Pratap and Kripa will be cousins.

9. B: The son of the daughter of P's sister will address P as maternal grandfather.

10. C: B is C's wife and A is C's father.
∴ A is father-in-law of B.

QUESTIONS RELATED TO DIRECTIONS

1	2	3	4	5	6	7	8	9	10
B	B	D	A	C	C	D	C	C	B
11	**12**	**13**							
D	B	C							

ARRANGING THE LETTERS TO MAKE MEANINGFUL WORDS

1. BLUE
2. COCHIN
3. URDU
4. IRON
5. PEACOCK
6. NARMADA
7. EARTH
8. PENCIL
9. TIGER
10. HOCKEY
11. SHIRT
12. MANGO
13. RICE
14. AGRA
15. CHAIR
16. HAND
17. RING
18. TAMIL
19. NEEM
20. TRAIN
21. PUNJAB
22. CRICKET
23. PETROL
24. GUITAR
25. BABY
26. KIDNEY
27. TONGUE
28. DONKEY
29. KRISHNA
30. KALIDAS
31. KASHI
32. PARIS
33. COPPER
34. GRAPE
35. RAMAYAN
36. AKBAR
37. BURMA
38. WATCH
39. BRIJNJAL
40. OXYGEN

ARRANGING WORDS IN THEIR NATURAL ORDER

1	2	3	4	5	6	7	8	9	10
C	C	D	C	D	C	C	D	D	B

MISCELLANEOUS

1. D.

2. A: School is to the west of hospital. Police post is to the north of the hospital. Court is to the north of the school. Therefore, the police post is to the each of court.

Court → E Police Post
N ↑ N ↑
School Hospital

3. D.

4. B.

5. C: B and E are the two short-sized students without spectacles.

6. D: The tallish Gandhi House student without spectacles is F.

7. C:

S. sized	S. sized	S. sized	Tallish	S. sized	Tallish
A	B	C	D	E	F
Nehru	House		Gandhi	House	
↓		↓	↓		
Spectacles	X	Spectacles	Spectacles	X	X

The Gandhi House short sized student without spectacles is E.

8. B: After exchanging positions with Kamal, Appu becomes sixth from the left and seventh from the right which means that there are twenty two children in the row. After exchanging position with Appu, Kamal will be fourth from the right and nineteenth from the left.

9. B: The eighteenth letter from the left will be I.

10. B.

11. A.

12. D.

13. D.

14. C.

15. A: The position of the five boys from the top was as under—Hari, Jayant, Krishna, Ram and Govind.

16. D: Dhulia > Amalner; Sri Rampur > Nasik; Jalgaon < Sri Rampur; Jalgaon > Amalner; Amalner < Nasik; Amalner > Manmad.

Dhulia, Nasik, Sri Rampur and Jalgaon are bigger than Amalner; Manmad is smaller than Amalner.

17. B.

18. C.

19. B: I + old man + old woman + wife + husband + child + wife + husband + child = 9 persons.

20. A.

21. D.

22. B.

23. A.

24. C: Apple is not at the bottom, so it cannot be opposite orange which is at the top. Melon and peach are opposite each other. So none of these will be opposite orange. Also, banana is one of its neighbours. So, the sixth fruit mango must be opposite the orange, and at the bottom.

25. C: 10 + Manisha + 10 = 21.

26. A: The second letter is E, the fourth is T, the sixth is N, the seventh is A, the eighth is N and the ninth letter is T. The meaningful word made from these letters is TENANT.

27. B: Since B and D are twins, therefore, D is also 3 years younger to A, and A is 3 years younger to C. Therefore, C is older than D by 3 + 3, *i.e.*, 6 years.

PLACE ARRANGEMENT

Place arrangement generally refers to the positioning of persons or objects in a manner indicated by set of information given. One has to understand the order of placement and then attempt questions following the given information.

EXERCISE

Directions : *In the following questions, under-stand the arrangement pattern and then select the right answer from the given options :*

1. Five boys are sitting in a row. Raghu is not adjacent to Shyam or Amit. Ajay is not adjacent to Shyam. Raghu is adjacent to Mayank. If Mayank is at the middle in the row, then Ajay is adjacent to whom out of the following?

A. Amit B. Raghu
C. Mayank D. Shyam
E. Data Inadequate

2. Mini is to the right of Rajni but to the left of Ananta. Saya is to the right of Mini but to the left of Jaya. Who is on the extreme left if all the girls are facing North?

A. Jaya B. Mini
C. Rajni D. Saya
E. Ananta

3. O, P, Q, R, S and T are standing on a bench according to their height. P is taller than O but shorter than S. Only S is taller than T. R is shorter than P but taller than Q. Who is the shortest?

A. O
B. Q
C. P
D. Cannot be said
E. None of these

4. Five personalities are living in a multistoried building. Mr. Effortless lives in a flat above Mr. Active, Mr. Charge lives in a flat below Mr. Diligent, Mr. Active lives in a flat above Mr. Diligent and Mr. Behaved lives in a flat below Mr. Charge. Who lives in the topmost flat?

A. Mr. Charge
B. Mr. Diligent
C. Mr. Effortless
D. Mr. Behaved
E. Cannot be said

5. In a pile of 10 books there are 3 of History, 3 of Hindi, 2 of Maths, and 2 of English. Taking from above there is an English book between a History and Maths book, a History book between a Maths and an English book, a Hindi book between an English and a Maths book, a Maths book between two Hindi books, and two Hindi books between a Maths and a History book. Book of which subject is at the sixth position from the top?

A. English B. Hindi
C. History D. Maths
E. Data Inadequate

6. Five persons P, Q, R, S and T are sitting in a row facing you such that S is on the left of R and Q is on the right of T. P is on the right of R and Q is on the left of S. If T occupies a corner position, then who is sitting in the centre?

A. P B. Q

C. R D. S

E. Data Inadequate

Directions (Qs. 7 to 11) : *Read the following statements and answer the questions given below :*

Nine family members are sitting in a theatre in one row. They are J, K, L, M, N, O, P, Q and R. L is at the right of M and at third place at the right of N. K is at one end of the row. Q is immediately next to O and P. O is at third place at the left of K. J is right next to the left of O.

7. Which of the following statement is true?

A. There is one person between L and O

B. R and P are neighbours

C. M is at one extreme end

D. N is at two seats away from J.

E. None of the above

8. The family members sitting on the right of O are :

A. RML B. JQP

C. QPK D. KPR

E. Cannot be determined

9. Who is sitting in the centre of the row?

A. L B. J

C. O D. Q

E. None of the above

10. Who are sitting next to L?

A. A and O B. M and J

C. M and O D. P and J

E. Data Inadequate

11. Who is at the other end of the row?

A. R B. J

C. P D. N

E. Q

Directions (Qs. 12 to 14) : (P) There are five friends; (Q) They are standing in a row facing south; (R) Jayesh is to the immediate right of Alok; (S) Pramod is between Babir and Subodh; (T) Subodh is between Jayesh and Pramod.

12. Who is at the extreme left end?

A. Alok

B. Babir

C. Subodh

D. Data inadequate

E. None of these

13. Who is in the middle?

A. Babir

B. Pramod

C. Subodh

D. Jayesh

E. Alok

14. To find answers to the above two questions, which of the given statements can be dispensed with?

A. None B. P only

C. Q only D. R only

E. S only

Directions (Qs. 15 to 17) : *Read the following information and answer the questions given below:*

(i) P, Q, R, S and T reside in a five-storey building.

(ii) Q and T do not reside on the ground floor.

(iii) S resides one storey above P and one storey below R.

(iv) T does not reside on the top floor.

15. On which floor does S reside?

A. Second B. Fourth

C. Fifth D. First

E. Data inadequate

16. How many of them do reside above R?

A. 3 B. 2

C. 4 D. 1

E. Data inadequate

17. To find out the answers to the above two questions, which of the four given statements can be dispensed with ?

A. Only *(iv)*

B. Only *(ii)* and *(iii)*

C. None

D. Only *(i)*

E. Only *(ii)* and *(iv)*

Directions (Qs. 18 to 20) : *Read the following information and answer the questions given below :*

(i) Six friends are playing a card game facing at the centre.

(ii) Subodh is to the right of Prabodh.

(iii) There is one person between Uma and Sudha.

(iv) Prabir is between Subodh and Uma and second to the left of Aloke.

18. Who is to the right of Sudha?

A. Prabodh B. Uma

C. Aloke D. Prabir

E. Data inadequate

19. If Aloke and Subodh interchange their positions, who will be second to the right of Prabir?

A. Prabodh

B. Subodh

C. Uma

D. Sudha

E. None of these

20. To answer the above two questions, which of the following statements can be dispensed with?

A. (iii) only B. (iv) only

C. (iii) or (iv) only D. None

E. (ii) only

EXPLANATORY ANSWERS

1. B. : The order of sitting is :
Amit, Shyam, Mayank, Ajay, Raghu

or

Ajay, Raghu, Mayank, Amit, Shyam

2. C. : The order in which the girls are positioned is :
Rajni, Mini, Ananta, Saya, Jaya

or

Saya, Jaya, Ananta

or

Saya, Ananta, Jaya

3. D. : In descending order of height, the standing positions are :

S		S
T		T
P	*or*	P
R		R
O		Q
Q		O

Either O or Q is the shortest. The informa-tion given is not enough to clarify the answer.

4. C. : The personalities living in flats in multi-storied building are in order given below :

Mr. Effortless
Mr. Active
Mr. Diligent
Mr. Charge
Mr. Behaved

5. B. : The pile of books is in the order :

1st — History
English
Maths
History
English
6th — Hindi
Maths
Hindi
Hind
10th — History

6. D. : Sitting order while facing us is :

P, R, S, Q, T

7. A. : Order of sitting for questions 23 to 27 is : N, R, M, L, J, O, Q, P, K.

8. C.

9. B.

10. B.

11. D.

12. A. : For questions 28 to 30 five friends are standing in this order :

Alok, Jayesh, Subodh, Pramod, Babir

13. C.

14. B.

15. D. : For answers 31 to 33 the manner of residing in a five-storey building is :

Q
T
R
S
Ground floor - P

16. B.

17. C.

18. A. : The manner of sitting is :

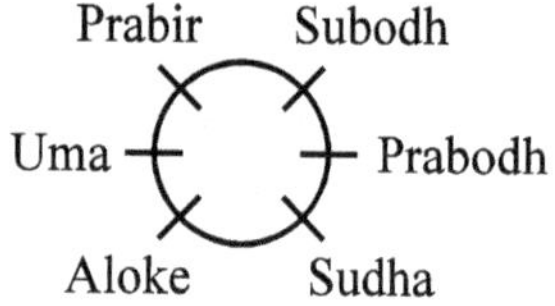

19. B. : After interchanging positions the order will be :

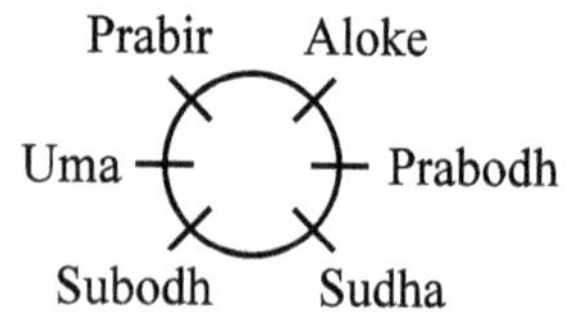

20. A.

DIAGRAMMATIC PUZZLES

In these problems one has to count the geometrical figures in a given complex figure. A little bit of systematic approach is needed to get the correct number of the asked figure. The shapes of all geometrical figures must be clear in mind.

EXERCISE

1. How many triangles are there in the figure given below?

A. 24 B. 27
C. 25 D. 26

2. How many parallelograms are there in this figure?

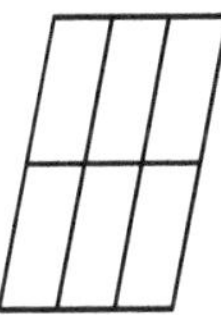

A. 9 B. 13
C. 15 D. 18

3. How many triangles are there in this figure?

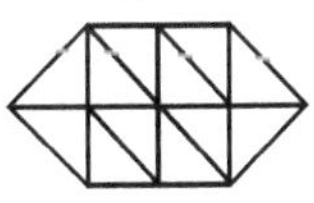

A. 16 B. 17
C. 18 D. 19

4. The number of rectangles in this figure are.

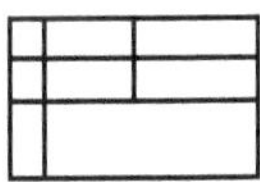

A. 21 B. 24
C. 23 D. 25

5. How many squares are hidden in this figure?

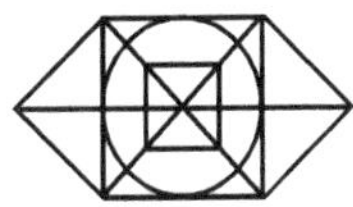

A. 7 B. 8
C. 9 D. 10

6. The number of triangles in this figure are.

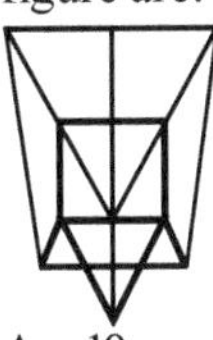

A. 19 B. 16
C. 21 D. 15

7. How many squares are there in the figure given below?

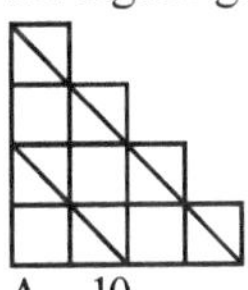

A. 10 B. 11
C. 13 D. 14

8. The number of circles in this figure is

A. 6 B. 5
C. 2 D. 3

9. How many triangles are there in the figure given below?

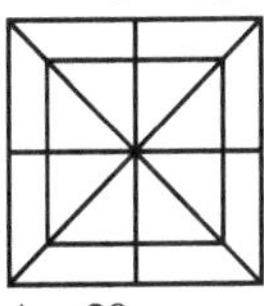

A. 28 B. 36
C. 24 D. 32

10. How many straight lines are needed to draw the figure in question 9?

A. 10 B. 12
C. 11 D. 13

11. How many squares are there in this figure?

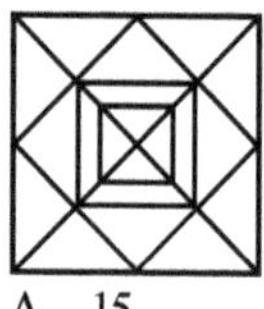

A. 15 B. 11
C. 8 D. 3

12. The number of squares in the figure below is

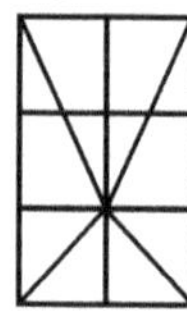

A. 6 B. 10
C. 8 D. 12

13. The number of triangles in the figure given in earlier question is

A. 15 B. 16
C. 17 D. 18

14. How many hexagons are there in the figure given below?

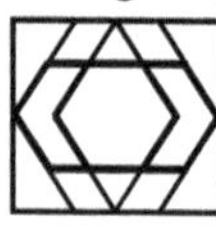

A. 1 B. 2
C. 4 D. 5

15. The number of parallelograms in this figure is

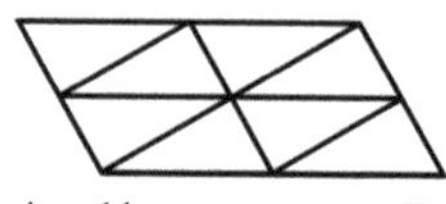

A. 11 B. 12
C. 9 D. 10

16. The number of squares in the figure given below is

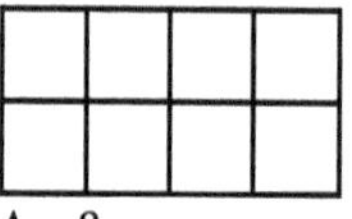

A. 8 B. 10
C. 11 D. 12

17. How many circles are there in the figure given below?

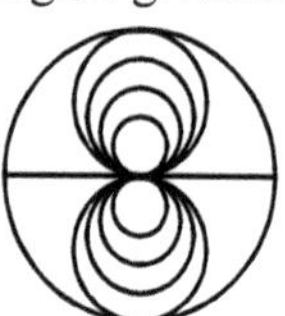

A. 5 B. 6
C. 8 D. 9

18. How many triangles are there in the figure?

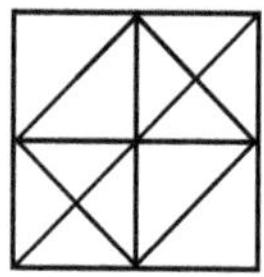

A. 26 B. 25
C. 28 D. 27

19. How many straight lines are used to make this figure?

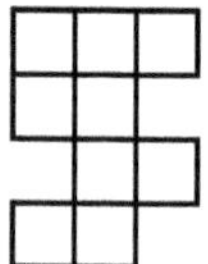

A. 7 B. 11
C. 8 D. 10

20. How many rectangles are there in the figure?

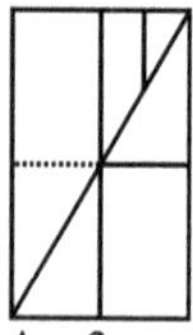

A. 3 B. 5
C. 6 D. 4

EXPLANATORY ANSWERS

1. B **2. D** **3. A** **4. C**

5. D **6. B**

7. C :

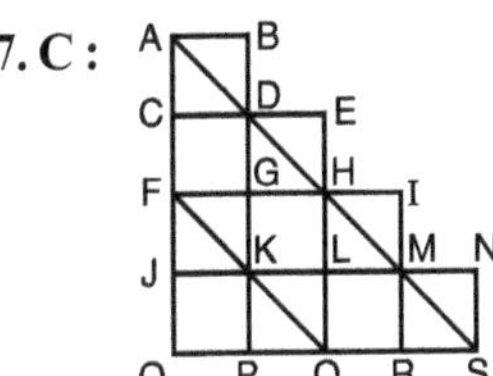

The simplest squares are : ABCD, CDFG, DEGH, FGJK, GHKL, HILM, JKOP, KLPQ, LMQR and MNRS *i.e.* – 10 squares.

Other squares are : CEJL, FHOQ and GIPR *i.e.* – 3 squares

So, the total number of squares is 10 + 3 = 13

8. A :

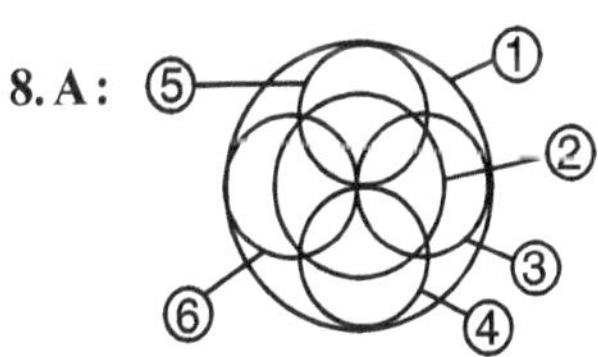

There are two main circles and four smaller circles intersecting each other.

So, the total number of circles is 2 + 4 = 6

9. D **10. B**

11. C :

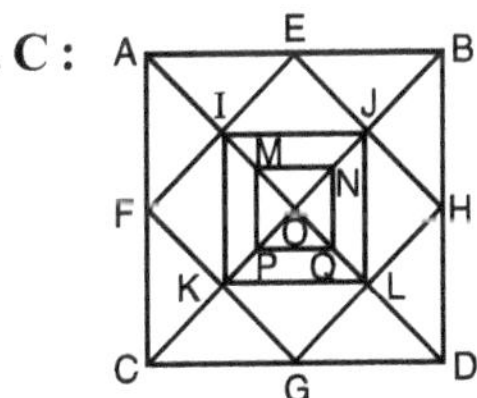

The main squares are : ABCD, IJKL, MNPQ and EFHG *i.e.* – 4 squares.

Other squares are. EIJO, IFKO, JOLH and OKGL *i.e.* – 4 squares

So, the total number of squares is 4 + 4 = 8

12. C :

The simplest squares are : AICK, CKEM, EMGN, IBKD, KDMF ad MFNH *i.e.* – 6 squares

Other squares are ABEF and CDGH *i.e.* – 2 squares.

So, the total number of squares is 6 + 2 = 8

13. B

14. C :

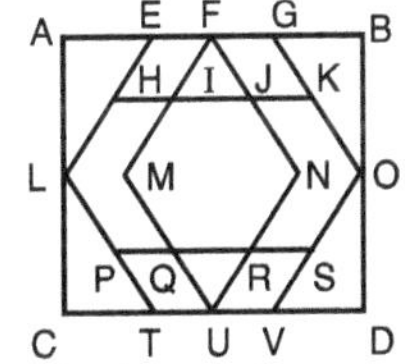

The larger hexagon is : EG – GO – GV – VT – TL – LE *i.e.* – 1 hexagon.

The smaller hexagons are : IJ – JN – NR – RQ – QM – MT, HJ – JN – NR – RP – PL – LH and IK – KO – OS – SQ – QM – MI, *i.e.*, –3, hexagons. So, the total number of hexagons is 1 + 3 = 4

(Hexagon is a figure having six side of equal length.)

15. A :

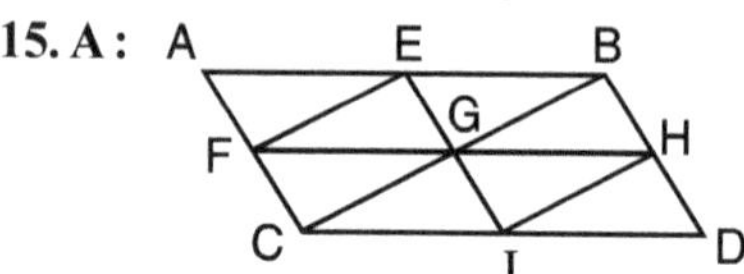

The main parallelogram in ABCD – *i.e.* – 1 parallelogram
The simplest parallelogram are : AEFG, FGCI, EBGH, GHID, FECG and GBIH *i.e.* – 6 parallelograms
Other parallelograms are : ABFH, FHCD, AECI and EBID *i.e.* – 4 parallelograms
So, the total number of parallelograms is
$1+6+4=11$

16. C

17. D :

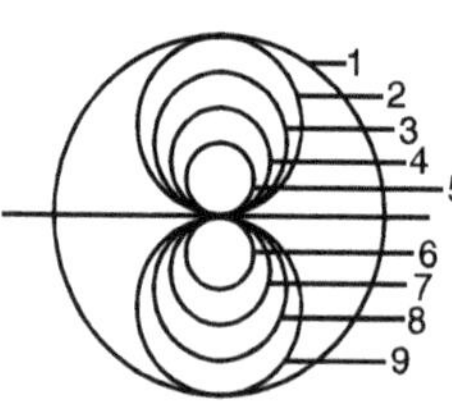

There is 1 main circle, 4 circles on the top of the horizontal lines and 4 circles below it.
So, the total number of circles is $1+4+4=9$

18. A

19. B :

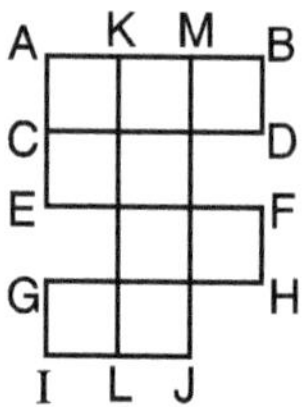

The horizontal lines are AB, CD, EF, GH and IJ *i.e.* – 5 lines
The vertical lines are AC, KL MJ, BD, FH and GI *i.e.* – 6 lines
So, the total number of lines used to draw this figure is 5 + 6 = 11

20. B :

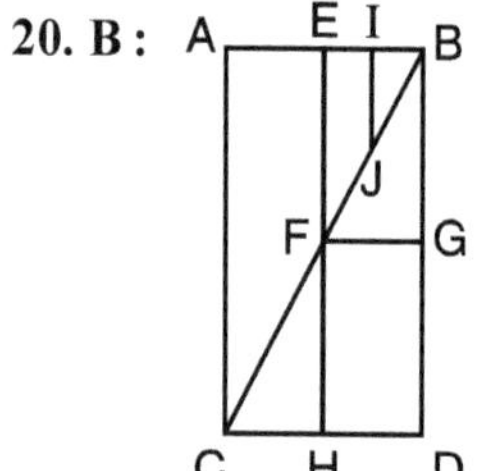

The main rectangle is ABCD *i.e.* – 1 rectangle
The simplest rectangles are AECH, EBFG and FGHD *i.e.* – 3 rectangles

CUBES AND DICES

The questions related to problems on cubes and dices are aimed to check the imaginative power of the candidate. The candidate must have the ability to visualise quickly in three-dimensional object for what is asked of it. To attempt such questions some basic facts should be kept in mind and the visualisation ability should be combined with fast and accurate calculations.

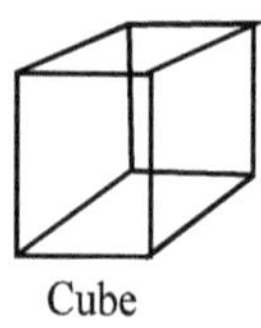
Cube

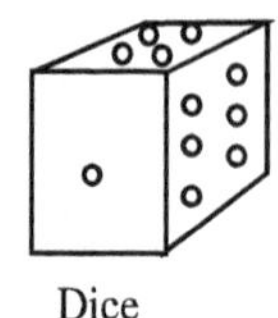
Dice

- Cube has six faces/sides and eight corners.
- Dice has six faces/sides.
- Problems are based on the same or different coloured faces.
- Problems are based only on the value occurring on the six faces.
- Problems are based on cutting the squares into specified number of smaller equal parts.

Diagrammatically, the explanation of a cube which is painted green on all sides can be understood easily taking one side of the cube.

a	b	a
b	c	b
a	b	a

This cube is divided into $3 \times 3 \times 3 = 27$ equal small cubes.

There are four corner pieces 'a'. so 4×2 *i.e.*, 8 pieces will be painted on 3 sides.

There are four middle pieces 'b', so 4×3 *i.e.*, 12 pieces will be painted on 2 sides

There is one middle piece 'c', so 1×6 *i.e.*, 6 pieces will be painted only on 1 side.

There will be one piece right in the centre of this cube *i.e.*, piece will not have paint at all.

So this cube has $8 + 12 + 6 + 1$ *i.e.*, 27 smaller cubes.

EXERCISE

1. Two positions of a dice are shown below. When there are two circles at the bottom, the number of circles at the top will be :

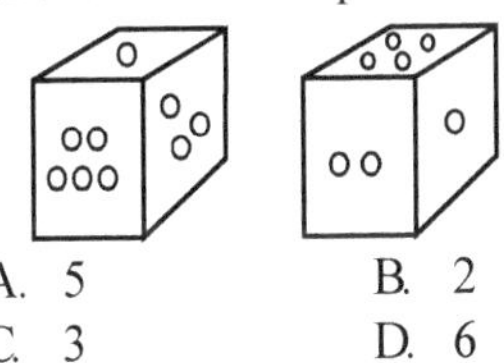

A. 5 B. 2

C. 3 D. 6

2. Two positions of a dice are shown below. When 4 is at the bottom, what number will be on the top?

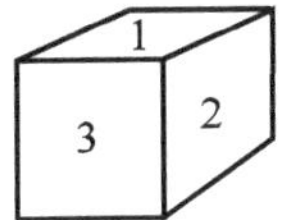

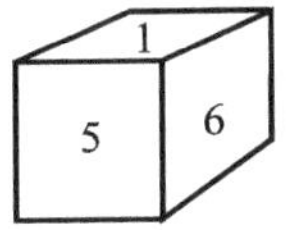

A. 1 B. 2

C. 5 D. 6

3. A cube is painted red on two adjacent faces and on one opposite face, yellow on two adjacent faces and green on the remaining face. It is then cut into 64 equal cubes. How many cubes have only one red and one green face?

A. 4 B. 8

C. 12 D. 16

4. Two positions of a dice with 1 to 6 dots on its sides are shown below. If the dice is resting on the side with three dots, what will be the number of dots on the side at the top?

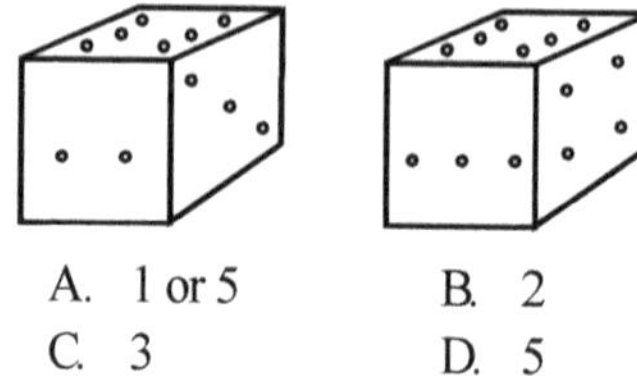

A. 1 or 5 B. 2
C. 3 D. 5

5. A cube, on whose sides letters have been written, is shown below in different positions as can be seen from different directions. Find the missing letter?

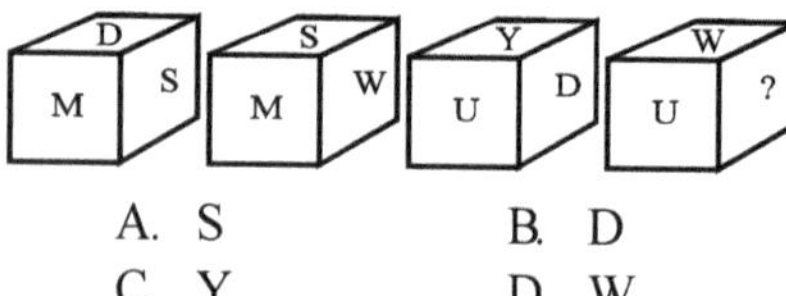

A. S B. D
C. Y D. W

6. If the total number of dots on opposite faces of a cubical block is always 7, find the figure which is correct?

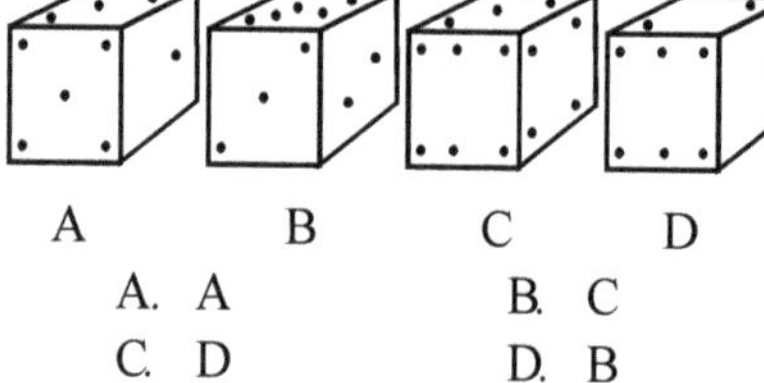

A B C D

A. A B. C
C. D D. B

7. The minimum number of colours required to paint all the sides of a cube so that no two adjacent faces may have the same colour, is :

A. 6 B. 4
C. 3 D. 2

8. In a dice a, b, c and d, are written on the adjacent faces, in a clockwise order and e and f at the top and bottom. When c is at the top, what will be at the bottom?

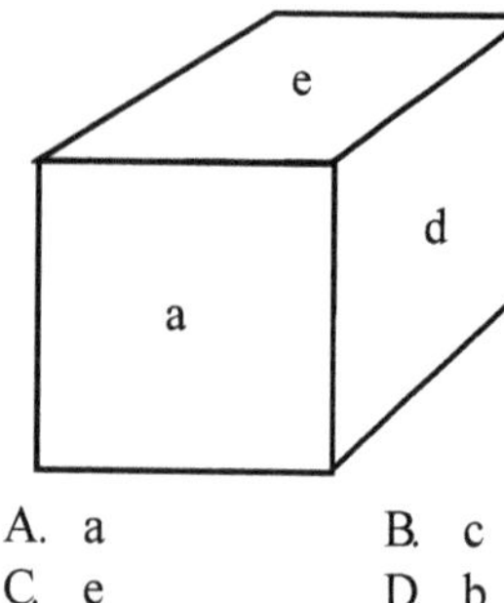

A. a B. c
C. e D. b

9. The number of cubes arranged one over the other in this figure will be :

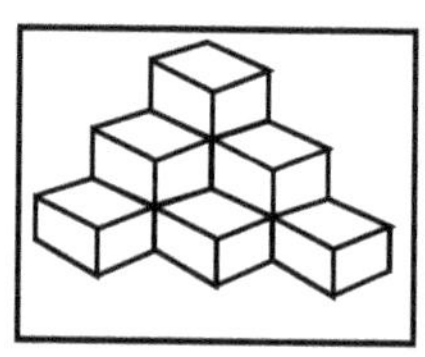

A. 8 B. 6
C. 5 D. 10

10. Two positions of a block are shown below. 5 and 6 are on opposite faces.

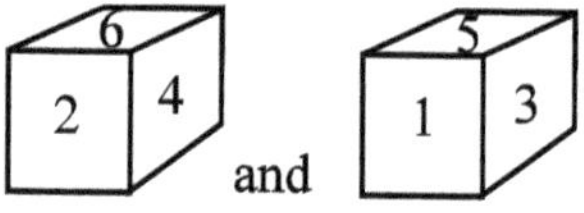

When 2 is at the bottom, what number will be at the top?

A. 1 B. 3
C. 4 D. 5

11. Two positions of a dice are given below. When 1 is at the top, which number will be at the bottom?

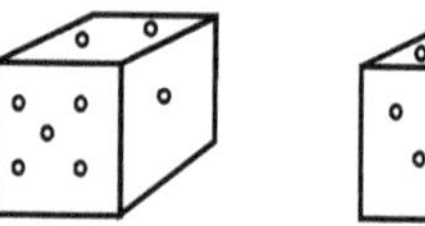

A. 3 B. 6
C. 2 D. 1

12. Two positions of a dice are shown below. When 2 is at the bottom, which number will be at the top?

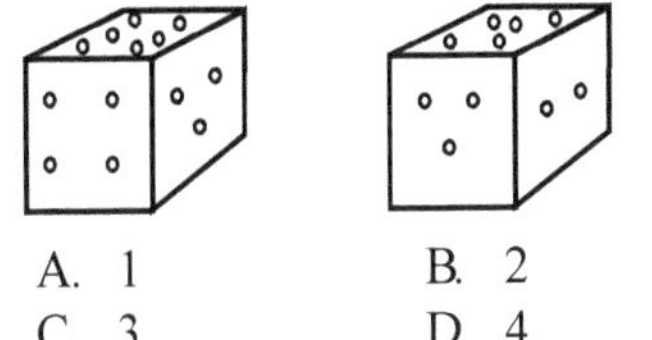

A. 1 B. 2
C. 3 D. 4

13. Study the three dices given below. What number will be opposite to the side bearing number 2?

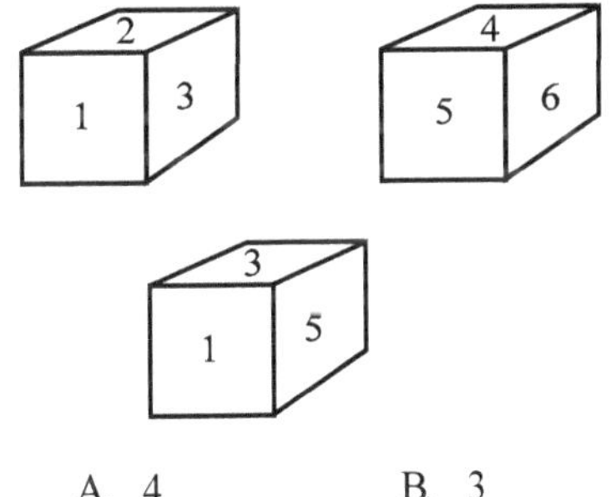

A. 4 B. 3
C. 6 D. 5

14. The sides of a cube are painted in different colours. Black side is opposite to red. White side is between black and red. Green side is adjacent to grey and blue side is adjacent to green. What colour will be on the side opposite to the white side of the cube?

A. Blue
B. Green
C. Grey
D. Data is insufficient

15. A cube is painted black on two adjacent faces and on one opposite face, red on two opposite faces and green on the remaining face. If it is cut into 64 equal cubes, then how many cubes will have only one black coloured face?

A. 32 B. 16
C. 12 D. 8

16. Six sides of a cube are coloured in the following manner

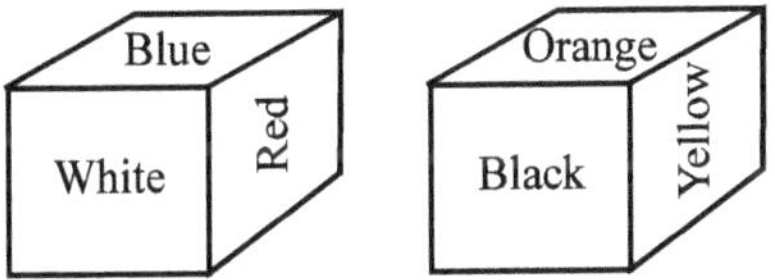

If blue and orange are opposite and red is on the top, which colour will be at the bottom?

A. Orange B. Purple
C. Black D. Yellow

17. A toy cube is painted orange on all sides. It is cut into 64 smaller cubes of equal size. How many smaller cubes are not painted at all?

A. 4 B. 8
C. 16 D. 20

18. A six centimetre cube is painted green on all sides. It is cut into two centimetre cubes. How many cubes will be there with two sides painted ?

A. 12 B. 8
C. 24 D. 4

19. What number in the dice, given below, will be on the side opposite to 6?

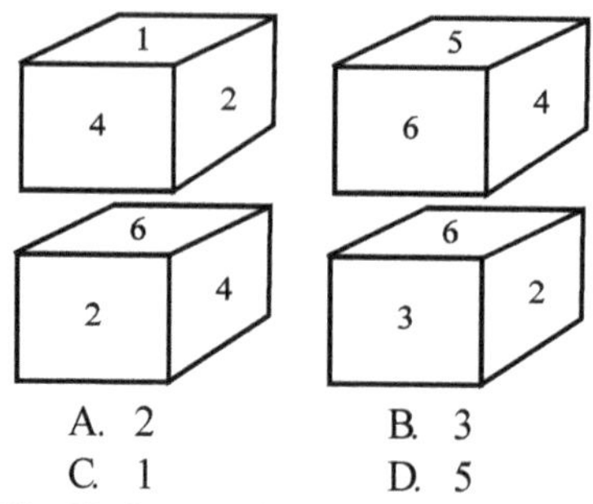

A. 2 B. 3
C. 1 D. 5

20. If the numbers on the opposite sides of the cube total as 7, which one of the following dices is definitely defective?

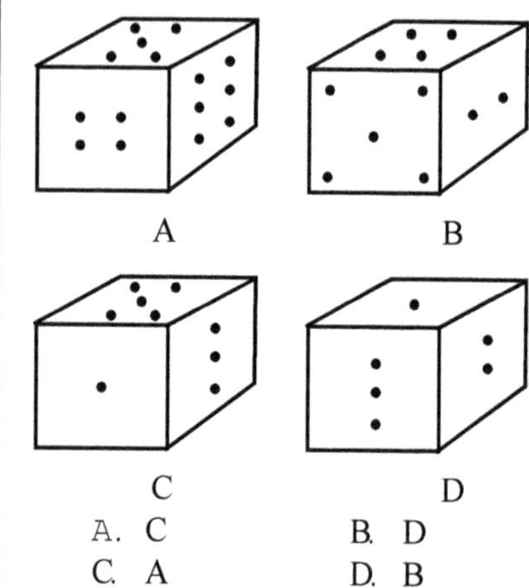

A. C B. D
C. A D. B

EXPLANATORY ANSWERS

1. A. : After observing the views of the same dice, the faces that can be clearly understood to be the opposites are : 2 — 5, 4 — 3 and 1— 6.

2. A. : In the given dice, the numbers adjacent to 1 are 3, 2, 5 and 6. So, the numbers on the opposite faces will be 1 and 4.

3. B

4. A. : It is, however, clear that the number on the face opposite 2 dots is the face with 4 dots. But it is not clear if the number 1 or 5 is on face opposite the face 3. The answer is either 1 or 5.

5. C. : The letters on the top and bottom sides are W and D respectively and the letters on the sides are U, Y, M and S clockwise.

6. A. : In this cubical block the number of dots on opposite faces will be 1—6, 3—4 and 5—2.

7. C. : A cube has six sides and two opposite sides can be painted in same colour.

8. A. : The two positions of dice will be :

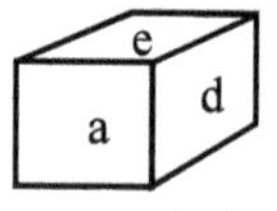

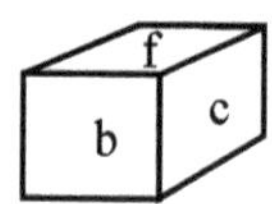

and the opposite sides will be a—c, b—d.

9. D

10. B. : When 5 and 6 are on opposite faces then the numbers on opposite faces will be 4—1 and 2—3. So, if 2 is at the bottom, 3 will be at the top.

11. B. : After observing the two views of the same dice, the faces that can be clearly understood to be the opposites are : 1—6, 2—4 and 3—5. So, when 1 is at the top, 6 will be at the bottom.

12. D. : The sides which are clearly understood to be the opposites are 1—3, 2—4 and 5—6. So, when 2 is at the bottom, 4 will be at the top.

13. D. : The numbers on the sides opposite to each other are 1 and 4; 2 and 5; 3 and 6.

14. B **15. C** **16. D** **17. B** **18. A**

19. C. : According to the given figures of the same dice, the numbers adjacent to 6 are 5, 4, 2 and 3. So, the number opposite to the side 6 will be 1.

20. D. : 5 and 2 are on adjacent sides instead of being on the opposite side.

ROWS AND RANKS

These type of problems need easy calculations to find out the number of objects in a row, lane or queue or to find a person's rank in a class of certain number of students; or to find the total number of students.

EXERCISE

1. In a row of trees, one tree is fifth from either end of the row. How many trees are in the row?

A. 11 B. 8
C. 10 D. 9
E. None of these

2. Jaya ranks 5th in a class of 53. What is her rank from the bottom in the class?

A. 49th B. 48th
C. 47th D. 50th
E. None of these

3. Mohan ranks twenty-first in a class of sixty-five students. What will be his (Mohan's) rank if the lowest candidate is assigned rank 1?

A. 44th
B. 45th
C. 46th
D. Data inadequate
E. None of these

4. If Rahul finds that he is 12th from the right in a line of boys and 4th from the left, how many boys should be added to the line such that there are 28 boys in the line?

A. 12 B. 14
C. 20 D. 13
E. None of these

5. In a row of boys, Rajan is tenth from the right and Suraj is tenth from the left. When Rajan and Suraj interchange their positions, Suraj will be twenty-seventh from the left. Which of the following will be Rajan's position from the right?

A. Tenth
B. Twenty-sixth

C. Twenty-ninth
D. Twenty-fifth
E. None of these

6. Mahesh and Suresh are ranked 11th and 12th respectively from the top in a class of 41 students. What will be their respective ranks from the bottom?
A. 32nd and 33rd
B. 29th and 30th
C. 30th and 31st
D. 31st and 30th
E. None of these

7. Uma ranked 8th from the top and 37th from bottom in a class. How many students are there in the class?
A. 47 B. 46
C. 45 D. 48
E. None of these

8. In a queue, Sadiq is 14th from the front and Joseph is 17th from the end, while Jane is in between Sadiq and Joseph. If Sadiq be ahead of Joseph and there be 48 persons in the queue, how many persons are there between Sadiq and Jane?
A. 5 B. 6
C. 7 D. 8
E. None of these

9. Rohan ranked eleventh from the top and twenty-seventh from the bottom among the students who passed the annual examination in a class. If the number of students who failed in the examination was 12, how many students appeared for the examination?
A. 48
B. 49
C. 50
D. Cannot be determined
E. None of these

10. Some boys are sitting in a row. P is sitting fourteenth from the left and Q is seventh from the right. If there are four boys between P and Q, how many boys are there in the row?
A. 19 B. 21
C. 25 D. 23
E. None of these

11. There are five different houses, P to T, in a row. P is to the right of Q and T is to the left of R and right of P, and Q is to the right of S. Which of the houses is in the middle?
A. Q B. P
C. S D. T
E. None of these

12. Madhav ranks seventeenth in a class of thirtyone. What is his rank from the last?
A. 13 B. 14
C. 15 D. 16
E. 17

13. Veena ranks 73rd from the top in a class of 182. What is her rank from the bottom if 22 students have failed the examination?
A. 88 B. 108
C. 110 D. 90
E. 93

14. Rakesh ranked 9th from the top and 38th from the bottom in a class. How many students are there in the class?
A. 47 B. 45

C. 46 D. 48

E. None of these

15. John ranks 19th in class and is 36th from the last. How many students are there in the class?

A. 53 B. 54

C. 51 D. 50

E. None of these

EXPLANATORY ANSWERS

1. D.:

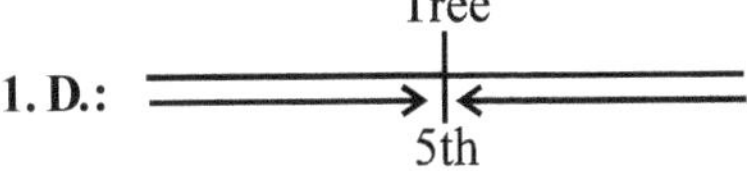

Total number of trees in the row are :
$(5+5)-1=9$

2. A. :

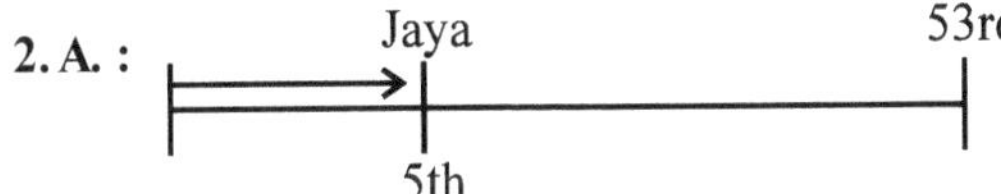

Jaya's rank from the bottom is :
$(53-5)+1=49$th.

3. B. :

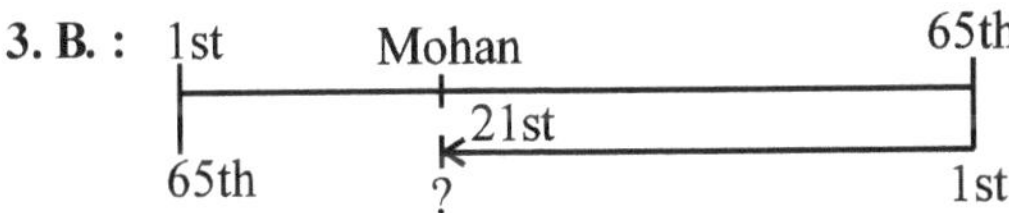

Note : Mohan's rank from the last or the question asked means the same.
Mohan's rank is $(65-21)+1=45$th

4. D. :

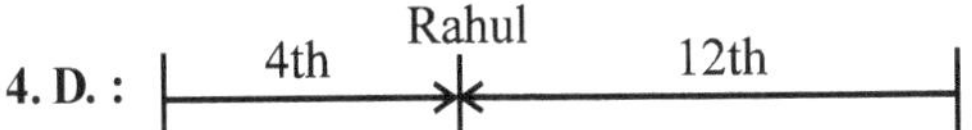

The number of boys in the line are :
$(4+12)-1=15$
To make a line of 28 boys, $(28-15)$ *i.e.* 13 more boys are needed.

5. E **6. D**

7. E. : Uma
8th 37th

Total number of students in the class are :
$(8+37)-1=44$

8. C **9. B**

10. C. :

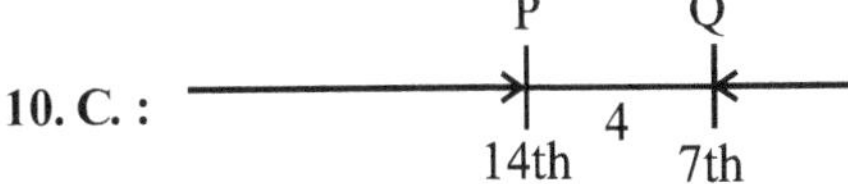

The number of boys in the row are : $(14+4+7)=25$

11. B. : The houses in the row are :
DBAEC

12. C. :

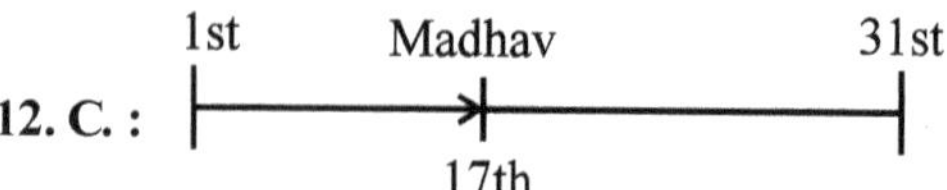

Madhav's rank from the last is :
$(31-17)+1=15\text{th}$

13. A

14. C. :

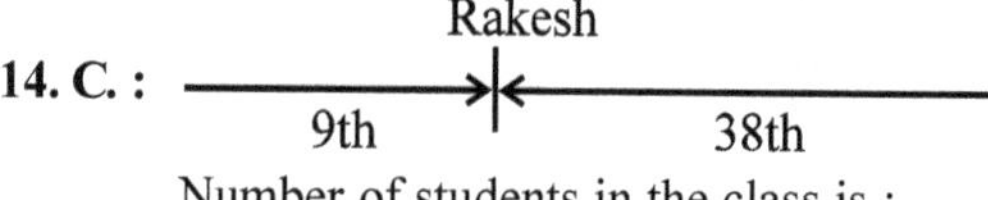

Number of students in the class is :
$(9+38)-1=46$

15. B. :

John

19th 36th

Number of students in the class is :
$(19+36)-1=54$

GENERAL ENGLISH

Error Detection

Directions : *In the following questions indicate which portion of the sentence marked A, B, C or D contains an error. If there is no error, mark E (Ignore punctuation errors, if any).*

1. They went (A)/to college (B)/after the rain (C)/stopped (D)/No error (E).
2. She had met (A)/me twice (B)/a week during (C)/the summer holidays (D)/No error (E).
3. Why does he (A)/not attend (B)/with what (C)/I am saying? (D)/No error (E).
4. We must (A)/not deviate (B)/of the (C)/right path (D) /No error (E).
5. The temperature (A)/has been (B)/upon (C)/the average recently (D)/No error (E).
6. They have (A)/enjoyed to talk (B)/to her about (C)/old times (D)/No error (E).
7. She made me (A)/to admire her (B)/to admire her for her beauty (C)/and intelligence (D)/ No error (E).
8. She asked her son (A)/if he was (B)/going to (C)/college today (D)/No error (E).
9. The doctor said to (A)/the patient (B)/not to eat (C)/fried things (D)/No error (E).
10. He is one of (A)/those boys (B)/who is (C)/physically strong (D)/No error (E).
11. Those who is (A)/punctual in attendence (B)/will be (C)/well rewarded (D)/No error (E).
12. If your mother (A)/will come again (B)/I shall report (C)/against you (D)/No error (E).
13. He is very poor (A)/to buy clothes/(B)/for his children (C)/and wife (D)/No error (E).
14. He is one of (A)/my those friends (B)/ who have achieved (C)/tremendous success in life (D)/No error (E).
15. Mumps are (A)/a disease (B)/with painful swelling (C)/in the neck (D)/No error (E).
16. No sooner (A)/I reached (B)/the station, (C)/than the train started (D)/No error (E).
17. Though he worked (A)/hard, still he (B)/could not pass (C)/the examination (D)/No error (E).
18. She is (A)/too happy (B)/to see you (C)/after so many days (D)/No error (E).
19. My friend has (A)/been living in London (B)/with her parents (C)/for the past three years (D)/No error (E).

20. He sat (A)/in the cafe (B)/when I met him (C)/the other day (D)/ No error (E).

21. All human beings (A)/have their roles (B)/to play in (C)/the theatre of this world (D)/No error (E).

22. Though lot of (A)/work has been done (B)/in the country, (C)/it is not enough (D)/No error (E).

23. Education can play (A)/an important role (B)/in creating (C)/communal harmony (D)/No error (E).

24. He felt that (A)/it was no longer necessary (B)/for him to hunt (C)/ down a job (D)/No error (E).

25. I know many men (A)/who had marked (B)/physical courage, but (C)/lacked moral courage (D)/No error (E).

26. Life is dear (A)/to a mute creature (B)/as it is (C)/to a man (D)/No error (E).

27. He walked up (A)/the end of (B)/ the road but (C)/found no flourist (D)/No error (E).

28. He has been (A)/appointed as (B)/President of (C)/the ruling party (D)/No error (E).

29. Fashion is very (A)/fickle, and keeping up (B)/with trends can (C)/be trying and expensive proposition (D)/No error (E).

30. The doctors told the family (A)/ that if the patient (B)/could survive for 24 hours (C)/he will have a chance (D)/No error (E).

31. They took (A)/more time (B)/for reaching there (C)/than we (D)/ No error (E).

32. Neither I nor (A)/she am to (B)/ apply for (C)/this teaching post (D)/No error (E).

33. Ten rupees are (A)/surely not a (B)/big sum to (C)/reckon with (D)/No error (E).

34. The speed of (A)/the sports car (B)/ is greater than the (C)/ other one (D)/ No error (E).

35. This dictionary is (A)/as good if (B)/not better than (C)/the other one (D)/No error (E).

36. None but (A)/those having (B)/ three years' experience (C)/need apply (D)/No error (E).

37. My father got (A)/angry before (B)/I said (C)/a word (D)/No error (E).

38. Tapan is the most (A)/irresponsible person (B)/and does not (C)/care for his belongings (D)/No error (E).

39. In spite of Jaya's (A)/faults my mother (B)/can not help (C)/but like her (D)/No error (E).

40. If she would have (A)/worked hard/(B)/she would have (C)/ passed the examination (D)/No error (E).

41. As the child is not (A)/feeling well, so he (B)/will not be able (C)/to attend the school (D)/No error (E).

42. After he returns (A)/from his official tour (B)/I will go and (C)/see him (D)/No error (E).

43. The maximum (A)/number of persons (B)/a boat (C)/is ten (D)/ No error (E).

44. If the day (A)/after tomorrow (B)/ is Friday, what day (C)/was yesterday (D)/No error (E).

45. Only well read person (A)/can make (B)/proper use (C)/of the English language (D)/No error (E).

46. She is one of (A)/the fashion designers (B)/which have (C)/ become famous (D)/No error (E).

47. Not only Harish (A)/but also Nikhil (B)/is involved in (C)/the social service programme (D)/No error (E).

48. Neither he (A)/or I have (B)/been called (C)/for the interview (D)/ No error (E).

49. We all know (A)/that he is (B)/ wiser (C)/than hardworking (D)/ No error (E).

50. I wish (A)/I was (B)/the Prime Minister (C)/of the country (D)/ No error (E).

51. Too calmly (A)/the hunter took (B)/careful aim (C)/and fired the bullets (D)/No error (E).

52. The court presented (A)/rigorous imprisonment to (B)/all the seven accused (C)/in the bank robbery case (D)/No error (E).

53. Amar was conscious to (A)/all that was (B)/going on (C)/around his place (D)/No error (E).

54. Hurry up (A)/if not (B)/you miss the bus (C)/to school! (D)/No error (E).

55. Till it stops raining (A)/I can not (B)/go to the (C)/market for shopping (D)/No error (E).

56. Only if (A)/I were rich (B)/ enough to buy I can (C)/buy my favourite car (D)/No error (E).

57. The thief mother (A)/pleaded (B)/for her (C)/son's innocence (D)/No error (E).

58. They plan their products (A)/and strategies little by little (B)/rather than (C)/take a long leap (D)/No error (E).

59. The last decade (A)/had witnessed a shift (B)/in business strategies (C)/all about the world (D)/No error (E).

60. Experience, good (A)/analytical skills (B)/and flair for innovation (C)/are called (D)/No error (E).

61. The Worker Union (A)/has given (B)/a written complaint (C)/to the Chairman (D)/No error (E).

62. Five armed miscreants (A)/broke through the house (B)/and decamped with (C)/jewellery and cash (D)/No error (E).

63. He is (A)/not scholar, (B)/he is (C)/an engineer (D)/No error (E).

64. On every (A)/Saturday night (B)/ we go (C)/to cinema (D)/No error (E).

65. I shall (A)/go to the library (B)/ to return books (C)/before the due date (D)/No error (E).

66. Her mother (A)/is an interior designer (B)/and earns thousands of rupees (C)/a month (D)/No error (E).

67. The leaf (A)/is always (B)/the green (C)/in colour (D)/No error (E).

68. The lion (A)/saw his (B)/shade in (C)/the water (D)/No error (E).

69. The child (A)/was walking (B)/ in the (C)/centre of the road (D)/ No error (E).

70. The fire (A)/that broke out (B)/ last night (C)/caused many damage (D)/No error (E).

71 Many people (A)/lost their life (B)/in the train accident (C)/last year (D)/No error (E).

72. The number of (A)/members of the club (B)/are increasing (C)/ day-by-day (D)/No error (E).

73. The colour (A)/of her hairs (B)/ is as black (C)/as coal (D)/No error (E).

74. The news (A)/of her recovery (B)/ from coma (C)/are unbelievable (D)/No error (E).

75. Very little (A)/people attended (B)/the function (C)/yesterday night (D)/No error (E).

76. Our long trip (A)/by train (B)/ was not (C)/at all comfortable (D)/No error (E).

77. All his savings (A)/are kept (B)/ in the locker (C)/of a nearby bank (D)/No error (E).

78. Jaya and me (A)/would rather (B)/ go to (C)/the library (D)/No error (E).

79. Just between (A)/you and I, (B)/ I do not want (C)/to meet him (D)/No error (E).

80. One should be (A)/aware of (B)/ his responsibility (C)/towards elders (D)/No error (E).

81. Divya is (A)/more beautiful (B)/ than (C)/her (D)/No error (E).

82. Rinku (A)/is intelligent (B)/than (C)/I (D)/No error (E).

83. Neither of (A)/the participants (B)/managed to score (C)/the qualifying points (D)/No error (E).

84. Any of (A)/these two dresses (B)/ has been tailored (C)/by the Choicest Tailors (D)/No error (E).

85. Mary has grown (A)/into (B)/a (C)/handsome woman (D)/No error (E).

86. Pinki is (A)/four years (B)/smaller (C)/than Asha (D)/No error (E).

87. The building (A)/on the next block (B)/is several metres (C)/ tall (D)/No error (E).

88. Children must (A)/keep (B)/their teeth (C)/clear (D)/No error (E).

89. All the students (A)/passed the examination (B)/accept the one (C)/who cheated (D)/No error (E).

90. Farther information (A)/on the matter (B)/is eagerly awaited (C)/ by all (D)/No error (E).

91. Mayank has been (A)/sick for (B)/ over (C)/two months (D)/No error (E).

92. He is (A)/my elder brother (B)/ and the man with him (C)/is his best friend (D)/No error (E).

93. Lie this (A)/book on (B)/the shelf (C)/over there (D)/No error (E).

94. He told (A)/me he (B)/would come back (C)/to Delhi (D)/No error (E).

95. This bank (A)/was stolen (B)/last night (C)/by some men (D)/ No error (E).

96. He wanted (A)/to lend a book (B)/from my (C)/best friend (D)/ No error (E).

97. He learnt (A)/me how (B)/to drive (C)/a car (D)/No error (E).

98. Can I (A)/be of (B)/some help (C)/to you? (D)/No error (E).

99. None fortunately (A)/saw us (B)/ there at (C)/the club (D)/No error (E).

100. Unless you (A)/do not (B)/leave early (C)/you can't catch the train (D)/ No error (E).

101. The teacher (A)/came always (B)/ late to (C)/our class (D)/No error (E).

102. Many remote areas (A)/are (B)/ rarely (C)/populated (D)/No error (E).

103. He is living (A)/in Patna (B)/ before he moved (C)/to Delhi (D)/No error (E).

104. I am sorry (A)/for not able to (B)/come to (C)/your Birthday Party (D)/No error (E).

105. Alas! (A)/the train (B)/stops (C)/ suddenly (D)/No error (E).

106. She is (A)/went to (B)/meet her (C)/parents after a long time (D)/ No error (E).

107. The child (A)/picked (B)/the ball (C)/from the ground (D)/No error (E).

108. God helps (A)/them (B)/who help (C)/themselves (D)/ No error (E).

109. Once on a time (A)/there lived (B)/a very wise (C)/and handsome king (D)/No error (E).

110. He thought (A)/that he could (B)/ win the first prize (C)/in the painting competition (D)/No error (E).

111. I refrained (A)/myself (B)/from expressing (C)/my views (D)/No error (E).

112. The official excuse (A)/was that (B)/the fourth general election (C)/was only 4 months aloof (D)/ No error (E).

113. Seven years (A)/was long (B)/a time (C)/to wait (D)/No error (E).

114. There are three major factors (A)/ which a recruiter (B)/must look for (C)/in a candidate (D)/No error (E).

115. Her mother had died (A)/when she was (B)/not yet (C)/two year old (D)/No error (E).

116. The sole objective (A)/of the trust (B)/is the warfare (C)/of mentally retarded children (D)/ No error (E).

117. All you have (A)/been hoping for (B)/will finally (C)/get accomplished (D)/No error (E).

118. Students are (A)/warned to (B)/ pay attention to (C)/their studies (D)/No error (E).

119. I have seen (A)/a beautiful (B)/ girl walking (C)/down the stairs yesterday (D)/No error (E).

120. Once he decided to (A)/build the temple (B)/the search for (C)/a suitable site started (D)/No error (E).

121. The robber was (A)/in poor shape (B)/but his spirit (C)/were not broken (D)/No error (E).

122. Inside a week (A)/I was asked (B)/to report to the Headquarters (C)/on deputation (D)/No error (E).

123. There is (A)/a clear division (B)/of opinion (C)/amidst the political parties (D)/No error (E).

124. The fighting (A)/broke out (B)/ later (C)/a dispute (D)/No error (E).

125. His lawyers (A)/have forbade (B)/ him to say (C)/anything (D)/No error (E).

EXPLANATORY ANSWERS

1. D : It should be 'had stopped'.

2. A : It should be 'she met'.

3. C : It should be 'to what'.

4. C : It should be 'from the'.

5. C : It should be 'above'.

6. B : It should be 'enjoyed talking'.

7. B : It should be 'admire her'.

8. D : It should be 'college that day'.

9. A : It should be 'The doctor advised'.

10. A : It should be 'who are'.

11. A : It should be 'Those who are'.

12. B : It should be 'comes again'.

13. A : It should be 'He is too poor'.

14. E :

15. A : It should be 'Mumps is'.

16. B : It should be 'did I reach'.

17. B : It should be 'hard, he'.

18. B : It should be 'very happy'.

19. D : It should be 'for the last three years'.

20. A : It should be 'He was sitting'.

21. C : It should be 'to play on'.

22. A : It should be 'Though a lot of'.

23. E :

24. D : It should be 'for a job'.

25. A : It should be 'I have known many men'.

26. A : It should be 'Life is as dear'.

27. B : It should be 'to the end of'.

28. B : It should be 'appointed'.

29. D : It should be 'be a trying and expensive proposition'.

30. D : It should be 'he would have a chance'.

31. C : It should be 'to reach there'.

32. B : It should be 'she is to'.

33. A : It should be 'Ten rupees is'.

34. C : It should be 'is greater than that of the'.

35. B : It should be 'as good as if'.

36. E :

37. C : It should be 'I had said'.

38. D : It should be 'take care of his belongings'.

39. D : It should be 'liking her'.

40. A : It should be 'If she had'.

41. B : It should be 'feeling well he'.

42. C : It should be 'I will go to'.

43. C : It should be 'on each boat'.

44. D : It should be 'was it yesterday'.

45. A : It should be 'only a well read person' OR 'only well read persons'.

46. C : It should be 'who have'.

47. E :

48. B : It should be 'nor I have'.

49. C : It should be 'more wise'.

50. B : It should be 'I were'.

51. A : It should be 'very calmly'.

52. A : It should be 'the court awarded'.

53. A : It should be 'Amar was conscious of'.

54. B : It should be 'lest'.

55. A : It should be 'Unless the rain stops'.

56. C : It should be 'I could'.

57. A : It should be 'The thief's mother'.

58. D : It should be 'taking a long leap'.

59. D : It should be 'all over the world'.

60. D : It should be 'are called for'.

61. A : It should be 'The Workers' Union'.

62. B : It should be 'broke into the house'.

63. B : It should be 'not a scholar'.

64. D : It should be 'to the cinema'.

65. C : It should be 'to return the books'.

66. E :

67. C : It should be 'green'.

68. C : It should be 'image in'

69. D : It should be 'middle of the road'.

70. D : It should be 'caused much damage'.

71. B : It should be 'lost their lives'.

72. C : It should be 'is increasing'.

73. B : It should be 'of her hair'.

74. D : It should be 'is unbeliev-able'.

75. A : It should be ' very few'.

76. A : It should be 'Our long journey'.

77. E :

78. A : It should be 'Jaya and I'.

79. B : It should be 'you and me'.

80. C : It should be 'one's responsi-bility'.

81. D : It should be 'she'.

82. B : It should be 'is more intelligent'.

83. A : It should be 'None of'.

84. A : It should be 'Either of'.

85. D : It should be 'beaufiful woman'.

86. C : It should be 'younger'.

87. D : It should be 'high'.

88. D : It should be 'clean'.

89. C : It should be 'except the one'.

90. A : It should be 'Further information'.

91. B : It should be 'ill for'.

92. E :

93. A : It should be 'Lay this'.

94. B : It should be 'me that he'.

95. B : It should be 'was robbed'.

96. B : It should be 'to borrow a book'.

97. A : It should be 'He taught'.

98. E :

99. A : It should be 'Fortunately no one'.

100. B : 'do not' is not needed in the sentence.

101. C : It should be 'always came'.

102. C : It should be 'scarcely'.

103. A : It should be 'He had been living'.

104. B : It should be 'for not being able to'.

105. C : It should be 'had stopped'.

106. B : It should be 'going to'.

107. B : It should be 'picked up'.

108. B : It should be 'those'.

109. A : It should be 'Once upon a time'.

110. E :

111. B : 'myself' is not needed in the sentence.

112. D : It should be 'was only four months away'.

113. B : It should be 'was too long'.

114. B : It should be 'that a recruiter'.

115. A : It should be 'Her mother died'.

116. C : It should be 'is the welfare'.

117. A : It should be 'All that you have'.

118. B : It should be 'advised to'.

119. B : It should be 'I saw'.

120. E :

121. D : It should be 'was not broken'.

122. A : It should be 'Within a week'.

123. D : It should be 'among the political parties'.

124. C : It should be 'after'.

125. B : It should be 'have forbidden'.

Synonyms

Directions : *In each questions below, out of the four alternatives, choose the one which best expresses the meaning of the given word.*

1. Odious
A. unpleasant B. dirty
C. silly D. constant

2. Hybrid
A. clean B. cross
C. superb D. serious

3. Detract
A. to redo B. delete
C. diminish D. change

4. Connoisseur
A. trustworthy B. expert
C. cheat D. corrupt

5. Luminous
A. quiet B. unbound
C. pressed D. glowing

6. Fractious
A. irritable B. shattered
C. partitioned D. unfair

7. Wanton
A. strict B. desired
C. playful D. unwanted

8. Spurious
A. genuine
B. false
C. readily available
D. outstanding

9. Verity
A. truth B. change
C. wholesome D. differ

10. Spendthrift
A. emptied B. consumer
C. worried D. wasteful

11. Vestibule
A. directed
B. investment
C. lobby
D. idling

12. Gullible
A. hungry B. foolish
C. insane D. cheeky

13. Bedeck
A. get off B. worker
C. decorate D. transfer

14. Infringe
A. filter B. disobey
C. boundary D. shrink

15. Adjourn
A. delay B. trip
C. bind D. court

16. Wobble
A. elastic B. heated
C. tremble D. jumpy

17. Drudgery
A. magic B. treatment
C. doubtful D. labour

18. Fugitive
A. crucial B. stormy
C. unstable D. mature

19. Profane
A. impure B. proud
C. survey D. certified

20. Niche
A. cost B. place
C. mark D. grip

21. Quirk
A. easy B. fancy
C. dumb D. recall

22. Mandatory
A. human B. heroic
C. required D. polite

23. Foster
A. cultivate B. dedicate
C. train D. achieve

24. Antiquity
A. age B. old
C. ancient D. thought

25. Complacent
A. confused B. unseen
C. thick D. pleased

26. Erudite
A. harsh B. strain
C. quick D. learned

27. Zenith
A. modest B. height
C. tussle D. shameful

28. Grimy
A. unclean B. shiny
C. greased D. slippery

29. Kindle
A. soft B. pity
C. fire D. make

30. Tedious
A. lively B. minute
C. tiring D. single

31. Yoke
A. embryo B. shout
C. desire D. bond

32. Jocular
A. faulty B. funny
C. idiotic D. uneven

33. Nefarious
A. evil B. friendly
C. ignorant D. many

34. Incur
A. gain B. arrive
C. speak D. force

35. Resolve
A. cancel B. total
C. decide D. balance

36. Overcast
A. announce B. project
C. dull D. carry

37. Vouch
A. rest B. certify
C. cheque D. purse

38. Supple
A. dark B. silly
C. agree D. elastic

39. Jeopardy
A. fun B. action
C. merry D. danger

40. Fidelity
A. manner B. faith
C. story D. charge

41. Zone
A. point B. issue
C. belt D. object

42. Decoy
A. spy B. ruin
C. trap D. fact

43. Amplify
A. boost B. remove
C. test D. value

44. Random
A. casual B. will
C. order D. limit

45. Extol
A. ending B. widen
C. force D. celebrate

46. Thorny
A. sharp
B. frightening
C. thorough
D. disable

47. Rugged
A. matted B. rough
C. strong D. grand

48. Forage
A. aged B. scare
C. food D. weak

49. Hoodwink
A. cheat B. viewer
C. honest D. decent

50. Smother
A. plain B. envelop
C. giggle D. hurry

Directions : *In the questions that follow, a set of three words is given with different meanings of a certain word. Choose that word from the options given after each set.*

51. Absurd, Droll, Comic
A. dainty B. insane
C. jocular D. stormy

52. Gracious, Daring, Manful
A. clanger B. gallivant
C. gallant D. wager

53. Lovable, Enchanting, Cuddly
A. beloved B. amiable
C. sonorous D. forage

54. Overwhelm, Crush, Destroy
A. overdue B. oppress
C. downfall D. engulf

55. Decode, Simplify, Interpret
A. observe
B. calculate
C. erase
D. translate

56. Mark, Note, Sign
A. symptom B. issue
C. letter D. order

57. Relish, Smack, Swallow
A. hurt B. praise
C. taste D. scold

58. Dreadful, Hellish, Titanic
A. uneven
B. monstrous
C. difficult
D. hated

59. Reduce, Cheaper, Exhaust
A. finish B. burn
C. wipe D. depress

60. Fancy, Request, Desire
A. covet B. worry
C. haste D. caution

61. Rough, Crude, Sharp
A. edged B. harsh
C. uneven D. witty

62. Devalue, Corrupt, Weaken
A. unwell B. alter
C. adulterate D. praise

63. Fence, Defend, Protect
A. barricade B. curtail
C. storm D. reserve

64. Graceful, Tender, Refined
A. pure B. lively
C. elegant D. legal

65. Lodge, Abide, Dwell
A. rule B. reside
C. dominate D. complain

66. Credit, Dignity, Glory
A. crown B. decent
C. mannerly D. honour

67. System, Method, Fashion
A. technique B. famous
C. unitary D. ability

68. Titan, Huge, Jumbo
A. time B. ample
C. fast D. gaint

69. Absurd, Amazing, Wonderful
A. silly
B. handsome
C. incredible
D. praise

70. Distant, Aloof, Careless
A. lazy
B. indifferent
C. away
D. secondary

71. Die, Expire, Vanish
A. perish B. last
C. want D. due

72. Thoughtful, Grave, Serious
A. ideal B. sacred
C. angry D. pensive

73. Sum, Number, Amount
A. whole B. count
C. quantity D. finance

74. Legal, Official, Lawful
A. court B. justice
C. valid D. rule

75. Insane, Dumb, Crazy
A. bright B. idiotic
C. clown D. wise

76. Reign, Empire, Kingdom
A. sovereignty
B. command
C. destruction
D. union

77. Nurse, Feed, Attend
A. nourish B. consume
C. present D. protect

78. Daily, Register, Gazette
A. journal
B. regular
C. attendance
D. always

79. Friendly, Warm, Cheerful
A. manly B. tepid
C. excited D. cordial

80. Cry, Moan, Sigh
A. wail B. groan
C. lease D. clamp

81. Imitate, Phoney, Counterfeit
A. mimic B. double
C. constitute D. forge

82. Creation, Inception, Source
A. genesis B. beget
C. sculpture D. trace

83. Protege, Aspirant, Entrant
A. nominee B. scholar
C. orator D. disposed

84. Force, Compel, Bind
A. solder B. unite
C. oblige D. activate

85. Derision, Contempt, Despite
A. ladle B. deface
C. berate D. scorn

86. Unfruitful, Barren, Unproductive
A. wasted B. marooned
C. pilfered D. sterile

87. Vanity, Arrogance, Pride
A. maturity B. exclusive
C. conceit D. terse

88. Douse, Satiate, Cool
A. freeze B. simplify
C. quench D. relax

89. Candid, Artless, Ingenuous
A. drab B. naive
C. fadded D. cheap

90. Guide, Symptom, Clue
A. measure B. index
C. effect D. aide

91. Baron, Mogul, Magnate
A. lure B. princely
C. tycoon D. genre

92. Mesmerize, Spellbind, Fascinate
A. hypnotize B. scrape
C. remember D. attract

93. Custom, Style, Trend
A. vogue B. tradition
C. lively D. fancy

94. Juvenile, Callow, Unfledged
A. shrewd
B. inexperienced
C. young
D. cunning

95. Struggle, Tussle, Scuffle
A. toil B. wrestle
C. debate D. error

96. Spiritual, Heavenly, Divine
A. learned
B. celestial
C. mythological
D. scholistic

97. Provide, Bestow, Reveal
A. convey B. engage
C. clear D. furnish

98. Husky, Gruff, Croaky
A. revile B. tactless
C. hoarse D. evident

99. Expression, Remark, Locution
A. distinct B. speech
C. phrase D. appeal

100. Contract, Guarantee, Pledge
A. undertake
B. soothe
C. offer
D. appropriate

101. Gauze, Swathe, Plaster
A. passage B. clean
C. fortify D. bandage

102. Opulence, Treasure, Prosperity
A. attainment
B. saving
C. fortune
D. support

103. Panic, Startle, Unnerve
A. dread B. release
C. corner D. alarm

104. Remove, Abstract, Recall
A. erase
B. unbound
C. remember
D. withdraw

105. Free, Frank, Direct
A. available
B. outspoken
C. orderly
D. approachable

106. Evildoer, Wrongdoer, Transgressor
A. corrupt B. killer
C. malefactor D. slave

107. Cripple, Hack, Disfigure
A. mutilate B. exercise
C. decrease D. beat

108. Baffle, Confuse, Bewilder
A. blend B. surprise
C. puzzle D. madden

109. Delight, Pleasure, Comfort
A. please B. luxury
C. happiness D. deceit

110. Slit, Gash, Notch
A. untie B. separate
C. stimulate D. incision

111. Core, Grain, Marrow
A. centre B. reality
C. kernel D. solid

112. Bolt, Lock, Hasp
A. rough B. latch
C. bound D. close

113. Notification, Statement, Account
A. presentation B. reminder
C. bulletin D. logic

114. Scrutinize, Investigate, Analyse
A. violate B. promote
C. explore D. exhibit

115. Precise, Methodical, Efficient
A. perfect B. calculated
C. systematic D. accurate

116. Sunny, Joyful, Debonair
A. Showy B. rampart
C. brisk D. buoyant

117. Academic, Speculative, Theoretical
A. hypothetical
B. educative
C. overwrought
D. unanimous

118. Confound, Dishevel, Tangle
A. jumble B. exchange
C. disobey D. affix

119. Paroxysm, Spasm, Outbreak
A. agony B. outburst
C. outset D. entry

120. Murmur, Breathe, Rustle
A. disturb B. whisper
C. inhale D. noise

ANSWERS

1	**2**	**3**	**4**	**5**	**6**	**7**	**8**	**9**	**10**
A	B	C	B	D	A	C	B	A	D
11	**12**	**13**	**14**	**15**	**16**	**17**	**18**	**19**	**20**
C	B	C	B	A	C	D	C	A	B
21	**22**	**23**	**24**	**25**	**26**	**27**	**28**	**29**	**30**
B	C	A	A	D	D	B	A	C	C
31	**32**	**33**	**34**	**35**	**36**	**37**	**38**	**39**	**40**
D	B	A	A	C	C	B	D	D	B
41	**42**	**43**	**44**	**45**	**46**	**47**	**48**	**49**	**50**
C	C	A	A	D	A	B	C	A	B
51	**52**	**53**	**54**	**55**	**56**	**57**	**58**	**59**	**60**
C	C	B	D	D	A	C	B	D	A

61	62	63	64	65	66	67	68	69	70
B	C	A	C	B	D	A	D	C	B
71	**72**	**73**	**74**	**75**	**76**	**77**	**78**	**79**	**80**
A	D	C	C	C	A	A	A	D	B
81	**82**	**83**	**84**	**85**	**86**	**87**	**88**	**89**	**90**
D	A	A	C	D	D	C	C	B	B
91	**92**	**93**	**94**	**95**	**96**	**97**	**98**	**99**	**100**
C	A	A	C	B	B	D	C	C	A
101	**102**	**103**	**104**	**105**	**106**	**107**	**108**	**109**	**110**
D	C	D	D	B	C	A	C	B	D
111	**112**	**113**	**114**	**115**	**116**	**117**	**118**	**119**	**120**
C	B	C	C	C	D	A	A	B	B

Antonyms

Directions : *In each questions below, out of the four alternatives, choose the word that is most nearly the opposite in meaning to the given word.*

1. Transient
A. passing B. brief
C. lucid D. eternal

2. Effective
A. potent B. able
C. futile D. sharp

3. Oust
A. spoil B. renew
C. induct D. outdo

4. Sustain
A. rule B. uphold
C. impose D. resist

5. Lofty
A. sublime B. flat
C. shrill D. terse

6. Venerable
A. similar B. young
C. accurate D. wise

7. Anticipation
A. surprise B. foresee
C. revival D. assurance

8. Embellish
A. obscure B. enrich
C. deface D. lavish

9. Deter
A. circulate B. induce
C. hamper D. encourage

10. Luscious
A. shining B. tasty
C. eerie D. sour

11. Revenue
A. income B. outlay
C. construct D. repeal

12. Tangible
A. independent B. unreal
C. material D. salient

13. Fiendish
A. corrupt B. angelic
C. valuable D. reverent

14. Headstrong
A. complaisant
B. mastermind
C. unorthodox
D. ponderous

15. Nebulous
A. clear B. confused
C. careful D. central

16. Questionable
A. subjective B. disputed
C. certain D. deductive

17. Slender
A. silky B. grim
C. stout D. coarse

18. Upright
A. inferior B. crooked
C. wrong D. engage

19. Tyrant
A. quiet B. accord
C. kind D. unjust

20. Sporadic
A. genuine B. blithe
C. peculiar D. frequent

21. Blemish
A. acclaim B. spotless
C. advance D. retard

22. Extravagant
A. frank B. credible
C. partial D. stingy

23. Stretch
A. prevail B. fondle
C. object D. curtail

24. Persecute
A. sanction B. patronize
C. authorise D. transact

25. Eternal
A. finite B. mystic
C. perpetual D. disjunct

26. Deviate
A. obscure B. magnify
C. persist D. restore

27. Vicious
A. moral B. chaste
C. faulty D. peevish

28. Subtle
A. artful B. coarse
C. delicate D. fragile

29. Ferocious
A. prolific B. strong
C. modest D. wild

30. Pertinent
A. relevant B. graphic
C. unfit D. prompt

31. Mighty
A. frail B. godly
C. potent D. uneasy

32. Onerous
A. exacting B. crushing
C. facile D. arduous

33. Transact
A. afflict B. loiter
C. waver D. persist

34. Mourn
A. maim B. deplore
C. revel D. truncate

35. Claim
A. quote B. waive
C. lively D. bright

36. Solemn
A. sedate B. cordial
C. artless D. vulgar

37. Zealot
A. devoted B. fickle
C. fanatic D. highest

38. Bewilder
A. astonish B. damage
C. enlighten D. distrust

39. Contempt
A. grace B. scorn
C. share D. accord

40. Hypocrisy
A. flattery B. charm
C. deceit D. honesty

41. Protract
A. refute B. clarify
C. curtail D. conceal

42. Uncouth
A. clownish B. attractive
C. unbiased D. reliable

43. Scarcity
A. pleasure B. galore
C. retrieval D. amass

44. Rejoice
A. neglect B. drain
C. obtuse D. lament

45. Partake
A. whole B. allot
C. divide D. sever

46. Just
A. unlawful B. partial
C. discreet D. fraction

47. Myth
A. legend B. story
C. fable D. fact

48. Unanimity
A. unity B. agreement
C. discord D. deception

49. Ghastly
A. inconstant B. spectral
C. gratified D. corporeal

50. Loathe
A. undress B. prefer
C. compromise D. dominate

ANSWERS

1	**2**	**3**	**4**	**5**	**6**	**7**	**8**	**9**	**10**
D	C	C	C	B	B	C	C	D	D
11	**12**	**13**	**14**	**15**	**16**	**17**	**18**	**19**	**20**
B	B	B	A	A	C	C	B	C	D
21	**22**	**23**	**24**	**25**	**26**	**27**	**28**	**29**	**30**
B	D	D	B	A	C	A	B	C	C
31	**32**	**33**	**34**	**35**	**36**	**37**	**38**	**39**	**40**
A	C	B	C	B	D	B	C	A	D
41	**42**	**43**	**44**	**45**	**46**	**47**	**48**	**49**	**50**
C	B	B	D	B	A	D	C	D	B

One Word Substitution

Directions : *Choose the most suitable 'one word' for each of the following expressions given below.*

1. The belief that good must prevail over evil in the end
A. Optimism
B. Sophtism
C. Truism
D. Radicalism

2. Hater of women
A. Misochist
B. Misogamist
C. Misogynist
D. Misanthropist

3. That cannot be seen through
A. Transparent
B. Translucent
C. Evanscent
D. Opaque

4. One who will never cease to exist
A. Immoral
B. Impassable
C. Immortal
D. Impassive

5. Custom or condition of marriage to more than one person at a time
A. Bigamy
B. Polygamy
C. Monogamy
D. Matriomony

6. Habit of walking in sleep
A. Sophtism
B. Somnambulism
C. Scepticism
D. Somniloquism

7. Person who talks too much or too often only about himself
A. Optimist
B. Critic
C. Egoist
D. Stoic

8. A summary or outline of a book
A. Precis
B. manuscript
C. Preface
D. Synopsis

9. Neat and smart in dress and appearance
A. Shabby B. Spruce
C. Rustic D. Sophist

10. Arrangement of events according to dates or times of occurrence
A. Chronology
B. Catalogue
C. Chronicle
D. Choreography

11. A person who has no means of livelihood
A. Beggar B. Refugee
C. Convict D. Pauper

12. A post supporting the handrail of a staircase
A. Banister B. Barrage
C. Barrister D. Barouche

13. A person who firmly believes that all the events are decided by fate

A. Forte B. Florist
C. Fugitive D. Fatalist

14. Easily cheated or duped

A. Naive B. Deceived
C. Gullible D. Forged

15. Things that can be easily set on fire

A. Inflammable B. Sparkler
C. Fiery D. Rabid

16. Instrument for testing the quality of milk

A. Altimeter
B. Lactometer
C. Barometer
D. Chronometer

17. A person who believes in the existence of God

A. Atheist B. Baptist
C. Theist D. Cynicist

18. Of, or like a cat

A. Furry B. Agile
C. Feline D. Canine

19. Extermination of a race or community by mass murder

A. Arson B. Coup
C. Pilferage D. Genocide

20. Given, done or obtained without payment

A. Award
B. Endowment
C. Gratuity
D. Grant

21. A cardboard box for holding goods

A. Carton B. Trunk
C. Chest D. Package

22. Person relying on experience and observation

A. Examiner
B. Eccentric
C. Empiric
D. Executioner

23. Group of lions

A. Shoal B. Pride
C. Flock D. Pack

24. An exceptionally brilliant or successful young person

A. Genius B. Maestro
C. Intellect D. Whiz-kid

25. Ruler who has absolute authority to run the government

A. Monarch
B. Dictator
C. Bureaucrat
D. Theocrat

26. Agreement during a war or battle to stop fighting for a time

A. Alliance
B. Treaty
C. Armistice
D. Concordant

27. A person who eats human flesh

A. Cannibal B. Obese
C. Dossier D. Laggard

28. An illusion or hope that cannot be realized

A. Mirage
B. Fantasy
C. Misconception
D. Perception

29. Something outdated or no longer in use or fashion

A. Absolute B. Obsolete
C. Retarded D. Regale

30. Complete failure to reach an agreement to settle a quarrel or grievance
A. Mishap B. Wreck
C. Omission D. Deadlock

31. Person who eats too much
A. Famished B. Glutton
C. Hungry D. Starved

32. Contrary to law
A. Inimical B. Adverse
C. Illegal D. Precept

33. A criminal who has often been in prison
A. Jailbird B. Jailor
C. Prisoner D. Jockey

34. Person using more words than needed
A. Gullible B. Talkative
C. Verbose D. Extrovert

35. Building where grain is stored
A. Stockyard B. Modicum
C. Iota D. Granary

36. A woman head of a family or tribe
A. Matriarch B. Patriarch
C. Frateral D. Ladybird

37. Crime of killing a small babe
A. Insensate
B. Infanticide
C. Innuendo
D. Infidel

38. Person of good appearance and manners
A. Debonair B. Adonis
C. Courteous D. Social

39. A change which is proposed or made to a rule, regulation etc.
A. Enhancement
B. Reform
C. Clarification
D. Amendment

40. A dull, slow or mindless person
A. Insane B. Zombie
C. Deranged D. Lunatic

41. A place where people often meet
A. Rendezvous
B. Club
C. Joint
D. Association

42. Reaching a conclusion from two statements
A. Reasoning
B. Comparison
C. Syllogism
D. Deduction

43. Being the only one of its sort
A. Specimen
B. Sample
C. Unique
D. Outstanding

44. Exposed to being attacked or harmed
A. Volatile
B. Vulnerable
C. Versatile
D. Voluptuary

45. Egg laying animals that creep or crawl
A. Reptiles B. Creepers
C. Primers D. Insects

46. A person who is free from national prejudices and feels at home in any country of the world
A. Orthodox
B. Conservative
C. Crusader
D. Cosmopolitan

47. Speech delivered without previous thought or preparation
A. Oration B. Jargon
C. Extempore D. Harangue

48. Irrelevant talk about God and sacred things
A. Sacrilege
B. Blasphemy
C. Profanity
D. Oblation

49. Company of persons making a journey together for safety
A. Travellers
B. Tourists
C. Campaign
D. Caravan

50. Animals feeding on flesh or other animal matter
A. Carnivore B. Omnivore
C. Barbarian D. Cannibal

ANSWERS

1	**2**	**3**	**4**	**5**	**6**	**7**	**8**	**9**	**10**
A	C	D	C	B	B	C	D	B	A
11	**12**	**13**	**14**	**15**	**16**	**17**	**18**	**19**	**20**
D	A	D	C	A	B	C	C	D	C
21	**22**	**23**	**24**	**25**	**26**	**27**	**28**	**29**	**30**
A	C	B	D	B	C	A	A	B	D
31	**32**	**33**	**34**	**35**	**36**	**37**	**38**	**39**	**40**
B	C	A	C	D	A	B	A	D	B
41	**42**	**43**	**44**	**45**	**46**	**47**	**48**	**49**	**50**
A	C	C	B	A	D	C	B	D	A

Idioms and Phrases

Directions : *From the alternatives given below each idiom/phrase select the one that best brings out the meaning of the idiom/phrase.*

1. By leaps and bounds
A. majority B. rapidly
C. easily D. fairly

2. In a daze
A. in bright light
B. ill and bedridden
C. facing a problem
D. confused and shocked

3. A broken reed
A. a broken affair
B. an unreliable person
C. discord
D. an easy task

4. Round the corner
A. curved
B. drift
C. easily available
D. not far off

5. A black sheep
A. a person of bad reputation
B. a breed of sheep
C. a dark room
D. unpleasant feeling

6. To cross one's mind
A. to get confused
B. to occur
C. to create tension
D. to tell a lie

7. Yeoman's service
A. render help
B. poor service
C. slavery
D. late delivery of goods

8. To lead a dog's life
A. to live in a small house
B. to behave inhumanly
C. to be loyal to others
D. to live in misery

9. An early bird
A. one who catches worms
B. a cock or hen
C. a lucky person
D. an early riser

10. A fool's errand
A. to work very slowly
B. to waste time
C. a useless task
D. a silly mistake

11. Fair and square
A. give reason
B. honest
C. smart person
D. a white cube

12. A feather in one's cap
A. a hole in the cap
B. an achievement
C. a light object
D. a dirty cap

13. A queer fish
A. a strange person

B. a dead fish
C. a secret plan
D. biased person

14. Flying colours
A. victory
B. modern art
C. rainbow
D. good news

15. Gift of the gab
A. well learned
B. an unexpected visitor
C. fluency in speech
D. a costly gift

16. Game for anything
A. prefer playing games to studies
B. full of life
C. easily impressed
D. a good player

17. To give a slip
A. to fall
B. to go unnoticed
C. to bunk the class
D. to escape

18. A white collar worker
A. a person doing a labourer's work
B. a person doing an officer's job
C. a person in white uniform
D. a foreign dignatory

19. By and large
A. expanded
B. without any trouble
C. an easy situation
D. in general

20. Dress someone up
A. get ready for a party
B. prepare to do something
C. disguise
D. plan

21. Let someone down
A. disappoint
B. push away
C. humiliate
D. say goodbye

22. To take after
A. to chase
B. to resemble
C. to follow
D. to walk behind

23. Fret and fume
A. shout loudly
B. burn a large fire
C. start a fight
D. show angry impatience

24. Practise what you preach
A. become a teacher
B. do what is right
C. do what one advises others to do
D. follow the leader

25. The top brass
A. a rich dealer of brass product
B. high ranking military officer
C. good trumpet player
D. of great value or importance

26. The ins and outs
A. entry and exit gates
B. secret information
C. the good and the bad
D. the full details

27. Hit the jackpot
A. have a great success
B. slap a foolish person
C. win in a gamble
D. hit the target

28. A casanova
A. to have fun
B. a sincere wish
C. an unfaithful lover
D. an unexpected good news

29. Straight from the horse's mouth
A. very outspoken
B. most powerful
C. heart warming speech
D. first hand news

30. To set forth
A. to impress
B. to express
C. to follow
D. to clear all doubts

31. Lay off
A. dismiss temporarily
B. to fall asleep
C. feel tired
D. postpone

32. To fall in with
A. form a group
B. work together
C. to decline
D. to agree to

33. Bring round
A. persuade
B. encircle
C. trap
D. draw a circle

34. Yawning gap
A. parted lips
B. a wide gap
C. on the other side
D. more than needed

35. A word of honour
A. an award
B. a sincere promise
C. a high military rank
D. an effort to win

36. Even walls have ears
A. holes in walls
B. very poor condition
C. there are spies around
D. face trouble

37. A stepping stone
A. a rung of ladder
B. to finish a given task
C. source of success
D. an opportunity

38. To smell a rat
A. to have a suspicion
B. foul smell
C. to be scared of
D. to sense trouble

39. Turning point
A. a busy crossroad
B. a point of change for the better
C. an important factor
D. a kind of bend

40. One of these days
A. recently B. recent past
C. finally D. shortly

41. To see eye to eye with
A. to cause a fight
B. to reason out
C. to get friendly with
D. to agree

42. Red tape
A. power
B. official delay
C. danger sign
D. unlucky person

43. To be in a saddle
A. to be in control

B. to ride a horse
C. to be in trouble
D. to be very excited

44. Under the table
A. unknown
B. secretly
C. well hidden
D. not in view

45. A rainy day
A. a time of trouble
B. the day of the onset of monsoon
C. a day when it rained continuously
D. the time to have fun

46. To put on
A. to mimic
B. to stay on
C. to offer for sale
D. to wear

47. To hold on
A. catch on to something
B. to save
C. to let someone wait
D. to continue

48. To read between the lines
A. to correct the errors
B. to see the hidden meaning
C. to study hard
D. to discover something new

49. Look after
A. to overlook
B. to ignore
C. to attend to
D. to take charge

50. Tom, Dick and Harry
A. three musketeers
B. many sided
C. ordinary person
D. three different pairs

ANSWERS

1	**2**	**3**	**4**	**5**	**6**	**7**	**8**	**9**	**10**
B	D	B	D	A	B	A	D	D	C
11	**12**	**13**	**14**	**15**	**16**	**17**	**18**	**19**	**20**
B	B	A	A	C	B	D	B	D	C
21	**22**	**23**	**24**	**25**	**26**	**27**	**28**	**29**	**30**
A	B	D	C	B	D	A	C	D	B
31	**32**	**33**	**34**	**35**	**36**	**37**	**38**	**39**	**40**
A	D	A	B	B	C	C	A	B	D
41	**42**	**43**	**44**	**45**	**46**	**47**	**48**	**49**	**50**
D	B	A	B	A	D	D	B	C	C

Mis-Spelt Words

Directions : *In each question below, groups of four words are given. In each group, one word is not spelt correctly. Find this mis-spelt word.*

1. A. bouquet B. eternal C. criple D. blurred

2. A. lodge B. rigime C. inhabit D. conduit

3. A. hostile B. entrence C. fervent D. typically

4. A. terminator B. border C. censer D. juicer

5. A. ruffian B. distortion C. brighten D. comedean

6. A. conterary B. persuade C. nostalgia D. proficient

7. A. spectators B. condemn C. priority D. analisis

8. A. percolate B. delimma C. fierce D. overwhelm

9. A. fabricate B. ethical C. optimist D. armistise

10. A. absente B. genuine C. heartily D. agitated

11. A. allot B. occurance C. faithful D. nativity

12. A. contradict B. realistick C. abstract D. brutal

13. A. profitable B. construct C. salwage D. authentic

14. A. engredients B. personal C. ruthless D. discrete

15. A. temprate B. virtuous C. fanfare D. smoulder

16. A. idling B. consumer C. protrution D. oblique

17. A. illegal B. condensed C. culpable D. boundry

18. A. prespire B. dribble C. acutely D. wither

19. A. stagnant B. profession C. quater D. inverted

20. A. ettiquete B. intrinsic C. probable D. crusading

21. A. reciprocate B. dehidration C. tournament D. circumvent

22. A. evacuate B. converge C. dissembark D. elegance

23. A. exemplary B. submerging C. cooperative D. managable

24. A. inundate B. smoulder C. stimulus D. generosity

25. A. dexterous B. kernel C. pagentry D. novice

26. A. wrestler B. numeros
C. festivity D. baptism

27. A. remorseful B. journalism
C. gurilla D. youngster

28. A. filanthropy B. ravenous
C. detergent D. unforeseen

29. A. inoccupied B. ensure
C. anatomy D. unwary

30. A. luminous B. abhorrent
C. vibrasion D. wretched

ANSWERS (WITH CORRECT SPELLING)

1. C : cripple
2. B : regime
3. B : entrance
4. C : censor
5. D : comedian
6. A : contrary
7. D : analysis
8. B : dilemma
9. D : armistice
10. A : absentee
11. B : occurrence
12. B : realistic
13. C : salvage
14. A : ingredients
15. A : temperate
16. C : protrusion
17. D : boundary
18. A : perspire
19. C : quarter
20. A : etiquette
21. B : dehydration
22. C : disembark
23. D : manageable
24. D : generosity
25. C : pageantry
26. B : numerous
27. C : guerilla
28. A : philanthropy
29. A : unoccupied
30. C : vibration

Word Usage

Directions : *In each question below, sentences are given with blanks to be filled in with appropriate words. From the given four alternatives, choose the correct word which meaningfully completes the given sentence.*

1. The suspect was too ..... to admit that he had committed the crime.
A. nervous B. clever
C. shy D. obstinate

2. The patient's condition would become ..... if timely medication is not given.
A. pathetic B. deadly
C. serious D. grave

3. He was ..... of his valuables.
A. cheated B. snatched
C. looted D. deprived

4. The child picked up the toy which ..... on the ground.
A. laid B. lay
C. lying D. was lie

5. I ..... a certain grace about the way she carried herself.
A. marked B. found
C. noticed D. assumed

6. The fact is that men in uniform make a ..... audience.
A. distinguished
B. cheerful
C. encouraging
D. experimental

7. Try to be ..... about your objectives.
A. clear B. confused
C. worried D. ignorant

8. One evening, all the children in the family ..... to go to a picnic.
A. fought B. panicked
C. decided D. needed

9. High pitched noises ..... the reader's mind.
A. crackled B. disturbed
C. dampened D. crossed

10. After the control, the ..... winner celebrated by partying with her friends.
A. eager B. solitary
C. expected D. radiant

11. Medication will also be ..... at the time of examination.
A. advised
B. made available
C. prescribed
D. distributed

12. Too much work will ..... your energy.
A. drain B. boost
C. enhance D. filter

13. The water ..... in a silver stream down on mountain slope.
A. seeped B. rushed
C. flowed D. drained

14. The film was ..... the 'Best Film' for its magnificent portrayal of the complex and moving emotions.
A. described B. directed
C. adjudged D. projected

15. He will not study ..... he is compelled to do so.
A. unless B. till
C. since D. until

16. Women have ..... strongly in our freedom movements during the Civil Disobedience Movement in 1930.
A. focussed
B. participated
C. protested
D. improved

17. The ..... he eats, the fatter he becomes.
A. less B. most
C. more D. lots

18. I felicitated him on his grand ..... at the Defence Service Examination.
A. party
B. success
C. authority
D. appointment

19. He ..... your helping him to do the sums.
A. criticises
B. praises
C. accomplishes
D. appreciates

20. The word 'caste' is ..... from the Portuguese word 'casta' signifying breed, race or kind.
A. extracted B. imposed
C. derived D. taken

21. She walked past us with her ..... in the air.
A. chin B. attention
C. nose D. hands

22. He ..... his back on his friends when he became a celebrity.
A. forced B. showed
C. detained D. turned

23. That multinational firm seeks to ..... engineers from all walks of disciplines to its various departments.
A. offer B. recruit
C. lay off D. impress

24. We all believe that change is the ..... of nature.
A. law B. force
C. habit D. part

25. Only ..... will you find a girl that combines both looks and is good at other things.
A. rarely B. often
C. naturally D. in films

26. There are a few parents, who can ..... to send their children to boarding schools.
A. reason out B. admit
C. afford D. try

27. His achievements in the field of social welfare are .....
A. creditable
B. exceptional
C. underestimated
D. manifold

28. The palatial building was ..... for the wedding occassion.
A. ignited
B. enlightened
C. lighted
D. illuminated

29. This is the ..... of the two questions.
A. hardest
B. unexpected
C. complex
D. easier

30. The court has ..... the final judgement.
A. decided B. awaited
C. examined D. passed

31. Nearly fifty countries are expected to ..... in the trade fair this year.
A. collaborate B. participate
C. franchise D. unite

32. The actor's fine performance undoubtedly deserved a great ..... from the audience.
A. applause B. criticism
C. proposal D. reward

33. The army offers exciting career ..... for the adventurous young people.
A. promotions B. perks
C. providents D. prospects

34. The model's face was ..... with heavy make-up.
A. coated B. painted
C. glued D. shaded

35. India is the largest ..... of films in the world.
A. producer B. maker
C. inventor D. creator

36. The naughty child was ..... by his mother.
A. loved B. defended
C. rebuked D. threatened

37. Even after hours of discussion the Board failed to reach a ..... decision.
A. biased
B. unanimous
C. unique
D. perplexed

38. He refused to sell that dress unless the price offered was .....
A. right B. true
C. correct D. realistic

39. Women in rural areas are capable of progressive thinking and have the ..... for viable social participation.
A. potential B. heart
C. knowledge D. courage

40. The unemployment rate in the country is ..... and ample measures should be taken to solve the problem.
A. stagnant
B. controversial
C. alarming
D. distinct

ANSWERS

1	2	3	4	5	6	7	8	9	10
D	C	D	B	C	A	A	C	B	D
11	**12**	**13**	**14**	**15**	**16**	**17**	**18**	**19**	**20**
C	A	B	C	A	B	C	B	D	C
21	**22**	**23**	**24**	**25**	**26**	**27**	**28**	**29**	**30**
C	D	B	A	A	C	A	C	D	D
31	**32**	**33**	**34**	**35**	**36**	**37**	**38**	**39**	**40**
B	A	D	A	A	C	B	A	A	C

Sentence Completion

Directions : *Following exercise is meant to test your ability to choose the right words to fill in the gaps of sentences. Read the sentence carefully and choose suitable preposition for the purpose.*

1. She is proud ..... her beauty.
A. at B. on
C. of D. about

2. Mohan belongs ..... the upper strata of the society.
A. from B. for
C. to D. of

3. They have invited us ..... attend the function.
A. for B. to
C. upto D. at

4. We offer heartiest congratulation ..... your success.
A. at B. on
C. upon D. for

5. M/s Ram Avtar & Sons are the famous dealers ..... sugar and wheat.
A. of B. in
C. at D. for

6. He showed much affection ..... me when I met him recently.
A. for B. to
C. with D. towards

7. He entered ..... the gate without any dificulty.
A. by B. from
C. in D. into

8. He aimed ..... the target and fired.
A. to B. at
C. on D. up

9. The trend ..... price rise is unfortunate.
A. in B. of
C. for D. with

10. Adulteration ..... food stuff is going unchecked.
A. with B. of
C. in D. into

11. So far that case is concerned, I have not dealt ..... it.
A. no preposition is required
B. in
C. into
D. with

12. The man killed ..... road accident was a stranger.
A. of B. by
C. in D. on

13. He did not go ..... the right direction.
A. to B. by
C. into D. in

14. The train reached ..... the station right time.
A. to
B. by
C. on
D. no preposition is required

15. Punjab Mail arrived ..... New Delhi Railway Station three hours late.
A. no preposition is required
B. on
C. at
D. to

16. He slipped away ..... the crowd to avoid arrest.
A. of B. from
C. by D. with

17. The man died ..... heart attack without receiving any treatment.
A. of B. with
C. in D. by

18. He called ..... me late at night to communicate the message.
A. upon B. on
C. to D. up

19. The accused ran away ..... the police custoday.
A. from B. off
C. by D. off

20. My friend called ..... me to offer congratulations on my success.
A. to B. upon
C. on D. off

21. This remark is not ..... your favour.
A. to B. for
C. in D. of

22. He acted well ..... accordance with law.
A. with B. by
C. in D. to

23. There is a provision ..... law to bail out the accused.
A. by B. of
C. with D. in

24. Parole can be granted ..... any convict under the provisions of law.
A. for B. to
C. into D. upon

25. The appeal has been moved ..... High Court by the party.
A. in B. to
C. for D. with

26. He filed an appeal ..... the higher court.
A. with B. to
C. in D. for

27. An appeal has been admitted ..... the Supreme Court.
A. by B. into
C. with D. in

28. The absentee was reported to be ..... bed since last three days.
A. at B. in
C. on D. into

29. When I entered the room he was lying ..... bed.
A. over B. at
C. on D. in

30. Please accompany me ..... my room to collect the material.
A. for B. to
C. upto D. into

31. He met me ..... the way near the park after a long time.
A. in B. by
C. on D. into

32. This item has been included ..... the agenda of the meeting.
A. into B. in
C. on D. with

33. He has made good progress ..... English now.
A. with B. in
C. into D. of

34. The colour of your coat is matching ..... that of the pant.
A. with
B. by
C. to
D. no preposition is required

35. Our team played a match ..... the Young Men's.
A. by B. with
C. to D. against

36. Will you go ..... the market just now?
A. in B. to
C. for D. into

37. Indian team had played ..... the M.C.C. last year.
A. with B. upon
C. against D. off

38. I am not going to contest Lok Sabha seat ...... Raebareli.
A. off B. from
C. by D. at

39. The substract can also be injected ..... human body.
A. with B. upon
C. into D. in

40. You must be very careful ..... reading the question paper.
A. for B. in
C. with D. against

41. The fare to Mumbai has been increased ..... sixty rupees from here recently.
A. to B. by
C. with D. upto

42. Fare to Chennai has now increased ..... eighty rupees from here instead of seventy-three.
A. by B. to
C. for D. upto

43. He is going to Kolkata ..... Punjab Mail.
A. by B. with
C. in D. through

44. Diwali is a festival ..... light.
A. of B. for
C. with D. by

45. I am not responsible ..... your personal safety.
A. of B. for
C. with D. about

46. He was run over ..... a speedy train.
A. of B. off
C. by D. under

47. The train reached the station ..... right time.
A. by
B. at
C. on
D. no preposition is required

48. He is good ..... chess.
A. for B. at
C. on D. with

49. Payments were made ..... cash at the Head Office.
A. in
B. by
C. through
D. no preposition is required

50. He called ..... John in the street and insulted him.
A. up B. at
C. down D. away

51. Preface ..... this book is very impressive.
A. for B. of
C. to D. on

52. Headlines of a newspapers are helpful ..... understanding the intro and follow-up of the news.
A. in B. for
C. about D. with

53. Title cover counts much ..... sale of any book.
A. in B. for
C. to D. on

54. He sent ..... his resignation last night.
A. for B. up
C. in D. to

55. He gave a ring ..... me yesterday.
A. for B. to
C. about D. by

56. He wants to appear ..... the university examination.
A. at B. in
C. for D. to

57. Respondent had appeared ..... the tribunal.
A. in B. at
C. before D. to

58. Witness was produced ..... the court today by the police.
A. to B. before
C. in D. at

59. The films produced ..... India lack of technical accomplishment.
A. by B. in
C. at D. from

60. In respect of films, India is ..... the largest producer of the world.
A. no preposition is required
B. from
C. among
D. into

61. Syce let ..... the horse from the carriage.
A. off B. away
C. up D. out

62. The cup was broken ..... pieces.
A. to B. into
C. with D. by

63. They are not ..... friendly terms now.
A. on B. with
C. in D. at

64. He was wearing a cap ..... his head.
A. over B. upon
C. on D. at

65. He had wrapped a handkerchief ..... his head.
A. over B. upon
C. around D. on

66. Who knocked at the door ..... this hour of night?
A. by B. in
C. at D. on

67. Alas! his ailing friend passed ..... last night.
A. off B. away
C. on D. out

68. Do not put ..... this urgent work on tomorrow.
A. away B. out
C. off D. down

69. An extra bogie was attached ..... Punjab Mail to accommodate the marriage party.

A. with
B. to
C. by
D. into

70. He pulled ..... the chain to stop the train.

A. up
B. down
C. away
D. off

71. They put ..... the cigarette before entering into the shrine.

A. down
B. off
C. out
D. away

72. There is a danger of epidemic break ..... in the flooded area.

A. out
B. up
C. away
D. off

73. There is an apprehension ..... breach of peace in the town.

A. for
B. of
C. with
D. into

74. The train was packed ..... capacity.

A. beyond
B. upto
C. over
D. to

75. The accused were awarded death penalty ..... the triple murder case.

A. for
B. in
C. into
D. against

76. He was listening ..... my advice attentively.

A. to
B. for
C. by
D. at

77. Servant put ..... the lights and went to sleep.

A. off
B. out
C. away
D. in

78. Due to on-rush ..... the traffic streets are jammed.

A. off
B. of
C. with
D. by

79. Survival of civil polity without fair administration justice cannot be imagined .....

A. at
B. by
C. no preposition is required
D. of

80. Aspirations ..... the people have remained unfulfilled in spite of much progress through planning.

A. by
B. of
C. in
D. for

81. We have entered ..... partnership of a reputable firm.

A. into
B. in
C. for
D. to

82. ..... the influence of wine, the man quarrelled with the conductor.

A. in
B. by
C. under
D. for

83. Our train will pass ..... that station during late hours of night.

A. through
B. by
C. from
D. with

84. Industrial production ..... the country has fallen due to labour trouble and power crisis.

A. in
B. of
C. into
D. within

85. Unemployment in the country is ..... the pitch of it.

A. on
B. at
C. to
D. in

86. Superfast trains are useful ..... long journey.

A. to
B. for
C. in
D. into

87. Don't take ill ..... it! my friend.
A. for B. of
C. on D. upon

88. Newspapers are an effective medium ..... public opinion in a democratic country.
A. for B. of
C. to D. into

89. All democratic governments show great respect ..... public opinion.
A. in B. for
C. to D. on

90. An independent judiciary is a must ..... social justice.
A. for B. to
C. unto D. upon

91. The facts as stated above are true ..... the best of my knowledge and belief.
A. in B. by
C. to D. from

92. He does not think ..... his future at all.
A. for B. on
C. upon D. of

93. Mohan is actively thinking ..... his future course of action.
A. of B. for
C. about D. upon

94. Wine is injurious ..... health.
A. for B. to
C. upon D. about

95. She alighted ..... the bus at Connaught Place.
A. off B. from
C. with D. by

96. He went abroad ..... the morning flight.
A. by B. from
C. with D. off

97. Orders have been issued to inquire ..... the matter.
A. about B. into
C. of D. off

98. One of your friends met me last night and inquired ..... your health.
A. into B. for
C. about D. of

99. Government has setup a court ..... inquiry to ascertain the facts.
A. for B. of
C. about D. on

100. He is a candidate ..... B.A. examination.
A. to B. for
C. in D. at

ANSWERS

1	2	3	4	5	6	7	8	9	10
C	C	B	B	B	B	D	B	B	C
11	**12**	**13**	**14**	**15**	**16**	**17**	**18**	**19**	**20**
D	C	D	D	C	B	A	D	A	C
21	**22**	**23**	**24**	**25**	**26**	**27**	**28**	**29**	**30**
C	C	B	B	A	C	A	C	D	B

31	**32**	**33**	**34**	**35**	**36**	**37**	**38**	**39**	**40**
B	A	B	D	D	B	C	B	C	B
41	**42**	**43**	**44**	**45**	**46**	**47**	**48**	**49**	**50**
B	B	A	A	B	C	D	B	A	C
51	**52**	**53**	**54**	**55**	**56**	**57**	**58**	**59**	**60**
B	A	B	C	B	B	C	C	B	A
61	**62**	**63**	**64**	**65**	**66**	**67**	**68**	**69**	**70**
A	B	A	C	C	C	B	C	B	B
71	**72**	**73**	**74**	**75**	**76**	**77**	**78**	**79**	**80**
C	A	B	D	B	A	B	B	D	B
81	**82**	**83**	**84**	**85**	**86**	**87**	**88**	**89**	**90**
A	C	B	B	B	B	B	B	B	A
91	**92**	**93**	**94**	**95**	**96**	**97**	**98**	**99**	**100**
C	D	C	B	B	A	B	C	B	B

Ordering of Sentences

Directions : *In the questions given below, the first and the last part of the sentences are numbered 1 and 6. The rest of the sentence is split into four parts P, Q, R and S which are not given in their proper order. From the given options after each questions, find out which of the four combinations is correct.*

1. 1. Looking at the history
P. can help us remember
Q. and perhaps encourage us
R. of everyday life
S. that every day is history
6. to live a little more intensely.
A. SQPR B. PQSR
C. QRPS D. RPSQ

2. 1. There are seven precautions.
P. of being a lightning casualty
Q. that can minimise your chances
R. if you cannot seek shelter
S. in a substantial building
6. or a hard-topped vehicle
A. SQRP B. SQPR
C. QSPR D. QPRS

3. 1. A large man
P. stood stiffly in the back
Q. to meet the wildly
R. of the vehicle
S. wearing a battered grey hat
6. cheering thousands
A. SPRQ B. SQPR
C. SQRP D. QSPR

4. 1. When it was learnt
P. the world price,
Q. that the cost of production
R. was more than three times
S. the government offered
6. lavish subsidies to farmers.
A. QRPS B. PQRS
C. PRQS D. QSRP

5. 1. Someone who has
P. sports or physical activity
Q. may not be
R. excelled only in studies
S. but has completely ignored
6. a good team player
A. PRQS B. SQRP
C. RSPQ D. QRPS

6. 1. Many top management executives
P. and therefore the pre-interview stage
Q. have realised the inadequacies
R. of the interview process
S. has become an important process

6. in weeding out the weaker candidates.

A. RPQS B. PRSQ
C. QSPR D. QRPS

7. 1. A large number

P. of party leaders feel

Q. only the judiciary

R. that it is

S. which can finally pave the way

6. for his selection as party chief.

A. SPQR B. PRQS
C. SQRP D. RQPS

8. 1. Fed up with

P. the villagers took turns staying awake

Q. in their neighbourhood,

R. the spate of robberies

S. to collar the uninvited visitor

6. on his next attempt to rob.

A. SPQR B. QSPR
C. RQPS D. PRSQ

9. 1. Law and order

P. who eliminate government officials

Q. terrorists and militants

R. are virtually at ransom

S. in the hands of

6. and panic crowds.

A. PRSQ B. RSQP
C. SQPR D. PSRQ

10. 1. It is not

P. but whether we can

Q. a question of whether

R. we can afford

S. to make nuclear weapons

6. afford not to

A. PQSR B. SRQP
C. QRSP D. RSPQ

11. 1. The most interesting feature

P. of the emancipation of women

Q. is that the woman's claim

R. accepted without any

S. to equality has been

6. demur or challenge.

A. PRQS B. SRQP
C. PQSR D. RQPS

12. 1. Hindi has

P. modern language and

Q. medium of instruction in

R. it is doing better as

S. rapidly developed as

6. schools and colleges.

A. SPRQ B. SRQP
C. PQRS D. PRSQ

13. 1. Cinema as a

P. used to educate childern

Q. as well as illiterates

R. can very effectively be

S. medium of instruction

6. under adult education scheme.

A. QRPS B. SQRP
C. PSQR D. SRPQ

14. 1. Most people with a layman's

P. do not go to a witchdoctor for one.

Q. is created by books and media

R. an awarness of which

S. knowledge of science,

6. but have recourse to medicine.

A. QSRP B. RQPS
C. SRQP D. PSQR

15. 1. The theories of Charles Darwin that

P. man was a special creation

Q. man was descended from the ape

R. of God and Adam and Eve

S. shook the religious belief that

6. were the first humans

A. RQPS B. QSPR
C. PSQR D. QRPS

16. 1. It is hard

P. responsibility for doing

Q. to work, to accept

R. often unpleasant

S. to teach youngsters

6. but necessary chores

A. SQPR B. RSPQ
C. PSRQ D. SRPQ

17. 1. Action speaks louder

P. provide the first

Q. parents need to be

R. conscious that they

S. than words and

6. role models for their children

A. PQSR B. SRQP
C. SQRP D. QRPS

18. 1. As a teenager

P. her singing talents

Q. under the watchful eye

R. Whitney Houston cultivated

S. of her mother, Cissy

6. founder of the 1960s group The Sweet Inspiration.

A. QPRS B. SQRP
C. PRSQ D. RPQS

19. 1. If however,

P. travel in winter, and

Q. do not mind

R. the cold and the snow,

S. you plan to

6. how about Europe?

A. PRSQ B. SPQR
C. RQSP D. RPSQ

20. 1. Talking excitedly,

P. the two walked on,

Q. eventually meeting

R. to be the father

S. a man who seemed

6. of one of them

A. SPRQ B. RQPS
C. PQSR D. QSPR

21. 1. Essentially, a mutual fund is

P. provided by

Q. a collective pool

R. purchased from money

S. of assets

6. a large number of investors.

A. QRPS B. QSRP
C. QPRS D. QSPR

22. 1. Renowned carnatic vocalist, T.R. Balamani,

P. teaching music for

Q. who has been

R. says that group lessons

S. the last 27 years,

6. have a certain advantage over private lessons.

A. QPSR B. SQRP
C. PQSR D. SRPQ

23. 1. A lot of friends
P. of their lives
Q. have made a shambles
R. I grew up with
S. and have got
6. into drugs and violent crime

A. RQPS B. QRSP
C. SQPR D. PSRQ

24. 1. Far more attention is
P. planning of kitchens today
Q. due to
R. than ever before,
S. being given to the
6. space constraints and modern appliances.

A. QRPS B. SPRQ
C. RSPQ D. PSQR

25. 1. A happy family is
P. the lessons of giving
Q. and sharing
R. the members learn
S. one in which
6. each other joys and sorrows.

A. QRSP B. SRQP
C. SRPQ D. RSQP

26. 1. It is important to keep
P. to maintain
Q. the various components
R. of nature in full harmony
S. a balance
6. in the environment

A. QRPS B. PSRQ
C. SQPR D. RQSP

27. 1. Not only
P. better than cats,
Q. the one better
R. are dogs
S. but in many ways
6. than humans

A. PSQR B. QSPR
C. RPSQ D. PQRS

28. 1. The mechanic was very busy
P. when I took my car
Q. in the waiting room
R. I settled down
S. for repairs, so
6. with a book I'd brought along.

A. PQRS B. RSQP
C. PSRQ D. RPQS

29. 1. Dressing up can be
P. an easy task of
Q. an honest manner
R. you can look at your figure
S. as its faults in
6. and then go about choosing something that's just right for you.

A. PQSR B. SPQR
C. QRPS D. PRSQ

30. 1. Some people
P. certainly they enjoy
Q. unhappy today but
R. may be
S. far greater comforts
6. than their forefathers ever did.

A. RQPS B. PSQR
C. SPRQ D. QSRP

ANSWERS

1	2	3	4	5	6	7	8	9	10
D	D	A	A	C	D	B	C	B	C
11	**12**	**13**	**14**	**15**	**16**	**17**	**18**	**19**	**20**
C	A	D	C	B	A	C	D	B	C
21	**22**	**23**	**24**	**25**	**26**	**27**	**28**	**29**	**30**
B	A	A	B	C	A	C	C	D	A

Comprehension

Directions : *Read the following passage carefully and choose the best answer to each of the questions out of the four alternatives given.*

PASSAGE-I

We talk about two people fighting like wild cats, but this is nothing compared to angry mongooses fighting. They grip each other with their mouths and front paws and they roll over and over, all the time screaming at each other. They seem to be tearing each other to pieces. Yet, when they finally part, neither of them shows even a scratch.

Mongooses can move as quickly as lightning. That is why they can kill snakes without hurting themselves. They sink their needle-sharp teeth into the back of the neck of a poisonous snake. Apart from its speed, its tail helps the mongoose when it fights with snakes. When the mongoose is angry the hairs on its tail stand out so that it looks like a brush. When it attacks it keeps wiping this brush across the face of its enemy.

Although, they kill snakes, the usual food of mongooses is rats, mice, lizards, insects and other small animals. They are also very fond of eggs. If it is caught when it is young, the mongoose can become very tame and it is a delightful pet. In India, many people keep mongooses in their homes as protection against snakes.

QUESTIONS

1. When two mongooses fight
A. they kill each other
B. they keep screaming
C. they tear each other to pieces
D. they scratch each other

2. A mongoose moves
A. only when asked to do so
B. very fast
C. all the time
D. round and round

3. When it fights a snake the mongoose uses
A. some needles
B. its nose
C. its sharp teeth
D. its ears

4. 'Apart from' (in paragraph 2), means
A. different from
B. away from
C. in addition to
D. far from

5. The mongoose uses its tail
A. to clean itself
B. to clean the face of the snake
C. instead of a brush
D. as a weapon

6. The ..... food of a mongoose is rats and mice

A. special B. ordinary
C. only D. raw

7. The mongoose likes to ..... eggs.

A. lay B. bury
C. hide D. eat

8. People, in India, keep mongooses at home

A. to guard the home
B. to catch mice
C. to protect themselves from snakes
D. to fight other mongooses

PASSAGE-II

The mosquito is a nuisance. It annoys people when they are sleeping and it is also dreaded as a carrier of malaria. For many years, all kinds of methods have been used to get rid of mosquitoes. In some parts of the world, people rub themselves with an oil that will keep mosquitoes away. The health authorities spend a lot of money spraying stagnant ponds and other places where mosquitoes breed, with a powerful fluid that kills all the harmful insects, including mosquitoes. In many tropical countries, people sleep under mosquito nets. If they sleep out in the open, they make sure that there is a fire to keep away mosquitoes.

The latest device for mosquito eradication is a machine called the 'Zapper' which is produced and sold by an American company. It kills mosquitoes and other small insects. A coloured light inside the machine attracts the mosquitoes. When they enter the Zapper a powerful ray kills the insects at once.

The machine which must be made to stand on the floor is four feet high and weighs thirty pounds. The Zapper does not cause any harm to human beings. The inventor of Zapper thinks that his machine is the best way to get rid of mosquitoes as well as other insects that bite human beings. Of course, insects such as flies and moths will also be killed if they enter the Zapper. The Zapper now works only on electricity. It is likely that in a few years somebody will invent a similar machine operated on battery.

QUESTIONS

1. Zapper is the ..... of a new machine.

A. inventor B. title
C. name D. colour

2. The Zapper is used for

A. catching mosquitoes
B. trapping flies
C. burning insects
D. killing mosquitoes

3. The mosquitoes are attracted by the ..... in the machine.

A. colours B. noise
C. beauty D. light

4. The Zapper should be

A. nailed to the wall
B. hung from the ceiling
C. placed on the ground
D. buried in the ground

5. Flies will be killed if they ..... the Zapper.

A. fly near

B. see
C. touch
D. come into

6. The Zapper can only be used in homes which have
A. electricity B. batteries
C. insects D. lights

7. The Zapper is a safe invention because it
A. is only four feet high
B. does not harm people
C. does not make noise
D. works on electricity

PASSAGE-III

Just as some men like to play football or cricket, so some men like to climb mountains. This is often very difficult to do, for mountains are not just big hills. Paths are usually very steep. Some mountain sides are straight up and down, so that it may take many hours to climb as little as one hundred feet. There is always the danger than you may fall off and be killed or injured. Men talk about conquering a mountain. It is a wonderful feeling to reach the top of a mountain after climbing for hours and may be, even for days. You look down and see the whole country below you. You feel god-like. Two Italian prisoners of war escaped from a prison camp in Kenya during the war. They did not try to get back to their own country, for they knew that was impossible. Instead, they climbed to the top of Mount Kenya, and then they came down again and gave themselves up. They had wanted to get that feeling of freedom that one has, after climbing a difficult mountain.

QUESTIONS

1. Some men like to climb a mountain because
A. they do not like to play football or cricket
B. they know the trick of climbing
C. they want to have a wonderful feeling
D. they like to face danger

2. To climb mountains is often difficult because
A. mountains are big hills
B. it consumes more time
C. prisoners often escape from camps and settle there
D. paths are steep and uneven

3. 'It is a wonderful feeling .....' 'It' refers to
A. the steep path
B. the prisoner
C. the mountain
D. mountaineering

4. Two Italian prisoners escaped from the camp and climbed to the top of Mount Kenya
A. to escape to Italy
B. to come down and give up
C. to get the feeling of freedom
D. to gain fame as mountaineers

5. Mountaineering is not a very popular sport like football or cricket because
A. there are no spectators in this sport
B. it may take many hours or even days

C. not many people are prepared to risk their lives
D. people do not want to enjoy a god-like feeling

PASSAGE-IV

Once, an ant who had come to drink at a stream fell into the water and was carried away by the swift current. He was in great danger of drowning. A dove, perched on a nearby tree, saw the ant's danger and dropped a leaf into the water. The ant climbed on to this, and was carried to safety.

Sometimes after this, a hunter, creeping through the bushes, saw the dove asleep, and took careful aim with his gun. He was about to fire when the ant, who was nearby, crawled forward and bit him sharply in the ankle. The hunter missed his aim, and the loud noise of gun awakened the dove from her sleep. She saw her danger and flew swiftly away to safety. Thus, the ant repaid the dove for having saved his life in the foaming current of the stream.

QUESTIONS

1. The ant came to stream to
A. fall into it
B. look at the swift current
C. to carry back some water
D. drink at it

2. The dove dropped a leaf into the water to
A. save the ant
B. drown the ant
C. help itself
D. perch on it

3. The dove was in danger because
A. a hunter wanted to care for it
B. there was a bush nearby
C. a hunter was about to shoot it
D. it had fell off the branch

4. The word 'aim' in this passage means
A. to point a gun at something or someone
B. to have an ambition
C. to try to reach somewhere
D. to look at something

5. The ant repaid the dove by
A. biting the hunter
B. warning the dove
C. crawling near the hunter
D. biting the dove

PASSAGE-V

Throughout in recorded history, India was celebrated for her fine textiles, her muslins and brocades of silver and gold. As a matter of fact, there is evidence that her textile industry goes back at least five thousand years, for Indian muslins were found urapped around mummies in Egyptian pyramids dating back to 3000 BC. The ancient Indian iron and steel industry was equally famous. The well-known Damascus steel for swords and armour used in the Crusades came from India. Thus, in countless industries and crafts, the Indian craftsman, worker, builder and artist created and prospered, and their products found favour both at home and abroad. And then, political disintegration and foreign conquest closed the long golden chapter of India's advancement and creative achievement.

QUESTIONS

1. India had a flourishing textile industry in the past, is proved by the fact, that
   A. India produced muslins and brocades of silver and gold
   B. the country was already famous for its fine textiles
   C. the industry claims to be five thousand year old
   D. Indian muslins were used for covering Egyptian mummies in 3000 BC.

2. According to the writer, the ancient Indian iron and steel industry was famous, because
   A. India supplied swords and armour to Damascus
   B. India provided steel with which swords and armour were made for the Crusaders
   C. Indian steel was famous among those fighting the Crusades
   D. Products of iron and steel were shipped to Damascus from India

3. Which one of the following statements is not true?
   A. There is a long history of excellence that the Indian craftsmen had achieved in various crafts
   B. Creations of Indian craftsmen brought to them prosperity
   C. Even after foreign conquest these crafts ensured India's industrial progress
   D. Indian crafts died out due to political division of the country

4. Which of the following is opposite in meaning to the word 'advancement' occurring in the passage?
   A. deterioration
   B. backwardness
   C. poverty
   D. failure

5. Which one of the following would be the most suitable title for the passage?
   A. The rise and fall of Indian crafts
   B. Ancient India's textile industry
   C. Indian iron and steel industry in the past
   D. Indian exports in the ancient times

PASSAGE-VI

A man may usually be known by the books he reads, as well as by the company he keeps; for there is a companionship of books as well as of men; and one should always live in the best compamy, whether it be of books or of men. A good book may be among the best of friends. It is the same today that it always was and it will never change. It is the most patient and cheerful of companions. It does not turn its back upon us in times of adversity or distress. It always receives us with the same kindness; amusing and interesting us in youth, comforting and consoling us in age.

QUESTIONS

1. According to the writer, 'a man may usually be known by the books he reads', because
   A. his reading habit shows that he is a scholar
   B. the books he reads affect his thinking and character
   C. books provide him a lot of knowledge
   D. his selection of books generally reveals his temperament and character
2. Which one of the following statements is not true?
   A. Good books as well as good men always provide the finest company
   B. A good book never betrays us
   C. We have sometimes to be patient with a book as it may bore us
   D. A good book serves as a permanent friend
3. The statement 'A good book may be among the best of friends', in the middle of the passage means that
   A. there cannot be a better friend than a good book
   B. books may be good friends, but not better than good men
   C. a good book can be included amongst the best friends of mankind
   D. our best friends read the same good books
4. Which of the following is opposite in meaning to the word 'adversity' occurring in the passage?
   A. happiness
   B. prosperity
   C. progress
   D. misfortune
5. Which one of the following would be the most suitable title for the passage?
   A. Books show the reader's character
   B. Books as man's abiding friends
   C. Books are useful in our youth
   D. The importance of books in old age

PASSAGE-VII

Honey bees make their own hives in hollow trees, or they use the hives that men make for them.

In each hive, there are worker bees who make the honey-comb out of wax and others who guard the beehive and collect food. There is a queen who lays an eggs in each cell of the honey-comb.

The young bees are fed on nectar and pollen. Honey is made in the bodies of the worker bees from the nectar and pollen of flowers.

Every year the old queen leaves the hive and she is followed by a 'Swarm' of bees.

QUESTIONS

1. Honey bees normally live
   A. on trees
   B. in houses
   C. in hives
   D. on roofs
2. The queen bee
   A. rules the other bees
   B. feeds on the other bees
   C. trains the worker bees
   D. lays the eggs
3. The honey-comb is made out of
   A. nectar
   B. flowers
   C. wax
   D. sugar
4. Honey is made by
   A. working men
   B. worker bees
   C. men in hives
   D. queens
5. Which of the following titles would be most suitable for the passage?
   A. The Queen
   B. Honey Bees
   C. Insects
   D. Worker Bees

PASSAGE-VIII

Birds are alike in many ways. Because they all have backbones. They are all vertebrates. They all have two legs and two wings. they all have lungs and are warm blooded. This means that their bodies are warm even when the weather is cold. All birds have feathers.

There are many different kinds of birds. Some, like the ostrich, are taller and heavier than a man. Some are very small, like the humming-bird. Many birds can fly very well. Swallows and ducks are excellent flyers. Some birds cannot fly at all. The pengum's wings cannot lift him off the ground.

QUESTIONS

1. According to the passage, all birds are vertebrates because they have
   A. feathers
   B. two legs and two wings
   C. backbones
   D. warm blood
2. When a bird is alive and well, its body is
   A. cold B. warm
   C. light D. heavy
3. One very large bird mentioned in the passage is the
   A. penguin
   B. humming-bird
   C. swallow
   D. ostrich
4. According to the passage, the humming-bird
   A. sings beautifully
   B. can fly very high
   C. is very small
   D. can fly very well
5. A penguin cannot
   A. fly in cold water
   B. stay on the ground
   C. fly very well
   D. fly at all

PASSAGE-IX

In order to measure distances, the surveyor lays out a series of straight lines which he calls survey lines. To do this, he uses his chain and ranging rods. The rods are not unlike broomsticks only longer, and they are usually coloured black and white or red and white so that they can be easily seen. Assuming that the surveyor wished to measure the distance between X and Y, he would place a rod at X while his assistant would walk towards Y. The surveyor would stand two or three yards behind X. Keeping X and Y in line; his assistant would then place one or more rods at intervals and in the same line, the surveyor guiding him as to whether or not all rods were in line.

QUESTIONS

1. Survey lines help a surveyor to
   A. make straight lines
   B. see easily and clearly
   C. range some rods
   D. measure distances
2. Two different things used by the surveyor to lay out his survey lines are
   A. a chain and some rods
   B. broomsticks and rods
   C. a tape and a chain
   D. a chain and broomsticks
3. Because they have to be easily seen, ranging rods are
   A. striaght
   B. carefully measured
   C. guided
   D. brightly coloured
4. When measuring the distance from X to Y, the surveyor stands
   A. in front of X
   B. behind X
   C. on a line between X and Y
   D. two or three yards behind Y
5. The surveyor has to guide his assistant to
   A. stand behind Y
   B. walk towards X
   C. find the rods
   D. keep the rods in a straight line

PASSAGE-X

Any person who wishes to be a candidate for election to the National Assembly must prepare four copies of the nomination paper in the prescribed form (Form E). He must also make a declaration in the prescribed form (Form F) stating that he is qualified to be a member of the Assembly. A day is specified in the election notice for the receipt of nominations. The nomination papers and the declaration must be delivered to the Returning Officer between 9 AM and 12 mid-day on that day. Delivery may be made by the candidate himself, or by the person who proposed or the person who seconded him.

QUESTIONS

1. The prospective candidate for elections has to
   A. make sure that he will win
   B. fill in a nomination paper

C. be a member of the Assembly
D. have a duplicate machine

2. How many different forms must be completed by the candidate?
A. Three
B. One
C. Two
D. Four

3. A candidate completes Form F to declare that he:
A. wants to vote
B. has paid the required deposit
C. is qualified to be a candidate
D. cannot vote

4. Nominations must be handed in
A. in nine o'clock on the day stated
B. at 12 mid-day on the day stated
C. during the afternoon of the day stated
D. during first half of the day stated

5. The completed forms can be delivered to the Returning Officer by
A. one of three people
B. any member of the candidate's family
C. the person who came second in the election
D. no-one but the candidate

PASSAGE-XI

Electricity is very useful as long as we do not get in its way. But it can make trouble for us if we do. Luckily, we have a way of avoiding this. We can wrap electric wires in coats of rubber or plastic. These coats are called insulation. Electricity cannot travel through a coat of insulation, and so it runs along safely inside the wire.

If a current of electricity runs through you, it gives you a shock and strong shocks are dangerous. They can kill you. So it is safest not to meddle with electric wires or machines. An electrician knows how to work with electricity, and he does not get hurt. Usually, he turns a switch so that no current at all comes into the wire on which he is working.

QUESTIONS

1. According to the passage, electricity becomes dangerous when
A. it is too hot
B. it is interfered with
C. the power fails
D. it cannot travel

2. Electric wires covered with rubber or plastic are
A. dangerous
B. insulated
C. live
D. troublesome

3. If a current of electricity runs through a person's body
A. it always kills him
B. he does not get hurt
C. it lights him up
D. he gets a shock

4. The advice given in the passage about electric wires and machines is

A. to cover them with rubber or plastic
B. to turn them off
C. to make them safe to meddle with
D. not to interfere with them

5. Electricians avoid getting shocks from electric wires by
A. switching off the current
B. not touching wires
C. going against the current
D. wearing insulated coats

PASSAGE-XII

Glaciers are formed by the continuous collection of snow on high peaks. The weight of additional snow compresses the earlier falls into ice which is slowly forced down into valleys.

Continental glaciers, or ice-sheets covering whole continents, are now found only in Greenland and the Polar regions. However, at one time similar ice-sheets covered most of Northern Europe, Canada and Northern USA. In the Southern Hemisphere, because of the smaller land surfaces, the effect of the ice-sheets was limited.

Much study has been devoted recently to the glaciers on Mt. Kenya. Here there are ten glaciers which appear to be slowly shrinking in size and five others have disappeared altogether. It is thought that the climate in this part of Africa may be getting progressively warmer, the giant groundsel plants on the slopes of Mt. Kenya were at one time known to grow much lower down but are now isolated plants near the peak.

QUESTIONS

1. According to the passage, glaciers are first formed
A. high up on mountains
B. in valleys
C. on ice
D. in ice-sheets

2. According to the passage, continental glaciers can now be fournd
A. on the continent
B. in northern Europe
C. in Greenland and at the Poles
D. on ice-sheets

3. The effect of te ice-sheets was limited in the Southern Hemisphere because
A. it is warmer than the Northern Hemisphere
B. it is smaller than the Northern Hemisphere
C. there is less land than in the Northern Hemisphere
D. there is more land than in the Northern Hemisphere

4. According to the passage, how many glaciers were there on Mt. Kenya at one time?
A. Ten B. Fifteen
C. Five D. None

5. What, according to the author, may be the cause of the disappearance of some of the glaciers on Mt. Kenya?
A. The climate is becoming colder
B. There is too much rain
C. Not enough snow is falling
D. The climate is becoming warmer

ANSWERS

Passage-I

1	2	3	4	5
B	B	C	C	D
6	**7**	**8**		
B	D	C		

Passage-II

1	2	3	4	5
C	D	D	C	D
6	**7**			
A	B			

Passage-III

1	2	3	4	5
C	D	D	C	A

Passage-IV

1	2	3	4	5
D	A	C	A	A

Passage-V

1	2	3	4	5
C	B	C	B	A

Passage-VI

1	2	3	4	5
B	C	C	B	B

Passage-VII

1	2	3	4	5
C	D	C	B	B

Passage-VIII

1	2	3	4	5
C	B	D	C	D

Passage-IX

1	2	3	4	5
D	A	D	B	D

Passage-X

1	2	3	4	5
B	C	C	D	A

Passage-XI

1	2	3	4	5
B	B	D	D	A

Passage-XII

1	2	3	4	5
A	C	C	B	D

Closet Test

Directions : *In the following passages, some of the words have been left out. First, read each passage over and try to understand what it is about, then fill in the blanks with the help of alternatives given.*

PASSAGE-I

He mentioned two factors being responsible ... (1) ... this telecom revolution. One is the ... (2) ... technological change, beginning ... (3) ... microelectronics ... (4) ..., the budget problems of most industrial countries ... (5) ... with free trade agreements ... (6) ... resulted in major liberalisation moves. Their aim ... (7) ... to increase the world economy through a ... (8) ... market at lower prices. In the process, most countries were, and still are, ... (9) ... to privatise part of their national telecom operator companies ... (10) ... order to survive.

1. A. to B. with C. from D. for

2. A. easy B. rapid C. real D. fast

3. A. with B. at C. by D. along

4. A. firstly B. truly C. rarely D. secondly

5. A. combination B. combined C. combine D. confusion

6. A. was B. will be C. had D. have been

7. A. are B. is C. was D. will be

8. A. many B. bigger C. busy D. largest

9. A. forcible B. pushed C. to go D. being forced

10. A. in B. at C. by D. with

PASSAGE-II

A long line of women were waiting ... (1) ... a shop. A man approached and immediately pushed ... (2) ... the front of the line. Angry shouts sent ... (3) ... retreating to the back. He tried again, ... (4) ... once more the women jostled and ... (5) ... him back again. Finally, giving ... (6) ..., he ... (7) ... his tie, ... (8) his ruffled hair and, with dignity, ... (9) ... , "Very well, ladies, ... (10) ... that's what you want, I won't open the shop."

1. A. beside B. outside C. against D. before

2. A. at B. forward
C. to D. behind

3. A. her B. his
C. she D. him

4. A. and B. also
C. because D. but

5. A. pushed B. broke
C. shook D. threw

6. A. in B. up
C. into D. on

7. A. straightened
B. messed
C. pressed
D. crushed

8. A. soothed
B. organised
C. smoothed
D. closed

9. A. told B. cried
C. said D. said that

10. A. all B. then
C. for D. if

PASSAGE-III

The skin is the body's ... (1) ... organ. With the exception of the palms and soles, the skin is ... (2) ... with hair follicles. The skin's ... (3) ... is to protect the body ... (4) ... regulating its temperature. The skin ... (5) ... of three layers. For a lovely skin one should ... (6) ... caring for it. Refresh the skin with a face mask from ... (7) ... . To prevent skin from losing vital oils use a moisturiser ... (8) ... cleansing. Moisturising prevents ... (9) ... loss of water from the skin ... (10) ... protecting and nourishing it.

1. A. longest B. larger
C. largest D. longer

2. A. scratched
B. covered
C. toned
D. dabbed

3. A. function B. reason
C. habit D. ability

4. A. by B. with
C. for D. unless

5. A. kinds B. parts are
C. is found D. consists

6. A. start B. detest
C. allow D. hate

7. A. morning till night
B. days
C. time to time
D. yesteryears

8. A. later B. beyond
C. ahead of D. after

9. A. undue B. wanted
C. little D. rare

10. A. hereby B. thereby
C. therefore D. hence

PASSAGE-IV

Many accidents take place at home, ... (1) ... it is up to the parents to take ... (2) ... . Open windows ... (3) ... dangerous ... (4) ... them with bars or grills. Also use child-proof electric circuits ... (5) ... the wall to ... (6) ... inquisitive little hands ... (7) ... getting shocks. Better ... (8) ... ensure ... (9) ... your home ... (10) ... earth-leak circuit breakers installed.

1. A. so B. also
C. for D. as

2. A. care
B. precaution
C. advise
D. help

3. A. are B. can be
C. prove D. appear

4. A. break B. seal
C. cover D. fill

5. A. inside B. over
C. on D. in

6. A. prevent B. let
C. allow D. encourage

7. A. against B. for
C. from D. behind

8. A. still B. thus
C. not D. quickly

9. A. regarding B. than
C. about D. that

10. A. had B. has
C. have D. may have

PASSAGE-V

He had lived nearly his ... (1) ... life not ... (2) ... from the house in ... (3) .. he was born and raised, and from the ... (4) ... of his brothers and sisters. That working class neighbourhood ... (5) ... big and rich ... (6) ... for him. Our family eventually joined him ... (7) ..., and on trips ... (8) ... the neighbourhood, he proudly ... (9) ... me ... (10) ... friends.

1. A. total B. complete
C. entire D. maximum

2. A. afar B. away
C. far off D. far

3. A. where B. what
C. why D. which

4. A. houses B. homes
C. dwelling D. inhabitat

5. A. was B. were
C. is D. are

6. A. only B. supply
C. enough D. amount

7. A. over B. together
C. there D. with

8. A. inside B. near
C. into D. through

9. A. threw
B. introduced
C. handed
D. presented

10. A. for B. to
C. like D. as

PASSAGE-VI

The boy was hurt ... (1) ... confused. What ... (2) ... seemed so beautiful now looked ... (3) ... the plastic, cheap thing ... (4) .... it was. He ... (5) ... outside to the back porch and ... (6) ... to cry ... (7) ... his mother appeared and ... (8) gently what was wrong. He explained ... (9) ... best he could. She listened, and then they ... (10) ... inside.

1. A. too B. and
C. so D. also

2. A. have B. has
C. has been D. had

3. A. alike B. like
C. same as D. as

4. A. that B. what
C. which D. who

5. A. brushed B. scurried
C. walked D. narrated

6. A. start B. acted
C. began D. got

7. A. early B. quick
C. fast D. soon

8. A. told B. cried
C. said D. asked

9. A. as B. it
C. on D. so

10. A. went B. go
C. will go D. were going

PASSAGE-VII

His appetite ... (1) ... research continued to set him apart from other investors. He ... (2) ... the heavy business manuals ... (3) ... the zest of a small boy reading comics. Line ... (4) ... line, he soaked up financial pages. His friends cheerfully accepted that he knew ... (5) ... about stocks than ... (6) ... . Nobody was going to tell you ... (7) ... stocks were a bargain; you had to ... (8) ... there on your own. And, so he ... (9) ... his homework. His independence of mind and ability to focus on his work ... (10) ... served him well.

1. A. for B. of
C. above D. with

2. A. weighed B. read
C. collected D. bought

3. A. around B. under
C. with D. like

4. A. from B. by
C. inside D. between

5. A. most B. more
C. all D. much

6. A. somebody
B. nobody
C. everybody
D. anybody

7. A. what B. that
C. which D. when

8. A. go B. come
C. arrive D. get

9. A. did B. do
C. made D. does

10. A. too B. also
C. together D. both

ANSWERS

Passage-I

1	2	3	4	5	6	7	8	9	10
D	B	A	D	B	C	C	B	D	A

Passage-II

1	2	3	4	5	6	7	8	9	10
B	C	D	D	A	B	A	C	C	D

Passage-III

1	2	3	4	5	6	7	8	9	10
C	B	A	A	D	A	C	D	A	B

Passage-IV

1	2	3	4	5	6	7	8	9	10
A	B	B	C	D	A	C	A	D	B

Passage-V

1	2	3	4	5	6	7	8	9	10
C	D	D	A	A	C	C	D	B	B

Passage-VI

1	2	3	4	5	6	7	8	9	10
B	D	B	A	C	C	D	D	A	A

Passage-VII

1	2	3	4	5	6	7	8	9	10
A	B	C	B	B	D	C	D	A	B

Miscellaneous Questions

Directions : *Choose the right question-word with which a question can be framed in respect to each of the following sentences. The italicised part of each sentence could be the answer to such a question.*

1. *Two clerks* had failed to report for duty.
A. Who B. What
C. Whom D. How

2. She is leaving the country *tomorrow.*
A. Why B. Where
C. When D. What

3. *Mr. Shah* is the Chairman of the newly-found committee.
A. Who B. What
C. How D. Why

4. The function was held *at the club.*
A. Whose B. Where
C. Whom D. Why

5. He scolded *the servant* for breaking the glass.
A. Who B. Whom
C. Whose D. What

6. This is *her* book.
A. Who B. Can
C. How D. Whose

7. The Dentist *told her to open the mouth.*
A. What B. Whom
C. Where D. Why

8. *This Grammar Book* is the better of the two books.
A. How B. Who
C. Which D. What

9. He went to the village *to visit his grand parents.*
A. Why B. Where
C. How D. What

10. *Yes,* I like it.
A. Will B. Do
C. Can D. have

Directions : *Choose the most appropriate meaning of each of the sentences given below.*

11. He secured 89% marks.
A. He stood first in class
B. He had faired well in his exams
C. He has done better than his friends
D. He will get the scholarship

12. The child is now cured.
A. The doctor is checking the child's pulse
B. The child is running around with joy
C. The child is eating chocolates
D. The child had been ill

13. Minni cannot sit on this chair.
A. There is dirt on the chair
B. Minni does not like the colour of the chairs

C. The chair is too small for Minni to sit on
D. Minni is sitting on the sofa

14. He only plays cricket.
A. He plays cricket and nothing else
B. He and nobody else plays cricket
C. He cannot play any other game
D. He plays cricket and nothing else worth-mentioning

15. Our guest came early.
A. Our guest came before the scheduled time
B. Our guest came earliest
C. Our guest came already
D. Our guest came too soon

16. She is Rhea's mother.
A. Rhea is her daughter
B. Only Rhea and nobody else is her daughter
C. She is not only Rhea's mother but also Ritu's mother
D. She is proud of her daughter

17. We missed the train.
A. The train had left the platform at 9.30 pm
B. The train had left right on time
C. We were late in reaching the station
D. The train did not wait for us

18. He is the richest man in the town.
A. A few men in the town are richer than him
B. No other man in the town is as rich as him
C. The town is full of rich men
D. He has recently purchased acres of land in this town

19. I want this book.
A. This book is very much in demand
B. This book is written by my favourite author
C. I want to present this book to my best friend
D. This book contains information useful for my research

20. She is drinking lemonade.
A. She is thirsty
B. She only drinks lemonade
C. She does not like any other drink
D. Only lemonade is served in the restaurant where she is sitting

Directions : *In the following questions, there are some bold words or phrase which have been given with four options. If another word or better expression is required for the bold part choose it from the group. If no change is required, choose 'D' as the answer.*

21. He **had left** for Kolkata tomorrow.
A. will go
B. is leaving
C. left already
D. no change is required

22. He is such **a clown man** that he can make anybody laugh.
A. clownish
B. a funny clown man
C. a serious joker
D. no change is required

23. **Many less** people attended the function.
A. very few
B. lesser
C. the least
D. no change is required

24. She is seventeen **ages** old.
A. age
B. year
C. years
D. no change is required

25. He is **a well student** and is admired by all
A. an expert student
B. a healthy student
C. a good student
D. no change is required

26. I **knocked at** the door before opening it.
A. banged
B. shouted at
C. kicked hard
D. no change required

27. **A much** pollution is caused by smoke from factories.
A. much
B. more
C. most
D. no change is required

28. You **are viewing at** the most beautiful girl.
A. are seeing at
B. are looking at
C. are viewing over
D. no change is required

29. Do not go near the fire, your clothes **may get burning.**
A. may get fired
B. may get burns
C. may catch fire
D. no change is required

30. The star **is burning** in the sky.
A. shines
B. is shone
C. was twinkling
D. no change is required

ANSWERS (WITH EXPLANATION)

1. D : How many clerks failed to report for duty?

2. C : When is she leaving the country?

3. A : Who is the Chairman of the newly found committee?

4. B : Where was the function held?

5. B : Whom did he scold for breaking the glass?

6. D : Whose book is this?

7. A : What did the Dentist tell her?

8. C : Which is the better of the two books?

9. A : Why did he go to the village?

10. B : Do you like it?

11	**12**	**13**	**14**	**15**	**16**	**17**	**18**	**19**	**20**
B	D	C	D	A	A	C	B	D	A
21	**22**	**23**	**24**	**25**	**26**	**27**	**28**	**29**	**30**
B	B	A	C	C	D	A	B	C	A

Objective General Knowledge

History

1. 'Abhinav Bharat' was organized by
A. Bhai Parmanand
B. Khudiram Bose
C. Vir Savarkar
D. None of these

2. The ancient name of Bengal was
A. Kamrupa B. Vasta
C. Gauda D. Vallabhi

3. Ashoka belonged to:
A. Maurya dynasty
B. Gupta dynasty
C. Kushan dynasty
D. Saka dynasty

4. Morish traveller, Ibn Batutah, came to India during the time of
A. Ala-ud-din Khilji
B. Firoz Shah Tughluq
C. Balban
D. Muhammad-bin-Tughluq

5. The relics of Indus Valley Civilisation indicates that the main occupation of the people was
A. Agriculture
B. Cattle rearing
C. Commerce
D. Hunting

6. The Mahabalipuram temples were built by the king of .... dynasty
A. Gupta
B. Chola
C. Pallava
D. Kushana

7. The first telegraph line between Calcutta (Kolkata) and Agra was opened in
A. 1852 B. 1853
C. 1854 D. 1855

8. The first discourse of Buddha in Sarnath is called
A. Mahabhiniskraman
B. Mahaparinirvana
C. Mahamastakabhisheka
D. Dharmachakrapravartan

9. The political and cultural centre of the Pandyas was
A. Vengi
B. Madurai
C. Kanchipuram
D. Mahabalipuram

10. What is the correct chronological order of the dynasties in which they invaded India?
1. Huns 2. Kushanas
3. Aryans 4. Greeks
A. 4, 3, 2, 1 B. 3, 4, 2, 1
C. 4, 2, 3, 1 D. 3, 4, 1, 2

11. Who wrote Mitakshara, a book of Hindu law?
A. Nayachandra
B. Amoghvarsa
C. Vijnaneswara
D. Kumban

12. Gupta empire declined in the fifth century A.D. as a consequence of
A. Chalukya raids
B. Greek invasion
C. Hun invasion
D. Pallava raids

13. Who founded the Hindu Shahi dynasty of Punjab?
A. Vasumitra
B. Kallar
C. Jayapala
D. Mahipala

14. The main external threat to the Sultanate of Delhi was posed by the
A. Mughals
B. Afghans
C. Iranians
D. None of these

15. Who among the following was a leading exponent of Gandhian thoughts?
A. J.L. Nehru
B. M.N. Roy
C. Vinoba Bhave
D. Jayaprakash Narayan

16. Who were the immediate successors of the Imperial Mauryas in Magadha?
A. Kushanas
B. Pandyas
C. Satvahanas
D. Sungas

17. Both Mahavira and Buddha preached during the reign of
A. Ajatashatru
B. Bimbisara
C. Nandivardhan
D. Uday

18. Jahangiri Mahal is located in
A. Delhi
B. Fatehpur Sikri
C. Agra Fort
D. Sikandara

19. The main contribution of the Chola dynasty is in the field of
A. Systematic provincial administration
B. A well planned revenue system
C. A well organised central government
D. An organised local self government

20. Who founded the philosophy of Pustimarga?
A. Chaitanya
B. Nanak
C. Surdas
D. Ballabhacharya

21. Which of the following battles changed the destiny of a Mughal ruler of India?
A. Haldighati
B. Panipat II
C. Khanwah
D. Chausa

22. "The Vedas contain all the truth" was interpreted by
A. Swami Vivekanand
B. Swami Dayanand
C. Swami Shraddhanand
D. S. Radhakrishnan

23. Match the colums

	Column I		**Column II**
(*a*)	Second Battle of Panipat	1.	Decline of Vijayanagar empire
(*b*)	Second Battle of Tarain	2.	British rule in India
(*c*)	Battle of Talikota	3.	Turkish rule in India
(*d*)	Battle of Plassey	4.	Mughal rule in India
		5.	Slave dynasty in India

Codes:

	(*a*)	(*b*)	(*c*)	(*d*)
A.	2	3	4	1
B.	3	1	2	4
C.	5	3	2	1
D.	4	3	1	2

24. Babur entered India for the first time from the west through
A. Kashmir B. Sind
C. Punjab D. Rajasthan

25. Which was the first among the following?
A. Doctrine of Lapse
B. Subsidiary Alliance
C. Permanent Settlement
D. Double Government

26. The name of Lord Cornwallis is associated with the
A. Dual government
B. Maratha wars
C. System of subsidiary
D. Permanent settlement

27. Sir Charles Wood's Despatch of 1854 dealt with
A. Administrative reforms
B. Social reforms
C. Economic reforms
D. Educational reforms

28. Which of the following pairs is correct?
A. Ashvaghosa — Vikramaditya
B. Banabhatta — Harshvardhan
C. Harisena — Kanishka
D. Kalidasa — Samudragupta

29. 4th July, 1776 is important in world history because
A. battle fo Plassey started
B. Sca routc to India was discovered
C. English King Charles II was executed
D. American Congress adopted the Declaration of Independence

30. Rawlatt Act was passed in the year
A. 1917 B. 1919
C. 1921 D. 1923

31. The court language of Delhi Sultanate was
A. Urdu B. Persian
C. Hindi D. Arabic

32. Where did Buddha attain Mahaparinirvana?
A. Kushinagar
B. Kapilvastu
C. Pava
D. Kundagramma

33. In Afghanistan, two towering Buddha statues were destroyed at
A. Kandahar B. Yakaolong
C. Bamiyan D. Mazar-i-Sharif

34. Kalibangan, the Indus Valley site is in
A. Rajasthan
B. Gujarat
C. Madhya Pradesh
D. Uttar Pradesh

35. Which of the following materials was mainly used in the manufacture of harappan seals?
A. Terracota B. Bronze
C. Copper D. Iron

36. The Grand Trunk Road in India was got constructed by
A. Ashoka B. Shershah Suri
C. Akbar D. Humayun

37. 'Tripitaka' is thc rcligious book of the
A. Jains B. Buddhists
C. Sikhs D. Hindus

38. Which among the following states was forced to merge itself with the Union of India after 1947?
A. Hyderabad
B. Kashmir
C. Patiala
D. Mysore

39. Alexander the Great died in 323 B.C. in
A. Persia
B. Babylon
C. Macedonia
D. Taxila

40. Who gave the slogan—"Jai Hind"?
A. Subhash Chandra Bose
B. Jawaharlal Nehru
C. Moti Lal Nehru
D. Mahatma Gandhi

41. The most glorious king of the Chola dynasty who conquered Ceylon was
A. Rajaraja I
B. Rajaraja II
C. Rajendra Chola
D. Gangai Konda Chola

42. Name the Chera King known as the "Red Chera", who built a temple for Kannagi?
A. Elara
B. Karikala
C. Senguttuvan
D. Nedenjerai Alan

43. The first Indian ruler to accept Subsidiary Alliance offered by Lord Wellesley in 1798 was
A. Nawab of Oudh
B. Nizam of Hyderabad
C. Nawab of Carnatic
D. King of Mysore

44. The first Viceroy of India was
A. Lord Hastings
B. Lord Canning
C. Lord Minto
D. Lord Curzon

45. The Satavahanas formerly worked as local officials under the
A. Nandas B. Mauryas
C. Cholas D. Cheras

46. Who was the first woman President of the Indian National Congress?
A. Sarojini Naidu
B. Bhikaji Cama
C. Annie Besant
D. Vijaya Lakshmi Pandit

47. During the Indian Freedom Struggle, who of the following founded the Parathana Samaj?
A. Atmaram Pandurang
B. Gopal Hari Deshmukh
C. Ishwar Chandra Vidyasagar
D. Keshav Chandra Sen

48. Which one of the following periodicals was published by Mahatma Gandhi during his stay in South Africa?
A. Afrikanes
B. Indian Opinion
C. India Gazette
D. Navjivan

49. During the Civil Disobedience Movement, who led the 'Red Shirts' of North-Western India?
A. Abul Kalam Azad
B. Khan Abdul Ghaffar Khan
C. Mohammad Ali Jinnah
D. Shaukat Ali

50. Match List-I with List-II and select the correct answer using the codes given below the lists—

List-I
(Name of the Author)

(a) Abul Fazal
(b) Nizamuddin Ahmed
(c) Krishnadeva Raya
(d) Kalhana

List-II
(Name of the Book)

1. Tabqat-i-Akbari
2. Akbarnama
3. Rajatarangini
4. Amuktamalyada

Codes:

	(a)	*(b)*	*(c)*	*(d)*
A.	2	4	1	3
B.	3	1	4	2
C.	2	1	4	3
D.	3	4	1	2

51. Which one of the following pairs is not correctly matched?

A. Sheikh Shihab-ud-din Suharawardi — Sufi Saint
B. Chaitanya Maha Prabhu — Bhakti Saint
C. Minhaj-us Siraj — Founder of Sufi order
D. Lalleshwari — Bhakti Saint

52. Who of the following kings was an ardent follower of Jainism?

A. Bimbisara
B. Mahapadma Nanda
C. Kharavela
D. Pulakesin II

53. To which dynasty did Ashoka belong?

A. Vardhana B. Maurya
C. Kushan D. Gupta

54. Which one of the following battles was fought between Babar and the Rajputs in 1527?

A. The First Battle of Panipat
B. The Battle of Khanwah
C. The Battle of Ghagra
D. The Battle of Chanderi

55. Aryabhat,ta and Varahamihira belong to which age?

A. Guptas B. Cholas
C. Mauryas D. Mughals

56. Consider the· following statements about Amir Khusro:

1. He was a disciple of Nizamuddin Auliya.
2. He was the founder of both Hindustani classical music and Qawwali.

Which of the statements given above is/are correct?

A. 1 only
B. 2 only
C. Both 1 and 2
D. Neither 1 nor 2

57. Panini, the first Grammarian of Sanskrit language in India, lived during the

A. 2nd Century B.C.
B. 6th-5th Century B.C.
C. 2nd Century A.D.
D. 5th-6th Century A.D.

58. Who among the following was associated with the foundation of Ghadar party?

A. Lala Lajpat Rai
B. Lala Hardayal
C. C.R. Das
D. Bipin Chandra Pal

59. The Treaty of Bassein (1802) was signed between

A. Madhav Rao and the British

B. Baji Rao II and the British

C. Mahadji Scindia and the British

D. Holkar and the British

60. The words 'Satyameva Jayate' in the State Emblem of India, have been adopted from which one of the following?

A. Brahma Upanishad

B. Mudgala Upanishad

C. Maitreyi Upanishad

D. Mundaka Upanishad

61. Match List-I with List-II and select the correct answer using the codes given below the lists—

List-I
(Symbol)

(*a*) Elephant

(*b*) Tree

(*c*) Empty Throne

(*d*) Horse

List-II
(Important event of life of Buddha)

1. Renouncement of worldly pleasures
2. Birth of Buddha
3. Enlightenment
4. Representation of royalty

Codes:

	(*a*)	(*b*)	(*c*)	(*d*)
A.	2	4	3	1
B.	3	1	4	2
C.	3	4	1	2
D.	2	3	4	1

62. When was Mahatma Gandhi, the father of the nation, born?

A. 1889 B. 1859

C. 1869 D. 1879

63. Chinese pilgrim Hiuen-Tsang came to and lived in India under whose rule?

A. Harshavardhan

B. Chandragupta Maurya

C. Ashok

D. Samudragupta

64. Who had founded the Slave dynasty in India?

A. Qutb-ud-din Aibak

B. Iltutmish

C. Mohammed Gauri

D. Balban

65. Which British Governor-General had started the *Doctrine of Lapse* policy in India?

A. Lord William Bentinck

B. Lord Dalhousie

C. Lord Canning

D. Lord Hardinge

66. "Liberty is our birth right, we shall seize it." Who said it?

A. Bhagat Singh

B. Ramprasad Bismil

C. Bal Gangadhar Tilak

D. Mahatma Gandhi

67. The most important Sufi shrine in India is located at

A. Pandua

B. Bidar

C. Ajmer

D. Shahjahanabad

68. The 'Ajivikas' were a

A. Sect contemporary to the Buddha

B. Breakaway branch of the Buddhists

C. Sect founded by Charvaka

D. Sect founded by Shankaracharya

69. The Indian Universities were first founded during the time of
A. Macaulay
B. Warren Hastings
C. Lord Canning
D. Lord William Bentinck

70. One of the following was ***not*** involved in the Chittagong Armoury Raid, 1934. Who was he?
A. Kalpana Dutt
B. Surya Sen
C. Pritilata Woddedar
D. Dinesh Gupta

71. Which of the following is associated with Sufi saints?
A. Tripitaka B. Dakhma
C. Khanqah D. Synagogue

72. Which Indian statesman used these, magic words, "Long years ago we made a tryst with destiny, and now the time comes when we shall redeem our pledge ... ""?
A. Mohandas Karamchand Gandhi
B. Sardar Vallabhbhai Patel
C. Netaji Subhas Chandra Bose
D. Jawaharlal Nehru

73. In which century did French Revolution begin?
A. 16th century
B. 17th century
C. 18th century
D. 19th century

74. Under whose patronage was the Khandariya Mahadco Tcmplc at Khajuraho built?
A. Solankis
B. Rashtrakutas
C. Tomaras
D. Chandellas

75. During the period of which of the following was 'Panchtantra' written?
A. Nandas B. Mauryas
C. Guptas D. Sungas

76. Who wrote the book called Kitab-i-Nauras?
A. Amir Khusro
B. Badauni
C. Ibrahim Adil Shah II
D. Ala-ud-din Bahmani

77. Who among the following, Mughal rulers granted the English Company *Dewani* over Bengal, Bihar and Orissa, by Treaty of Allahabad?
A. Ahmad Shah
B. Alamgir II
C. Shah Alam II
D. Akbar Shah II

78. During the Indian freedom struggle, what accusation was made against Master Amir Chand, Awadh Bihari, Bal Mukund and Basant Kumar Biswas?
A. Assassination of the Commissioner of Poona
B. Throwing a bomb on Viceroy's procession in Delhi
C. Attempt to shoot the Governor of Punjab
D. Looting an armoury in Bengal

79. Which of the following pairs is/are correctly matched?
1. Regulating Act : IIastings
2 Widow Remarriage Act : Bentinck
3. Vernacular Press Act : Lytton

Select the correct answer using the codes given below:

A. 1 only B. 2 and 3

C. 1 and 3 D. 1, 2 and 3

80. Which among the following is referred to as the Montague-Chelmsford Reforms?

A. Indian Council Act, 1909

B. Government of India Act, 1919

C. Rowlatt Act

D. Government of India Act, 1935

81. Consider the following statements:

1. Lord Cornwallis introduced the Permanent Land Settlement in Bengal.
2. Lord Wellesley introduced the Subsidiary Alliance system.

Which of the statements given above is/are correct?

A. 1 only

B. 2 only

C. Both 1 and 2

D. Neither 1 nor 2

82. Who was the Governor-General when the Revolt of 1857 started?

A. Lord Canning

B. Lord Cornwallis

C. Lord Dalhousie

D. Lord Ellenborough

83. Which of the following pairs is correctly matched?

A. Mahatma Gandhi : Home Rule

B. Annie Besant : Non-Cooperation Movement

C. Jawaharlal Nehru : Khilafat Movement

D. Lala Hardayal : Hindustan Ghadar Party

84. For which of the following movements did Mahatma Gandhi give the slogan "Do or Die"?

A. Kheda Satyagraha

B. Non-Cooperation Movement

C. Civil Disobedience Movement

D. Quit India Movement

85. Who among the following was the founder of the Servants of India Society?

A. Bal Gangadhar Tilak

B. Dadabhai Naoroji

C. Gopal Krishna Gokhale

D. Lala Lajpat Rai

86. Which of the following pairs is ***not*** correctly mathced?

A. Lord Wellesley : Subsidiary Alliance

B. Lord Dalhousie : Doctrine of Lapse

C. Lord Ripon : Vernacular Press Act

D. Lord Curzon : Partition of Bengal

87. Which of the following territories was outside the boundaries of the Mughal Empire during the reign of Akbar?

A. Khandesh B. Kabul

C. Bijapur D. Kashmir

88. Which Sultan of Delhi enforced a strict market control system during his time?

A. Ala-ud-din Khilji

B. Mohammad-bin-Tughlaq

C. Firoz Shah Tughlaq

D. Bahlol Lodi

89. Which of the following pairs is *not* correctly matched?

A. Kautilya : Arthashastra
B. Hala : Gathasaptasati
C. Banabhatta: Buddha Charita
D. Kalidasa : Abhijnana Shakuntalam

90. With which of the following countries is the famous 'October Revolution' associated?

A. China B. Cuba
C. France D. Russia

91. Who is the author of "Das Kapital"?

A. Karl Marx
B. Friedrich Engels
C. Joseph Stalin
D. Vladimir Lenin

92. Who was the Commander of the American forces during the American War of Independence?

A. Alexander Hamilton
B. Thomas Jefferson
C. George Washington
D. Major Samuel Shaw

93. Who fought the Battle of Buxar?

A. Humayun and Sher Shah Suri
B. Ahmad Shah Abdali and Marathas
C. English and Mir Kasim
D. English and Marathas

94. Who of the following started the newspaper 'Samvad Kaumudi' in the early 19th century?

A. Ishwar Chandra Vidyasagar
B. Keshav Chandra Sen
C. Raja Rammohan Roy
D. Satyendranath Tagore

95. Match List-I (Movements) with List-II (Leaders) and select the correct answer using the codes given below the lists:

List-I (Movements)	List-II (Leaders)
A. Home Rule movement	1. Maulana Abul Kalam Azad
B. Bhudan movement	2. Bal Gangadhar Tilak
C. Aligarh movement	3. Sayyid Ahmad Khan
D. Khilafat movement	4. Vinoba Bhave

Codes:

	(a)	*(b)*	*(c)*	*(d)*
A.	1	4	3	2
B.	2	4	3	1
C.	2	3	4	1
D.	1	3	4	2

96. When the Moroccan traveller Ibn Batutah visited India, who was the Delhi Sultan?

A. Jalaluddin Khilji
B. Ala-ud-din Khilji
C. Giasuddin Tughlaq
D. Muhammad-bin Tughlaq

97. The Lingaraja Temple built during the medieval period is at

A. Bhubaneswar
B. Khajuraho
C. Madurai
D. Mount Abu

98. Which of the following is Considered as an encyclopaedia of Indian medicine?

A. Charakasamhita
B. Lokayata

C. Brihatsamhita
D. Suryasiddhanta

99. Which of the following is not included in the 'eight-fold path' of Buddhism?
A. Right Speech
B. Right Contemplation
C. Right Desire
D. Right Conduct

100. During India's freedom struggle, the 'Sepoy Mutiny' started from which of the following places?
A. Agra B. Gwalior
C. Jhansi D. Meerut

Geography

101. Match List-I (Historical Site) with List-II (State) and select the correct answer using the codes given below the lists:

List-I (Historical Site)	List-II (State)
(*a*) Shore temple	1. Karnataka
(*b*) Bhimbetka	2. Tamil Nadu
(*c*) Kesava temple (Hoysala (Monuments)	3. Kerala
(*d*) Hampi	4. Madhya Pradesh
	5. Rajasthan

Codes :

	(*a*)	(*b*)	(*c*)	(*d*)
A.	3	5	2	1
B.	2	4	1	1
C.	3	4	2	2
D.	2	5	1	4

102. Where are the maximum numbers of major ports located in India?
A. Maharashtra
B. Kerala
C. Goa
D. Tamil Nadu

103. Match List-I (Beach Resort) with List-II (State) and select the correct answer using the codes given below the lists:

List-I (Beach Resort)	List-II (State)
(*a*) Digha	1. Kerala
(*b*) Covelong	2. West Bengal
(*c*) Cherai	3. Maharashtra
(*d*) Murud-Janjira	4. Tamil Nadu

Codes :

	(*a*)	(*b*)	(*c*)	(*d*)
A.	2	4	1	3
B.	3	1	4	2
C.	2	1	4	3
D.	3	4	1	2

104. Match List-I (Produce) with List-II (Major Producer State) and select the correct answer using the codes given below the lists:

List-I (Produce)	List-II (Major Producer State)
(*a*) Rubber	1. Andhra Pradesh
(*b*) Soyabean	2. Tamil Nadu
(*c*) Groundnut	3. Madhya Pradesh
(*d*) Wheat	4. Kerala
	5. Uttar Pradesh

Codes :

	(a)	(b)	(c)	(d)
A.	4	1	2	5
B.	5	3	1	4
C.	4	3	1	5
D.	5	1	2	4

105. Match List-I (Railway Zone) with List-II (Headquarters) and select the correct answer using the codes given below the lists:

List-I (Railway Zone)	**List-II (Headquarters)**
(a) East-Central Railway	1. Hubli
(b) North-Western Railway	2. Allahabad
(c) North-Central Railway	3. Hajipur
(d) South-Western Railway	4. Jabalpur
	5. Jaipur

Codes :

	(a)	(b)	(c)	(d)
A.	3	5	2	1
B.	2	1	4	5
C.	3	1	2	5
D.	2	5	4	1

106. Match List-I (Wildlife Sanctuary) with List-II (State) and select the correct answer using the codes given below the lists:

List-I (Wildlife Sanctuary)	**List-II (State)**
(a) Bhitar Kanika	1. Andhra Pradesh
(b) Pachmarhi	2. Karnataka
(c) Pocharam	3. Madhya Pradesh
(d) Sharavathi	4. Orissa
	5. Uttar Pradesh

Codes :

	(a)	(b)	(c)	(d)
A.	4	2	1	3
B.	1	3	5	2
C.	4	3	1	2
D.	1	2	5	3

107. Which one of the following is ***not*** a tributary of the river Godavari?

A. Koyna B. Manjra
C. Pranhita D. Wardha

108. Which one of the following is the correct statement?

A. Spring tides occur on the full moon day only
B. Neap tides occur on the new moon day only
C. The West coast of India experiences tides four times a day
D. Tides do not occur in the gulfs

109. Which one of the following pairs is ***not*** correctly matched?

	City	**River**
A.	Ahmedabad:	Sabarmati
B.	Hyderabad :	Musi
C.	Lucknow :	Gomti
D.	Surat :	Narmada

110. Match List-I (Famous Place) with List-II (Country) and select the correct answer using the codes given below the lists:

List-I (Famous Place)	List-II (Country)
(*a*) Alexandria	1. Turkey
(*b*) Blackpool Pleasure Beach	2. Great Britain
(*c*) Constantinople	3. Italy
(*d*) Florence	4. Greece
	5. Egypt

Codes :

	(*a*)	(*b*)	(*c*)	(*d*)
A.	1	3	4	2
B.	5	2	1	3
C.	1	2	4	3
D.	5	3	1	2

111. Match List-I (Institute) with List-II (City) and select the correct answer using the codes given below the lists:

List-I (Institute)	List-II (City)
(*a*) Rashtriya Sanskrit Vidyapeeth	1. Hyderabad
(*b*) Maharishi Sandipani Rashtriya Veda Vidhya Pratishthan	2. Varanasi
(*c*) Central Institute of Indian Languages	3. Mysore
(*d*) Central Institute of English and Foreign Languages	4. Tirupati
	5. Ujjain

Codes :

	(*a*)	(*b*)	(*c*)	(*d*)
A.	2	3	1	5
B.	4	5	3	1
C.	2	5	3	1
D.	4	3	1	5

112. Consider the following statements:

1. Kaziranga National park is a World Heritage Site recognised by the UNESCO
2. Kaziranga National Park is a home to sloth bear and hoolock gibbon.

Which of the statements given above is/are correct?

A. 1 only
B. 2 only
C. Both 1 and 2
D. Neither 1 nor 2

113. Which country among the following is the biggest producer of cotton?

A. China
B. India
C. Indonesia
D. USA

114. Where is the Holy Shrine of Imam Ali in Najaf located?

A. Saudi Arabia
B. Iraq
C. Iran
D. Kuwait

115. Match List-I (Institute) with List-II (Location) and select the correct answer using the codes given below the lists:

List-I (Institute)	List-II (Location)
(*a*) Indian Institute of Public Administration	1. Faridabad

(*b*)	V.V. Giri National Labour Institute	2. Bangalore
(*c*)	National Institute of Financial Management	3. NOIDA
(*d*)	National Law School of India University	4. Mumbai
		5. Delhi

Codes :

	(*a*)	(*b*)	(*c*)	(*d*)
A.	1	2	4	3
B.	5	3	1	2
C.	1	3	4	2
D.	5	2	1	3

116. Which river feeds "Tehri dam"?
A. Alaknanda
B. Bhagirathi
C. Gandak
D. Ghaghara

117. Which of the following winds are known as "Anti-trade winds"?
A. Chinook
B. Cyclones
C. Typhoons
D. Westerlies

118. Geostationary orbit is at a height of
A. 6 km
B. 1000 km
C. 3600 km
D. 36000 km

119. The orbits of planets around the Sun can be
A. Elliptic and parabolic
B. Parabolic and hyperbolic
C. Circular and hyperbolic
D. Circular and elliptic

120. What is Super Nova?
A. A black hole
B. A dying star
C. An asteroid
D. A comet

121. Which State is irrigated by the Gang Canal?
A. Uttar Pradesh
B. Bihar
C. West Bengal
D. Rajasthan

122. Among the following Indian cities, which one is located most southward?
A. Hyderabad
B. Visakhapatnam
C. Panaji
D. Belgaum

123. Match List I (National Highway) with List II (Connected Cities) and select the correct answer using the codes given below the Lists:

List-I (National Highway)	**List-II (Connected Cities)**
A. NH 3	1. Delhi-Lucknow
B. NH 4	2. Agra-Bikaner
C. NH 11	3. Agra-Mumbai
D. NH 24	4. Chennai-Thane (Mumbai)

Codes :

	(*a*)	(*b*)	(*c*)	(*d*)
A.	3	1	2	4
B.	2	4	3	1
C.	3	4	2	1
D.	2	1	3	4

124. Match List-I (Defence Institute) with List-II (City) and select the correct answer using the codes given below the Lists:

List-I (Defence Institute)	List-II (City)
(*a*) College of Defence Management	1. Panchmarhi
(*b*) Army Air Defence College	2. Bengaluru
(*c*) Army Supply Corps (ASC) Centre and College	3. Secunderabad
(*d*) Army Education Corps (AEC) Training College and Centre	4. Gopalpur

Codes :

	(*a*)	(*b*)	(*c*)	(*d*)
A.	3	4	2	1
B.	1	2	4	3
C.	3	2	4	1
D.	1	4	2	3

125. Which of the following are Defence Public Sector Undertakings?

1. Goa Shipyard Limited
2. The Bharat Dynamics Limited
3. Mishra Dhatu Nigam Limited

Select the correct answer using the codes given below:

A. 1 and 2 B. 2 and 3
C. 1 and 3 D. 1, 2 and 3

126. Which one of the following pairs is ***not*** correctly matched?

A. Gol Gumbaz : Hyderabad
B. Tomb of Itmad-ud-daula : Agra
C. Tomb of Sher Shah : Sasaram
D. Tomb of Rani Rupmati : Ahmedabad

127. Where is the Baglihar Hydro-electric Project located?

A. Firozepur District of Punjab
B. Doda District of Jammu and Kashmir
C. Faridkot District of Punjab
D. Baramulla District of Jammu and Kashmir

128. Match List-I (Temple/Cathedral) with List-II (Place) and select the correct answer using the code given below the Lists:

List-I (Temple/Cathedral)

(*a*) Brihadeswara Temple
(*b*) Vishwanatha Temple
(*c*) Kamakhya Temple
(*d*) Santhom Cathedral

List-II (Place)

1. Guwahati
2. Chennai
3. Thanjavur
4. Khajuraho

Codes :

	(*a*)	(*b*)	(*c*)	(*d*)
A.	3	2	1	4
B.	1	4	3	2
C.	3	4	1	2
D.	1	2	3	4

129. Match List-I (World Heritage Site) with List-II (State) and select the correct answer using the code given below the Lists:

List-I (World Heritage Site)

(*a*) Manas Wildlife Sanctuary
(*b*) Mahabodhi Temple Complex
(*c*) Group of Monuments, Pattadakal
(*d*) Nandadevi National Park

List-II (State)

1. Bihar
2. Uttarakhand
3. Asom
4. Karnataka

Codes :

	(*a*)	(*b*)	(*c*)	(*d*)
A.	2	4	1	3
B.	3	1	4	2
C.	2	1	4	3
D.	3	4	1	2

130. Consider the following statements:

1. Black soils occur mainly in Maharashtra, Western Madhya Pradesh and Gujarat.
2. Alluvial soils are confined mainly to the northern plains.

Which of the statements given above is/are correct?

A. 1 only
B. 2 only
C. Both 1 and 2
D. Neither 1 nor 2

131. What is the new name of the old colony of Northern Rhodesia?

A. Zambia B. Zimbabwe
C. Uganda D. Tanzania

132. Which is the smallest (in area) of the following Union Territories?

A. Chandigarh
B. Dadra and Nagar Haveli
C. Daman and Diu
D. Lakshadweep

133. The Sundarbans or the 'Mangrove' forests are found in

A. Kutch Peninsula
B. Western Ghats
C. Konkan Coast
D. Deltaic West Bengal

134. On which river has the Hirakud dam been built?

A. Mahanadi
B. Godavari
C. Cauvery
D. Periyar

135. Where is "Ground Zero"?

A. Greenwich
B. New York
C. Indira Point
D. Sriharikota

136. The maximum concentration of scheduled caste population is in the

A. Indo-Gangetic Plains
B. North-East India
C. Western Coast
D. Eastern Coast

137. When was the first passenger train run in India?

A. January 1848
B. April 1853
C. May 1857
D. April 1852

138. Which is the major area where 'Garba' dance form is common?

A. Maharashtra B. Gujarat
C. Rajasthan D. Punjab

139. Where is India's most prized tea grown?
A. Jorhat B. Darjeeling
C. Nilgiris D. Mannar

140. Which is the largest cotton growing State in India?
A. Maharashtra
B. Madhya Pradesh
C. Andhra Pradesh
D. Gujarat

141. Which one of the following is the first shipyard of India?
A. Cochin
B. Visakhapatnam
C. Mazagaon
D. Paradeep

142. Which of the following Indian States is the largest producer of Cardamom?
A. Kerala
B. Tamil Nadu
C. Karnataka
D. Jammu & Kashmir

143. Vikram Sarabhai Space Centre is located in
A. Peenya
B. Ahmedabad
C. Thiruvananthapuram
D. Dehradun

144. The Sardar Sarovar Dam is associated with
A. Tapti river valley project
B. Mahanadi river valley project
C. Narmada project
D. Bhakra-Nangal project

145. In which of the following states in India is the bird, Great Indian Bustard found?
A. Rajasthan
B. Bihar
C. Karnataka
D. Andhra Pradesh

146. The Indian state with smallest population is
A. Sikkim
B. Arunachal Pradesh
C. Goa
D. Mizoram

147. On which of the following rivers Nasik is situated?
A. Ganges
B. Krishna
C. Godavari
D. Cauvery

148. Atacama Desert is in
A. South America
B. North America
C. South Africa
D. Russia

149. Which place in India is a reference for determining Indian Standard Time?
A. Delhi B. Allahabad
C. Kolkata D. Mumbai

150. Which of the following does not share a boarder with India?
A. Pakistan
B. Bangladesh
C. Burma
D. Afghanistan

151. The Dachigam Wildlife Sanctuary is in
A. Himachal Pradesh
B. Asom
C. Jammu & Kashmir
D. Karnataka

152. How many days does the moon take to complete 1 revolution around the earth?

A. $26\frac{1}{3}$ days

B. $27\frac{1}{3}$ days

C. $24\frac{1}{3}$ days

D. $28\frac{1}{2}$ days

153. A high growth rate of population is characterised by

A. High birth and high death rates

B. High birth and low death rates

C. Low birth and low death rates

D. Low birth and high death rates

154. The Indian Sub-continent was originally a part of

A. Jurassic-land

B. Angara-land

C. Aryavarta

D. Gondwana-land

155. The tropical grassland is called

A. Pampas B. Llanas

C. Savanah D. Veld

156. The atmosphere is heated mainly by

A. Insolation

B. Conduction

C. Radiation

D. Convection

157. Which one of the following countries is the largest producer of uranium in the world?

A. Canada B. South Africa

C. Namibia D. USA

158. Which of the following methods does not help in conserving soil fertility and moisture?

A. Contour ploughing

B. Dry farming

C. Strip cropping

D. Shifting agriculture

159. Mudumalai Wildlife Sanctuary is located in the State of

A. Kerala

B. Karnataka

C. Tamil Nadu

D. Andhra Pradesh

160. The narrow stretch of water connecting two seas is called

A. Bay B. Peninsula

C. Isthmus D. Strait

161. The topography of plateau is ideal for

A. Cultivation

B. Forestry

C. Mining

D. Generation of hydel power

162. Naga Khasi and Garo hills are located in

A. Purvanchal Ranges

B. Karakoram Ranges

C. Zaskar Ranges

D. Himalayas Ranges

163. In which of the following States, Jawahar Tunnel is located?

A. Himachal Pradesh

B. Jammu & Kashmir

C. Uttarakhand

D. Goa

164. Where was India's first submarine museum established?
A. Kochi
B. Panjim
C. Visakhapatnam
D. Mumbai

165. Which two countries are connected by an under-water tunnel?
A. England and Spain
B. Malaysia and Singapore
C. England and Belgium
D. France and England

166. Which of the following is correctly matched with regard to thermal power projects?
A. Korba — Uttar Pradesh
B. Ramagundam — Tamil Nadu
C. Talcher — Andhra Pradesh
D. Kawas — Gujarat

167. Sundarbans of Eastern India is an example of
A. Forest Ecosystem
B. Mangrove Ecosystem
C. Grassland Ecosystem
D. Marine Ecosystem

168. The deepest trench of the world—'The Mariana Trench' is located in the
A. Indian Ocean
B. Atlantic Ocean
C. Arctic Ocean
D. Pacific Ocean

169. Which of the following is a landlocked sea?
A. Timor Sea
B. Arafura Sea
C. Greenland Sea
D. Aral Sea

170. Match the dams and the states in which they are situated:

	Dam	**State**
(*a*)	Hirakud	1. Chhattisgarh
(*b*)	Mettur	2. Orissa
(*c*)	Mahanadi	3. Karnataka
(*d*)	Almatti	4. Tamil Nadu

Codes :

	(*a*)	(*b*)	(*c*)	(*d*)
A.	3	2	4	1
B.	2	4	1	3
C.	1	3	2	4
D.	4	1	3	2

171. Which of the following territories does not have a border with Arunachal Pradesh?
A. Asom
B. Nagaland
C. Bhutan
D. Manipur

172. Which of the following 'rivers does ***not*** originate in the Indian territory?
A. Mahanadi
B. Brahamaputra
C. Ravi
D. Chenab

173. Land and sea-breezes occur due to
A. Conduction
B. Convection
C. Radiation
D. Tides

174. Which of the following is ***not*** correctly matched with regard to Project Tiger Reserves?
A. Sariska — Alwar
B. Valmiki — Hazaribagh
C. Pench — Garhwal
D. Nagarjunasagar — Sri Sailam

175. Trade winds blow from the
A. Equatorial low pressure
B. Polar high pressure
C. Subtropical high pressure
D. Subpolar low pressure

176. Most of the Indians belong to which of the following racial stocks?
A. Caucasoid
B. Negroid
C. Australoid
D. Mongoloid

177. Which of the following signifies the American Indians living in the US?
A. Bushmen
B. Alpine
C. Amerindus
D. Mestizoes

178. Which region is most famous for citrus fruits?
A. Deserts
B. Monsoon regions
C. Temperate grasslands
D. Mediterranean regions

179. The leading sulphur producing country in the world is
A. USA B. Russia
C. Japan D. Mexico

180. The largest producer of mercury is
A. USA B. Canada
C. China D. Spain

181. The largest amount of saffron comes from
A. Uttar Pradesh
B. Tamil Nadu
C. Jammu and Kashmir
D. Kerala

182. The boundary between Germany and Poland is called the
A. Hindenberg Line
B. Maginot Line
C. Durand Line
D. 17th Parallel

183. The boundary between North and South Korea is marked by the
A. Radcliffe Line
B. 38th Parallel
C. 49th Parallel
D. 17th Parallel

184. Which countries are separated by the 49th Parallel?
A. France and Germany
B. USA and Mexico
C. USA and Canada
D. Russia and China

185. Echo-sounding is the technique applied to
A. Measure the depth of the sea
B. Measure the amplitude of sound waves
C. Record earthquake waves
D. Record the density of air in the atmosphere

186. On which of the rivers is the famous Kariba Dam situated?
A. Nile B. Niger
C. Zambezi D. Amazon

187. The northernmost limit of India is
A. 36°4' N latitude
B. 37°8' N latitude
C. 37°6' N latitude
D. 36°12' N latitude

188. The length of India's coastline is about
A. 4,500 km
B. 5,900 km
C. 7,000 km
D. 7,516 km

189. The total area of India is about
A. 31 lakh sq km
B. 33 lakh sq km
C. 320 lakh sq km
D. 35 lakh sq km

190. Where is the Gulf of Mannar located?
A. West of Gujarat
B. East of Tamil Nadu
C. West of Kerala
D. South of Kanyakumari

191. The Sivaliks stretch between
A. Indus and Sutlej
B. Potwar Basin and Teesta
C. Sutlej and Kali
D. Sutlej and Teesta

192. The territorial waters of India extend up to
A. 12 nautical miles
B. 6 nautical miles
C. 15 nautical miles
D. 10 nautical miles

193. The deepest lake in the world is
A. Pushkar Lake
B. Lake Superior
C. Victoria Lake
D. Baikal Lake

194. Simlipal Tiger Reserve is located at
A. Assam
B. Gujarat
C. Orissa
D. Bihar

195. Which of the following rivers flow through a rift valley?
A. Ganga
B. Narmada
C. Brahmaputra
D. Krishna

196. What is the most important characteristic of the islands (Indian) located in the Arabian Sea?
A. They are all very small in size
B. They are all of coral origin
C. They have a very dry climate
D. They are extended parts of the mainland

197. The Thar Desert is believed to be expanding. The most suitable way to check it would be by
A. Afforestation
B. Artificial rain
C. Canal irrigation
D. Using the area for cattle rearing

198. Which one is a land-locked State?
A. Gujarat
B. Andhra Pradesh
C. West Bengal
D. Bihar

199. Which area in India gets the summer monsoon?
A. The Himalayas
B. The Eastern Ghats
C. The Western Ghats
D. The Indo-Gangetic plains

200. In which of the following areas is maximum precipitation received from the summer monsoon?
A. The Coromandel coast

B. The North-Eastern hilly region
C. The Central Indian hills
D. The Western Himalayas

Indian Polity and Constitution

201. Which Schedule of the Constitution lists the languages recognised by it?
A. Eighth Schedule
B. Sixth Schedule
C. Seventh Schedule
D. Ninth Schedule

202. Which of the following Union Territories has a Chief Minister?
A. Andaman and Nicobar Islands
B. Puducherry
C. Chandigarh
D. Dadra and Nagar Haveli

203. Who among the following administers the Oath of Office to the President of India?
A. The Vice-President of India
B. The Chief Justice of India
C. The Chairman of Rajya Sabha
D. The Prime Minister

204. Parliament of India consists of
A. Directly elected members only
B. Directly elected and nominated members
C. Directly elected and indirectly elected members
D. Directly elected, indirectly elected and nominated members

205. In a Unitary Government
A. All powers are vested in the Centre
B. Powers are divided between the Centre and the States under a Constitution
C. Powers are divided by mutual consent of the Centre and the States through Parliamentary statute
D. The Judiciary must be independent

206. Article 360 of the Constitution of India relates to
A. National Emergency
B. Emergency in a State
C. To conduct Parliament Elections
D. Financial Emergency

207. Panchayati Raj was recommended by
A. Sarkaria Commission
B. Fazlali Commission
C. Balwantrai Mehta Committee
D. Rajamannar Committee

208. Name the first woman Governor of an Indian State
A. Padmaja Naidu
B. Lakshmi N. Menon
C. Sarojini Naidu
D. Sucheta Kriplani

209. Gangtok is the capital of
A. Nagaland
B. Meghalaya
C. Sikkim
D. Arunachal Pradesh

210. Who appoints the Chief Justice of a High Court in India?

A. The President of India
B. The Governor of the State concerned
C. The Chief Justice of the Supreme Court
D. An Appointment Committee in the Union Ministry of Law

211. In India, how did the Planning Commission come into existence?
A. By an Act of Parliament
B. By an executive order
C. Under the provisions of the Constitution
D. As an attached office of the Union Ministry of Finance

212. Which is the first executive tier of the Panchayati Raj system from below?
A. Gram Sabha
B. Gram Panchayat
C. Mandal Parishad
D. Panchayat Samiti

213. After the Constitution of India, came into force, when did the Parliament enact the Untouchability (Offences) Act?
A. 1953 B. 1954
C. 1955 D. 1956

214. Which of the following pairs is ***not*** correctly matched?

	State/U.T.	High Court
A.	Goa	— Bombay
B.	Andaman and Nicobar Islands	— Calcutta
C.	Sikkim	— Guwahati
D.	Puducherry	— Madras

215. The procedure for the Amendment of the Constitution of India is given under
A. Article 315
B. Article 358
C. Article 360
D. Article 368

216. Which of the following Articles of the Constitution of India has provision for the President to proclaim emergency?
A. Article 352
B. Article 355
C. Article 356
D. Article 360

217. Which of the following offices is held during the pleasure of the President of India?
A. Vice-President
B. Chief Justice of India
C. Governor of a State
D. Chairman of the Union Public Service Commission

218. Article 370 of the constitution is applicable to the state of
A. Nagaland
B. Mizoram
C. Manipur
D. Jammu & Kashmir

219. In the parliamentary practices when did the "Zero-hour" interventions emerge in India?
A. 1952 B. 1962
C. 1972 D. 1982

220. "Vote on Account" means legislative vote
A. On the Appropriation Bill
B. On the Finance Bill

C. On the accounts and audit report submitted by the CAG
D. Authorising expenditure in respect of the demands for grants pending the passing of the Appropriation Bill

221. Which of these words is not in the preamble of the constitution of India?
A. Socialist
B. Sovereign
C. Secular
D. Public Welfare

222. Which of the following has ***not*** been mentioned in the Indian Constitution as a Right?
A. Political and Social Rights
B. Educational Rights
C. Economic Rights
D. Religious Rights

223. Which one of the following is ***not*** stated in the Preamble of the Indian Constitution?
A. Justice
B. Fraternity
C. Adult franchise
D. Equality of status

224. In framing the Constitution of India, from which country did we borrow the scheme of the federal set up?
A. U.S.A. B. U.K.
C. Canada D. Switzerland

225. Who among the following was ***not*** a member of the Constituent Assembly set up in July 1946?
A. Dr. Rajendra Prasad
B. K.M. Munshi
C. Mahatma Gandhi
D. Abul Kalam Azad

226. Which article of the Indian Constitution provides for the institution of Panchayati Raj?
A. Art. 36 B. Art. 39
C. Art. 40 D. Art. 48

227. Which of the following is a bulwark of personal freedom?
A. Mandamus
B. Habeas Corpus
C. Quo Warranto
D. Certiorari

228. Who is the highest civil servant of the Union Government?
A. Attorney-General
B. Cabinet Secretary
C. Home Secretary
D. Principal Secretary to the Prime Minister

229. Article 1 of the Constitution declares India as
A. Federal State
B. Quasi-Federal State
C. Unitary State
D. Union of States

230. Which functionary can be invited to give his opinion in the Parliament?
A. Attorney-General of India
B. Chief Justice of India
C. Chief Election Commissioner of India
D. Comptroller and Auditor-General of India

231. Which of the following countries has an Unwritten Constitution?
A. USA B. UK
C. Pakistan D. India

232. The Drafting Committee of the Constitution, including the chairman, comprised of

A. Seven members

B. Five members

C. Nine members

D. Three members

233. Which one of the following exercised the most profound influence on the Indian Constitution?

A. The Government of India Act 1935

B. The US Constitution

C. British Constitution

D. The UN Charter

234. Which one of the following features was borrowed by the Indian Constitution from the British Constiution?

A. Parliamentary system of government

B. Rule of Law

C. Law-making procedure

D. All the above

235. India borrowed the idea of a federal system with a strong centre from

A. USA B. Canada

C. Australia D. New Zealand

236. The emergency provisions of the constitution of India were greatly influenced by

A. The Government of India Act 1935

B. The Weimar Constitution of Germany

C. The Constitution of United States

D. The Constitution of Canada

237. India borrowed the idea of Directive Principles of State Policy from the Constitutions of

A. The Weimar Republic of Germany

B. The Republic of Ireland

C. The South Africa

D. None of the above

238. If the President wishes to tender his resignation before the expiry of his normal term, he has to address the same to

A. The Vice-President of India

B. The Speaker of Lok Sabha

C. The Chief Justice of India

D. The Election Commission

239. Who among the following got the Bharat Ratna Award before becoming the President of India?

A. Dr. Zakir Hussain

B. Dr. Rajendra Prasad

C. V.V. Giri

D. Dr. S. Radhakrishnan

240. The Council of Ministers is collectively responsible to

A. The President of India

B. The Parliament

C. The Prime Minister

D. The Rajya Sabha

241. The office of the Prime Minister of India

A. Has been created by the Constitution

B. Is extra-constitutional growth

C. Has been created by a Parliamentary Statute

D. Is the combination of all the above

242. The minimum age at which a person can be appointed Prime Minister of India?
A. 21 years B. 25 years
C. 30 years D. 35 years

243. The first Amendment of the constitution was made in the year:
A. 1950 B. 1949
C. 1954 D. 1958

244. Which of the following is the maximum time limit of 'Zero Hour' during the Parliament session in India?
A. 30 minutes
B. One hour
C. Two hours
D. None of the above

245. Who among the following summons the joint session of Lok Sabha and Rajya Sabha?
A. Speaker
B. Chairman of Rajya Sabha
C. President
D. Minister of Parliamentary Affairs

246. Which of the following is India's Contribution to parliamentary system of democracy?
A. Zero Hour
B. Cut Motion Resolution
C. Adjournment Motion
D. Guillotine

247. The total number of members in the Legislative Council of a State cannot exceed
A. one-fourth of the total number of members in the Legislative Assembly
B. one-third of the total number of members of the legislative Assembly
C. one-sixth of the total number of members of the Legislative Assembly
D. No such limit has been fixed

248. Sikkim was made an integral part of India under the
A. 42nd Amendment
B. 40th Amendment
C. 39th Amendment
D. 36th Amendment

249. The number of Anglo-Indians who can be nominated by the President to the Lok Sabha is
A. 2 B. 3
C. 4 D. 5

250. Money Bills can be introduced in the State Legislature with the prior consent of
A. the Speaker
B. the Chief Minister
C. the Governor
D. the President

Economy

251. The apex bank for industrial credit in India is
A. RBI B. NABARD
C. ICICI D. IDBI

252. The prominent function of the Central Statistical Organisation is
A. To determine the money supply
B. To collect national income estimates
C. To collect employment details
D. To determine prices

253. Planning and control are related in such a way that
A. Planning precedes control
B. Control precedes planning
C. Both are concurrent
D. Both go hand in hand with each other in a cyclical manner

254. 'Gresham's Law' states that
A. Good money drives away bad money out of circulation
B. Bad money drives away good money out of circulation
C. Good money promotes bad money in the system
D. Bad money promotes good money in the system

255. National income refers to
A. Money value of goods and services produced in a country during a year
B. Money value of stocks and shares of a country during a year
C. Money value of capital goods produced by a country during a year
D. Money value of consumer goods produced by a country during a year

256. Which of the following taxes is/ are lived by the Union and collected and appropriated by the States?
A. Service tax
B. Stamp duties
C. Estate duty
D. Passenger and goods tax

257. Which of the following is ***not*** shared by the Centre and the States?
A. Income tax
B. Excise duty
C. Corporation duty
D. Sales tax

258. Expenditure on which of the following is ***not*** considered as an investment in the theory of income determination?
A. Factory construction
B. A computer
C. Increase in stocks of unsold goods
D. Stocks or shares in a joint stock company

259. With what aspect of commerce are "Bull" and "Bear" associated?
A. Banking
B. E-Commerce
C. International trade
D. Stock market

260. FDI means—
A. Foreign Direct Investment
B. Full Dog Cost
C. Full Direct Cost
D. Finance Institute

261. If the tax rate increases with the higher level of income, it shall be called
A. Proportional tax
B. Progressive tax
C. Lump sum tax
D. Regressive tax

262. In India, one-rupee coins and notes and subsidiary coins are issued by
A. The Reserve Bank of India
B. The Central Government
C. The State Bank of India
D. The Unit Trust of India

263. Which is the highest body that approves Five-Year Plans in the country?
A. NITI Aayog
B. Union Cabinet
C. National Development Council
D. Parliament

264. Prime cost is equal to
A. Variable cost plus administrative cost
B. Variable cost plus fixed cost
C. Variable cost only
D. Fixed cost only

265. New capital issue is placed in
A. Secondary market
B. Grey market
C. Primary market
D. Black market

266. Bank deposits that can be withdrawn without notice are called
A. Account payee deposits
B. Fixed deposits
C. Variable deposits
D. Demand deposits

267. An expenditure that has been made and cannot be recovered is called
A. Variable cost
B. Opportunity cost
C. Sink cost
D. Operational cost

268. The practice of selling goods in a foreign country at a price below their domestic selling price is called
A. 'Diplomacy'
B. 'Discrimination'
C. 'Dumping'
D. 'Double pricing'

269. Who propounded the 'market law'?
A. Adam Smith
B. J.B. Say
C. T.R. Malthus
D. Dravid Ricardo

270. National income is based on the
A. total revenue of the state
B. production of goods and services
C. net profit earned and expenditure made by the state
D. the sum of all factors of incomes

271. 'Utility' in economics means the capacity to
A. provide comforts
B. earn an income
C. satisfy human wants
D. satisfy human motives

272. Labour welfare does not include
A. education facilities
B. health facilities
C. housing facilities
D. quick promotion in job

273. 'Sellersmarket' denotes a situation where
A. Commodities are available at competitive rates
B. Demand exceeds supply

C. Supply exceeds demand
D. Supply and demand are evenly balanced

274. "Legal Tender Money" refers to
A. Cheques
B. Drafts
C. Bills of exchange
D. Currency notes

275. The sum total of incomes received for the services of labour, land or capital in a country is called
A. Gross domestic product
B. National income
C. Gross domestic income
D. Gross national income

276. The measurement of poverty line is based on the criteria of
A. Their dwelling houses
B. The nature of employment
C. Coloric consumption
D. Level of education

277. Capital is that wealth
A. Which is used for the production of wealth
B. Which is kept in boxes and lockers
C. Which is buried in the land
D. Which is stored for consumption

278. The poverty line has been defined in the
A. Seventh Five–Year Plan
B. Sixth Five–Year Plan
C. Eight Five–Year Plan
D. Fifth Five–Year Plan

279. Perfect market means there are
A. Many sellers and many buyers
B. A few sellers and a few buyers
C. A few sellers and many buyers
D. A few buyers and many sellers

280. A hard currency is the one
A. Whose external value is increasing
B. Which can be acquired only with official permission
C. Which can be obtained only against sale of gold
D. Which is really accepted in international transactions

281. Which of the following is not a Central Government Tax?
A. Income Tax
B. Customs
C. Land Revenue
D. Corporation Tax

282. Who is called the father of White Revolution?
A. Dr. Kurien Verghese
B. Nanjunda Swamy
C. M.S. Swaminathan
D. U.R. Rao

283. The major source of revenue in India is through
A. Direct Taxes
B. Indirect Taxes
C. Internal Borrowings
D. External Borrowings

284. The Reserve Bank of India was established in
A. 1927 B. 1935
C. 1947 D. 1949

285. Finance Commission is appointed by
A. Prime Minister
B. President of India
C. Ministry of Finance
D. None of these

286. Which of the following groups suffer the most from inflation?
A. Debtors
B. Creditors
C. Business class
D. Holders of real assets

287. Which one of the following is not an example of indirect tax?
A. Sales tax
B. Excise duty
C. Customs duty
D. Expenditure tax

288. The major aim of devaluation is to
A. Encourage imports
B. Encourage exports
C. Encourage both exports and imports
D. Discourage both exports and imports

289. Which of the following is a cash crop?
A. Wheat
B. Rice
C. Sugarcane
D. Maize

290. NAFED is connected with
A. Animal husbandry
B. Conservation of fuels
C. Agricultural marketing
D. Agricultural implements

291. Which Commission replaced Planning Commission in 2015?
A. NIYAM Aayog
B. NAGRIK Aayog
C. NITI Aayog
D. None of these

292. The one-rupee notes bear the signatures of the
A. Governor, Reserve Bank of India
B. Secretary, Ministry of Finance
C. Deputy Governor, Reserve Bank of India
D. Joint Secretary, Ministry of Finance

293. Whose approval is necessary before the Five-Year Plan can start?
A. The Finance Minister
B. National Development Council
C. The Prime Minister
D. Parliament

294. NABARD stands for
A. National Bank of Agriculture and Regional Development
B. National Bank for Agriculture and Rural Development
C. National Bureau of Aeronautical Research and Development
D. None of these

295. 'Bottle neck inflation' means
A. No rise in prices despite increase in aggregate demand
B. Rise in prices without increase in the aggregate demand

C. Decline in prices due to increase in aggregate demand
D. None of these

296. The main cause of International Trade is
A. Equal cost difference
B. Absolute cost difference
C. Comparative cost difference
D. Equal and comparative cost difference

297. Which one of the following taxes is not shared by the Central Government with the States?
A. Union excise duties
B. Customs duty
C. Income tax
D. Estate duty

298. A dualistic economy is one in which
A. both rich and poor people co-exist side by side
B. it has both foreign trade and internal trade
C. industry and agriculture exist side by side
D. modern sector and traditional sector exist side by side

299. Whose signatures are found on the 10 rupee note in India?
A. Prime Minister of India
B. President of India
C. Finance Minister of India
D. Governor, Reserve Bank of India

300. "Green Revolution" began in India during the year
A. 1967-68 B. 1966-67
C. 1968-69 D. 1969-70

General Science

301. Deep blue colour is imparted to glass by the presence of
A. Cobalt Oxide
B. Cupric Oxide
C. Ferrous Oxide
D. Nickel Oxide

302. Which of the following fibres is least prone to fire?
A. Nylon B. Cotton
C. Rayon D. Terry Cott

303. Which of the following is used as a filler in rubber tyres?
A. Carbon black
B. Coal
C. Coke
D. Graphite

304. Which of the following alloys is used for making magnets?
A. Duralumin
B. Stainless Steel
C. Alnico
D. Magnalium

305. Which of the following elements is obtained from sea weeds?
A. Argon
B. Sulphur
C. Vanadium
D. Iodine

306. Where are Mesons found?
A. Cosmic rays
B. X-rays
C. γ-rays
D. Laser beams

307. Milk tastes sour when kept in the open for sometime due to the formation of
A. Lactic acid
B. Citric acid
C. Acetic acid
D. Carbonic acid

308. Polythene is industrially prepared by the polymerisation of
A. Methane
B. Styrene
C. Acetylene
D. Ethylene

309. Which of the following chemicals responsible for the depletion of ozone layer in the atmosphere?
A. Nitrous oxide
B. Carbon dioxide
C. Chlorofluorocarbons
D. Sulphur dioxide

310. Plants die in winter by frost because
A. There is no transpiration
B. No photosynthesis takes place at such low temperatures
C. Respiration ceases at such low temperatures
D. Of desiccation and mechanical damage to tissues

311. Which of the following is ***not*** a constituent of chlorophyll?
A. Hydrogen
B. Magnesium
C. Carbon
D. Calcium

312. Which is the chief nitrogenous waste in humans?
A. Ammonia
B. Urea
C. Uric acid
D. Ammonium nitrate

313. Which is the largest living bird?
A. Peacock B. Ostrich
C. Dodo D. Turkey

314. Hormones are normally absent in
A. Rat B. Monkey
C. Bacteria D. Cat

315. Dengue fever is caused by
A. Fungi B. Bacteria
C. Protozoa D. Virus

316. Which of the following is considered to be good cholesterol?
A. VLDL B. LDL
C. HDL D. Triglycerides

317. "Thalassaemia" is a hereditary disease affecting
A. Blood B. Kidney
C. Lungs D. Heart

318. Which of the following is a proper food chain showing a producer, a herbivore and the carnivore?
A. Grass-Insect-Elephant
B. Plants-Rabbit-Tiger
C. Fish-Insect-Whale
D. Tiger-Rabbit-Owl

319. Aspirin is
A. Methoxy Benzoic acid
B. Methyl Salicylate
C. Acetyl Salicylic acid
D. Phenyl Salicylate

320. The medical instrument sphygmomanometer is used to examine
A. hormonal activity
B. brain tumor
C. the functions of intestine
D. blood pressure

321. Onion is a modified form of
A. stem B. root
C. leaves D. fruit

322. Weight of the body
- A. remains the same everywhere on the earth's surface
- B. is maximum at the poles
- C. is maximum at the equator
- D. is more on mountains than plains

323. Most of the nutrients are absorbed into blood through
- A. large intestine
- B. mouth
- C. small intestine
- D. abdomen

324. The path of Halley's comet in its orbit around the Sun is
- A. circular
- B. elliptical
- C. parabolic
- D. hyperbolic

325. Atoms of the same element having the same atomic number but different atomic weights are called
- A. Isotopes B. Polymers
- C. Isomers D. Isobars

326. The chief constituent of gobar gas is
- A. Nitrogen
- B. Ethane
- C. Hydrogen
- D. Methane

327. Law of heredity was put forward by
- A. Mendel B. Mendeleev
- C. Pavlov D. Koch

328. A device used for converting a.c. into d.c. is called
- A. Transformer
- B. Rectifier
- C. Induction oil
- D. Dynamo

329. An antibiotic is
- A. A chemical synthesised by a human cell against a micro-organism
- B. A chemical synthesised by a micro-organism against another micro-organism
- C. A substance produced by blood cells against bacteria
- D. A substance produced by blood cells against infection

330. Which one of the following can be synthesized by Liver?
- A. Vitamin-A
- B. Vitamin-E
- C. Vitamin-D
- D. Vitamin-K

331. Fluid part of blood devoid of corpuscles is called
- A. Tissue fluid
- B. Plasma
- C. Serum
- D. Lymph

332. Heart murmur indicates a
- A. Defective valve
- B. Poor oxygenation
- C. Dislocation of the heart
- D. Improper development of muscles

333. The language used in writing the scientific name of animals is
- A. French B. Latin
- C. German D. Dutch

334. Energy of Ultra-violet rays is greater than
- A. Infra-red rays

B. Gamma rays
C. X-rays
D. Cosmic rays

335. By-product obtained by soap-industry is
A. Caustic soda
B. Glycerol
C. Naphthalene
D. Caustic potash

336. Ripe grapes contain
A. Fructose
B. Sucrose
C. Galactose
D. Glucose

337. Polythene is polymer of
A. Ethylene
B. Propylene
C. Acetylene
D. Aniline

338. Which one of the following is pure water?
A. Rain water
B. Filter water
C. Tubewell water
D. Distilled water

339. Which silver salt is used for making film for photography?
A. Silver bromide
B. Silver chloride
C. Silver sulphate
D. Silver nitrate

340. To an astronaut sky appears
A. White
B. Rich blue
C. Light blue
D. Dark

341. The instrument used to measure the speed of the wind is
A. Altimeter
B. Anemometer
C. Chronometer
D. Dosimeter

342. Who defined the law of gravitation?
A. Newton B. Archimedes
C. Galileo D. Faraday

343. The metal used to make lightning conductors is
A. Iron B. Aluminium
C. Copper D. Zinc

344. 'IC' in computers stands for
A. Integrated Charge
B. Integrated Current
C. Integrated Circuits
D. Internal Circuits

345. A hydrogen balloon floats up because of
A. Air pressure decreases with decrease in height
B. Air pressure decreases with decrease in weight
C. Weight of the balloon is less than the weight of air displaced by it
D. The pressure inside the balloon is more than the pressure outside it

346. In a rechargeable cell what kind of energy is stored within the cell?
A. Electrical energy
B. Potential energy
C. Chemical energy
D. Kinetic energy

347. M.R.I. stands for
A. Metered Resonance imaging
B. Magnetic Resonance Imaging

C. Magnetic Reaction Imaging
D. Metered Reaction Imaging

348. The American space shuttle which exploded in space killing astronaut Kalpana Chawla, was known as
A. Challenger
B. Columbia
C. Discovery
D. Columbus

349. For determination of the age of which among the following is carbon dating method used?
A. Fossils
B. Rocks
C. Trees
D. A and B

350. Which is the hottest planet in the Solar System?
A. Jupiter B. Saturn
C. Venus D. Uranus

State

351. Telangana became India's 29th State in
A. 2014 B. 2013
C. 2012 D. 2011

352. In which State would you find Jim Corbett National Park?
A. Assam
B. Uttar Pradesh
C. Maharashtra
D. Uttarakhand

353. Jharia mines are situated in which of the following States?
A. Jharkhand
B. West Bengal
C. Bihar
D. Odisha

354. 'Sardar Sarovar' project is in which of the following States?
A. Rajasthan
B. Madhya Pradesh
C. Uttar Pradesh
D. Gujarat

355. The new name of Rajasthan canal is
A. Gandhi canal
B. Indira Gandhi canal
C. Jawahar canal
D. Subhash canal

356. Which of the following lakes in Rajasthan is saline?
A. Ana Sagar
B. Pichola
C. Sambhar
D. Jaisamand

357. In which state is the district of Udham Singh Nagar situated?
A. Punjab
B. Uttarakhand
C. Uttar Pradesh
D. Rajasthan

358. Which amongst the following States has the highest population density as per census 2011?
A. Kerala
B. Madhya Pradesh
C. Uttar Pradesh
D. Bihar

359. Which one among the following states is smallest in area?
A. Andhra Pradesh
B. Gujarat
C. Karnataka
D. Tamil Nadu

360. In which State is Nalsarovar Bird Sanctuary located?

A. Maharashtra
B. Odisha
C. Gujarat
D. Rajasthan

361. Which of the following is the 28th State of India?
A. Jharkhand
B. Uttarakhand
C. Chhattisgarh
D. Gorkhaland

362. In which State is Ghana Bird Sanctuary located?
A. U.P.
B. M.P.
C. Assam
D. Rajasthan

363. Which of the following States does not have border with China?
A. Uttarakhand
B. U.P.
C. H.P.
D. Sikkim

364. What is the capital of the State of Chhattisgarh?
A. Raipur
B. Patna
C. Jamshedpur
D. Bokaro

365. With which State would you associate the festival of Dev Devali?
A. Bihar
B. West Bengal
C. Uttar Pradesh
D. Maharashtra

366. Areawise, which is the smallest State in India?
A. Goa B. Sikkm
C. Manipur D. Tripura

367. The capital of Lakshadweep is
A. Aizwal B. Port Blair
C. Kavaratti D. Agartala

368. The famous Kanha Wildlife Sanctuary is located in the State of:
A. Assam
B. Bihar
C. Madhya Pradesh
D. Karnataka

369. Which one of the following State is most populous?
A. Odisha
B. Uttar pradesh
C. Maharashtra
D. Bihar

370. Bhangra is a folk dance of
A. Punjab
B. Madhya Pradesh
C. Odisha
D. Assam

371. Kaziranga Animals Sanctuary is situated in the State of
A. Assam
B. Uttar Pradesh
C. Madhya Pradesh
D. Rajasthan

372. Konark temple is situated in the State of
A. Odisha
B. Kerala
C. Madhya Pradesh
D. Andhra Pradesh

373. The State which produces maximum Uranium in India is
A. Rajasthan
B. Kerala
C. Jharkhand
D. West Bengal

374. Lumbini, the birth place of Gautam Buddha is in
A. Bihar B. Sikkim
C. Nepal D. Uttar Pradesh

375. Which of the following is the least densely populated State?
A. Sikkim
B. Meghalaya
C. Mizoram
D. Arunachal Pradesh

376. "Dudhawa National Park" is situated in
A. Madhya Pradesh
B. Bihar
C. Uttar Pradesh
D. Karnataka

377. Sandal wood is found in
A. Tamil Nadu
B. Himachal Pradesh
C. Karnataka
D. Maharashtra

378. The chief producer of 'Jute' in India is
A. West Bengal
B. Karnataka
C. Tamil Nadu
D. Asom

379. The Ghat and Bhor Ghat are the important passes in
A. Kerala
B. Maharashtra
C. Gujarat
D. Rajasthan

380. The famous monolithic statue of Jain Saint Bahubali is situated in the state of
A. Andhra Pradesh
B. Bihar
C. Karnataka
D. Tamil Nadu

381. Which state of India is the largest exporter of marine products?
A. Andhra Pradesh
B. Gujarat
C. Kerala
D. Maharashtra

382. After Uttar Pradesh, which State leads in the production of sugarcane?
A. Bihar
B. Andhra Pradesh
C. Maharashtra
D. Tamil Nadu

383. Goa was liberated from the Portuguese in
A. 1964 B. 1961
C. 1963 D. 1962

384. The State which accounts for more than 90 per cent of total rubber production in India is
A. Karnataka
B. Kerala
C. Tamil Nadu
D. Andhra Pradesh

385. Which one of the following States has no common border with UP?
A. Punjab
B. Haryana
C. Madhya Pradesh
D. Uttarakhand

386. Name the State in which the Hirakud Dam is located?
A. Orissa B. Karnataka
C. U.P. D. Gujarat

387. Panna in Madhya Pradesh is associated with
A. Manganese
B. Mica
C. Copper
D. Diamond

388. The holy city Hardwar is in which of the State?
A. Uttar Pradesh
B. Haryana
C. Bihar
D. Uttarakhand

389. According to the census of 2011 the only State in India that shows excess of females over males is
A. Uttar Pradesh
B. Kerala
C. Maharashtra
D. Jammu and Kashmir

390. Which States share the Tungabhadra multipurpose project?
A. Karnataka and Madhya Pradesh
B. Orissa and Madhya Pradesh
C. Andhra Pradesh and Karnataka
D. Tamil Nadu and Andhra Pradesh

Organisations

391. The headquarter of World Trade Organisation (WTO) is located at
A. Rome
B. New York
C. Geneva
D. Washington DC

392. Which of the following countries is not a member of SAARC?
A. Nepal
B. China
C. Pakistan
D. India

393. Where is SAARC secretariat situated?
A. Islamabad
B. Colombo
C. New Delhi
D. Kathmandu

394. What is the activity of the INTERPOL?
A. Central record keeping agency of the international crimes
B. Investigative agency of the UN
C. An organisation to coordinate the police activities of the participating nations
D. A terrorist outfit

395. The six official languages of the UN are Russian, Chinese, English, French, Spanish and
A. Hindi B. Urdu
C. Arabic D. Japanese

396. What does SAPTA stands for?
A. South Asian Preferential Trade Agreement
B. South Asian Post Trade Agreement
C. SAARC Preferential Trade Agreement
D. SAARC Prevention Trade Agreement

397. The Association of South East Asian Nations (ASEAN) has its headquarters at
A. Manila
B. Jakarta
C. Kuala Lumpur
D. Bangkok

398. The normal term of office of UN Secretary General is
A. 3 years
B. 4 years
C. 5 years
D. 6 years

399. Which of the following countries is not a member of the G-7 Group?
A. France
B. Italy
C. Spain
D. Germany

400. Which of the following is NOT a permanent member of the UN Security Council?
A. Germany
B. France
C. Great Britain
D. China

401. The first Secretary General of the United Nations was:
A. Mrs. Vijay Lakshmi Pandit
B. Trygve Lie
C. Dag Hammarskjoeld
D. U. Thant

402. Who was the first Indian to be the President of U.N. General Assembly?
A. Natwar Singh
B. V.K. Krishna Menon
C. Smt. Vijay Lakshmi Pandit
D. Romesh Bhandari

403. Where is the headquarters of the International Court of Justice?
A. The Hague (Netherlands)
B. Paris (France)
C. Rome (Italy)
D. Washington (U.S.A)

404. How many Judges are there in the International Court of Justice?
A. 9 B. 10
C. 11 D. 15

405. When was the United Nations Organisation founded?
A. 20th October, 1945
B. 11th, November, 1944
C. 24th October, 1945
D. 26th June, 1945

406. The headquarters of the Organisation of Petroleum Exporting Countries is at
A. Teheran
B. Vienna
C. Abu Dhabi
D. Doha

407. How many members does the Security Council of UN have?
A. Ten B. Fifteen
C. Sixteen D. Twenty

408. Which country is not a member of ASEAN?
A. Indonesia
B. Cambodia
C. Singapore
D. Philippines

409. Where is the Head Quarter of Asian Development Bank?
A. Washington
B. Manila
C. Paris
D. Canberra

410. The headquarters of the U.N.O. is located in
A. Washington
B. New York
C. Philadelphia
D. Chicago

Awards

411. 'Pulitzer' prizes are awarded to Americans for excellence in
A. Films
B. Social work
C. Journalism
D. Medicine

412. When was the Nobel Prize started?
A. 1901 B. 1905
C. 1934 D. 1900

413. 'Bharat Ratna' Award was given for the first time in
A. 1956 B. 1957
C. 1952 D. 1954

414. Saraswati Samman is awarded by
A. K.K. Birla Foundation
B. Government of India
C. Bharatiya Jnanpith
D. Sahitya Academy

415. Who was the first Asian to win a Nobel Prize?
A. Hideki Yuka
B. Har Gobind Khurana
C. C.V. Raman
D. Rabindranath Tagore

416. The highest Gallantry Award given in India is
A. Ashok Chakra
B. Mahavir Chakra
C. Param Vir Chakra
D. None of these

417. On which day every year National Awards for Teachers are announced?
A. September 5
B. November 14
C. November 19
D. August 15

418. Dronacharya Awards are given
A. to outstanding athletes
B. to outstanding coaches
C. for best performance in archery
D. for invention in science

419. Dr. C.V. Raman was awarded Nobel Prize in
A. Chemistry
B. Literature
C. Physics
D. Medicine

420. The first recipient of Rajiv Gandhi Khel Ratna Award is
A. Leander Paes
B. Viswanathan Anand
C. Kapil Dev
D. Limba Ram

421. The highest civilian award of India is
A. Bharat Ratna
B. Padam Vibhushan
C. Padam Bhushan
D. Padma Shri

422. Which of the following Indians awarded 'Legion D Award', the highest civilian award of France?
A. Satyajit Ray
B. Pandit Ravi Shankar
C. Lok Nayak Jayaprakash
D. J.L. Nehru

423. Dhanvantari Awards are given for the best performance in the field of
A. Medical Sciences
B. Nuclear Sciences
C. Economics
D. Space Research

424. Nobel Prizes are not given for which of the following fields?
A. Music B. Chemistry
C. Peace D. Physics

425. Dadasaheb Phalke Award is given for:
A. drama B. social welfare
C. films D. literature

426. In which year Nehru Award for International Understanding was instituted?
A. 1969 B. 1984
C. 1964 D. 1966

427. Who among the following has not been awarded the Bharat Ratna?
A. Indira Gandhi
B. Mahatma Gandhi
C. Sardar Patel
D. Radhakrishnan

428. Which one of the following is the second highest Civilian award in India?
A. Padma Shri
B. Bharat Ratna
C. Padma Bhushan
D. Padma Vibhushan

429. 'Victory Medal' is awarded in:
A. the USA
B. the UK
C. Russia
D. France

430. National film Awards were instituted in the year
A. 1954 B. 1950
C. 1961 D. 1969

431. In which year was the Nobel Prize for Economics announced for the first time?
A. 1969 B. 1901
C. 1919 D. 1970

432. Borlaug Award was instituted for recognising outstanding contribution in the field of
A. agriculture
B. ecology
C. journalism
D. medicine

433. Jesse Owens Global Award is given in the field of
A. Literature
B. Journalism
C. Science
D. Sports

434. Noble Alfred Bernhard after whom Nobel Prizes are given was
A. Engineer
B. Chemist
C. Both (A) and (B)
D. Doctor

435. Who was the first winner of Nehru Award for International Understanding?
A. Martin Luther King
B. Mother Teresa
C. U. Thant
D. Dr. Jonas Salk

Sports

436. In which International Championship, 'Thomas Cup' is given
A. Football
B. Cricket
C. Badminton
D. Tennis

437. 'Gambit' is related to which among the followings sports?
A. Carrom B. Bridge
C. Chess D. Billiards

438. The term 'Grandmaster' is used in which of these games?
A. Chess B. Judo
C. Bridge D. Karate

439. In the game of Volleyball, the number of players on each side is
A. Eight B. Five
C. Seven D. Six

440. The term ''Cue'' is associated with which game?
A. Hockey B. Football
C. Billiards D. Cricket

441. With which game is Geet Sethi Associated?
A. Basketball
B. Snooker
C. Chess
D. Tennis

442. How many players are there in each side in the game of Netball?
A. 7 B. 6
C. 9 D. 11

443. 'Uber Cup' is associated with which of the following?
A. Tennis B. Badminton
C. Chess D. Cricket

444. Where is the annual Australian Open Tennis tournament held?
A. Sydney B. Melbourne
C. Canberra D. Brisbane

445. The Olympic Motto is
A. Health is wealth
B. Promote Universal brotherhood
C. Faster, higher, stronger
D. Excellence is the goal

446. The term 'Tee' is associated with which of the following sports?
A. Polo B. Table Tennis
C. Golf D. Judo

447. Which Indian sportsman is known as Hockey Wizard throughout the world?
A. A.B. Subbiah
B. Jude Felix
C. Dhyan Chand
D. Ajitpal Singh

448. When did India become World Cricket champion?
A. 1980 B. 1982
C. 1983 D. 1986

449. ''Googly'' is associated with:
A. Cricket B. Table-Tennis
C. Hockey D. Billiards

450. With which game are the terms bull's eye, muzzle and plug associated?
A. Shooting B. Solitaire
C. Billiards D. Rowing

451. Who is the first Indian to take a hat trick in an international test?
A. Kapil Dev
B. Jasu Patel
C. Harbhajan Singh
D. B.S. Chandrashekhar

452. Who was declared by wisden as '' The Best Indian Bowler of the Century'' (20th Century)?
A. Kapil Dev
B. B.S. Chandrashekhar

C. B.S. Bedi
D. Subhash V. Gupte

453. " Jab" and "Parry" are terms used in which sport?
A. Wrestling
B. Boxing
C. Billiards
D. Weightlifting

454. India's national game is
A. Football B. Cricket
C. Tennis D. Hockey

455. Davis Cup is associated with the sport of
A. Tennis B. Football
C. Cricket D. Hockey

456. The term 'breast stroke' is associated with:
A. Skating
B. Croquet
C. Swimming
D. Rifle Shooting

457. What is the National Game of the USA?
A. Cricket B. Baseball
C. Soccer D. Billiards

458. Roger Federer is associated with
A. Hockey B. Lawn Tennis
C. Golf D. Badminton

459. 'Merdeka Cup' is associated with
A. Golf B. Football
C. Squash D. Hockey

460. Who among the following has become the first woman in the world to swim across seven seas?
A. Shikha Tandon
B. Bula Chowdhury
C. Amanda Beard
D. Arti Saha

Books

461. The famous book 'Geet Govind' is written by
A. Banabhatt
B. Jaydev
C. Mirabai
D. Kalidas

462. 'Ain-e-Akbari' was written by
A. Farista B. Ibn Batuta
C. Abul Fazal D. Birbal

463. Who wrote " Vande Mataram"?
A. Rabindra Nath Tagore
B. Sumitra Nandan Pant
C. Bankim Chandra Chatterji
D. Vivekanand

464. Who among the following is the author of 'Das Kapital'?
A. Lenin
B. J.M. Keynes
C. Robert Owen
D. Karl Marx

465. 'Panchatantra' was written by
A. Jai Dev
B. Ved Vyas
C. Bhavbhuti
D. Vishnu Sharma

466. Patanjali is well known for the compilation of
A. Yoga Sutra
B. Panchatantra
C. Brahma Sutra
D. Ayurveda

467. Who among the following has written the book, 'The Wings of Fire: An Autobiography'?
A. K.R. Narayan
B. Sobha De

C. A.B. Vajpayee
D. A.P.J. Abdul Kalam

468. Who compiled the 'Adi Granth'?
A. Guru Nanak
B. Guru Ramdas
C. Guru Arjun
D. Guru Gobind Singh

469. The famous book 'Anandmath' was authored by
A. Rabindranath Tagore
B. Bankim Chandra Chattopadhyaya
C. Sarojini Naidu
D. Sri Aurobindo

470. Which one of the following pairs is ***not*** correctly matched?
A. Mudrarakshasa : Visakhadatta
B. Rajtarangini : Kalhana
C. Kadambari : Bana Bhatta
D. Ratnavali : Bilhana

471. 'Harry Potter and the Deathly Hallows' is written by
A. Robert Ludlum
B. J.K. Rowling
C. Sidney Sheldon
D. Spencer Johnson

472. 'Arthashastra' was written by
A. Kalidas
B. Kautilya
C. R.K. Narayan
D. Bana Bhatta

473. Name the author of book "The Post Office (Dak Ghar)"?
A. R.K. Narayan
B. Rabindra Nath Tagore
C. Prem Chand
D. Krishan Chandra

474. Who wrote the nursery rhyme, "Twinkle, twinkle, little star"?
A. Lovelace
B. Ann Taylor
C. William Ross Wallace
D. William Shakespeare

475. Ashtadhyayi is a book written by
A. Panini
B. Patanjali
C. Vishnu Sharma
D. None of these

476. 'Prithviraj Raso' was written by:
A. Kalhan
B. Chand Bardai
C. Bhavbhuti
D. Bhule Shah

477. The book 'Prison Diary' was written by
A. Mahatma Gandhi
B. V.D. Savarkar
C. Jai Prakash Narayan
D. Morarji Desai

478. "Runs and Ruins" is written by
A. Nawab Pataudi
B. Vivian Richards
C. Clive Lloyd
D. Sunil Gavaskar

479. Who is the author of the book, 'The God of small Things'?
A. Ali Sardar Jafri
B. Vikram Chandra
C. Padma Seth
D. Arundhati Roy

480. India-2020 is a book written by
A. Montek Singh Ahluwalia
B. A.P.J. Abdul Kalam
C. G. Ganeshan
D. Indra Kumar Gujral

Computer

481. Which one of the following has earned the title "Father of Modern Computer"?
A. Blaise Pascal
B. Charles Babbage
C. Herman Hollerith
D. Jack Kilby

482. Which one of the following is the first generation computer?
A. UNIVAC-1
B. EDVAG
C. IBM 1201
D. IBM 1104

483. Which one of the following is a hardware?
A. Integrated circuit
B. Compiler
C. DOS
D. FORTRAN

484. What is the measuring unit of memory?
A. Watt B. Words
C. Bit D. None of these

485. How many bits are there in one byte?
A. 1 B. 2
C. 8 D. 1024

486. Digital computers deal with
A. discrete quantities
B. physical quantities
C. both discrete and physical quantities
D. neither discrete nor physical quantities

487. What is nibble?
A. A group of 2 bits
B. A group of 4 bits
C. A group of 8 bits
D. A group of 12 bits

488. Which one of the following is not a package?
A. BASIC
B. dBase
C. Pagemaker
D. Wordstar

489. Who invented the punched card?
A. Jack Kilby
B. John Napier
C. Gottfried Leibnitz
D. None of these

490. Which of the following does not represent an I/O device?
A. Speaker which beeps
B. Plotter
C. Joystick
D. ALU

491. A set of instructions is called a
A. compiler B. program
C. assembler D. information

492. Data is a collection of
A. raw material
B. number of alphabets
C. facts and entities relevant to user
D. input material for a computer

493. Which one of the following is part of the CPU?
A. Memory
B. Compiler
C. Control unit
D. Joystick

494. Which one of the following is not a system software?
A. Operating system
B. Compiler

C. Assembler
D. Software for railway reservation

495. What are the main limitations of computers?
A. Lack of decision-making power
B. Zero IQ
C. Lack in innovations
D. All the above

496. What do you understand by IPO cycle?
A. Information and Programming Operations cycle
B. Innovating and Programming Operations cycle
C. Input-Program-Output cycle
D. None of these

497. Calculations are made in computer with the help of its
A. Memory
B. ALU
C. CU
D. Input device

498. Results are obtained from computer through its
A. input unit
B. output unit
C. CPU
D. memory

499. Who, among the following invented the method of logarithm?
A. John Napier
B. Blaise Pascal
C. Joseph Jacquard
D. Charles Babbage

500. The modern age of data processing began with the completion of the computer
A. Analytical Engine
B. Napier's 'Logs' and 'Bones'
C. ENIAC
D. Leibnitz's Calculator

Miscellaneous

501. Who is called the First Citizen of India?
A. President of India
B. Prime Minister of India
C. Mahatma Gandhi
D. Dr. B.R. Ambedkar

502. Panini was a famous scholar of
A. Language and grammar
B. Ayurveda
C. Astronomy
D. Biology

503. Which of the following is not a mineral?
A. Slate
B. Limestone
C. Coal
D. Calcite

504. The state of rising prices due to an enhancement in the quantity of money in circulation, is termed as
A. Inflation
B. Deflation
C. Demonetisation
D. Devaluation

505. Name the minerals that are essential for bone and teeth formation in human
A. Calcium and Phosphorus
B. Magnesium and Potassium
C. Sodium and Iron
D. Iodine and Sulphur

506. Ripe mangoes contain
A. Vitamin A
B. Vitamin B
C. Vitamin C
D. Vitamin E

507. In which one of the following places, the boiling point of water is the highest?
A. Dead Sea
B. Mt. Everest
C. Nile Delta
D. Sunderbans Delta

508. The primary colours used in a colour TV are
A. Green, Yellow, Violet
B. Violet, Red, Orange
C. Blue, Green, Red
D. Blue, Geen, Violet

509. Which one of the following is not a Fundamental Right guaranteed by the Indian Constitution?
A. Freedom to manage religious affairs
B. Free and compulsory education up to primary stage
C. Prohibition of employment of children in factories
D. Freedom to propagate religion

510. The chief merit of a federal government is that it
A. Ensures a strong government at the centre
B. Integrates national unity with regional autonomy
C. Keeps a check on the multiparty system
D. Is very less expensive

511. The first Assamese to become the President of India was
A. Saiyeda Anowara Taimur
B. Gopinath Bordoloi
C. Fakhruddin Ali Ahmed
D. Syed Abdul Malik

512. Match List I with List II and select the correct answer using the codes given below the lists:

List-I	**List-II**
(*a*) Amjad Ali Khan	1. Flute
(*b*) Bismillah Khan	2. Sarod
(*c*) Hari Prasad Chaurasia	3. Tabla
(*d*) Alla Rakha	4. Shehnai

Codes:

	(*a*)	(*b*)	(*c*)	(*d*)
A.	2	1	3	4
B.	4	2	1	3
C.	2	4	1	3
D.	1	2	3	4

513. A dentist's mirror is a
A. Cylindrical mirror
B. Plane mirror
C. Convex mirror
D. Concave mirror

514. Which of the following is the largest producer of raw silk?
A. Asom
B. Karnataka
C. Andhra Pradesh
D. Jammu and Kashmir

515. The Gandhara School of Sculpture was a blend of
A. Indian and Greek styles
B. Indian and Persian styles
C. Purely Indian in origin
D. Indian and South East Asian style

516. Which one of the following languages is used in Tripura?
A. Hindi B. Mizo
C. Khasi D. Bengali

517. How many schedules are there in the Constitution of India?
A. Eight B. Ten
C. Twelve D. Fourteen

518. The term 'cloning' is related with
A. Environment
B. Genetics
C. Space technology
D. Trade

519. The planet nearest to the Earth is
A. Jupiter B. Venus
C. Mercury D. Mars

520. Hard water can be used in
A. Boilers
B. Textile industry
C. Paper industry
D. Drinking

521. Ras Leela, Yaosang, Lai Haraoba are the festivals of
A. Assemese people
B. Karbi people
C. Manipuri people
D. Bodo people

522. The Tigris river flows mainly through
A. Turkey B. Syria
C. Iraq D. Iran

523. "India is a secular State". It means that the Indian State
A. Favours irreligious citizens
B. Favours the religions of the majority community
C. Favours the religions of the minority community
D. Favours no particular religion

524. The second largest linguistic unit in India is
A. Tamil B. Hindi
C. English D. Telugu

525. The oldest inhabitants of India are considered to be
A. Mongoloids
B. Negritos
C. Indo-Aryan
D. Mediterranean

526. The International Date Line passes through
A. Malacca Strait
B. Gibraltar Strait
C. Bering Strait
D. Florida Strait

527. The last three digits of a PIN code represent
A. Zone
B. Subzone
C. Sorting District
D. Mailing route

528. Which state has the largest number of sugar mills?
A. Punjab
B. Haryana
C. Tamil Nadu
D. Uttar Pradesh

529. The first oil well in India was dug at
A. Bombay High
B. Moran
C. Digboi
D. Naharkatiya

530. Which of the following is ***not*** a rabi crop?
A. Wheat B. Maize
C. Mustard D. Gram

531. The state with the largest area under waste land is
A. Gujarat
B. Madhya Pradesh
C. Jammu and Kashmir
D. Rajasthan

532. Mixed farming involves
A. Growing more than one crop on a farm
B. Growing specialised crops
C. Growing crops and keeping livestock
D. Intensive and extensive agriculture

533. The country with the highest population density is
A. China B. Bangladesh
C. India D. France

534. When the first metal came into being, it was used for
A. Pot making
B. House-building
C. Clearing jungles
D. Making wheels

535. To whom does Vasudeva-Krishna address all his teachings in the Bhagvad Gita?
A. Arjuna
B. Duryodhana
C. Yudhishthira
D. The common people

536. Who raised the simple slogan 'Do or Die' for the Quit India Movement?
A. Mahatma Gandhi
B. Subhash Chandra Bose
C. Jawahar Lal Nehru
D. J.B. Kripalani

537. The salary and perquisities of the Prime Minister of India are decided by the
A. Constitution
B. Cabinet
C. Parliament
D. President

538. At what age can one exercise the right to vote in the general elections?
A. 18 years B. 21 years
C. 25 years D. 19 years

539. The Supreme Court was set up
A. By an act of Parliament
B. By the Constitution
C. Under the Government of India Act, 1935
D. By the Presidential order

540. A party to be recognised as a National Party must be in at least_____states.
A. Three B. Four
C. Five D. Six

541. Which of the following places is well known for the embroidery form of ''Chikankari''?
A. Hyderabad
B. Jaipur
C. Bhopal
D. Lucknow

542. Match the following

Folk form	**States where popular**
(*a*) Heer song	1. Bengal
(*b*) Bhatiali song	2. Punjab

(*c*) Garba dance		3. U.P.
(*d*) Raas dance		4. Gujarat

	(*a*)	(*b*)	(*c*)	(*d*)
A.	1	2	3	4
B.	1	3	2	4
C.	2	1	4	3
D.	2	3	4	1

543. Which is the most ancient musical instrument of India?
A. Flute B. Tabla
C. Veena D. Sitar

544. Who was the pioneer of the Bengal School of Art?
A. Nandlal Bose
B. B.C. Sanyal
C. Jamini Roy
D. Abanindranath Tagore

545. The proposed sea-route ''Sethu Samudram'' is a canal through which of the following sea-lanes?
A. Gulf of Mannar
B. Malacca Strait
C. Gulf of Kutch
D. Andaman and Nicobar Islands

546. The English established their first factory in India at
A. Bombay (Mumbai)
B. Surat
C. Sutanati
D. Madras (Chennai)

547. Which one of the following is a political right?
A. Right to freedom
B. Right to contest elections
C. Right to equality before law
D. Right to life

548. The main function of the judiciary is
A. Law formulation
B. Law execution
C. Law adjudication
D. Law application

549. 'Sakshat' is
A. A missile
B. An artificial satellite
C. A railway project
D. A website

550. Who started the first English newspaper in India?
A. Bal Gangadhar Tilak
B. Raja Rammohan Roy
C. J.A. Hickey
D. Lord William Bentinck

551. Mahatma Gandhi's autobiography—'My Experiments with Truth' was originally written in—
A. English B. Hindi
C. Marathi D. Gujarati

552. Who commanded the army of Bahadur Shah Zafar in 1857 revolt in Delhi ?
A. Azimulla
B. General Bakht Khan
C. Haqim Ahsanulla
D. Khan Bahadur

553. People greet one another in French language with—
A. GutenTag
B. Bonjour
C. Ahlan Wasahlan
D) None of these

554. Which among the following is ***not*** a correct match—
A. Thomas Cup—Badminton
B. Rovers Cup—Hockey
C. Deodhar Trophy—Cricket
D. Durand Cup—Football

555. What is Gene ?
A. A segment of RNA, DNA and Histone
B. A segment of DNA and RNA
C. A segment of DNA
D. A segment of DNA and Histone

556. Water pollution is mainly caused by-
A. Pesticides
B. NH_3
C. Industrial waste
D. Detergent

557. In the constitution of India, India has been described as—
A. A federation
B. A secular of federation
C. A quasi-federal organization
D. A union of states

558. Damodar Valley Project is sponsored by West Bengal and—
A. Orissa
B. Jharkhand
C. U.P.
D. All the above

559. Which among the following is a riverine port ?
A. Cochin B. Kolkata
C. Kanca D. Mormugao

560. Budapest is the capital of—
A. Haiti
B. Honduras
C. Hungary
D. Czech Republic

561. Among the following, which state capital is not situated near the bank of a river ?
A. Lucknow B. Patna
C. Bombay D. Kolkata

562. Which is the storehouse of salt in human body ?
A. Liver B. Skin
C. Kidneys D. Neck

563. Pyorrhoea affects which part of the body ?
A. The gums
B. The teeth
C. Salivary glands
D. Lips

564. Who was the author of 'Geet Govind' ?
A. Vidyapati B. Jayadeva
C. Magha D. Sriharsha

565. Thermocole is made from—
A. Polystyrene
B. Perspex
C. Polythene
D. Teflon

566. Printing for the blind was invented by—
A. Berliner
B. N.R.Finsen
C. Louis Braile
D. J. L. Baird

567. Which is the heaviest flying bird?
A. Bustard
B. Penguin
C. Ostrich
D. Vulture

568. Economic development of a country is directly based on—
A. Natural resources
B. Capital formation
C. Availability of market
D. None of these

569. The term Ikebana is associated with which country ?
A. Thailand B. Japan
C. England D. Australia

570. The largest irrigation canal in India is called the—
A. Yamuna canal
B. Sirhind canal
C. Lower Baridoab canal
D. Indira Gandhi canal

571. Horns of most mammals are made of—
A. Bones B. Cartilage
C. Keratin D. Chitin

572. Rigveda is divided into how many Mandals ?
A. 10 mandals
B. 7 mandals
C. 15 mandals
D. 20 mandals

573. The constitution of UNO is known as—
A. Peace agreement
B. Magna Carta
C. Declaration
D. Charter

574. December 10 is observed as—
A. World Mental Health Day
B. World Sight Day
C. World Red Cross Day
D. Human Rights Day

575. The Durand Line is the international border between—
A. Afghanistan and Pakistan
B. Iran and Syria
C. India and Bangladesh
D. India and Nepal

576. Washington is situated at the bank of—
A. Vistula B. Moskava
C. Potomac D. Tagus

577. The term 'Rook' is linked with—
A. Golf B. Archery
C. Chess D. Badminton

578. 'Fan', a widely spoken language of the world belongs to—
A. Laos B. Kenya
C. Tibet D. Myanmar

579. Which among the following is matched incorrectly ?
A. Mahatma Gandhi — Bapu
B. Lajpat Rai — Punjab Kesari
C. C.F. Andrews— Deshabandhu
D. Subhash Chandra Bose — Netaji

580. Supreme Court in India was established in Calcutta in :
A. 1771 B. 1774
C. 1775 D. 1776

581. The first radio-programme in India was broadcast by Radio Club of Bombay in:
A. 1924 B. 1923
C. 1926 D. 1927

582. In India, the first state to institute a Human Rights Commission is :
A. A.P. B. Kerala
C. W. Bengal D. Rajasthan

583. The 'Vikram Sarabhai Space Centre is located at :
A. Bangalore
B. Hyderabad
C. Chennai
D. Thiruvananthapuram

584. The first film actor to be nominated to Rajya Sabha was :
A. Ashok Kumar
B. Dilip Kumar
C. Jeevan
D. Prithviraj Kapoor

585. The first Indian Institute of Technology was set up in India in 1950 at :

A. Kolhapur B. Kanpur
C. Kharagpur D. Bangalore

586. Which state has the maximum forest cover amongst all Indian States and Union Territories?

A. T.N. B. A.P.
C. M.P. D. U.P.

587. Manas Wildlife Sanctuary housing tigers is in:

A. Sikkim
B. Asom
C. Karnataka
D. Arunachal Pradesh

588. Who wrote 'Long Walk To Freedom' ?

A. Nelson Mandela
B. Aung San Su Kyi
C. Abraham Lincoln
D. Moti Lal Nehru

589. The currency of Bhutan is :

A. Lote B. Rupiah
C. Ngultrum D. Shekel

590. Who discovered X-rays in 1895 ?

A. Mackintos
B. B. Certois
C. Belard
D. Prof. Roentgen

591. The melting point of iron is :

A. 1600°C B. 1535°C
C. 1765°C D. 1650°C

592. The headquarters of European Union is :

A. Rome B. Paris
C. Brussels D. Dublin

593. Commonwealth Day is observed by Member Countries on :

A. 26 August
B. 24 May
C. 27 December
D. 29 January

594. IMF (International Monetary Fund) was established in :

A. 1950 B. 1965
C. 1945 D. 1980

595. The distance covered by wheeled vehicle is measured by :

A. Sextant
B. Odometer
C. Speedometer
D. Stroboscope

596. Diphtheria, a disease, attacks :

A. Lungs B. Eyes
C. Gums D. Throat

597. Phrenology is the study of :

A. Language
B. Teeth
C. Skull and brain
D. Nerves

598. If the President of India wants to submit his resignation, to whom, would he submit his resignation?

A. Speaker of the Lok Sabha
B. Chief Justice of Supreme Court
C. Vice President
D. Prime Minister

599. Rose is the national emblem of :

A. Italy B. Iran
C. Israel D. Iraq

600. 'Akash' is India's—

A. Air to air missile
B. Anti-tank guided missile
C. Surface to surface missile
D. Surface to air missile

601. Tapti river originates from :
A. Amarkantak
B. Panchmarhi
C. Trimbakeshwar
D. Satpura range

602. The first municipal corporation in India was established in Madras in :
A. 1687 B. 1699
C. 1685 D. 1690

603. RAW (Research and Analysis Wing) works under:
A. Ministry of Home
B. Ministry of Personnel
C. PMO
D. Cabinet Secretariat

604. The first spacecraft sent by Europe to the moon is :
A. Atlantis B. Discovery
C. Odyssey D. SMART-I

605. Siyam is the old name of :
A. Vietnam B. Thailand
C. Myanmar D. Laos

606. The number of states which do not touch international boundary and are completely landlocked is :
A. 3 B. 7
C. 5 D. 6

607. Which state of India touches the boundary of most other states?
A. A.P. B. M.P.
C. Asom D. U.P.

608. Which of the Mughal rulers promoted painting most?
A. Babar B. Akbar
C. Jahangir D. Shahjahan

609. The subject matter of the fourth schedule of the Constitution of India is :
A. Administration of tribal areas
B. Forms of oath or Affirmation
C. Languages
D. Allocation of seats of the Rajya Sabha to states

610. Vice-President is the part of :
A. Legislature
B. Executive
C. Rajya Sabha
D. None of these

ANSWERS

1	2	3	4	5	6	7	8	9	10
C	C	A	D	C	C	B	D	B	B
11	**12**	**13**	**14**	**15**	**16**	**17**	**18**	**19**	**20**
C	C	C	D	C	D	B	C	D	D
21	**22**	**23**	**24**	**25**	**26**	**27**	**28**	**29**	**30**
B	B	D	B	D	D	D	B	D	B
31	**32**	**33**	**34**	**35**	**36**	**37**	**38**	**39**	**40**
B	A	C	A	A	B	B	B	A	A
41	**42**	**43**	**44**	**45**	**46**	**47**	**48**	**49**	**50**
C	C	B	B	B	C	A	B	B	C
51	**52**	**53**	**54**	**55**	**56**	**57**	**58**	**59**	**60**
C	C	B	B	A	C	B	B	B	D

61	62	63	64	65	66	67	68	69	70
D	C	A	A	B	C	C	A	C	D
71	**72**	**73**	**74**	**75**	**76**	**77**	**78**	**79**	**80**
C	D	C	D	C	C	C	B	C	B
81	**82**	**83**	**84**	**85**	**86**	**87**	**88**	**89**	**90**
C	A	D	D	D	C	C	A	C	D
91	**92**	**93**	**94**	**95**	**96**	**97**	**98**	**99**	**100**
A	C	C	C	B	D	A	A	C	D
101	**102**	**103**	**104**	**105**	**106**	**107**	**108**	**109**	**110**
B	D	A	C	A	C	A	A	D	B
111	**112**	**113**	**114**	**115**	**116**	**117**	**118**	**119**	**120**
B	C	A	B	B	B	D	D	D	B
121	**122**	**123**	**124**	**125**	**126**	**127**	**128**	**129**	**130**
D	C	C	A	D	A	D	C	B	C
131	**132**	**133**	**134**	**135**	**136**	**137**	**138**	**139**	**140**
B	D	D	A	B	A	B	B	B	D
141	**142**	**143**	**144**	**145**	**146**	**147**	**148**	**149**	**150**
B	A	C	C	A	A	C	A	B	D
151	**152**	**153**	**154**	**155**	**156**	**157**	**158**	**159**	**160**
C	B	B	C	C	D	A	D	C	D
161	**162**	**163**	**164**	**165**	**166**	**167**	**168**	**169**	**170**
B	D	B	C	D	D	B	D	D	B
171	**172**	**173**	**174**	**175**	**176**	**177**	**178**	**179**	**180**
D	B	B	C	C	C	A	D	A	C
181	**182**	**183**	**184**	**185**	**186**	**187**	**188**	**189**	**190**
C	A	B	C	B	C	C	D	B	D
191	**192**	**193**	**194**	**195**	**196**	**197**	**198**	**199**	**200**
D	A	D	C	B	B	A	D	D	C
201	**202**	**203**	**204**	**205**	**206**	**207**	**208**	**209**	**210**
A	B	B	D	A	D	C	C	C	A
211	**212**	**213**	**214**	**215**	**216**	**217**	**218**	**219**	**220**
B	B	C	C	D	A	C	D	B	D
221	**222**	**223**	**224**	**225**	**226**	**227**	**228**	**229**	**230**
D	C	C	A	C	C	B	A	D	A
231	**232**	**233**	**234**	**235**	**236**	**237**	**238**	**239**	**240**
B	A	A	A	A	B	B	A	D	B
241	**242**	**243**	**244**	**245**	**246**	**247**	**248**	**249**	**250**
D	B	A	B	C	C	B	D	A	C
251	**252**	**253**	**254**	**255**	**256**	**257**	**258**	**259**	**260**
D	B	D	B	A	B	C	D	D	A

261	**262**	**263**	**264**	**265**	**266**	**267**	**268**	**269**	**270**
B	A	C	C	C	D	C	C	B	B
271	**272**	**273**	**274**	**275**	**276**	**277**	**278**	**279**	**280**
C	D	B	D	D	C	A	D	A	D
281	**282**	**283**	**284**	**285**	**286**	**287**	**288**	**289**	**290**
C	A	B	B	B	B	D	B	C	C
291	**292**	**293**	**294**	**295**	**296**	**297**	**298**	**299**	**300**
C	B	D	B	B	C	B	D	D	A
301	**302**	**303**	**304**	**305**	**306**	**307**	**308**	**309**	**310**
A	B	A	C	D	A	A	D	C	A
311	**312**	**313**	**314**	**315**	**316**	**317**	**318**	**319**	**320**
D	C	B	C	D	C	A	B	C	D
321	**322**	**323**	**324**	**325**	**326**	**327**	**328**	**329**	**330**
A	B	C	B	A	D	A	B	B	D
331	**332**	**333**	**334**	**335**	**336**	**337**	**338**	**339**	**340**
B	A	B	A	C	C	A	A	D	D
341	**342**	**343**	**344**	**345**	**346**	**347**	**348**	**349**	**350**
B	A	B, C	C	C	C	B	B	A	C
351	**352**	**353**	**354**	**355**	**356**	**357**	**358**	**359**	**360**
A	D	A	D	B	C	B	D	D	C
361	**362**	**363**	**364**	**365**	**366**	**367**	**368**	**369**	**370**
A	D	B	A	D	A	C	C	B	A
371	**372**	**373**	**374**	**375**	**376**	**377**	**378**	**379**	**380**
A	A	C	C	D	C	C	A	B	C
381	**382**	**383**	**384**	**385**	**386**	**387**	**388**	**389**	**390**
D	C	B	B	A	A	D	D	B	C
391	**392**	**393**	**394**	**395**	**396**	**397**	**398**	**399**	**400**
C	B	D	C	C	A	B	C	C	A
401	**402**	**403**	**404**	**405**	**406**	**407**	**408**	**409**	**410**
B	C	A	D	C	B	B	B	B	B
411	**412**	**413**	**414**	**415**	**416**	**417**	**418**	**419**	**420**
C	A	D	A	D	C	A	B	C	B
421	**422**	**423**	**424**	**425**	**426**	**427**	**428**	**429**	**430**
A	A	A	A	C	C	B	D	A	A
431	**432**	**433**	**434**	**435**	**436**	**437**	**438**	**439**	**440**
A	A	D	B	C	C	C	A	D	C
441	**442**	**443**	**444**	**445**	**446**	**447**	**448**	**449**	**450**
B	A	B	B	C	C	C	C	A	A
451	**452**	**453**	**454**	**455**	**456**	**457**	**458**	**459**	**460**
C	B	B	D	A	C	B	B	B	B

461	462	463	464	465	466	467	468	469	470
B	C	C	D	D	A	D	C	B	D
471	472	473	474	475	476	477	478	479	480
B	B	B	B	B	B	C	D	D	B
481	482	483	484	485	486	487	488	489	490
B	A	A	D	C	A	B	A	D	D
491	492	493	494	495	496	497	498	499	500
B	C	C	D	D	D	B	B	A	A
501	502	503	504	505	506	507	508	509	510
A	A	C	A	A	A	A	C	C	B
511	512	513	514	515	516	517	518	519	520
C	C	D	A	A	D	C	B	B	A
521	522	523	524	525	526	527	528	529	530
C	C	D	D	B	C	C	D	C	C
531	532	533	534	535	536	537	538	539	540
D	C	B	A	A	A	C	A	B	B
541	542	543	544	545	546	547	548	549	550
D	C	A	D	A	B	B	C	D	C
551	552	553	554	555	556	557	558	559	560
D	B	B	B	C	C	D	B	B	C
561	562	563	564	565	566	567	568	569	570
C	B	A	B	A	C	A	B	B	D
571	572	573	574	575	576	577	578	579	580
C	A	D	D	A	C	C	D	C	B
581	582	583	584	585	586	587	588	589	590
B	C	D	D	C	C	B	A	C	D
591	592	593	594	595	596	597	598	599	600
B	C	B	C	B	D	C	C	B	D
601	602	603	604	605	606	607	608	609	610
B	A	D	D	B	C	D	C	D	B

1904

www.ingramcontent.com/pod-product-compliance
Ingram Content Group UK Ltd.
Pitfield, Milton Keynes, MK11 3LW, UK
UKHW021709190726
13853UKWH00001B/478

9 789386 845337